カラー版

英語でつくる和食

食の歳時記

Annual events of
Japan and
recipes of dishes

ナヴィ インターナショナル 編著

ナツメ社

春夏秋冬
日本の伝統行事を知り、
季節の料理を楽しむ

はじめに

　日本には四季（春夏秋冬）折々の自然があり、さまざまな歳時記（年中行事）がある。それぞれの行事には必ずといってよいほど料理がふるまわれてきた。

　新年を迎える「お正月」には、子孫の繁栄を願う数の子、五穀豊穣を願う田作り、家族の健康を願う黒豆、一年を喜びながら生活できるようにと願うこぶ巻きなどの「おせち料理」を食べて新年を祝う習わしがある。

　春には女の子のすこやかな成長を願う雛祭り、男の子が丈夫に成長することを願う端午の節句などの行事があり、それを祝う料理がある。夏は無病息災などを願う夏祭り、花火大会、ご先祖をまつる仏事のお盆などがある。秋は紅葉狩り、運動会、女の子と男の子の成長の無事を願う七五三などがある。

　本書は、日本の伝統的な歳時記の由来やすごし方、そして四季の移ろい、歳時記にふるまわれる日本の料理と旬を感じる野菜類、魚介類などの食材を使った料理などの作り方が数多く紹介されている。まさに日本ならではの魅力が詰まっている。

　また、料理ページには、メインの食材を使ったバリエーション料理や、作り方、調味料などの材料はそのままにメインの食材を他の食材に代える情報、食材の栄養と効能、食材、料理などの豆知識をコラムとして紹介している。

　本書のすべての内容が日本語と英訳の対訳で紹介されているので、英語の勉強になるのはもちろんのこと、外国の方に日本の素晴らしい文化と和食の作り方を知ってもらうのにも役立つ一冊である。本書を手に取った方が、改めて日本の魅力に気づき、その魅力を世界に伝える手助けになれば幸いだ。

Preface

Japan has four distinct seasons (spring, summer, fall and winter), each of which has its own natural features and a variety of annual events. At each of the regular events, unique dishes have been enjoyed in families and served to guests.

On New Year's Day and the first few days of January, Japanese people eat *osechi-ryori* (traditional New Year food), such as herring roe eaten to pray for family prosperity and descendants, *tazukuri* (small sardines, dried and then boiled slowly in sugar and soy sauce), to wish for a bumper crop, black soybeans cooked in sugar, to hope for the health of the family and kelp rolls, to pray for a year-round happy life.

In spring, Japanese have the Girls' Festival to pray for the healthy growth of girls and the Boys' Festival, to wish boys good health, when special food is served to celebrate these events. In summer, there are summer festivals to pray for good health, fireworks displays, and *Obon*, the Buddhist event for worshipping ancestors. In addition, in fall, people have excursions to view the autumn leaves, sports days, and *Shichi-go-san*, the event wishing for the healthy growth of boys and girls.

This book describes the history of traditional events in Japan, how people celebrate them, the changes of the four seasons, the Japanese dishes served at each event, and the recipes for the food cooked using seasonal vegetables, fish, shellfish, and other materials. Its pages are packed with many attractions unique to Japan.

In the cooking sections, pages contain various dishes prepared using main ingredients and their recipes, information about variations of the recipes using different main ingredients with the same seasonings, the nutrition and efficacy of the food, and useful hints about food materials and dishes.

Every page of this book is bilingual, with an English translation alongside the Japanese text. Therefore, this book will help Japanese readers studying English, while also encouraging non-Japanese readers to get to know many attractive aspects of Japanese culture and food. We will be very happy if the readers will rediscover the attraction of Japan and thus contribute to the dissemination of the country's attractive features to people worldwide.

目次
Contents

和食の基礎知識 ··············· 281～291
Basic Knowledge of Japanese Cuisine

コラム ●Column

春を彩る
日本の歳時記と和食

Japanese Events and Food in Spring

春の歳時記と和食
Events and Food in Spring

さまざまな草花が芽吹き、樹々には薄緑色の葉がつきはじめ、自然の生命力を感じることができる春。里山には花々が咲き乱れ、ふきのとうが顔を出し、梅や桜、桃の花を求めて人々は花見へとくり出す。うぐいすが鳴き、日差しもポカポカと暖かくなり、なんとも気持ちのよい季節である。そんな生命力がいっぱいの山菜をはじめ、春ならではの旬の食材を使った料理をいただくと、生きていくエネルギーをいただいたように感じる。そして雛祭り（桃の節句）や端午の節句など、古くから伝わる伝統文化がとりおこなわれる。

Spring is the season when various flowering plants bloom and trees begin to shoot light green leaves, bringing home the vitality of nature to you. In hills and fields, a wealth of flowers bloom, the flower-buds of Japanese butterburs appear and people go to view the beautiful blossoms of *ume* (Japanese apricot), cherries, and peaches. Spring is a very pleasant season when bush warblers sing and the sunlight grows warmer. When you eat dishes prepared using edible wild plants full of the vitality of spring and other seasonal foods available only in spring, you will feel these dishes give you the power to live. In this season, you also celebrate traditional events, including *Hina-Matsuri* (also known as Girls' Festival) and *Tango-no-Sekku* (a.k.a. Boys' Festival).

芽吹き●Buds put forth
雪どけがはじまる初旬になると、いろいろな植物が芽吹く。まさに春到来を感じさせる。
In early March, the snow begins to melt and various plants shoot buds, which heralds the arrival of spring.

菜の花●Rape blossoms
春の里山や川岸などを黄色く染める菜の花。まさに春を代表する花といってよい。
Rape blossoms adorn hills, fields, and river banks with their yellow flowers. This plant should really be called the representative plant for spring in Japan.

梅● *Ume* Japanese apricot blossoms
早い地方では2月初旬から咲くが、3月が盛期。300種以上もの品種がある。
The Japanese apricot starts blooming in early February in warmer areas, peaking in March. This plant has as many as 300 varieties or more.

桃●Peach blossoms
3月下旬から4月上旬頃に咲く。山梨県の桃畑が有名で、一面が濃いピンク色に染まる。
Peach blossoms bloom in late March to early April. The peach fields in Yamanashi Prefecture are famous; they are all covered with the dark pink colors of peach blossoms in season.

桜●Cherry blossoms
沖縄は1月だが、3月下旬〜5月上旬が盛期の桜。ソメイヨシノ、カン桜などが有名。
Cherry blossoms bloom in January in Okinawa but its best seasons elsewhere in Japan are from late March to Early May. *Someiyoshino* and Chinese primrose are among the well-known varieties.

たんぽぽ●Dandelions
日本たんぽぽと西洋たんぽぽがあるが、白花は日本たんぽぽになる。春を代表する花だ。
Both Japanese and Western dandelions exist, and those with white flowers belong to the former variety. This plant is also representative in Japan.

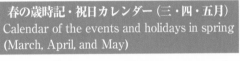

春の歳時記・祝日カレンダー（三・四・五月）
Calendar of the events and holidays in spring (March, April, and May)

雛祭り（桃の節句）・三月三日●Hina-Matsuri (Girls' Festival) —March 3

花見（梅）・二〜三月●Hanami (Ume blossom viewing)—February to March

花見（桜）・三〜五月●Hanami (Cherry Blossom viewing) —from March to May

花見（桃）・四〜五月●Hanami (Peach blossom viewing)—April to May

彼岸・三月十八〜二十四日●Higan (Buddhist equinoctial week) —March 18-24

春分の日・三月二十日もしくは二十一日●Spring equinox—March 20 or 21
※年によって十九日、二十二日もある。
※Some years have this event on March 19 or 22.

昭和の日・四月二十九日●Day of Showa—April 29

憲法記念日・五月三日●Constitution Day —May 3

みどりの日・五月四日●Midori-no-Hi (Greenery Day) —May 4

こどもの日（端午の節句）・五月五日●Tango-no-Sekku (Boys' Festival) —May 5

れんげ草●Chinese milk vetches
正式名はげんげで、中国原産。春に薄赤い花を田んぼなどで咲かせ、緑肥になる。
This plant is generally known as *rengeso* in Japan but its formal Japanese name is *genge*. It is native to China. In spring, this plant bears light red flowers in paddy fields, etc. and is used as green manure.

新緑●Fresh green
日差しが暖かくなると樹々に薄い緑色の葉がつき、春の息吹を感じさせてくれる。
As the sunshine grows ever-warmer, trees shoot light green leaves, causing you to feel a breath of spring.

雛祭り Hina-Matsuri (Girls' Festival)

春を代表する伝統行事の雛祭り。女の子がすこやかに成長することと、幸せを願い雛人形を飾り、雛祭り用の料理を親しい人たちといただく。日本ならではのなんとも美しく、歴史のある行事のひとつである。

Hina-Matsuri or the Girls' Festival is a traditional and representative spring event in Japan. To pray for the healthy growth and happiness of their daughters, parents display dolls, and special dishes prepared for the festival are eaten together with close friends. *Hina-Matsuri* is a very beautiful event, peculiar to Japan and with a long history.

雛祭りの歴史と由来 Origin and history of *Hina-Matsuri* (Girls' Festival)

　三月三日は家に女の子のいる家では、雛人形を飾って女の子のすこやかな成長と幸せを祈る。この雛祭りの由来は、平安朝時代の宮廷貴族の子供たちが、"ひいな"と呼ばれる紙製の人形やさまざまな調度品を供えて遊んでいたことを"ひいな遊び"といっていたことからといわれている。

　また、雛祭りは桃の節句、上巳の節句ともいわれる。桃の節句は、古くから桃が邪気を祓うため、女の子の成長を無事願う雛祭りに適していることと、三月が桃の開花の季節だったことが由来である。

　上巳の節句とは、中国で上巳の日(三月第一の巳の日のこと)に水辺で祓いの行事を行い、自分自身の身代わりになる"ひと形"(紙型の人形など)に穢れを移してから川に流して無病息災を願ったものが、平安時代に日本に伝わり、貴族たちがひと形で体をなでさすり、体と心の汚れを移したあと、そのひと形を川に流して身を清めたのが由来である。

　江戸時代になると、紙の人形も上焼きの豪華な人形となり、宮廷生活を模して男女一対の内裏雛、左大臣、右大臣、三人官女(三賢女)、五人囃子、衛士とお茶道具などの調度品を飾るようになった。

On March 3, parents wish their daughters' healthy growth and happiness by displaying traditional dolls at home. This festival is said to have its origins in the *hiina-asobi*, the name given to the play enjoyed by the children of noble families in the court in the Heian Era (794-1192) where paper dolls (called *hiina*) and various accessories were used.

Hina-Matsuri is also known as the Peach Festival and the Festival on the Day of *Joshi*. The name Peach Festival originated in the fact that peaches have long been believed to drive out noxious vapors from the body and are suited for the Girls' Festival to wish ones' daughters healthy growth and that this plant blooms in March.

The origin of the name Festival on the Day of *Joshi* can be found in China: In that country, an event was held on the Day of *Joshi* (the first day of *Mi* or snakes, the sixth of the twelve signs of the Chinese zodiac, in March) during which a purification ceremony was held at the riverside. After transferring uncleanness from their body to *hitogata* (paper dolls, etc.), which would act as substitutes for them, people discharged the *hitogata* into the river to pray to the gods for good health. This custom was imported to Japan in the Heian Era, and nobles began to purify themselves and pray for their good health by rubbing their body with *hitogata* to transfer pollution from their minds and bodies into a paper doll, and throwing it into the river.

Later in the Edo Era (1603-1867), luxurious best quality ceramic dolls began to be used in place of traditional paper dolls. In addition, reflecting court life, people started to display Emperor and Empress dolls, dolls of the Minister of the Left and Right, three court lady dolls (or three wise women dolls), five musician dolls, and guard dolls as well as tea ceremony utensils and other beautiful accessories.

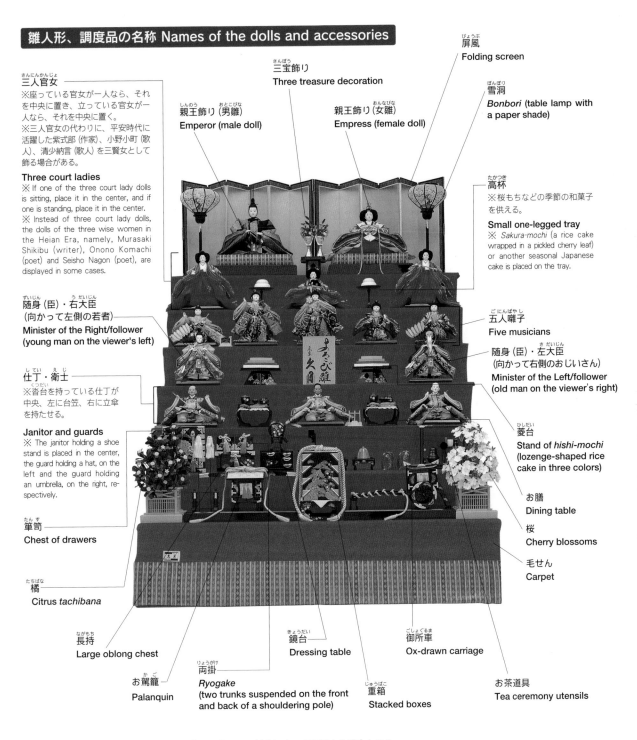

びょうぶ
屏風
Folding screen

さんぼう
三宝飾り
Three treasure decoration

ぼんぼり
雪洞
Bonbori (table lamp with a paper shade)

さんにんかんじょ
三人官女
※座っている官女が一人なら、それを中央に置き、立っている官女が一人なら、それを中央に置く。
※三人官女の代わりに、平安時代に活躍した紫式部 (作家)、小野小町 (歌人)、清少納言 (歌人) を三賢女として飾る場合がある。

Three court ladies
※ If one of the three court lady dolls is sitting, place it in the center, and if one is standing, place it in the center.
※ Instead of three court lady dolls, the dolls of the three wise women in the Heian Era, namely, Murasaki Shikibu (writer), Onono Komachi (poet) and Seisho Nagon (poet), are displayed in some cases.

しんのう　おとこびな
親王飾り (男雛)
Emperor (male doll)

おんなびな
親王飾り (女雛)
Empress (female doll)

たかつき
高杯
※桜もちなどの季節の和菓子を供える。

Small one-legged tray
※ *Sakura-mochi* (a rice cake wrapped in a pickled cherry leaf) or another seasonal Japanese cake is placed on the tray.

ずいじん　しん　う だいじん
随身 (臣)・右大臣
（向かって左側の若者）
Minister of the Right/follower
(young man on the viewer's left)

ごにんばやし
五人囃子
Five musicians

ずいじん　しん　さ だいじん
随身 (臣)・左大臣
（向かって右側のおじいさん）
Minister of the Left/follower
(old man on the viewer's right)

してい　えじ
仕丁・衛士
※沓台を持っている仕丁が中央、左に台笠、右に立傘を持たせる。

Janitor and guards
※ The janitor holding a shoe stand is placed in the center, the guard holding a hat, on the left and the guard holding an umbrella, on the right, respectively.

ひしだい
菱台
Stand of *hishi-mochi* (lozenge-shaped rice cake in three colors)

ぜん
お膳
Dining table

さくら
桜
Cherry blossoms

もうせん
毛せん
Carpet

たんす
箪笥
Chest of drawers

たちばな
橘
Citrus *tachibana*

ながもち
長持
Large oblong chest

きょうだい
鏡台
Dressing table

ごしょぐるま
御所車
Ox-drawn carriage

りょうがけ
両掛
Ryogake
(two trunks suspended on the front and back of a shouldering pole)

かご
お駕籠
Palanquin

じゅうばこ
重箱
Stacked boxes

お茶道具
Tea ceremony utensils

※ここで紹介する雛人形は江戸風の七段飾りのもので、地方によっては異なる場合もある。
※The above is the Edo-style seven-tier display of dolls, and the display method differs in some areas.

子供が初めて生まれた時、初めて迎える節句を〝初節句〟といって、子供が女の子の場合は、妻の実家から男女一対の内裏雛を贈るしきたりがある。さらに親戚や親しい知人が、内裏雛以外の人形や調度品を贈る習慣がある。これらの習慣は都市では少なくなっているが、まだ地方には残っている。

祝い方にこれといった決まりはないが、両親、友人、親戚、親しい近所の人などを自宅に呼び祝う。もちろん雛人形や調度品を雛壇に飾り、雛祭りの伝統的なお祝い膳の、ちらし寿し、はまぐりのお吸いもの、白酒、桜餅、菱餅、雛あられなどを準備してもてなす。また、地方によって異なるが、小豆入りのおこわや赤飯、お煮しめ、小だい、車えび、ぬたあえなどがお祝い膳として出されるところもある。現在は子供たちの好きなもの、大人も楽しめる料理、飲みものになっている。

祝いがはじまる前に、〝うれしいひなまつり〟を皆んなで歌いたい。

▲菱餅は雛祭りにはかかせない
Hishi-mochi is a must for the Girls' Festival

▼雛祭りを祝う代表的なお祝い膳のちらし寿し
Chirashi-zushi, a typical dish for celebrating the Girls' Festival

雛あられ▶
Hina-arare

The Boys' or Girls' Festival that comes first after the birth of a baby is called the baby's first Boys' or Girls' Festival. There is a tradition that if the baby is a girl, the parents of the mother present a pair of dolls of the Emperor and Empress to their daughter's family. There is also the custom that the relatives and friends of the family having a baby girl present the family with other dolls and accessories. While these practices are vanishing in cities, they can still be observed in rural districts.

There is no rule about how to celebrate *Hina-Matsuri* but in general, parents having a daughter invite their parents, friends, relatives, and close neighbors to celebrate the event with them. They display dolls and accessories on the tiered stand and serve guests traditional dishes for the occasion, including *chirashi-zushi* (garnished *sushi*), hard-shell clam clear soup, white *sake*, *sakura-mochi*, *hishi-mochi* and *hina-arare* (pink and white grilled pieces of rice cakes for *Hina-Matsuri*). In some areas, they serve their guests with *sekihan* (glutinous rice steamed with red beans), *nishime* (vegetables stewed in soy sauce), small red sea bream, prawns, and *nuta* (vegetables marinated with a sauce of vinegar and *miso*). Today, children's favorite food, as well as dishes and drinks that adults can enjoy, are generally served.

Before the party is started, sing "*Ureshii Hina-matsuri* (Happy *Hina-Matsuri*)" together with the participants.

雛祭りの遊びといえば、平安時代から伝わる〝貝合わせ〟である。はまぐりに金箔を塗り、その上に平安朝時代の貴族たちの生活様式などを描いたものや和歌を書いたものを、裏返して置き、同じ絵を当てるか、和歌の上の句と下の句を合わせるなどの遊びである。

また、はまぐりは二枚貝を代表する貝だが、二枚ある殻が他の殻とは絶対に合わないため、「よい伴侶に巡り合える」といわれている。

The typical game played at the Girls' Festival is *Kai-awase*, the concentration game with clamshells that has been passed down from the Heian Era. The tools are clamshells, plated with gold inside, and depicting either the life, etc. of nobles in the Heian Era or the first or second half of *tanka* (31-syllable Japanese

poems) drawn or written on the inside. These shells are randomly placed on the floor face down. The players try to guess any two shells with the same picture on them, or the shell with the first half of the *tanka* and another with the second half of the same *tanka*.

Hard-shell clams are representative of bivalves, and in Japan, it is said that because one of the two shells of a hard-shell clam never matches the shells of any other hard-shell clam, this shellfish will help girls find a good husband in future.

雛人形を片づけないと結婚が遅れるって本当？

Is it true that the marital age of a girl rises unless dolls are put away at the proper time?

雛祭りがすぎても雛人形を片づけないと、結婚が遅れるといわれている。これは昭和初期にいわれた迷信である。

旧暦では梅雨の時期が間近で、雛人形を片づけないと人形にカビが生えることからいわれるようになったらしい。

ちなみに雛人形は、立春の二月四日頃からか、二月中旬に飾りたい。遅くても節句の一週間前に飾ろう。片づけは節句がすんだら、天気のよい乾燥している日にしまうのがベスト。遅くとも三月中旬には片づけたい。

In Japan, it is said that if dolls are not put away promptly after the Girls' Festival ends, the marital age of a girl rises. This is a superstition that became pervasive in the early years of the Showa Era (1926-1989).

In the lunar calendar, the rainy season comes soon after the Girls' Festival, hence dolls are likely to get moldy unless they are put away quickly.

This is probably the reason that the belief was shaped.

Dolls should be displayed on around February 4, the first day of spring in the lunar calendar or by mid-February. You should display them no later than a week before the Girls' Festival. The best way is to put dolls away on a fine, dry day soon after the Festival. Dolls should be put away by mid-March at the latest.

雛祭りを楽しむレシピ
Recipe to enjoy *Hina-matsuri*, or Girls' Festival

ちらし寿し
雛祭りをとっておきの食材を使った色鮮やかなちらし寿しで祝う

about
45
min

Chirashi-zushi
Garnished *Sushi*

Celebrate *Hina-matsuri* with colorful *chirashi-zushi* using special ingredients

■材料・2人分

寿し飯	………………………	2合分
にんじん	………………………	約4cm

A
だし汁	………………………	80cc
砂糖	………………………	小さじ1
しょう油	………………………	少々
塩	………………………	少々

干ししいたけ	………………………	3枚

B
だし汁（干ししいたけの戻し汁と合わせる）………………………		100cc
しょう油	………………………	小さじ2
砂糖	………………………	大さじ1
酒	………………………	大さじ1/2
みりん	………………………	大さじ1/2

れんこん（細めのもの）	………………………	約3cm

C
酢	………………………	大さじ2
砂糖	………………………	大さじ1
塩	………………………	ひとつまみ
水	………………………	大さじ3

卵	………………………	2個

D
塩	………………………	少々
酒	………………………	少々

殻つきえび	………………………	6尾
いくら	………………………	大さじ2
絹さや	………………………	6枚
白ごま	………………………	大さじ1
塩	………………………	適量

※工程時間に干ししいたけを戻す時間は含まれていません

Ingredients (serves 2)

Vinegared rice, cooked with 1 1/2 U.S. cups rice
1 1/2 inches carrot

A
- 1/3 U.S. cup stock
- 1 tsp sugar
- Small quantity of soy sauce
- Small quantity of salt

3 dried *shiitake* mushrooms

B
- 2/5 U.S. cup stock (mixed with the water the *shiitake* has been soaked in)
- 2 tsps soy sauce
- 1 Tbsp sugar
- 1/2 Tbsp *sake*
- 1/2 Tbsp *mirin* sweet cooking *sake*

About 1 inch lotus root (thin)

C
- 1 Tbsp vinegar
- 1 Tbsp sugar
- Pinch of salt
- 3 Tbsps water

2 egg

D
- Small quantity of salt
- Small quantity of *sake*

6 shrimps
2 Tbsps salmon roe
6 snow peas
1 Tbsps white sesame seeds
Salt

※ The cooking time does not include the time for softening the dried *shiitake* mushroom.

【作り方】

1 寿し飯を準備する。（P22、23参照）

2 にんじんは皮をむいて2cmの長さのせん切りにし、Aを加えて煮る。

3 干ししいたけは水で戻し、やわらかくなったらBで煮て冷めたら半分に切り、さらに薄切りにする。

4 れんこんは皮をむき、薄切りにしてさっと塩ゆでし、熱いうちにCに漬け甘酢れんこんを作る。

5 卵は溶いてDを加え薄焼き卵を焼き、冷めたらせん切りにして錦糸卵にする。

6 えびは背わたを取り除き、殻つきのまま塩ゆでにし、冷めたら殻をむく。

7 絹さやは筋を取り除いたら、塩ゆでにする。

8 寿し飯がまだ温かいうちに汁けをきった2のにんじん、3の干ししいたけ、白ごまを加え切り混ぜる。

※具材と寿し飯をへらやしゃもじでやわらかく切り混ぜるようにすること。混ぜすぎるとご飯がつぶれてべたついた寿しになるので注意したい。

9 器に8を盛り、4の甘酢れんこん、5の錦糸卵、6のゆでえび、7の絹さや、いくらを彩りよく散らす。

【DIRECTIONS】

1 Make vinegared rice. (See p.22 and 23.)

2 Peel the carrot and cut into 3/4 inch strips, and cook in **A**.

3 Soak dried *shiitake* mushrooms in cold water to soften. When softened, cook the *shiitake* in **B**. When cool, cut the *shiitake* in halves, and then cut into narrow strips.

4 Peel the lotus root, and thinly slice. Boil the lotus root in salty water, and marinate it in **C** while hot to make sweet-vinegared lotus root.

5 Beat the eggs and add **D**. Make paper-thin omelets, and cut into julienne strips when cool.

6 Devein the shrimps, and boil them in their shells in salty water. When cool, shell the shrimps.

7 String the snow peas, and boil them in salty water.

8 While the vinegared rice is still warm, add the drained carrot prepared in **2**, cut the *shiitake* mushrooms, add the white sesame seeds, and mix them.
※ Use a flat wooden spoon or spatula in a sideways cutting motion to mix the ingredients with vinegared rice. Be careful not to over stir the rice to prevent it from being mashed and sticky.

9 Place the vinegared rice on a plate, and scatter over the sweet-vinegared lotus root, strips of omelets, boiled shrimps, boiled snow peas, and salmon roe.

2-a

にんじんを2cmの長さに切る
Cut carrot into a 3/4 inch length

2-b

にんじんをAで煮る
Cook carrot in A

3-a

干ししいたけを水で戻す
Soak dried *shiitake* mushrooms in cold water to soften

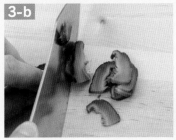

3-b

しいたけを薄切りにする
Cut *shiitake* mushrooms into narrow strips

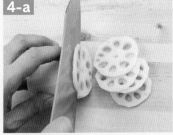

4-a

れんこんを薄切りにする
Slice lotus root thin

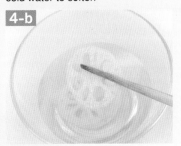

4-b

塩ゆでしたれんこんをCに漬ける
Marinate salty-water boiled lotus root in C.

5-a

溶き卵とDを混ぜる
Mix beaten eggs with D

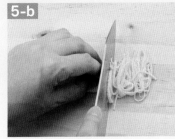

5-b

せん切りにして錦糸卵をつくる
Cut omelets into julienne strips

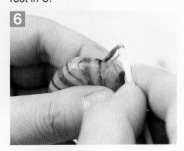

6

えびの背わたを取る
Devein shrimps

7

絹さやの筋を取る
String snow peas

8

寿し飯ににんじん、しいたけ、白ごまを加え切り混ぜる
Use a flat wooden spoon in a sideways cutting motion to mix the drained carrot, cut *shiitake* mushrooms, and white sesame seeds with vinegared rice.

9

仕上げにいくらを散らす
Scatter over salmon roe as a finishing touch

雛祭りを楽しむレシピ
Recipe to enjoy *Hina-matsuri*, or Girls' Festival

はまぐりの潮汁
雛祭を祝うちらし寿しとともにいただく、はまぐりの潮汁

about
10
min

Hard-Shell Clam *Ushio-Jiru*
Hard-shell clam *ushio-jiru* goes with the celebratory dish of *chirashi-zushi* for the Girl's Festival

■材料・2人分

はまぐり（小） ……………………………4個
※大きなはまぐりの場合は、2個でOK

昆布 ………………………………約6〜7cm
水 …………………………………400cc
酒 …………………………………大さじ1
塩 …………………………………適量
三つ葉 ……………………………適量
ゆず ………………………………適量

Ingredients (serves 2)

4 live small hard-shell clams
※ Use 2, if the clams are large.

About 2 1/2 inches *konbu* kelp
1 2/3 U.S. cups water
1 Tbsp *sake*
Salt
Trefoil stalks
Yuzu Japanese lime rind

※ Basically, *ushio-jiru* is a type of clear soup which is made without stock.

【作り方】

1 はまぐりは塩水（分量外）で砂出しをする。

2 三つ葉は水洗いし、ざく切りにする。ゆずは皮をせん切りにする。

3 鍋に**1**のはまぐりと水、昆布、酒を入れ火にかけ、煮立ったら昆布を取る。はまぐりの口が開いたら器に取る。汁は塩で味を調える。

4 **3**の汁を器に注ぎ、**2**の三つ葉とゆずの皮を添える。

【DIRECTIONS】

1 Leave the clams in salty water (extra quantity of salt) to allow them to expel sand.

2 Rinse the trefoil stalks with water, and roughly cut them. Cut the *yuzu* rind into julienne strips.

3 Put the clams prepared in **1**, water, *konbu* kelp and *sake* in a pot, and heat. When it boils, remove the *konbu* kelp. When the clams open, remove them from the soup to put them in bowls. Add salt to season the soup.

4 Pour the soup into bowls, and add the cut trefoil and julienne strips of *yuzu* rind.

吸い物の具のバリエーション
Variations of Clear Soup Ingredients

★かまぼこと三つ葉

Kamaboko fish paste and trefoil

★てまり麩とわかめ、絹さや

Temari-fu ball-shaped dried wheat gluten, *wakame* seaweed and *kinusaya* snow peas

★鶏肉とかまぼこ、かいわれ大根

Chicken, *kamaboko* fish paste and young giant white radish shoot

寿し飯の作り方
ちらし寿し、巻き寿し、いなり寿しなどに使う寿し飯の作り方を覚えよう

How to Prepare Vinegared Rice
Let's learn how to make vinegared rice for garnished *sushi*, *sushi* rolls, or *sushi* pockets

■材料・2〜3人分（出来上がり約700g）

米	2合
湯	400cc
昆布	5〜6cm長さ1枚
酢	大さじ3
砂糖	大さじ2と1/2
塩	小さじ1

■ Ingredients (serves 2 or 3, about 24 1/2 oz)

1 1/2 U.S. cups rice
1 2/3 U.S. cups hot water
About 2 inches *konbu* kelp
3 Tbsps vinegar
2 1/2 Tbsps sugar
1 tsp salt

【作り方】

1 米は炊く30分前にとぎ、ざるに上げて水けをきる。炊飯器に米を入れ、湯と昆布を加えて炊く（湯炊き）。

※通常は米を炊く時は水で炊き上げるが、寿し飯などの大量の米を炊く場合、湯炊きにする場合もある。湯炊きにすると寿し飯がサラリと、むらなく炊き上がる利点がある。

2 小鍋に酢、砂糖、塩を合わせ火にかけ、煮立たせないようにして砂糖と塩を溶かす。

3 1のご飯を水でしめらせた飯台にあけ、2の合わせ酢を回しかけ、しゃもじで切るように手早く合わせる。

※飯台に移すことで余分な水分が抜け、ご飯がべたっとしない。

4 合わせ酢がご飯に均等になじんでほぐれたら、うちわであおぎながらさらに切り混ぜ、余分な酢けをとばす。人肌くらいになれば寿し飯の出来上がり。水にしめらせ固く絞った清潔な布巾をかけておく。

※ぬれた布巾をかけておくことによって、ご飯の乾燥を防ぐことができる。

【DIRECTIONS】

1 Wash the rice 30 min before cooking, and drain on a sieve. Place the rice in a rice cooker, add hot water and *konbu* kelp, and cook. (Hot-water rice cooking)

※ Cold water is usually used to cook rice. But when cooking a large quantity of rice for *sushi* and other dishes, hot water is sometimes used. With hot-water, rice is cooked evenly, which makes vinegared rice firm.

2 Put the vinegar, sugar and salt in a small pot, and heat until the sugar and salt dissolve. Do not boil the solution.

3 Put the cooked rice in a wooden *sushi* bowl, and sprinkle the vinegar dressing prepared in **2** in a circular motion. Use a flat wooden spoon to mix it quickly in a cutting motion.

※ A wooden *sushi* bowl helps to remove extra moisture, preventing the rice from being sticky.

4 When the rice is loosened without any lumps left, evenly mix with the vinegar dressing, mix the rice further with the wooden spoon quickly in a sideways slicing motion, while cooling it with a hand fan, to allow the extra vinegar to evaporate. When the rice cools down to body temperature, it's done. Cover the rice with a clean cloth moistened with water and tightly squeezed.

※ The moistened cloth covering protects the rice from drying out.

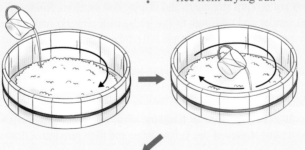

合わせ酢を外側から回しかける

Sprinkle the vinegar dressing from the edge in a circular motion.

全体にまんべんなく回しかける

Sprinkle evenly all over the rice.

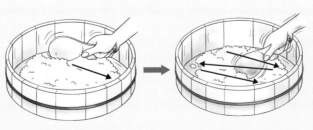

うちわであおぎながら、しゃもじでご飯を切るように混ぜる

Using a flat wooden spoon, toss the rice with horizontal, cutting strokes while cooling the rice with a hand fan.

ご飯がベタつかないように手早く切り混ぜる

Mix swiftly using a sideways cutting motion to prevent the rice from becoming mushy.

端午の節句 *Tango-no-Sekku* (Boys' Festival)

男の子の立身出世や、無病息災などを願って、鯉のぼりや武者人形、兜などを飾り、願いを込めて祝う端午の節句。男の子を持つ家庭では、江戸時代から脈々と続くこの伝統を守り、我が子のすこやかな成長を願うのである。

Tango-no-Sekku is the day when carp streamers are put up and doll warriors, war helmet decorations, and other items are displayed to wish boys social success and good health. At this event, parents with a son follow this long tradition that has continued since the Edo Era and pray for the healthy growth of their son.

端午の節句の歴史と由来 Origin and history of *Tango-no-Sekku* (Boys' Festival)

　五月五日には、男の子がいる家庭では、鯉のぼりを立て、武者人形、金太郎人形、鎧、兜などを飾り、粽や柏餅を飾り、いただく。また、菖蒲が入った湯や、菖蒲を鉢巻として締めたりする。

　現在のような端午の節句の様式になったのは、江戸時代の武家からだといわれている。その当時は、男児の出世を願って、庭先で紙、布、不織布などに鯉の絵を描き、鯉の形に模した吹き流しを立ててなびかせていたらしい。これが鯉のぼりのはじまりである。この鯉のぼりは、中国の故事で、黄河の急流にある竜門と呼ばれる滝を鯉のみが登りきって竜になれたことから、立身出世ができるといわれたことが由来である。

　武者人形、兜は武士の大将を表わし、立身出世と強いものの象徴である。金太郎人形は相撲で熊にも勝つほど強いため、やはり強いものの象徴であり、子供が丈夫に強く育つことを願って飾る。

　菖蒲は尚武 (武術を修練し、戦いの攻防技術に通じ、心身を強健にし、力と勇気をたずさえること)、勝負に例えられる。また、古くから薬草とされている菖蒲の葉や根をお風呂に入れて入浴することで、邪気を払い子供の無病息災を願った。

On May 5, families with a boy put up carp streamers and display doll warriors, *Kintaro* (baby warrior) dolls, armor and war helmet decorations and similar and offerings to the gods, with *chimaki* (cake wrapped in bamboo leaves) and *kashiwa-mochi* (rice cake wrapped in oak leaves). People often take a bath scented with iris leaves and also wear an iris leaf around their heads.

The form of the Boys' Festival, as it is held today, is said to have originated in the families of *bushi* in the Edo Era. At first, it appears that to pray for the social success of their son, the parents put up streamers in their garden, modeled after carp and made of paper, cloth or unwoven cloth, etc. on which carp were drawn. These are the origins of the present day carp streamers. According to Chinese tradition, of all fishes, only the carp was able to leap the waterfall known as *Ryumon* located in a rapid stream of the Yellow River and then turn into a dragon, meaning the carp became a symbol of social success.

Doll warriors and war helmet decorations express generals and are symbols of success in life and great strength. *Kintaro* is a legendary hero who was strong enough as to beat a bear in a *sumo* wrestling and thus also symbolizes strength. Parents display *Kintaro* dolls to wish their sons healthy growth.

Shobu is the Japanese word for iris but has two homonyms: one of which means martial spirit (training in martial arts familiarizing with strategies for battles, making the mind and body strong, and having power and courage) and the other, a fight. Iris has also long been used as a medicinal herb. By taking a bath to which the leaves and roots of this plant are added, people hoped that noxious vapors would be driven out from the body and their children would have sound health.

鯉のぼりの名称 Names of the parts of the carp streamer

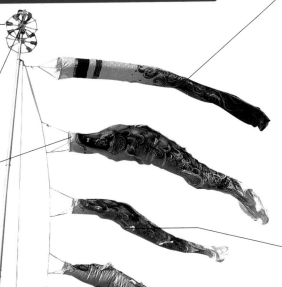

矢車
※魔よけの意味がある。

Arrow wheels
※People believed that these wheels would drive out noxious vapors from their body.

回転球か籠玉
Revolving ball or cage ball

黒鯉 (真鯉)
※黒く、大きい真鯉はお父さんを表わす。

Black carp
※The large black carp represents the father.

吹き流し
※吹き流しは五色で、これは古代中国の「五行説」に由来している。「五行説」とは、万物は木・火・土・金・水の五つの要素で形成されているという考え方。
※木＝青、火＝赤、土＝黄、金＝白、水＝黒を表わす。
※魔よけの意味や家を象徴している。

Streamer
※ The streamer has five colors, which originate in the Chinese doctrine of the five elements. This is the belief that all things are composed of five elements, i.e. wood, fire, earth, metal, and water.
※ Wood is shown by blue, fire by red, earth by yellow, metal by white, and water by black.
※ The streamer has the function of a talisman to protect people from evil and symbolizes the household.

赤鯉 (緋鯉)
※赤い緋鯉はお母さんを表わす。

Red carp
※The red carp represents the mother.

青鯉 (子鯉)
※子供たちを表わす。

Blue carp
※ The blue carp represents children.

端午の節句の祝い方と祝い膳 How to celebrate the Boys' Festival and special food for the event

　子供が初めて迎える初節句の場合は、お嫁さんの実家や親戚などから、五月人形、鎧、兜、鯉のぼりのいずれかを贈る習慣がある。

　ちなみに五月人形の段飾りは三段が多く、上段に鎧や兜を、武者人形は中段に、下段に粽や柏餅を飾る。

　雛祭りのような豪華な祝い膳を食べることはないが、中国の故事にならい、災いを除けるために粽をいただく。また、柏餅を包む柏は、新芽が出ないと古い葉は落ちないため、「子供が生まれるまで親は死なない」といわれ、「跡継ぎが途絶えない」「子孫繁栄」の意味を込めて端午の節句に柏餅を食べるようになった。

There is a tradition that at the first Boys' Festival celebrated for a baby boy, the parents or relatives of the mother present dolls for the festival, armor, war helmet decorations or carp streamers to the baby's family.

Three-tier decorations are mostly used for the display of dolls for the Boys' Festival: armor and war helmet decorations are placed on the top tier, doll warriors on the middle one and *chimaki* and *kashiwa-mochi* on the bottom one.

While no sumptuous dishes are served at the Boys' Festival in comparison to those for the Girls' Festival, people have *chimaki* to avoid evil in line with the Chinese tradition. Oak, whose leaves are used to wrap *kashiwa-mochi*, does not drop old leaves before sending out new shoots. Because of this, people believe that if you eat *kashiwa-mochi*, you will never die before your child is born, will always have an heir and your descendants will prosper. This is why *kashiwa-mochi* began to be eaten at the Boys' Festival.

端午の節句を楽しむレシピ
Recipe to enjoy *Tango-no-Sekku*, or Boys' Festival

手巻き寿し

子供たちの大好きな具材を準備して、端午の節句を祝う

about
20
min

Hand-Rolled *Sushi*

Celebrate *Tango-no-Sekku* with hand-rolled *sushi* with children's favorite ingredients

■材料・2〜3人分

寿し飯	2合分		**B** [レモン汁	少々
焼きのり	5〜6枚		マヨネーズ	大さじ2
まぐろ（刺身用さく）	5〜6cm		きゅうり	1/2本
サーモン（刺身用さく）	5〜6cm		ラディッシュ	2個
ほたて貝柱（刺身用）	2個		スプラウト	1/2パック
いくら	大さじ2		大葉	5〜6枚
卵	2個		プリーツレタス	3〜4枚
A [砂糖	小さじ2		コーン（缶詰）	適量
酒	小さじ2		万能ねぎ	適量
しょう油	少々		わさび	適量
塩たらこ	1/2腹		しょう油	適量

Ingredients (serves 2 or 3)

Vinegared rice, cooked with 1 1/2 U.S. cups rice
5-6 sheets toasted *nori* seaweed
About 2 inches tuna block (for *sashimi*)
About 2 inches salmon (for *sashimi*)
2 scallop abductor muscles (for *sashimi*)
2 Tbsps salmon roe
2 eggs

A ⎡ 2 tsps sugar
⎢ 2 tsps *sake*
⎣ Small quantity of soy sauce

1/2 piece salted cod roe

B ⎡ Small quantity of lemon juice
⎣ 2 Tbsps mayonnaise

1/2 cucumber
2 radishes
1/2 pack white radish sprouts
5-6 green perilla leaves
3-4 leaves of leaf lettuce
Canned corn
Bannou-negi onion
Wasabi
Soy sauce

【作り方】

1 寿し飯を準備する。（P22、23参照）

2 まぐろ、サーモンは巻きやすいよう細切りにする。

3 ほたて貝柱は薄切りにする。焼きのりは1/4に切る。

4 卵を溶いてAを加えて混ぜ、卵焼きを焼く。冷めたら棒状に切る。

5 塩たらこは皮を除いてほぐし、Bを加え混ぜる。

6 きゅうりは細切りに、ラディッシュは薄切りに、万能ねぎは小口切りにする。

7 スプラウトは根を切り取る。水洗いした大葉は固い軸を取る。プリーツレタスは食べやすい大きさにちぎる。コーンは水けをきる。

8 2～7（プリーツレタス以外）の具材やいくらを盛り合わせ、お好みのものを焼きのりまたはプリーツレタスで巻いて、わさび、しょう油でいただく。

【DIRECTIONS】

1 Make vinegared rice. (See p.22 and 23.)

2 Cut the tuna and salmon into easy-to-roll size strips.

3 Thinly slice the scallops. Cut the *nori* seaweed sheets into 4 pieces.

4 Beat the eggs, and mix with **A**. Make an omelet, and cut it into stick shapes when cooled.

5 Skin the cod roe, loosen and mix with **B**.

6 Cut the cucumber into thin strips. Thinly slice the radish. Cut the *bannou-negi* onion into small pieces.

7 Cut off the roots of the white radish sprouts. Rinse the green perilla leaves, and cut off their hard stalks. Tear the leaves of leaf lettuce into bite-sized pieces. Drain the canned corn.

8 Arrange ingredients 2-7 (except for the leaves of leaf lettuce) and salmon roe on a serving plate. Roll your favorite ingredients with the *nori* or leaves of leaf lettuce at the table, and eat with some *wasabi* and soy sauce.

花見 *Hanami* (viewing of cherry and other blossoms)

はなみ

春になると桜前線が気になるという人も多いことだろう。花見はまさに春を彩る行事といってよいほど日本人は好きである。桜、梅、桃の花の下をゆっくり歩きながら花を愛でるのもよし、親しい人と好きな食べものを持ち寄って宴を開くのもよいだろう。

When spring has come, many Japanese will be anxious about the movement of the cherry-blossom front. *Hanami* or blossom viewing is so loved by Japanese that it is an event that represents spring for them. You can enjoy the beauty of cherry, *ume* (Japanese apricot), or peach blossoms while strolling under the trees or can also hold a party under these trees with your friends, with people bringing their favorite food.

花見の歴史と由来 Origin and history of *Hanami* (viewing of cherry and other blossoms)

　花見というと私たちはすぐに桜を思い浮かべるが、実は最初の花見は梅や桃だった。奈良時代に中国から伝来した梅を当時の貴族たちが鑑賞していたことがわかっている。

　平安時代になると梅に代わって桜が鑑賞されるようになり、花見といえば桜になった。記録に残っている最初の花見は、弘仁三年（812年）に嵯峨天皇が、神泉苑で花宴を催したと『日本後紀』に記されている。

　室町時代になると貴族たちの花見は、武士階級まで広がった。その当時は将軍の自邸でおこなわれていたらしい。その後、織田信長、豊臣秀吉らが野外に出て花見をするようになった。中でも豊臣秀吉の〝醍醐の花見〟は豪華で有名だ。江戸時代になると八代将軍の徳川吉宗が江戸の各地に桜を植えさせ、花見を奨励したことから庶民に広まったといわれている。

The word *hanami* easily brings to mind cherry-blossom viewing for Japanese people today, but *hanami* in the early days was the viewing of *ume* or peach blossoms. It is known that nobles in the Nara Era (710-793) started to enjoy the beauty of *ume* blossoms, which were imported from China during this era.

During the Heian Era, cherry blossoms took the place of *ume* in blossom viewing. The first cherry-blossom viewing was the party held by Emperor Saga at *Shinsen-en* Park in 812 that was recorded in *Nihon-koki*, an official chronicle.

In the Muromachi Era (1392-1477), the practice of *hanami* spread from nobles to warriors. In those days, *hanami* seems to have been held in the residence of the *shogun*. Subsequently, Oda Nobunaga, Toyotomi Hideyoshi and others began to hold *hanami* outdoors. In particular, Daigo no Hanami (*Hanami* party held in Daigo), as given by Toyotomi Hideyoshi, is well known for its magnificence. In the Edo Era, Tokugawa Yoshimune, the eighth shogun, made people plant cherry trees everywhere in Edo (present Tokyo) and encouraged them to enjoy *hanami*, which helped popularize cherry-blossom viewing among the people.

花見を初めてした嵯峨天皇は、文人たちを招いて詩を吟じさせたといわれる。その後、庭に楽所（がくしょ）を設け、夜になると庭火をたいて夜桜を楽しんだらしい。

江戸時代になると、桜の名所（江戸の桜の名所は上野（うえの）、向島（むこうじま）、飛鳥山（あすかやま）など、京都では嵐山（あらしやま）、清水（きよみず）、知恩院（ちおんいん）、八坂（やさか）など）には、焼餅、団子、そば、うどんなどを売る多くの露店が並んだといわれる。「花より団子」といわれる言葉は、この江戸時代に売っていた花見団子（桜色、白色、緑色の三色の団子を串に刺したもの）に由来している。これは、花の鑑賞もせず、団子という実質的なものを選ぶ行動を揶揄（やゆ）したものである。

現在は、料理を持ち寄ったり購入して、お酒を飲みながら花を愛でることが多い。料理はちらし寿しや煮ものなどが定番だろう。公園内で火をおこしたり、カラオケは近隣の迷惑になるのでひかえたいものだ。

また、『徒然草（つれづれぐさ）』に「酒のみ連歌して、はては、大きなる枝、心なく折り取りぬ」と紹介されているように、酔って桜の枝を折るなどという行為は田舎者だといっている。この教えのようにけっして桜の枝を折ったり、登ってはいけない。

It is said that Emperor Saga, who first gave *hanami*, invited poets and poetesses and had them recite poems. After that when night came, the Emperor and other participants seem to have kindled a fire in the garden and enjoyed cherry blossoms at night while listening to music played at the open-air stage built for the event.

In the Edo Era, it is said that at places famous for beautiful cherry blossoms (e.g. Ueno, Mukojima and Asukayama in Edo, present-day Tokyo, and Arashiyama, Kiyomizu, Chion-in Temple and Yasaka in Kyoto), many stalls of *yakimochi* (toasted rice cake), dumplings, buckwheat noodles, wheat noodles, and others were set up for visitors during the season. The proverb "Dumplings rather than blossoms (which means that bread

is better than birdsong)" has its origin in *hanami-dango* or dumplings for cherry-blossom viewing (pink, white, and green dumplings on a skewer). This pokes fun at people's preference for dumplings (substantial things) to cherry blossoms (non-substantial things).

絵は江戸時代の上野の花見風景
（東京都江戸東京博物館「東都上野花見」歌川広重（二代）・複製禁止）

This picture shows a scene of *hanami* in Ueno in the Edo Era (Touto Ueno Hanami by Utagawa Hiroshige II, the Edo-Tokyo Museum, Tokyo; reproduction prohibited)

At present, people bring or buy food and drinks and enjoy the cherry blossoms while drinking under the trees in most cases. The typical dishes eaten are probably *chirashi-zushi* and simmered food. Some people make fires and sing with *karaoke* accompaniment during cherry-blossom viewing but these practices should be avoided because they will disturb residents in the neighborhood.

Tsurezure-gusa, a collection of short essays written in 1330 to 1331, says: "Some people drink sake and sing songs loudly and even snap large branches of cherry trees thoughtlessly." The author wrote that the act of breaking branches of cherry trees while getting drunk is that of a bumpkin. As this writer said, you should never snap the branch of cherry trees and climb the trees during *hanami*.

江戸時代には、桜色、白色、緑色の三色団子が、桜の名所地で売られていた

In the Edo Era, three-color *hanami-dango*, as shown on the right, was sold at places known for beautiful cherry blossoms.

日本各地にある名桜の中でも、歴史があり、枝ぶりなども見事な名木を日本三大桜といっている。
The top three cherry trees are those having a very long history and very elegant branches.

三春滝桜 Miharu-Taki-Zakura

樹齢1000年以上もある巨木の三春滝桜は、福島県田村郡三春町にある。この桜は江戸彼岸系の紅枝垂桜で満開になると、名のごとく滝のように見える。国の天然記念物に指定されている。

Taki-zakura is a huge cherry tree, with a history of over 1,000 years and exists in Miharu-machi, Tamura-gun, Fukushima Prefecture. This tree is a rouge weeping cherry of the Edo-higan variety. When it comes into full bloom, the cherry blossoms resemble waterfalls, as the name suggests. This tree is designated as the country's natural monument.

山高神代桜 Yamataka-Jindai-Zakura

山梨県北杜市武川町にある樹齢約2000年もの神代桜。日本武尊が植えた伝説や、日蓮が衰え始めたこの桜を回復させたという逸話がある。幹の周囲13.5mもある。

This is a *jindai-zakura* (cherry tree in the age of the gods) 2,000 years old located in Mukawa-machi, Hokuto, Yamanashi Prefecture. There is a legend that this tree was planted by Yamato-Takeru-No-Mikoto, an Imperial prince in ancient times and that Nichiren, the founder of the Nichiren sect of Buddhism, recovered this cherry when it began to weaken. The peak girth of this tree is as much as 13.5m.

淡墨桜 Usuzumi-Zakura

今から1550余年前に男大迹王（26代継体天皇）が、植えたものと伝えられている。樹高16.3m、幹回り9.91m、枝張り東西26.90m、南北20.20mもある巨木だ。満開になると白色で、散りぎわに淡い墨色を帯びてくるのが名の由来。岐阜県本巣市にある。

This cherry tree is said to have been planted by Oto-No-Oh (26th Emperor Keitai) over 1,550 years ago. This is a giant tree, with a height of 16.3m, a peak girth of 9.91m and an expansion of branches of 26.90m from east to west and 20.20m from north to south. The name originates in the fact that in full bloom, the blossoms are initially white and then become light gray before beginning to fall. This cherry exists in Motosu, Gifu Prefecture.

日本三大夜桜 Top three sights of cherry blossoms at night

昼間の桜も風情があるが、夜にライトアップされた桜も、実に神秘的で美しい。ここでそんな日本三大夜桜を紹介しよう。

While cherry blossoms in daytime are elegant, those lit up at night also look very mysterious and beautiful. Here are the top three sights of cherry blossoms at night.

高田公園 Takada Park

新潟県上越市にある高田公園。約4000本もの満開の桜と三重櫓、お堀がライトアップされてなんとも美しく、幻想的だ。

Takada Park is located in Joetsu, Niigata Prefecture. As many as 4,000 cherry trees in full bloom as well as the three-tier turret and the moat are lit up, creating very beautiful and fantastic scenes.

弘前公園 Hirosaki Park

青森県弘前市にある城跡が残る弘前公園内には日本最古のソメイヨシノをはじめとする約52種の桜が約2600本もある。

Hirosaki Park is located in the ruins of a castle in Hirosaki, Aomori Prefecture. This park has about 2,600 cherries of about 52 varieties, including the oldest *somei-yoshino* cherries in Japan.

上野公園 Ueno Park

江戸時代より桜の名所として知られる東京の上野公園内には約1100本ものソメイヨシノがあり、ライトアップされた満開の桜は見事だ。

Ueno Park in Tokyo has been known for beautiful cherry blossoms since the Edo Era. The park has about 1,100 *somei-yoshino* cherry trees, and the illuminated cherry blossoms in full bloom present really wonderful scenes.

上野観光連盟（撮影者：須賀一）
Photos courtesy of the Ueno Tourist Federation (photographer: Hajime Suga)

桜の代表品種 Main varieties of cherry trees

【ソメイヨシノ・染井吉野】
Somei-yoshino
日本全国で見られる観賞用桜の代表品種で、咲きはじめは淡紅色で、満開になると白色になってくる。
This is a representative variety of cherries for cherry-blossom viewing seen all over Japan. The blossoms are light rouge when they begin to shoot and turn white as they come into full bloom.

【エドヒガン・江戸彼岸】
Edo-higan
淡白紅の花を咲かせる。主に本州、四国、九州に分布する。別名アズマヒガン（東彼岸）ともいわれる。
This variety has light whitish-rouge blossoms. It is distributed mainly in the Honshu, Shikoku and Kyushu regions. *Edo-higan* is also known as *azuma-higan*.

【カスミ桜・霞桜】
Kasumi-zakura (haze cherry blossoms)
北海道、本州、四国に分布する。白色か微紅色の花を咲かせる。花柄、葉などに毛があるため、ケヤマ桜（毛山桜）ともいわれる。
This variety is distributed in the Hokkaido, Honshu and Shikoku regions and has white or light rouge blossoms. Because the peduncles, leaves, etc. of this tree have fuzz, it is also called *ke-yamazakura* (mountain cherry tree with fuzz).

【シダレ桜・枝垂桜】
Shidare-zakura (weeping cherry)
エドヒガンの変種のシダレ桜は、枝が長く、名の通り枝がしだれているのが特徴。ヤエベニシダレ（八重紅枝垂）などがある。
Shidare-zakura is a variety of *Edo-higan* and is characterized by long weeping branches, as the name suggests. This variety includes *yaebeni-shidare* (double-petaled rouge weeping cherry).

花見を楽しむレシピ
Recipe to enjoy a picnic under the cherry blossoms

五種類の野菜とそぼろのちらし寿し
花を愛でながら、体にやさしい五種類の野菜のちらし寿しをいただく

about
90
min

Chirashi-Zushi, or Garnished *Sushi*, with 5 Vegetables and *Soboro* Minced Chicken

Savor *chirashi-zushi* with 5 healthy vegetables, while enjoying the beauty of the flowers

■材料・3人分

米	………………………………………	2合
水	………………………………………	360cc
昆布	………………………………………	約10cm

A
酢	………………………………………	大さじ3
砂糖	………………………………………	大さじ2
塩	………………………………………	小さじ1/2

干ししいたけ	………………………………	3枚

B
だし	………………………………………	1/3カップ
砂糖	………………………………………	大さじ2
しょう油	………………………………	大さじ2

にんじん	………………………………	1/3本

C
だし	………………………………………	1/3カップ
砂糖	………………………………………	小さじ1
塩	………………………………………	少々

れんこん	………………………………	1/4節

D
だし	………………………………………	大さじ2
酢	………………………………………	大さじ1
砂糖	………………………………………	小さじ2
塩	………………………………………	少々

ごぼう	………………………………	1/3本

E
だし	………………………………………	1/3カップ
砂糖	………………………………………	小さじ2
しょう油	………………………………	小さじ1

絹さや	………………………………	15枚
鶏ひき肉	………………………………	100g

F
しょう油	………………………………	大さじ1
砂糖	………………………………………	大さじ1
みりん	………………………………	大さじ1
酒	………………………………………	大さじ1/2
しょうが汁	…………………………	小さじ1

▦ Ingredients (serves 3)

1 1/2 U.S. cups rice
1 1/2 U.S. cups cold water
About 4 inches *konbu* kelp

A
- 3 Tbsps vinegar
- 2 Tbsps sugar
- 1/2 tsp salt

3 dried *shiitake* mushrooms

B
- 1/3 U.S. cup stock
- 2 Tbsps sugar
- 2 Tbsps soy sauce

1/3 carrot

C
- 1/3 U.S. cup stock
- 1 tsp sugar
- Small quantity of salt

1/4 block of lotus root

D
- 2 Tbsps stock
- 1 Tbsp vinegar
- 2 tsps sugar
- Small quantity of salt

1/3 burdock

E
- 1/3 U.S. cup stock
- 2 tsps sugar
- 1 tsp soy sauce

15 snow peas
3 1/2 oz minced chicken

F
- 1 Tbsp soy sauce
- 1 Tbsp sugar
- 1 Tbsp *mirin* sweet cooking *sake*
- 1/2 Tbsp *sake*
- 1 tsp ginger juice

【作り方】

1 寿し飯を作る。（P22, 23を参照）
米は炊く30分前にといでざるに上げておき、炊飯器に水とさっと洗った昆布を入れて炊き、約10分蒸らしたら、飯台またはボウルに入れて、**A**を合わせて作った寿し酢を数回に分けて加え、ご飯をしゃもじで切るように混ぜ合わせ、うちわであおいでつやを出す。

2 干ししいたけは水でやわらかく戻して軸を切り、小鍋に**B**のだしと砂糖を入れて弱火で4〜5分煮込み、しょう油を加えて汁けが少なくなるまで煮ふくめ、冷めたら薄切りにする。

3 にんじんは皮をむいて、2cmの長さの拍子切りにし、小鍋に入れて**C**でやわらかくなるまで煮ふくめる。

4 れんこんは皮をむいていちょう切りにし、水にさらしてから熱湯でゆで、合わせた**D**につけておく。

5 ごぼうは包丁で皮をこそげて約5mm角に切ったら水にさらし、小鍋に入れて**E**のだしと砂糖を入れて弱火で4〜5分煮込み、しょう油を加えて汁けが少なくなるまで煮ふくめる。

6 絹さやは筋を取って塩（分量外）を入れた湯でゆでてから冷水に取り、せん切りにしておく。

7 鍋に鶏ひき肉、合わせた**F**を入れてポロポロになるようにかき混ぜながら炒り、肉に味を煮ふくませる。

8 1の寿し飯に7の鶏ひき肉、2の干ししいたけ、5のごぼう、3のにんじん、4のれんこんの順に入れてごはんを切るように混ぜ、6の絹さやを散らせば出来上がり。

【DIRECTIONS】

1 Make vinegared rice. (See p.22 and 23.)
Wash the rice 30 min before cooking, and leave it on a seive to drain. Place the rice, water, and the lightly rinsed *konbu* kelp in a rice cooker, and cook. After cooking finishes, leave the cooker covered for about 10 min to allow the grains to settle. Put the rice in a bowl or a wooden *sushi* bowl, and pour **A** in several parts. Use a flat wooden spoon to mix the rice in a cutting motion, while cooling it with a hand fan to make the rice shine.

2 Soak the dried *shiitake* mushrooms in cold water to soften. When softened, cut off the stalks, and put the mushrooms in a small pot with **B**. Cook over a low heat for 4-5 minutes. Add the soy sauce, and continue simmering until most of the liquid has evaporated. After cooling, slice the mushrooms.

3 Peel the carrot, and cut into 3/4 in-long bar rectangles. Cook the carrot in **C** in a small pot until soft.

4 Peel the lotus root, and cut it into quarter rounds. After soaking in cold water, boil the cut lotus root in hot water. Marinate it in **D**.

5 Scrape off the skin of the burdock with a kitchen knife. Cut the burdock into 1/5 inch squares, and soak them in cold water for a while. Put the cut burdock in a small pot together with **E**, and simmer over a low heat for 4-5 min. Add the soy sauce, and continue simmering until most of the liquid has evaporated.

6 String the snow peas, and boil them in water with salt (extra quantity). Cool them in cold water, and cut them into narrow strips.

7 Put the minced chicken and the mixture of **F** in a pot, and cook while mixing the meat to make it crumbly. Allow the chicken to absorb the liquid.

8 Put on the vinegared rice prepared in **1** in the order of the minced chicken, cut *shiitake* mushrooms, burdock, carrot, and lotus root. Use a flat wooden spoon in a cutting motion to mix the ingredients with the rice. Scatter over the snow peas as a finishing touch.

バリエーション

★春らしく、ゆでたけのこの短冊切りにし、**C**で煮ふくめたもの。ふき（ゆでたふきの皮を取ったものを約2〜3cmの長さに切り、それをせん切りにしたもの）を**D**につけたものを加えても少し苦味があって美味しい。

VARIATION

★Cut boiled bamboo shoot into rectangles, and cook in **C**. It's a good ingredient for the springtime. It would also be good to add Japanese butterburs, whose slight bitterness will add some tastiness. (Boil Japanese butterburs, and peel them. Cut them into a length of about 1 inch, and cut into julienne strips. Marinate in **D**.)

潮干狩り *Shiohigari* (shellfish gathering)

潮が引いた広い砂浜で、あさりやはまぐりを探す。まさに、水ぬるむ春の
風物詩といってもよいだろう潮干狩り。

People enjoy shellfish gathering on the large beach at low tide. This can really be called a special attraction of spring in Japan when the water gets warmer.

潮干狩りの歴史と由来 Origin and history of *Shiohigari* (shellfish gathering)

三月の上旬からはじまる潮干狩り。干潮と満潮の差が大きい〝大潮〟の日が潮干狩りに適している。

今まで海だった所が潮が引いて、砂浜になる。安全で小さな子供たちでもできるとあってファミリーにも人気があるレジャーである。

そんな潮干狩りだが、もともとは現在のようなレジャーとしてではなく、信仰行事だった。旧暦の三月三日の日は、雛（紙でかたどったもの）を水に流す（雛流し）ために海辺に出かけ、潮水で自らもけがれをはらい、魚や貝類を取って遊ぶ日だったのだ。

沖縄では旧暦の三月三日には、家にいてはいけないといわれ、村中の人が弁当を持って海に繰り出したといわれている。これはアカマターといわれる蛇が若者に化け、村の娘を誘惑して身ごもらせたが、娘が若者の本当の正体に気づき、三月三日に浜に下って身を清めたという話が起源だとされている。

他には古くからおこなわれていた磯遊びが起源だともいわれる。

Shiohigari or shellfish gathering starts in early March. The best day for *shiohigari* is the day of a spring tide when the difference between low and high tides peaks. At spring tide, the tide goes out, turning the sea into a sandy beach. *Shiohigari* is safe and can also be done by little children; thus it is a very popular leisure activity among families.

Originally, *shiohigari* was not a leisure activity as today but an event for religious faith. On March 3 in the lunar calendar, people went to the seaside to discharge paper dolls; they purified themselves with seawater and then enjoyed catching fish and shellfish.

In Okinawa, they say that people believed that they should not be at home on March 3 in the lunar calendar and all of them went to the seaside, taking a lunch box along with them. This custom is said to have originated in the old tale of a village girl: a snake named Akamatah disguised as a young man and seduced the girl, making her pregnant. Becoming aware that the young man was really a snake, the girl went to the nearby beach and purified herself there.

Another theory says that playing at the beach, as was done from olden times, was the origin of *shiohigari*.

潮干狩りでとれる主な貝の種類 Main shellfish caught in *shiohigari*

　日本近海には、およそ5000種類もの貝が生息しているが、そのうち食用にされるのは、あさり、はまぐり、ほたて、あわびなど約50種がいる。
　ちなみに潮干狩りの代表的な貝といえば、あさりだが、「浅い所にすむ貝だから」とか魚や貝をとる「漁り」が名の由来といわれている。

In the sea off Japan, as many as 5,000 or so shellfish species live, of which about 50, including short-neck clams, hard-shell clams, scallops and abalones, are edible.

Typical shellfish gathered in *shiohigari* are short-neck clams. The short-neck clam is called *asari* in Japan, and this Japanese name is said to have originated in the fact that this clam lives in shallow (*asai* in Japanese) places or in *asari*, a Japanese word meaning catching fish and shellfish.

【あさり・浅蜊】
Short-neck clam

潮干狩り場でとれるものは、稚貝放流したものが多い。日本を代表する食用貝で日本各地の内湾に分布する。殻の色や模様はさまざま。

The short-neck clams caught in *shiohigari* are mostly those released into the sea. This clam is the representative edible shellfish in Japan and is distributed in deep bays nationwide. The color and pattern of its shells vary from clam to clam.

【はまぐり・蛤】
Hard-shell clam

名の由来は、小石（ぐり）のように見えることと、まるで栗のような形に見えることから。焼きはま、酒蒸し、汁の実などにされる。

The Japanese name *hamaguri* comes from the fact that this shellfish resembles a *guri* (small stone) and also that its shape also resembles that of a chestnut (*kuri* in Japanese: pronounced *guri* euphonically). Hard-shell clams are eaten by broiling or steeping them in *sake* and then steaming or as ingredients for soup.

【ばか貝・馬鹿貝】
Hen clam

別名あおやぎ（青柳）とも呼ばれる。殻から出た赤い足が、まるでばか者のように見えることが、ばか貝の名の由来である。

Also known as *aoyagi* (trough shell). The Japanese name *baka-gai* (fool shell) originated in the fact that the red foot protruding from the shells looks somewhat foolish.

【まて貝・馬刀貝】
Jack-knife clam

北海道南部から九州に分布。干潟や浅海の砂泥底に巣穴を作ってすむ。塩焼きや、ゆでたものを酢みそあえなどにする。

This shellfish is distributed in the areas off southern Hokkaido to Kyushu and lives in the nest it makes in tidal flats or in the sandy and muddy bottoms of the shallow sea. This shellfish is eaten mainly by sprinkling with salt and broiling or by boiling it and marinating with vinegar and *miso*.

写真提供：ぼうずコンニャクの『市場魚貝類図鑑』（ばか貝、まて貝）

金色のはまぐりを探せ！ Search for golden clams!

　けっして金色のはまぐりが生息しているわけではなく、潮干狩りのシーズンに漁協がおこなっているイベントのひとつ。
　このはまぐりをみつけると、地元特産品がプレゼントされるという。ちなみに赤や銀のあさりもある潮干狩り場があるらしい。また、他の潮干狩り場でさまざまなイベントをしているので、各漁協などのホームページにアクセスしてみよう。

No golden clams actually exist. This is a catchphrase for an event promoted by the fisheries cooperative during the *shiohigari* season.

According to the promoting cooperative, those who successfully find a golden clam hidden in sand will win local specialties. There are rumored to be *shiohigari* sites where red and silver short-neck clams are hidden. Various other events are held at *shiohigari* sites, too; let's access the website of fisheries cooperatives to find fun events!

潮干狩りを楽しむレシピ
しお ひ が

Recipe to enjoy shellfish gathering

あさりご飯

捕れたての砂抜きした新鮮なあさりを炊き込みご飯でいただく

about
12
min

Short-Necked Clam Rice

Savor short-necked clams fresh out of the sea and cleaned in seasoned rice

■材料・2〜3人分

米	2カップ
あさりのむき身	100g
あさつき	5〜6本
しょうが	1片
塩	少々
水	2カップ
酒	大さじ1
薄口しょう油	大さじ1と1/2
塩	小さじ1/4

Ingredients (serves 2 or 3)

1 2/3 U.S. cups rice
3 1/2 oz shucked short-necked clams
5-6 *asatsuki* chives
1 knob ginger
Small quantity of salt
1 2/3 U.S. cups water
1 Tbsp *sake*
1 1/2 Tbsps light soy sauce
1/4 tsp salt

【作り方】

1 米は炊く30分前にとぎ、ざるに上げて水をきっておく。

2 あさりはざるに入れ、塩を少々ふって軽くもみ、水でふり洗いをし、水けをきる。
★塩でもむとぬめりが出てくるので、それをふり洗いする。

3 炊飯器に、米、酒、薄口しょう油、塩を入れ水を加減しながら注ぎ入れ、その上に**2**のあさりを入れて炊く。

4 炊き上がったら、10分ほど蒸らして軽くかき混ぜ、小口切りにしたあさつき、皮をむいてせん切りにし、水にさらした針しょうがを散らしていただく。

【DIRECTIONS】

1 Wash the rice 30 min before cooking, and drain in a sieve.

2 Sprinkle a small quantity of salt on the short-necked clams in a sieve. Lightly rub the clams, rinse in water by gently shaking, and drain.
★ A slimy substance comes out from the clams when rubbed with salt. Rinse off the slime by shaking the sieve in water.

3 Put into a rice cooker the rice, *sake*, light soy sauce, and salt, and pour over the proper quantity of water. Place the clams on top, and cook.

4 When the rice is done, keep the cooker covered, and let it stand for about 10 min to allow the grains to settle. Open the cover, and lightly mix the rice. Sprinkle with the *asatsuki* chives (cut into small rounds), and ginger needles (cut into julienne strips and soaked in water), before serving.

Column

あさりを使った江戸前の味 〝深川丼〟
"*Fukagawa-don*," One-Bowl Meal Using Short-Necked Clams from Tokyo Bay

江戸時代の深川（現在の東京都江東区深川）は、海に面した小さな漁師町だった。もちろん前の海であさりもたくさん捕れた。

当時の漁師たちは朝漁に出る時間が早く、のんびりと朝食を食べている時間がなかったことから、前の晩に食べた〝あさりのみそ汁〟を温かいご飯にかけて食べたのが、この〝深川丼〟のはじまりである。

In the Edo Era, Fukagawa (presently Fukagawa, Koto Ward, Tokyo) was a small fishing town facing Tokyo Bay. At that time, short-necked clams were plentiful in the sea.
Fishermen in those days left home to go fishing very early, having only limited time to have breakfast. So, they poured hot rice *miso* soup over short-necked clams left over from the previous night, and gulped it down. This is the origin of *Fukagawa-don*.

深川丼の作り方
How to make *Fukagawa-don*

■材料・2人分

あさり（新鮮なむき身） …200g
しょうが …………………2かけ
長ねぎ ……………………適量
万能ねぎ …………………適量

A
みそ ……………大さじ1と1/2
しょう油 ………大さじ1と1/2
酒 ………………大さじ1と1/2
みりん …………大さじ1と1/2
砂糖 ……………………小さじ1
水 ………………………大さじ2

刻みのり …………………適量
ご飯（小さめの丼） ……2杯分

▥ Ingredients (serves 2)

7 oz fresh shucked short-necked clams
2 knobs ginger
Naga-negi onion
Bannou-negi onion

A
1 1/2 Tbsps *miso*
1 1/2 Tbsps soy sauce
1 1/2 Tbsps *sake*
1 1/2 Tbsps *mirin* sweet cooking *sake*
1 tsp sugar
2 Tbsps water

Thin strips of *nori* seaweed
2 bowls cooked rice (relatively small *donburi* bowl)

【作り方】

1 あさりを海水より薄めの塩水（分量外）で洗い、水けをきる。

2 しょうがをせん切りにする。長ねぎは斜め切りにする。

3 鍋にAを入れ、2のしょうがを加えて煮立ったら、1のあさりを入れて、身がぷくっとふくらんだら、いったん取り出しておく。

4 3の煮汁を3分の2くらいまで煮詰めたら、3のあさりを入れ、2の長ねぎを加えてさっと煮る。

5 器にご飯を盛り、4のあさりを汁ごとかけ、万能ねぎの小口切りを散らし、最後に刻みのりをのせる。

[DIRECTIONS]

1 Wash the short-necked clams in salty water (extra quantity salt) that is less salty than seawater, and drain.

2 Cut the ginger into julienne strips. Cut the *naga-negi* onion diagonally.

3 Put the ingredients of **A** and the ginger strips in a pot. When the liquid comes to the boil, add the clams. When the clams inflate, remove from the pot.

4 Boil down the liquid until the quantity is reduced to about 2/3rd. Add the clams and the *naga-negi* onion, and cook briefly.

5 Put the rice in a serving bowl. Put the clams and liquid together on top of the rice, and sprinkle with the chopped *bannou-negi* onion and *nori* strips as a finishing touch.

春の和食レシピ

Recipes of Japanese Food in Spring

春を彩る旬の食材
Seasonal Ingredients in Spring

寒い冬がすぎ、草木が芽ぶきはじめると、さまざまな野菜、山菜、魚介類が店頭に並び、私たちの食卓をにぎやかに飾ってくれる春の旬の食材。わらび、ぜんまい、うどなどの山菜はアクを抜いてからいただく。真だいは一年で一番美味しい季節。あさり、はまぐりなどの貝類は身が太って美味しくなる。美味しいものが数多い春の息吹をめいっぱい楽しみたい。

When the cold winter has passed and trees and plants begin to bud, various vegetables, *sansai* (edible wild plants) and fish and shellfish appear at grocery stores. These are the seasonal food materials in spring that are spread on the table. Bracken, royal fern, *udo*, and other *sansai* are eaten after removing harshness from them. Spring is the best season for *madai* red sea bream. Short-neck clam, hard-shell clam, and other shellfishes have fattened and become delicious. Let's fully enjoy spring, a season full of abundant tasty food.

※本書で紹介する食材の旬は基本的なものを紹介している。地方によって異なる場合もある。
※The typically best season for the ingredients in this book is given, and this may differ in some areas.

つくし（土筆）
Fertile shoots of field horsetail

つくしとはスギナの胞子茎で、春を代表する山菜である。はかまといわれる部分を取り除いてから、佃煮、天ぷら、おひたし、あえものなどに使用される。

The fertile shoot of field horsetail is a typical *sansai* in spring. After removing the portion known as the *hakama* (sheath), the shoot is used to prepare *tsukudani* (food broiled down in soy sauce), *tempura*, *ohitashi* (boiled food), *aemono* (marinated dishes) and other dishes.

わらび（蕨）
Bracken

春を代表する山菜のわらびは、日当たりのよい林緑、草地、土手などに生えている。アクを抜いてから、おひたし、あえもの、炒めものなどに使用される。現在、栽培ものもある。

Bracken, another representative *sansai* in spring, grows in sunny places, such as the surroundings of forests, grasslands and banks. After removing the harshness, bracken is used mostly for *ohitashi*, *aemono*, and *itamemono* (stir-fried food). Artificially cultivated bracken is now also available.

ぜんまい（薇）
Royal fern

ぜんまいは収穫してすぐには食べられない。灰汁でゆでてから、もみながら乾燥させ、食べる直前に水で戻してから、煮もの、炒めものなどに使用される。

Gathered royal fern cannot be eaten immediately. It is boiled in lye and dried while rubbing it. Just before cooking it, the dried royal fern is soaked in water and used mainly for *nimono* (food boiled with soy sauce and some sugar) and *itamemono*.

なのはな (菜の花)
Rape blossoms

春を代表する花として親しまれているなのはな。花がまだ蕾のうちに切り、束にして販売されている。あえもの、おひたし、炒めものなどに使用する。別名ナバナという。

Rape blossoms are a representative flower in spring popular among Japanese. This plant is picked when the flower is still a bud and sold in a bundle. It is used mainly for *aemono*, *ohitashi*, and *itamemono*. This plant is also known as *nabana*.

みつば (三葉)
Trefoil

セリ科の多年草で、野生のものと栽培もの (根三つ葉、切り三つ葉、糸三つ葉) がある。おひたし、すいもの、鍋料理などに使用する。ビタミンCが豊富。

Trefoil is an umbelliferous perennial plant, with both wild and cultivated varieties (*ne-mitsuba* [root trefoil], *kiri-mitsuba* [cut trefoil] and *ito-mitsuba* [thread trefoil]). This plant is used mainly for *ohitashi*, soup and *nabe-ryori* (one-pot dishes cooked at the table). It is rich in Vitamin C.

せり (芹)
Japanese parsley

日本原産の野菜のひとつのせりは、湿地などに自生する野生のものと、栽培したものとがある。香りがよく、あえもの、おひたし、汁の実、鍋料理などに使用する。写真は栽培もの。

Japanese parsley is one of the vegetables native to Japan and includes wild varieties that grow in wetlands, as well as cultivated ones. It has a good scent and is used mainly for *aemono*, *ohitashi*, soup, and *nabe-ryori*. The photo shows the cultivated variety.

うど (独活)
Udo

自生する野生のものと、軟化栽培したものとがある。独特な風味があり、アク抜きが必要。あえもの、酢のもの、煮もの、炒めもの、天ぷらなどに使用される。写真は野生のもの。

Udo includes wild varieties and those raised by softening culture. It has a unique taste, and its harshness should be removed before cooking. Its main uses are *aemono*, *sunomono* (vinegared dishes), *itamemono* and *tempura*. The photo shows wild *udo*.

ふき (蕗)
Japanese butterbur

日本原産の野菜のひとつで、野生のものと、栽培のものがある。茎の部分をゆでて、皮をむいてから、炒めもの、煮ものなどに使用する。ふきの若い花房をふきのとうという。

This plant is another vegetable native to Japan, with both wild and cultivated varieties. The stem of the Japanese butterbur is used mainly for *itamemono* and *nimono* after boiling and peeling. The young flower cluster of butterbur is known as *fuki-no-tou* butterbur flower stalk.

にら (韮)
Chinese chives

一年中出まわるにらだが、春のものはやわらかくて美味しい。炒めもの、あえもの、汁の実、鍋料理などに使用する。軟化した黄にら、花茎がついている花にらもある。

While Chinese chives proliferate year-round, they are softer and better in spring. Their main uses are *itamemono*, *aemono*, soup, and *nabe-ryori*. There are also softened yellow chives and flower chives with scape, too.

わさび（山葵）
Wasabi (Japanese horseradish)

日本を代表するスパイスのひとつで、根の部分の皮をむいたものをすって薬味にする。ツーンと抜ける辛さは、わさび独特なもの。葉は漬けものにすると美味しい。

Wasabi is one of the representative spices in Japan, and its roots are grated after removing the skin and used as spice. *Wasabi* has a unique sharp taste. The pickled leaves of *wasabi* are tasty.

たけのこ（筍）
Bamboo shoots

地方によって異なるが、2月下旬頃から市場に出まわるたけのこ。モウソウチク、ハチクなどが有名で、アク抜きしてから煮もの、あえもの、揚げものなどにする。

Bamboo shoots arrive on the market around late February, though this differs somewhat from area to area. The main varieties are *mousouchiku* bamboo and *hachiku* bamboo. After removing the harshness, bamboo shoots are used for *nimono*, *aemono*, and *agemono* (deep-fried dishes).

たらのめ（楤の芽）
Taranome (sprout of the Japanese angelica tree)

山菜の王様ともいわれるたらの芽。野生のものと、栽培ものがある。たらのきの枝先につく若芽をあえもの、天ぷらなどに使用する。少しくせがあるが美味しい。

Taranome is called the king of *sansai* in Japan and comes in both wild and cultivated varieties. The young sprout appearing on the tip of branches of Japanese angelica tree is used for *tempura*, among others. The sprout has a peculiar taste but is good.

めばる（目張）
Rockfish

春告魚といわれる春が旬のめばる。目が張っているのが名の由来。体色が黒褐色の黒めばると、体色が赤い赤（沖）めばるに大別できる。煮つけ、塩焼き、刺身などにされる。

Known as the fish signaling the advent of spring, rockfish is in season in spring. The Japanese name *mebaru* has its origin in the fish's swollen eyes (*me* = eyes; *baru* = *haru* pronounced euphonically meaning swelling). This fish can roughly be divided into categories of black rockfish with a blackish brown body color and red (offing) rockfish with a red body color. Rockfish are mainly eaten by boiling with soy sauce and some sugar, sprinkling with salt and broiling or as *sashimi* (sliced raw fish).

さわら（鰆）
Sawara spanish mackerel

魚に春と書いてさわらというように、春を代表する魚のひとつ。くせのない身で、新鮮なものは寿し、刺身に使用されるし、焼きもの、粕漬け、味噌漬けも美味しい。

The Chinese character for this fish is composed of an element meaning fish and another part meaning spring. As this suggests, Spanish mackerel is one of the typical fishes in spring. Its meat has no specific taste; while fresh varieties are used for *sushi* and *sashimi*, the *yakimono* (grilled food) of this fish and that pickled in *sake* lees or in *miso* are also delicious.

まだい（真鯛）
Red sea bream

一年中出まわるまだいだが、春が一番美味しいといわれている。日本の祝ごとにかかせない魚である。白身で刺身、煮もの、塩焼き、蒸しものなど、どんな料理にも合う。

This fish is sold all year round but is said to be best in spring. Red sea bream is a must for celebrations in Japan. It has white meat and suits any kind of dishes, including *sashimi*, *nimono*, *shioyaki* (broiled food after sprinkling with salt) and *mushimono* (steamed food).

さより（細魚）
Halfbeak fish

体長は細長く、下あごが上あごより長いのが特徴。きれいな白身だが、腹が黒い膜でおおわれているので、腹黒い人を〝さよりのような人〟といわれる。刺身が美味しい。

This fish is characterized by its oblong body and the lower jaw, which is larger than the upper jaw. It has white meat but its belly is covered with black film. Because of this, a wicked (*hara-guroi* in Japanese: *hara*=the belly; *guroi*=*kuroi* pronounced euphonically meaning black) person is often called a fellow like a halfbeak fish. The *sashimi* of this fish is delicious.

あさり（浅蜊）
Short-neck clam

あさりは春になると身が太り、より美味しくなる。砂抜きした殻付きのものは、味噌汁、酒蒸し、炒めもの、蒸しものなど、むき身でかき揚げ、炊き込みご飯にする。

Short-neck clam fattens in spring and becomes more delicious. This clam is used with shells mainly for *miso* soup, *sakamushi* (steeping in *sake* and steaming), *itamemono* and *mushimono* after removing sand, while shelled short-neck clams are used for *kakiage* (food fried in batter) and *takikomi-gohan* (rice seasoned with soy sauce and boiled with meat or seafood and certain vegetables).

はまぐり（蛤）
Hard-shell clam

今や日本産は少なく、中国産、韓国産などが数多く流通されている。焼きもの、吸いもの、蒸しもの、鍋料理、クラムチャウダーのような煮ものなどにされる。

Currently, in the market, the number of hard-shell clams caught in Japan is decreasing, and those caught in China and South Korea are more widely sold. This shellfish is mainly used for *yakimono*, *suimono* (soup), *mushimono*, *nabe-ryori* and *nimono*, such as clam chowder.

かれい（鰈）
Flounder

日本では約40種ものかれいがいるが、中でもよく流通しているのは、まこがれい、いしがれい、まがれい、めいたがれいなど。煮つけ、揚げもの、焼きもの、刺身などにされる。

As many as about 40 species of flatfish live off Japan and the most widely distributed are marbled sole, stone flounder, brown sole, and frog flounder. The dishes of flatfish include *nimono*, *agemono*, *yakimono* and *sashimi*.

さざえ（栄螺）
Top shell

殻につの（突起）があるものと、つののない丸腰といわれるものがいる。新鮮なものは刺身、壷焼きなどにされる。身のコリコリ感と磯くささがなんとも美味しい。

Some of the top shells have small projections on the shell, while others have none. Fresh top shells are eaten as *sashimi* and *tsuboyaki* (shellfish cooked in the shell). The crunchy meat with the sea smell is very good.

その他の旬の食材
Other Seasonal Ingredients

えんどう豆（豌豆）●Peas
春キャベツ●Spring cabbage
ほうれん草（菠薐草）●Spinach
あしたば（明日葉）● *Ashitaba*(Angelica keiskai)
あいなめ（鮎並、愛魚女）●Greenling
にしん（鰊、鯡）●Pacific herring
きびなご（吉備奈子）●Blue sprat
ほたるいか（蛍烏賊）●Firefly squid
いいだこ（飯鮹）●Webfoot octopus
あかがい（赤貝）●Bloody clam
あおやぎ（青柳）●Hen clam
とこぶし（床伏）●Japanese abalone
さくらえび（桜海老）● *Sakura* shrimp
うに（海胆）●Sea urchin
わかめ（和布、若布）● *Wakame* seaweed

たけのこの木の芽あえ

about **20** min

木の芽の爽やかな香りとたけのこの甘さが春を感じさせてくれる

Bamboo Shoot with *Kinome* Dressing

The refreshing flavor of *kinome*, or young leaves of *sansho* Japanese pepper, and the sweetness of bamboo shoot make you feel the arrival of spring

■材料・2人分	
ゆでたけのこ	100g
いか（胴の部分）	1/2杯

A	だし汁	1/2カップ
	みりん	小さじ1
	薄口しょう油	小さじ1/2
	塩	小さじ1/4

B	西京みそ	30g
	みりん	大さじ1
	砂糖	大さじ1/2

ほうれん草（葉先）	3枚
木の芽	10枚

▌ Ingredients (serves 2)

3 1/2 oz boiled bamboo shoot
1/2 squid (body part)

A
2/5 U.S. cup stock
1 tsp *mirin* sweet cooking *sake*
1/2 tsp light soy sauce
1/4 tsp salt

B
1 oz *Saikyo miso*
1 Tbsp *mirin* sweet cooking *sake*
1/2 Tbsp sugar

3 spinach leaves
10 *kinome*, or young leaves of *sansho* Japanese pepper

■作り方

1 たけのこは短冊切りにし、鍋に**A**の調味料と一緒に入れて煮立てたらそのまま冷ましておく。

2 いかは皮をむいて鹿の子（縦横か斜めに交差する切り目）に包丁目を入れ、たけのこと同じくらいの大きさの短冊切りにし、さっと湯通しをしてざるに上げ、しっかりと水けをきっておく。

3 木の芽みそを作る。
★少量の場合は電子レンジを使って簡単に！
(a) 耐熱容器に**B**を入れてラップをし、電子レンジ（600W）で約30秒加熱し、手早く混ぜ合わせて、練りみそを作る。

(b) ほうれん草は水洗いしたあと、耐熱皿にのせてラップをし電子レンジ（600W）で約30秒加熱したら水にさらしてアクを抜き、汁けを絞って細かく刻んでからすり鉢でする。

(c) (b) のすり鉢に葉だけをつんだ木の芽を入れて香りが出るようにすりつぶしたら (a) の練りみそを入れて合わせる。

4 食べる直前に汁けをきった、**1**のたけのこと**2**のいかを**3**の (c) の木の芽みそであえて器に盛る。

■DIRECTIONS

1 Cut the bamboo shoot into rectangles. Put the bamboo shoot in a pot together with **A**, bring to the boil, and allow it to stand to cool.

2 Skin the squid, and make shallow cuts in the *kanoko* pattern (parallel vertical and horizontal lines or diagonal lines crossing each other). Cut the squid into the same size pieces as the bamboo shoot. Blanch the squid, and thoroughly drain it on a sieve.

3 Make *kinome miso*.
★If the quantity is small, use a microwave to cook simply!

(a) Put **B** in a heat-resistant vessel, and cover it with plastic wrap. Microwave (600w) for about 30 sec, and swiftly stir to make a thick *miso* sauce.

(b) Rinse the spinach with cold water, put it in a heat-resistant container covered with plastic wrap, and microwave (600w) for about 30 sec. Soak the spinach to remove the bitterness. Squeeze the spinach, finely chop, and grind in a mortar.

(c) Add only the *kinome* leaves to the mortar and grind until the flavor emerges. Add the thick *miso* sauce prepared in (a), and mix.

4 Just before serving, mix the drained bamboo shoot and squid with the *kinome miso* sauce, and place it on a serving dish.

若たけ煮

ほのかに甘いたけのこの風味と食感で春を感じる

about **30** min

Simmered Bamboo Shoots

Feel the arrival of spring with the aroma and texture of slightly sweet bamboo shoots

■ **材料・2人分**

ゆでたけのこ ………………………	200g
生わかめ …………………………	15g

A
だし汁 ………………………	2と1/2カップ
酒 ……………………………	1/4カップ
砂糖 …………………………	大さじ2
みりん ………………………	大さじ1
薄口しょう油 ………………	大さじ1
塩 ……………………………	小さじ1/4

かつお節 …………………………	20g
木の芽 ……………………………	適宜

■ Ingredients (serves 2)

7 oz boiled bamboo shoot
1/2 oz fresh *wakame* seaweed

A
- 2 1/8 U.S. cups stock
- 1/5 U.S. cup *sake*
- 2 Tbsps sugar
- 1 Tbsp *mirin* sweet cooking *sake*
- 1 Tbsp light soy sauce
- 1/4 tsp salt

2/3 oz dried bonito flakes
Kinome, or young leaves of *sansho* Japanese pepper

■作り方

1 たけのこは穂先の部分と根元に切り分け、穂先を縦6等分に切り、根元の部分は厚さ約1cmの半月に切る。

2 生わかめは水洗いしたら湯通しをし、ざく切りにして水けをきっておく。

3 かつお節は、ガーゼや木綿の袋に詰めるか、キッチンペーパーの中央において左右、上下の順に折畳んで口が開かないように閉じておく。

4 鍋にAの煮汁と1のたけのこを入れ、3のかつお節を落としぶたの代わりにのせ、弱火で20分煮ふくめたら、かつお節を取り除き、2の生わかめを加えてひと煮立ちさせる。

5 器に4のたけのことわかめを汁ごと入れ、上に木の芽をのせる。

■ DIRECTIONS

1 Cut the bamboo shoot to separate the top part from the bottom. Cut the top into 6 equal parts, and cut the bottom part into 3/8 inch-thick half moons.

2 Wash the *wakame*, and blanch. Cut it coarsely, and drain.

3 Put the dried bonito flakes in a gauze or cotton bag, or wrap them with kitchen paper— Put the flakes in the center of the paper, fold the paper from the sides first, and then the top and bottom. Close the wrapping to prevent it from opening while cooking.

4 Put **A** and the bamboo shoot in a pot, and place the wrapped bonito flakes on top so that it serves as a lid. After simmering over a low heat for 20 minutes, remove the bonito bag, add the *wakame*, and bring the stock to the boil briefly.

5 Place the bamboo shoot, *wakame*, and liquid on a serving dish, and garnish with *kinome* on top.

たけのこのみそマヨネーズ焼き

たけのこの食感とみそマヨネーズの風味がベストマッチ

Toasted Bamboo Shoot with *Miso*-Mayonnaise

The texture of bamboo shoot best matches the flavor of *miso*-mixed mayonnaise

■材料・2人分

ゆでたけのこ（根元の部分）	約100g

A
みそ	大さじ1
はちみつ	小さじ1/2
マヨネーズ	大さじ2

ピザ用チーズ	約40g
パルメザンチーズ	大さじ1/2
芽ねぎ	少々

■ Ingredients (serves 2)

3 1/2 oz boiled bamboo shoot (bottom part)

A
- 1 Tbsp *miso*
- 1 tsp honey
- 2 Tbsps mayonnaise

1 1/3 oz pizza cheese
1/2 Tbsp grated Parmesan cheese
Small quantity of young green onion

■作り方

1 たけのこは約（根元の部分）1cmの厚さの半月切りにして、アルミホイルをしいたトースターの天板にのせる。

2 Aを混ぜ合わせ、みそマヨネーズを作り、1のたけのこの上面に塗る。

3 2にピザ用チーズとパルメザンチーズをふりかけ、オーブントースターで焼き色がつくまで焼き、芽ねぎを散らせば出来上がり。

■ DIRECTIONS

1 Cut the bamboo shoot (bottom part) into 3/8 inch-thick half moons, and place on the aluminum-foil-covered baking tray of a toaster.

2 Mix the ingredients of **A** together to make *miso-mayonnaise*, and spread on the surface of the cut bamboo shoot.

3 Sprinkle the pizza cheese and Parmesan cheese on the bamboo shoot covered with the *miso* mayonnaise, and toast it till brown. Sprinkle over the young green onion as a finishing touch.

コラム
Column

たけのこの種類
Types of Bamboo Shoot

　春になると市場に出まわり、食卓を彩るたけのこ。私たちがたけのこといっているほとんどが、モウソウチク（孟宗竹）のことだが、他にはどんなたけのこがあるのだろうか……。

　他には、関東地方以南で栽培されている地方名でダイミョウチクとも呼ばれるカンザンチク（寒山竹）、肉はやや薄く、えぐみが少ないハチク（淡竹）、竹皮が包装用に用いられるマダケ（真竹）、北海道、東北地方などでよく食べられるネマガリダケ（根曲竹）が食用にするタケノコの代表といえるだろう。

　ちなみにモウソウチクは、薩摩藩主の島津吉貴によって、元文1年（1736年）に中国から琉球経由で入った株を植えたのが最初だといわれている。

モウソウチク（孟宗竹）▶
Mousouchiku bamboo

When spring comes, bamboo shoots appear on the market, and lend flair to the dining table. What we call *takenoko*, or bamboo shoots, are mostly the shoots of *mousouchiku* bamboo. What else is available?

Other species of edible bamboo shoots include *kanzanchiku*, cultivated in areas south of the Kanto region and locally called *daimyochiku*; *hachiku*, which has thin flesh and less harshness; *madake*, whose skin is often used for wrapping; and *nemagaridake*, popularly consumed in Hokkaido and Tohoku. *Mousouchiku* is said to have been first planted in Japan by the feudal lord of *Satsuma*, Shimazu Yoshitaka, in 1736. The first plant is said to have come from China via *Ryukyu* (present-day Okinawa).

たけのこご飯

甘くシャクシャクとした食感のたけのことほのかに香るだしを吸ったご飯が美味しい

Bamboo Shoot Rice

Delicious rice with sweet and crispy bamboo shoot and the delicate aroma of stock

■材料・3人分	
米	2合
ゆでたけのこ	150g
油揚げ	1枚

A	だし汁	1/3カップ
	酒	大さじ2
	薄口しょう油	大さじ1
	みりん	大さじ1

B	だし汁	1/3カップ
	薄口しょう油	大さじ1
	塩	小さじ1/4

木の芽	適宜

Ingredients (serves 3)

1 1/2 U.S. cups rice
5 1/4 oz boiled bamboo shoot
1 *abura-age* deep-fried *tofu*

A
1/3 U.S. cup stock
2 Tbsps *sake*
1 Tbsp light soy sauce
1 Tbsp *mirin* sweet cooking *sake*

B
1/3 U.S. cup stock
1 Tbsp light soy sauce
1/4 tsp salt

Kinome, or young leaves of *sansho* Japanese pepper

■作り方

1 米は炊く30分前に洗い、ざるに上げておく。
※米の洗い方、炊き方はP260・261参照。

2 たけのこはやわらかい穂先の部分と根元の硬い部分に切り分け、穂先の部分は縦4等分に切ってから薄く放射状に切り、根元の部分は薄い短冊切りにし、小鍋にAと入れて汁けをからませるようにひと煮立ちさせたらそのまま冷ます。

3 油揚げは熱湯で煮て油抜きをしてから約2cmの長さの短冊切りにする。

4 炊飯器に1の米とBを入れてひと混ぜし、上に汁ごと2のたけのこと、3の油揚げをのせて炊く。

5 炊き上がったら約10分蒸らしてから全体をかき混ぜ、器に盛り木の芽を散らしていただく。

■DIRECTIONS

1 Wash the rice 30 min before cooking, and leave it on a sieve to drain.
※ For the washing and cooking of rice, see p.260 and 261.

2 Cut the bamboo shoot to separate the tender top part and hard bottom part. Cut the top part vertically into 4 equal parts and then into thin wedges. Cut the bottom part into thin rectangles. Put the bamboo shoot in a small pot together with **A**, and bring it to the boil briefly so that the bamboo shoot is covered with liquid. Turn off the heat and leave it to cool down.

3 Boil the *abura-age* to remove excess oil, and cut it into about 3/4 inch-long rectangles.

4 Put the rice prepared in **1** and **B** in a rice cooker, and mix lightly. Add the ingredients of **2** (bamboo shoot with liquid) and the cut *abura-age*, and cook.

5 When it's done, leave the cooker covered for about 10 min to allow the grains to settle. Then open the lid, and mix the rice. Place the rice in a serving dish, and sprinkle *kinome* as a finishing touch.

ふきの土佐煮

ふきの滋味溢れる風味にかつお節の風味がよく合う一品

about 15 min

Simmered Japanese Butterbur, *Tosa*-Style

The flavor of Japanese butterbur matches well with the aroma of dried bonito

■材料・2人分

ふき（下ゆでしたもの）…150g

A ┌ だし汁 ……1と1/2カップ
　├ 酒……………………大さじ1
　├ 砂糖…………………小さじ1
　└ みりん………………大さじ1

塩 …………………………小さじ1/4
薄口しょう油 ……小さじ1/2
かつお節 ……………………5g
木の芽……………………適宜

Ingredients (serves 2)

5 1/4 oz Japanese butterbur (parboiled)

A ┌ 1 1/4 U.S. cups stock
　├ 1 Tbsp *sake*
　├ 1 tsp sugar
　└ 1 Tbsp *mirin* sweet cooking *sake*

1/4 tsp salt
1/2 tsp light soy sauce
1/6 oz dried bonito flakes
Kinome, or young leaves of *sansho* Japanese pepper

1 ふきは4〜5cmの長さに切る。

2 1のふきをさっと洗い、塩（分量外）をふり、まな板の上で両手でころがす。たっぷりの湯で1分ぐらいゆでて冷水に取る。皮と筋をむき、きれいな水につけておく。

※水につけることで、ふきのアクを抜くことができる。

3 鍋にAを入れて煮立てたら、2のふきを入れてさっと煮る。

4 3が煮立ってきたら塩と薄口しょうゆ、かつお節を加えてからませ、火からおろしてそのまま冷ます。

5 器に4を盛り、木の芽を飾る。

■DIRECTIONS

1 Cut the butterbur into a length of about 2 inches.

2 Rinse the cut butterbur, sprinkle salt (extra quantity), and roll it on a cutting board with both hands. Boil the butterbur in plenty of hot water for about 1 min, and put it in cold water. Skin and string the butterbur, and soak it in clean water.
※ The bitterness of butterbur is removed while soaked in water.

3 Put **A** into a pot, bring to the boil, add the butterbur and cook briefly.

4 When it comes to the boil, add salt and light soy sauce, as well as the bonito flakes, and stir to allow the flakes to cover the butterbur. Remove the pan from the heat, and allow it to cool down.

5 Place in a serving dish, and garnish with *kinome* on top.

コラム
Column

ふきの栄養
Nutrition of Japanese Butterbur

春を代表する野菜（山菜）のふきは独特な香りや苦味があり、煮ものや炒めものによく使用されるが、栄養について知っている人は少ないのではないだろうか……。

ふきは食物繊維が豊富で便秘を予防してくれる働きをする。さらに低カロリーなためダイエットにも効果がある。他にはカロテン、免疫力を高め、疲労回復の働きや美肌効果のあるビタミンC、ビタミンA、鉄分などが含まれている。

また、ふきの香りは、古くからたん切り、せき止め、消化（老廃物を排出する）などに効果があるといわれている。

ちなみにふきのとうには、カロテン、ビタミンC、鉄分が、ふきより多く含まれている。

The Japanese butterbur, a popular vegetable (edible wild plant) in spring, has a peculiar aroma and bitterness. It is often used for simmered or stir-fried dishes. But few people may know about its nutrition value.
The Japanese butterbur is rich in dietary fiber, which helps to prevent constipation. It has a low caloric value. So it's good for those on a diet. The butterbur also contains carotene, vitamin C, vitamin A, and iron, which are effective for enhancing immunity, recovering from fatigue, and producing beautiful skin.
The aroma of the Japanese butterbur has long been believed to be effective for loosening phlegm, stopping coughs, and aiding digestion (to eliminate waste matter).
Incidentally, its flower-buds contain a higher amount of carotene, vitamin C, and iron than the stalks and leaves.

ふきと油揚げの炒め煮

だしがしみ込んだ油揚げとふきとがよくマッチした定番のおかず

Simmered Japanese Butterbur and *Abura-Age*

Standard dish featuring stock-soaked *abura-age* deep-fried *tofu* and Japanese butterbur

■ 材料・2人分

ふき（下ゆでしたもの）	150g
油揚げ	1枚
サラダ油	大さじ1
A 酒	大さじ3
A 砂糖	大さじ1
だし汁	1/2カップ
しょう油	大さじ1

■ Ingredients (serves 2)

5 1/4 oz Japanese butterbur (parboiled)
1 *abura-age* deep-fried *tofu*
1 Tbsp vegetable oil

A [3 Tbsps *sake*
A [1 Tbsp sugar

2/5 U.S. cup stock
1 Tbsp soy sauce

■作り方

1 ふきは3〜4cmの長さに切り、油揚げは熱湯で煮て油抜きをしてから約3cmの長さの短冊切りにする。

2 鍋にサラダ油を熱し、1のふきと油揚げを炒めたら火からはずし、**A**を加えて全体にからませる。

3 2にだし汁を入れて火にかけ、しばらく煮たらしょう油を加えて煮汁が少なくなるまで煮込めば出来上がり。

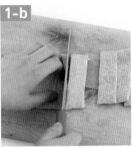

1-a 1-b

■DIRECTIONS

1 Cut the butterbur to a length of 1.5 inches. Lightly boil the *abura-age* to remove excess oil, and cut it into about 1 1/5 inch-long rectangles.

2 Heat the vegetable oil in a pot, and sauté the cut butterbur and *abura-age*. Remove the pot from the heat, and add **A** to allow it to coat the ingredients.

3 Pour the stock over the ingredients of **2**, and heat for a while. Add the soy sauce, and continue to simmer to reduce the liquid.

コラム
Column

ふきの種類
Types of Japanese Butterbur

ふきは日本原産の数少ない野菜のひとつで、北海道から沖縄まで分布している。平安時代から野菜として栽培されている歴史を持つ。

そんなふきは、日本全国の野山に自生している赤ぶき（葉柄が赤い）と青ぶき（葉柄が緑色）、そして栽培種とがある。

スーパーなどの店頭に並ぶのは、栽培種の代表品種である愛知早生ふきがほとんどで、他には、京都と奈良で栽培されているやわらかく、苦味が少ない水ふき（京ふき）がある。

他には葉径は1mにもなる北海道のラワンブキ、秋田県の秋田ふきが有名だが、ただしこの2つは固いので、あまり野菜としては出まわることはない。

写真は秋田ふき　The photo shows *akitafuki*

The Japanese butterbur is one of the rare vegetables native to Japan, and is distributed across the country from Hokkaido to Okinawa. It has been cultivated since the Heian Era.
There are 2 wild species seen across Japan — *akabuki* with red stalks and *aobuki* with green stalks — and some cultivated species.
Most of the butterburs available at grocery stores are Aichi *wasefuki*, a cultivated species. Also available is *mizufuki* (*kyofuki*), cultivated in Kyoto and Nara. It is tender and contains less bitterness.
Rawanbuki from Hokkaido and *akitafuki* from Akita Prefecture are known for their size — their leaves can be as large as 3 feet or more in diameter. But they are not commonly distributed as edible vegetables, as they are too tough.

ひじきの煮もの

古くから伝わる日本の伝統食。ボリュームもあって美味しい

Simmered *Hijiki* Seaweed

Traditional Japanese food that has been passed down over generations.
Hearty and tasty

■材料・4人分

ひじき（乾燥）	40g
厚揚げ	1枚
にんじん	5〜6cm
桜えび	5g
絹さや	8枚
だし汁	200cc
A 酒	大さじ3
しょう油	大さじ3
みりん	大さじ3
砂糖	小さじ2
サラダ油	大さじ2

Ingredients (serves 4)

1 1/3 oz dried *hijiki* seaweed
1 *atsu-age* thick fried *tofu*
1/3 carrot
1/6 oz *sakura* shrimp
8 snow peas
4/5 U.S. cup stock

A
3 Tbsps *sake*
3 Tbsps soy sauce
3 Tbsps *mirin* sweet cooking *sake*
2 tsps sugar

2 Tbsps vegetable oil

■作り方

1 ひじきを耐熱ボウルに入れ、水をたっぷり加える。ラップをかけて電子レンジで3分加熱する。水けをきり、新しく水をはったボウルに入れ、軽くかき混ぜるようにしてふり洗いし、ざるに上げる。

2 厚揚げは熱湯を回しかけて油抜きし、厚みを半分に切り、さらに縦半分に切ってから5〜6mm幅に切る。にんじんは2〜3cm長さの細切りにする。絹さやは筋を取り、さっと塩（分量外）ゆでして斜めせん切りにする。

3 鍋にサラダ油を熱し、中火で2のにんじんを炒め、1のひじきを加えて炒め合わせ、だし汁を加える。

4 3が煮立ったらAの調味料、2の厚揚げ、桜えびを加えざっと混ぜ、落としぶたをして約10分煮て火を止め、2の絹さやを加え混ぜ、盛りつける。

- -

■ DIRECTIONS

1 Put the *hijiki* seaweed in a heat-resistant bowl, and add 3 1/3 U.S. cups of water. Cover the bowl with plastic wrap and cook it in a 500-watt microwave on "high" for 3 min. Drain, and put *hijiki* in clean water in a bowl. Clean *hijiki* by gently stirring it in the water, and drain on a sieve.

2 Pour boiling water on the *atsu-age* fried *tofu* to remove excess oil. Cut it horizontally in half, then, vertically in half, and cut into a width of 1/5 inch. Cut the carrot into about 1 1/2 to 2-inch-long thin strips. String the snow peas, briefly boil in salty water (extra quantity of salt), and cut diagonally into julienne strips.

3 Heat the vegetable oil in a pot, stir-fry

絹さやとひじきのごまあえ
Snow Peas and *Hijiki* with Sesame Dressing

■材料・2人分

絹さや	80g
芽ひじき（乾）	3g
油揚げ	1/2枚
サラダ油	大さじ1/2
炒り白ごま	大さじ2
A ┌ だし汁	大さじ3
├ 砂糖	小さじ2
└ しょう油	小さじ2

■ INGREDIENTS (serves 2)

2 4/5 oz snow peas
1/10 oz dried young *hijiki* seaweed
1/2 *abura-age* deep-fried *tofu*
1/2 Tbsp vegetable oil
2 Tbsps roasted white sesame seeds

A ┌ 3 Tbsps stock
　├ 2 tsps sugar
　└ 2 tsps soy sauce

【作り方】

1 芽ひじきは水につけてやわらかく戻して水けをしっかりときり、絹さやは筋を取っておき、油揚げは熱湯で油抜きしてから約2cmの長さの短冊切りにする。

2 炒り白ごまは包丁で粗く切って切りごまにしておく。

3 フライパンにサラダ油を熱し、1の芽ひじき、油揚げを炒めたら、絹さやを加えて炒め合わせ、全体に油がまわったらAを入れて味を煮ふくませて火を止め、2の切りごまを加えてあえる。

【DIRECTIONS】

1 Soak the dried young *hijiki* in water to soften, and thoroughly drain. String the snow peas. Remove excess oil from the *abura-age* in boiling water, and cut into 3/4 inch-long rectangles.

2 Coarsely chop the roasted white sesame seeds with a kitchen knife.

3 Heat the vegetable oil in a frying pan, and stir-fry the drained *hijiki* and the cut *abura-age*. Add the snow peas, and continue to stir-fry. When all the ingredients are dressed with the oil, add **A**, and cook the ingredients. Turn off the heat, and add the chopped white sesame seeds, and mix.

---

the cut carrot over a medium heat, add the drained *hijiki* and stir-fry together. Add the stock.

4 When it comes to the boil, add **A**, the cut *atsu-age*, and *sakura* shrimps, and roughly stir. Cover with a drop lid, and simmer for about 10 min. After turning off the heat, mix the cut snow peas, and place on a serving dish.

菜の花の中華風塩炒め

色鮮やかにゆであげた菜の花を素早く炒めてシャキッと仕上げる

Chinese-Style Fried Rape Blossoms Seasoned with Salt

Quickly stir-fry brightly-colored boiled rape blossoms to enjoy the crisp texture

■材料・2人分

菜の花	1束
にんにく	1片
赤唐辛子	1本
サラダ油	大さじ1
紹興酒	大さじ1
中華スープ	大さじ3
塩・黒こしょう	少々

■ Ingredients (serves 2)

1 bundle rape blossoms
1 clove garlic
1 red chili pepper
1 Tbsp vegetable oil
1 Tbsp shaoxing rice wine
3 Tbsps Chinese soup stock
Small quantity of salt and black pepper

■作り方

1 菜の花は4cmの長さに切り、にんにくはみじん切り、赤唐辛子はへたを切り取り、種を取っておく。

2 鍋にお湯を沸かし、塩（分量外）を入れて1の菜の花の茎の硬い部分、穂先の順に入れてさっと湯通しし、ざるなどに上げて水けをきっておく。

3 フライパンにサラダ油、1のにんにく、赤唐辛子を入れて熱し、香りが出てきたら2の菜の花を入れて強火で炒め合わせ、紹興酒と中華スープを入れ、塩・黒こしょうで味を調えれば出来上がり。

■DIRECTIONS

1 Cut rape blossoms into a length of 1 1/2 inches. Finely chop the garlic. Remove the calyx and seeds of the red chili pepper.

2 Boil water in a pot and add salt (extra quantity). Blanch the rape blossoms. Put in the hard stalks first, and then the top part. Drain them on a sieve.

3 Heat the vegetable oil, and put the chopped garlic and chili pepper prepared in **1** in a frying pan. When the aroma begins to emerge, stir-fry the drained rape blossoms over a high heat. Add the shaoxing wine and Chinese soup stock, and season the ingredients with salt and black pepper.

菜の花のナムル
Marinated Rape Blossoms

■材料・2人分

菜の花	1/2束

┌ にんにく（すりおろし）
│ 　　　　　　　　　小さじ1/4
A │ すりごま 大さじ1
│ 白ごま 小さじ1
│ ごま油 大さじ1/2
└ 塩 小さじ1/4

【作り方】

1 鍋に湯を沸かし、塩（分量外）を入れて菜の花をゆで、冷水に取ったらざるに上げて水けをしっかりとキッチンペーパーなどでふいておく。

2 1の菜の花は約3～4cmの食べやすい長さに切る。

3 ボウルに2の菜の花と、**A** を入れてあえれば出来上がり。

■Ingredients (serves 2)

1/2 bundle rape blossoms

┌ 1/4 tsp grated garlic
│ 1 Tbsp ground sesame
│ 　seeds
A │ 1 tsp white sesame seeds
│ 1/2 Tbsp sesame oil
└ 1/4 tsp salt

〖DIRECTIONS〗

1 Boil water in a pot, and add salt (extra quantity). Boil the rape blossoms, cool in cold water, and drain them on a sieve. Use kitchen paper to dry the rape blossoms.

2 Cut the drained rape blossoms into a length of about 1 1/2 inches or bite-sized pieces.

3 Put the cut rape blossoms and **A** in a serving bowl and mix them together.

春野菜の天ぷら

ほろ苦くて美味しい春の野菜と山菜を天ぷらでいただく

about 15 min

Spring Vegetable *Tempura*

Enjoy *tempura* of spring vegetables and wild plants, tasty with slight bitterness

■材料・2人分

うどの穂先	2本分
ふきのとう	4個
たらの芽	4個

A ┌ 冷水＋卵黄1個 … 3/4カップ
　└ 薄力粉 … 3/4カップ

片栗粉	適宜
揚げ油	適宜
塩	適宜
すだち	適宜

Ingredients (serves 2)

2 tips *udo*
4 Japanese butterbur flower buds
4 *taranome*, or sprout of the Japanese angelica tree

A ┌ 3/5 U.S. cup chilled water + 1 egg yolk
　│ 3/5 U.S. cup *hakurikiko*
　└ low-gluten cake flour

Starch powder
Oil for deep frying
Salt
Sudachi Japanese lime

■作り方

1 うどの穂先は切り離し、ふきのとうは外側の汚れた部分を取り除いてからつぼみを丁寧に開いて水にさらしてから、水けをキッチンペーパーなどでふいておく。たらの芽はとげに注意しながら根元の茶色いがくの部分を包丁でむき、太ければ根元に十字に切り込みを入れておく。

2 **A**で天ぷらの衣を作る。
軽量カップに卵黄を入れ、冷水を150ccの所になるまで注ぎ入れてかき混ぜ、冷やしたボウルに移し

てから、ふるって冷やしておいた薄力粉を入れてかるく混ぜ合わせる。

3 揚げ鍋に揚げ油を160℃に熱し、**1**のうどの穂先、ふきのとう、たらの芽それぞれに薄く片栗粉をはたきつけてから天ぷらの衣にくぐらせて揚げ、しっかりと油をきる。

4 器に天ぷらを盛り、塩とすだちでいただく。

■ DIRECTIONS

1 Cut off the top part of *udo*. Remove the outer dirty part of the butterbur buds, open the buds carefully, and soak in cold water. Dry them with kitchen paper. Peel the brown bottom part of the *taranome* buds to remove the calyxes, while taking precautions against their thorns. If the stalk is thick, put cross cuts on the bottom.

2 Make the batter for *tempura* with the ingredients of **A**.
Put the egg yolk in a measuring cup, add chilled water to 150 ml (3/5 U.S. cup), and mix. Put the mixture into a chilled bowl, add the sieved and chilled *hakurikiko* low-glutten cake flour, and stir lightly.

3 Heat the oil in a deep frying pan to 320°F. Dust with starch powder on the tips of *udo*, butterbur buds, and *taranome*, which have been prepared in **1**. Coat them with the batter, and deep-fry. Drain the oil well.

4 Place them on a serving dish, and serve with salt and *sudachi*.

春野菜の下ごしらえ

春野菜（山菜）にはアクがあるので、このアクの下処理をしないと、えぐみが強くて食べられないものもある。アクの取り方と下ごしらえを覚えておきたい。

Preparing Spring Vegetables

Spring vegetables including wild plants require preparations before cooking, as they contain bitterness or harshness. Otherwise, some vegetables are inedible because of the too strong taste. Learn how to remove bitterness and harshness to prepare spring vegetables.

【たけのこのアク抜き】

1 たけのこは皮についている泥をたわしでこすって洗い落とし、穂先の部分を斜めに切り落とし、縦に1本切り込みを入れる。

2 大きな鍋にたけのこ、たけのこがかぶるくらいの水、米ぬか1カップ、赤唐辛子2本を入れて落としぶたをして火にかける。煮立ったら弱火にして約1時間くらい加熱し、根元の固い部分に竹串がすっと刺さるまで煮る。

3 そのままある程度冷めるまで放置したら水洗いし、皮の切り込みのところから皮をむく。根元のイボや残った皮などは包丁でこそげ取る。

4 すぐに使わない時は、たっぷりの水に浸して冷蔵庫に入れ、1日1回水を変えれば4～5日は保存できる。
※たけのこは冷凍するとすが入るので冷凍保存はNG！

【 How to remove harshness from bamboo shoots 】

1 Wash the bamboo shoot with a brush to clean the mud on the sheath. Cut off the tip diagonally, and put a vertical cut along the length of the body.

2 Place the bamboo shoot in a large pot, and add water deep enough to immerse the bamboo shoot, 4/5 U.S. cup of rice bran, and 2 red chili peppers. Cover with a drop lid, and turn on the heat. When it comes to the boil, turn down the heat to low, and boil for about 1 hour. Pierce the bottom part with a bamboo skewer. If the skewer goes into the flesh smoothly, it's done.

3 Leave the pot to allow it to cool down to some extent. Wash the bamboo shoot with water, and remove the sheath from the vertical cut. Scrape off the warts near the bottom and remaining skin.

4 If you don't use the parboiled bamboo shoot immediately, immerse it in plenty of water, and store in a refrigerator. It can last for 4 to 5 days, if water is changed once every day.
※ Do not freeze bamboo shoots, as they become spongy.

穂先の部分を斜めに切り落とし、縦に1本切り込みを入れる。

Cut off the tip diagonally, and put a vertical cut along the length.

大きな鍋にたけのこがかぶるくらいの水、米ぬか1カップ、赤唐辛子2本を入れた鍋に1のたけのこを加え、落としぶたをして火にかける。煮立ったら弱火にして約1時間煮て、根元に竹串が刺さるまで煮る。

Place the bamboo shoot in a large pot, and add water deep enough to immerse the bamboo shoot, 4/5 U.S. cup of rice bran, and 2 red chili peppers. After covering with a drop lid, turn on the heat. After it comes to the boil, turn down the heat to low, and cook for about 1 hour until the base part of the bamboo shoot becomes soft enough for a bamboo skewer to smoothly penetrate the flesh.

2を冷めるまで置き、冷めたら水洗いし、皮の切り込みから写真のように皮をむく。

Leave the pot until cool. Wash the bamboo shoot with water, and remove the sheath from the cut, as shown in the photo.

【ふきのアク抜き】

1 ふきはゆでやすい適当な長さに切り、塩を多めにふってまな板の上で転がして板ずりをする。

2 たっぷりのお湯を鍋に沸かし、あれば重曹を小さじ1杯程度入れ、ふきがやわらかくなるまでゆでる。

3 ゆで上がったふきを冷水に取り、1本ずつ皮をむき、しばらくきれいな水にさらしておいてから料理に使う。

4 すぐに使わない時は、たっぷりの水に浸して冷蔵庫に入れ、1日1回水を変えれば4〜5日は保存できる。

【How to remove the bitterness from Japanese butterburs】

1 Cut the Japanese butterburs into a length convenient for boiling. Sprinkle over a rather large quantity of salt, and roll the butterburs on a cutting board with both hands.

2 Boil plenty of water in a pot, add about 1 tsp of baking soda, if available, and boil the butterburs until soft.

3 Put the boiled butterburs in cold water, and skin them one by one. Soak them in clean water for a while before cooking.

4 If you don't use the butterburs immediately, immerse them in plenty of water, and store in a refrigerator. They can last for 4 to 5 days, if water is changed once every day.

塩で板ずりをすることで、ふきのアクを抜くことができるし、ふきのきれいな色をそのままでゆでることができる。

Rolling on the cutting board with salt removes bitterness, and retains the clear color of the butterburs even after being boiled.

写真のようにふきがやわらかくなるまでゆでる。

Boil the butterburs until soft as shown in the photo.

ふきの皮を手で1本ずつていねいにむいていく。少しでも皮が残っていると食感が悪くなるので注意したい。

Remove the skin carefully one by one. Be careful, because even a trace of skin will spoil the butterburs' texture.

すぐに料理しない場合は、たっぷりの水に浸して、冷蔵庫に入れ、1日1回水を変えれば4〜5日は保存できる。

If you don't use the butterburs immediately, immerse them in plenty of water, and put in a refrigerator. They can last for 4 to 5 days, if water is changed once every day.

【ふきのとう】

ふきのとう（天然もの）は、がくの部分に土などの汚れが入っている可能性があるので、がくが開いているものは、ボウルに水を入れた中できっちりと汚れを取ること。

【Flower buds of Japanese butterburs】

The flower buds of wild Japanese butterburs may be smeared with mud inside the calyxes. So, clean the buds carefully in water in a bowl, if their calyxes are open.

【うど】

うどにはアクがあるため、使用する大きさ（長さ、厚さ）に切ったら、酢水（水2カップに対して、酢小さじ1程度の割合）に、約5〜10分つけておくと変色を防ぎ、アクがぬける。ただし長くつけすぎると風味が悪くなるので注意したい。

【Udo】

Udo contains harshness. After cutting *udo* into an appropriate length or thickness, soak it in vinegared water (at the ratio of 1 tsp of vinegar for 1 2/3 U.S. cups of water) for 5 to 10 min. This removes the bitterness and prevents *udo* from discoloring. But be careful, too long soaking will spoil the flavor.

真だいの薄造り

春に美味しい真だいの薄造りを、あっさりとぽん酢しょう油でいただく

Thinly-Sliced *Madai* Red Sea Bream

Enjoy thinly-sliced *madai* red sea bream, tasty especially in spring, simply with soy sauce and citrus juice

■材料・1人分

真だい（刺身用さく）………………	約4～5cm
万能ねぎ…………………………………	2本
大根………………………………………	約5～6cm
鷹の爪……………………………………	1本
ぽん酢しょう油…………………………	適量

■ Ingredients (serves 1)

1 1/2 to 2 inch block *madai* red sea bream (for *sashimi*)
2 *bannou-negi* onions
About 2 inches *daikon* giant white radish
1 red chili pepper
Ponzu soy sauce (citrus-juice-mixed soy sauce)

■作り方

1 大根は皮をむき、箸で穴をあけ、鷹の爪のへたを切ったものを刺し、そのままおろし金でおろし、もみじおろしを作る。

2 万能ねぎは水洗いし、約4cmの長さに切る。

3 真だいのさくを薄造りにする。

4 器に3の真だいの薄造り、1のもみじおろし、2の万能ねぎをバランスよく盛る。ぽん酢しょう油でいただく。

※真だいの薄造りの身を広げ、2の万能ねぎを2〜3本乗せて端からたいの身を巻き、1のもみじおろしを適量身に乗せてぽん酢しょう油でいただく。

■DIRECTIONS

1 Peel the *daikon*. Dig a hole with a chopstick, and insert the red chili pepper (the calyx removed). Grate the *daikon* with a grater to make *momiji-oroshi*.

2 Wash the *bannou-negi* onions, and cut into a length of 1 1/2 inches.

3 Thinly slice the *madai* block.

4 Arrange the sliced madai, *momiji-oroshi*, and the *bannou-negi* onion on a plate beautifully. Serve with *ponzu* soy sauce.
※ When eating, spread out a slice of *madai*, put 2, 3 strips of *bannou-negi* onion, and roll up the slice. Put some *momiji-oroshi* on it, and soy sauce with citrus juice.

もみじおろしの作り方
How to Make
Momiji-Oroshi

■材料
※P66参照

【作り方】

1 大根の皮をむく。鷹の爪はへたを切る。

2 箸で**1**の大根の切り口の面中央部に穴をあける。

3 **2**の大根の穴に**1**の鷹の爪を差し込む。

4 **3**の大根をおろし金でおろす。
※大根が大きい場合は使用する鷹の爪の本数を増やすとよいだろう。

▥ Ingredients
※ See p.66

[DIRECTIONS]

1 Peel *daikon* giant white radish. Cut off the calyx of a red chili pepper.

2 Use a chopstick to dig a hole in the middle of the cut surface.

3 Insert the red chili pepper into the hole of the *daikon*.

4 Grate the *daikon* with a grater.
※ For a large *daikon*, use more cone peppers.

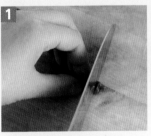

真だいの木の芽焼き

ほのかに香る木の芽の風味が、甘い真だいをやさしく包む

Grilled *Madai* Red Sea Bream with *Kinome*

The faint aroma of *kinome*, or young leaves of *sansho* Japanese pepper, gently covers sweet *madai* red sea bream

■材料・2人分

真だい（切り身）	……………	2切れ
A しょう油	……………	大さじ1
みりん	……………	大さじ1
酒	……………	大さじ1/2
木の芽（刻んだもの）	……………	少々
はじかみ	……………	2本
木の芽（仕上げ用）	……………	適量

※木の芽の代わりに大葉でも可

■ Ingredients (serves 2)

2 fillets *madai* red sea bream

A
1 Tbsp soy sauce
1 Tbsp *mirin* sweet cooking *sake*
1/2 Tbsp *sake*
Small quantity of *kinome* (chopped)

2 *hajikami* sweet-vinegared ginger sticks
Kinome (for finishing)
※Green perilla leaves can replace *kinome*.

■作り方

1 Aを混ぜ、真だいを入れて約30分つける。仕上げ用の木の芽も刻んでおく。

2 1の真だいをグリルで両面焼く。焼いている途中で、1のつけ汁を表面に塗って表面を香ばしく焼く。

3 2の真だいを器に盛り、はじかみを添え、1の刻んだ木の芽を散らす。

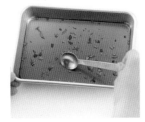

■DIRECTIONS

1 Mix the ingredients of **A**, and marinate the *madai* for about 30 min. Chop the *kinome* for finishing.

2 Grill both sides of the *madai*. Apply more of the marinating sauce of **1** to the surface of the *madai* while grilling, to make it more savory.

3 Place the *madai* on a serving dish, garnish it with the *hajikami* ginger sticks, and sprinkle over chopped *kinome* as a finishing touch.

コラム
Column

真だいの栄養と効能
Nutrition and Efficacy of *Madai* Red Sea Bream

日本のお祝いごとに欠かせない真だいは、古来から「たいは大位なり、こいは小位なり」といわれたように、魚の王様といっても過言ではない。

しかし、古くから日本人に愛されてきた白身魚の代表ともいえる真だいの栄養と効能を知っている人が、どれだけいるだろうか……。

皮膚や粘膜の健康維持を助ける働きをするナイアシンをはじめ、免疫力を高めてくれるビタミンA、疲労回復に役立つビタミンB1、血液サラサラ効果や生長期の栄養に欠かせないビタミンB2を多く含んでいる。さらにコレステロールや血圧を下げてくれる働きや、胃腸障害、皮膚疾患などにも効果がある。

Madai has been an indispensable foodstuff for celebratory occasions in Japan. As indicated in an old saying, the Japanese have traditionally valued *madai* more highly than carp, which is also a symbol of good luck. It is not too much to say that *madai* is the king of fish.

Although *madai* is one of the most popular white-meat fish loved by the Japanese people, I wonder how many people actually know the nutrition value and efficacy of *madai*.

Madai abundantly contains niacin that helps to maintain healthy skin and mucous membranes; vitamin A that enhances immunity; vitamin B1 that relieves fatigue; and vitamin B2 that is effective for preventing blood from clotting, and is indispensable for the growth of children. The fish also reduces blood pressure and cholesterol, and is effective for gastrointestinal problems and skin problems.

さわらの西京焼き

しっとりしたさわらの身とほのかに香るみそが食欲をかきたてる

about **40** min

Griddled *Sawara* Mackerel, Saikyo-Style

The tender flesh of the *sawara* mackerel and the faint aroma of *miso* stimulate your appetite

■材料・2人分

さわら（切り身）	2切れ
塩	適量
A 西京みそ	300g
みりん	60cc
みょうが（甘酢漬け）	適宜

■ Ingredients (serves 2)

2 fillets *sawara*, or Japanese Spanish mackerel
Salt

A 10 1/2 oz Saikyo *miso*
1/4 U.S. cup *mirin* sweet cooking *sake*

Mioga (pickled in sweetened vinegar)

※調理時間にさわらのつけ込み時間は含まれていない

※The time needed for cooking does not include the time for pickling the fish.

■作り方

1 Aをよく混ぜ合わせて、みそ床を作る。

2 さわらの両面に軽く塩をふり、約30分おいて水けが出てきたらペーパータオルなどでふき取る。
※さわらから出てくる水けが、生ぐさみの原因になるのできっちりと取りたい。

3 タッパーに1のみそ床の半量を入れ、へらなどでのばし、ガーゼをしいて2のさわらをおく。さわらをガーゼでおおい、残りのみそ床をのせ均等にのばす。

4 3を冷蔵庫に入れ約1日つけ込む。

5 4のさわらのみそをふき取り、弱火から中火で香ばしく焼き上げる。

6 5を器に盛り、みょうが（甘酢漬け）を添える。

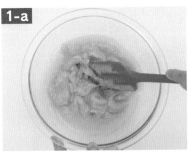

■DIRECTIONS

1 Mix **A** well to make *miso* paste.

2 Sprinkle salt over the *sawara* and leave it for 30 min to allow fluid to be released. Wipe off the fluid with a paper towel.
※ Thoroughly wipe off the fluid being released from the *sawara*, as it could cause a fishy odor.

3 Put the half quantity of the *miso* paste in an airtight container, and spread with a spatula. Lay gauze fabric on the *miso* paste, and place the *sawara* on it. Cover the *sawara* with the gauze, and evenly spread the remaining *miso* paste on it.

4 Leave the container in a refrigerator for 1 day.

5 Wipe off the *miso* paste from the *sawara*, and grill over a low to medium heat.

6 Put the grilled *sawara* on a serving dish, and serve with the *mioga* (pickled in sweetened vinegar.)

子持ちかれいの煮つけ

煮汁がしみ込んだやわらかいかれいの身と、しっとりした卵が美味しい

Simmered Flounder with Roe

Soft flesh of flounder that has absorbed soup and moist roe are delicious

■材料・2人分

子持ちかれい（切り身）	……	2切れ
A	水	…… 400cc
	酒	…… 50cc
	しょう油	…… 50cc
	みりん	…… 大さじ1と1/2
しょうが（薄切り）	……	4枚
絹さや	……	4枚
針しょうが	……	適量

▌Ingredients (serves 2)

2 fillets flounder with roe

A
- 1 2/3 U.S. cups cold water
- 1/5 U.S. cup *sake*
- 1/5 U.S. cup soy sauce
- 1 1/2 Tbsps *mirin* sweet cooking *sake*

4 slices ginger
4 snow peas
Ginger needles

■作り方

1 子持ちかれいは、表面に飾り包丁を入れる。

2 絹さやはさっとゆでておく。

3 鍋に**A**としょうがの薄切りを入れ煮立たせ、**1**の子持ちかれいを入れて落としぶたをし、弱火にして約20分煮て卵に火を通す。
※強火にしてだらだらと煮ると身が硬くなるので注意したい。

4 器に**3**の子持ちかれいを盛りつけ、**2**の絹さやと針しょうがを添える。

■ DIRECTIONS

1 Put decorative cuts on the surface of the flounder with roe.

2 Boil the snow peas briefly.

3 Put **A** and the sliced ginger in a pot, and bring it to the boil. Put the flounder in the pot, and cover with a drop lid. Turn down the heat, and simmer for about 20 min so that the roe is cooked.
※Note that cooking over a high heat for a long time makes the fish tough.

4 Place the flounder on a serving dish, and garnish with the snow peas and ginger needles. Put decorative cuts on the flounder.

コラム
Column

かれいの種類
Types of Flounder

かれいは世界で約100種、日本近海で約40種生息しているといわれている。しかし、市場によく出まわるのは、まこがれい、まがれい、いしがれい、むしがれい、あかがれい、めいたがれい、やなぎむしがれい、くろがしらかれい、そうはちなどになる。

特にまこがれいは肉厚で美味とされる。全国的に有名な大分県のしろしたがれいは、このまこがれいのことである。いしがれいはある表側に石状突起があることが名前の由来。他のかれいに比べると生ぐさみが多少強い。そうはち、くろがしらかれい、めいたがれいは、東北、北海道でよく食べられる。

他には今や高級魚のほしがれい（体表に星のような黒い斑紋があるのが名の由来）、まつかわ（体表が松の樹皮のようにざらざらしているのが名の由来）などがいる。

There are about 100 species of flounders around the world, and about 40 species are said to live in the seas around Japan. Commonly available on the market in Japan are the *mako-garei* (marbled sole), *ma-garei* (brown sole), *ishi-garei* (stone flounder), *mushi-garei* (roundnose flounder), *aka-garei* (flathead flounder), *meita-garei* (frog flounder), *yanagimushi-garei* (willowy flounder), *kurogashira-garei* (crest-head flounder), and *souhachi* (point-head flounder).

Of them, the marbled sole has thick and delicious flesh. The famous delicacy of Oita, *shiroshita-garei*, is actually the marbled sole. The stone flounder was named such because it has stone-like projections on its surface. Compared to other species, the stone flounder has a slightly stronger fishy odor. The point-head flounder, crest-head flounder and frog flounder are popularly consumed in Hokkaido.

Other species include the spotted plaice (named for the star-like black spots on its surface), which is now a prized fish, and barfin flounder, whose Japanese name is *matsukawa* (pine tree bark), as its skin is coarse like tree bark.

あさりと菜の花のバター炒め

にんにくの香りとバターとあさりと菜の花がベストマッチ

Butter-Sautéed Short-Necked Clams and Rape Blossoms

The aroma of garlic, butter, short-necked clams and rape blossoms is the best match

■ 材料・2人分

あさり	200g
菜の花	1束
バター	大さじ1
にんにく（みじん切り）	小さじ1/2
酒	大さじ2
こしょう	少々

■ Ingredients (serves 2)

7oz short-necked clams
1 bundle rape blossoms
1 Tbsp butter
1/2 tsp chopped garlic
2 Tbsps *sake*
Small quantity of ground pepper

■作り方

1 あさりは塩水（分量外）につけ、砂出しをする。
※水1カップに対して、塩小さじ1の割合の塩水を作り、最低でも30分はつけて砂出しをするとよい。
※砂をはかせたあさりは殻と殻を手でこすり合わせて水でよく洗って使用する。

2 菜の花はさっと塩（分量外）ゆでし、水けを絞って半分に切る。

3 フライパンにバターを入れて熱し、にんにくを加えて香りが出たら、**1** のあさりを入れてざっと炒める。酒を入れてふたをして蒸らす。

4 **3** のあさりの殻が開いたら、**2** の菜の花を加え、強火で炒める。こしょうをふり、器に盛る。

■DIRECTIONS

1 Immerse the short-necked clams in salty water (extra quantity of salt), to allow them to expel sand and dirt.
※Make salty water at a ratio of 1 tsp of salt for 4/5 U.S. cup of water. Leave the clams immersed for at least 30 min to allow them to expel sand and dirt.
※After this process, rub the clams together with both hands, and wash well in water before use.

2 Boil the rape blossoms briefly in salty water (extra quantity of salt), squeeze out the water, and cut in half.

3 Heat the butter in a frying pan, and add the garlic. When their aroma emerges, add the short-necked clams, and stir-fry briefly. Add the *sake*, and cover with a lid to steam the ingredients.

あさりの酒蒸し
Sake-steamed Short-Necked Clams

■材料・2人分

あさり	300g
水	1カップ
酒	1/2カップ
昆布（5×10cmのもの）	1枚
しょう油	少々
小口切りの万能ねぎ	適宜

【作り方】

1 鍋に水1カップ、酒 1/2カップ、昆布、しょう油少々と下処理したあさりを入れて中火にかけ、ふたをする。

2 **1** を5～6分煮て、あさりの殻が完全に開いたら、あさりを皿に盛り煮汁をかけ、小口切りの万能ねぎを散らせていただく。

■Ingredients (serves 2)

10 1/2 oz short-necked clams
4/5 U.S. cup water
2/5 U.S. cup *sake*
1 (2×4 inch) *konbu* kelp
Small quantity of soy sauce
Edge-cut *bannou-negi* onion

[DIRECTIONS]

1 Put 4/5 U.S. cup water, 2/5 U.S. cup *sake*, *konbu* kelp, a small amount of soy sauce and the clams into a pot, and place over a medium heat. Cover the pot.

2 Simmer for 5 to 6 min. When the shells have fully opened, arrange the clams in a bowl and pour on the simmered liquid and sprinkle edge-cut *bannou-negi* onion.

砂出しをする
Allow the clams to expel sand and dirt.

手でこすり合わせる
Rub the clams together with both hands.

4 When the clamshells open, add the cut rape blossoms, and stir-fry over a high heat. Sprinkle over the ground pepper, and place on a serving dish.

めばるの煮つけ

ほろほろとやわらかい春告魚の身を甘辛いたれでいただく

about **25** min

Simmered *Mebaru* Rockfish

Enjoy the tender flesh of the fish heralding the arrival of spring, with sweet and salty sauce

■材料・2人分

めばる ……2尾（1尾約260g）

A
水 ……………………200cc
酒 ……………………大さじ1
みりん ………………大さじ1
しょう油 ……………大さじ3
砂糖 …………………大さじ3

しょうが（薄切り）………4枚
ごぼう ……………………1/4本

▌Ingredients (serves 2)

2 whole *mebaru* rockfish
(about. 9 oz each)

A
4/5 U.S. cup water
1 Tbsp *sake*
1 Tbsp *mirin* sweet
cooking *sake*
3 Tbsps soy sauce
3 Tbsps sugar

4 thin slices ginger
1/4 burdock

■作り方

1 めばるのうろこを取り、えらを包丁（キッチンバサミ）で切り取る。隠し包丁を入れて腹わたを取り出し、血合いを洗う。表面に飾り包丁を入れる。

2 1を平ざるにのせ熱湯をまわしかけ、霜降りにする。
※魚の生ぐさみが取れ、旨味を閉じこめることが出来るので、必ず霜降りにすること。

3 ごぼうは包丁で皮をこそげ落とし、約4〜5cmの長さに切り、太ければさらに縦半分に切り、さっとゆでておく。

4 鍋にAとしょうがの薄切りを入れ煮立たせる。
※必ず煮汁が沸騰してから魚を入れること。煮汁が沸騰していないと魚の生ぐさみが出てしまうので注意したい。

1-a

1-b

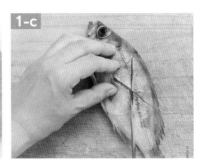

1-c

2

4

■ DIRECTIONS

1 Scale the *mebaru* rockfish, and cut off the gills with a kitchen knife, or scissors. Make cross-shape cuts on the body to facilitate soup penetration, and gut them.

2 Place the fish on a flat basket, and pour boiling water in a circular motion to allow the surface of the fish to lightly cook.
※Do not skip this process, as blanching removes the bad fishy odor, and contains *umami* (delicious taste).

3 Scrape off the skin of the burdock, and cut into a length of 1 1/2 to 2 inches. If the root is too thick, cut it vertically. Briefly boil the burdock.

4 Put **A** and the sliced ginger in a pot, and bring it to the boil.
※Make sure the sauce is boiling, before putting the fish in it. Otherwise, the fish will have a bad fishy odor.

5 2のめばる、**3**のごぼうを入れて落としぶた（アルミホイル、中央部に穴を開けたキッチンペーパーでもよい）をし、途中煮汁をめばるにかけながら、弱火にして約15分煮る。

※身が崩れてしまうため、煮ている時に絶対にめばるを裏返してはいけない。落としぶた（アルミホイル、キッチンペーパー）をしているため、めばる全体に煮汁がまわり、火が通るため大丈夫。

6 器に**5**をバランスよく盛りつけ、煮汁をかける。

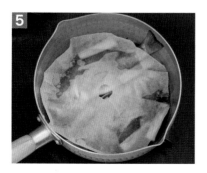

5 Put the *mebaru* prepared in **2** and the parboiled burdock in the pot, and cover with a drop lid. (A piece of aluminum foil, or kitchen paper with a hole in its center will suffice.) Turn down the heat, and cook for about 15 min, while occasionally pouring the liquid on the fish.

※Do not turn the fish while cooking, as the flesh could fall apart. Do not worry, as the drop lid (either of aluminum foil or kitchen paper) helps the liquid to circulate and cook the fish well.

6 Arrange the fish on a serving dish, and pour the liquid on them.

コラム
Column

めばるの種類
Types of *Mebaru* Rockfish

めばるは大別すると、黒めばると赤めばる（沖めばる）に分類することができる。名の通り体色が黒褐色、黒灰色などをしているものを黒めばるという。沖合い生息していて体色が赤色をしているものを赤めばるという。

赤めばるは、よく市場に出まわるウスメバル（体表の模様がやや薄くて不鮮明）、やや小型で斑紋が濃いのが特徴のトゴットメバル、エラブタの黒色斑紋が特徴でパンダメバルともいわれるウケクチメバルが代表である。

めばるは春告魚と呼ばれるように、春からよく出まわるため、やはり春が旬のタケノコと一緒に煮ると美味しいことから〝タケノコメバル〟とも呼ばれるが、実はタケノコメバルという名のメバルがいるのでお間違いのないように……。

The *mebaru* rockfish can be roughly categorized into the black *mebaru* and red *mebaru*. As the names indicate, the black *mebaru* has a blackish brown or grey body, while the red *mebaru*, living in offshore areas, has a reddish body.

Species often available on the market among the red *mebaru* are the *usu-mebaru*, or goldeye rockfish, whose body patterns are unclear; the *togotto-mebaru*, or jetner stingfish, which is rather small and has dark spots; and *ukekuchi-mebaru*, also known as *panda mebaru*, which has characteristic black spots on its operculum.

As often called the fish heralding the arrival of spring, the rockfish begin to appear on the market from spring. Because the fish is tasty if cooked with bamboo shoots, a typical spring vegetable, it is sometimes called "*takenoko* (bamboo shoot) *mebaru*." But be careful, as there is actually a species of *mebaru* with the same name.

夏を彩る
日本の歳時記と和食

Japanese Events and Food in Summer

夏の歳時記と和食
Events and Food in Summer

梅雨が終わるといよいよ暑い夏の到来である。薄緑だった樹々の葉も深緑になり、海も強い日差しでキラキラと輝き、海開きになった海水浴場は多くの人で賑わう。そして色鮮やかなあじさいやひまわりなどの花々などが咲きみだれ、日本全国の夜空を色鮮やかな花火が明るくする。そして、豪華絢爛な神輿を担いだ男衆が町をねり歩く。日本の暑い夏はとてもエネルギッシュでエキサイティングだ。そんな祭りやお盆のための料理が食卓を飾る。

When the rainy season is over, the summer gets really hot. The leaves of the trees turn from light to dark green. The sea glitters brightly reflecting the strong sunlight. Ocean beaches opened to swimmers buzz with many people. Colorful summer flowers, such as Japanese hydrangeas and sunflowers, bloom profusely, while the night sky all over Japan is brilliant with fireworks. At summer festivals, men carrying magnificent *mikoshis* (portable shrine) on their shoulders parade along the streets. The summer in Japan is vibrant with energy and excitement. Special dishes for summer festivals and the *Bon* Festival are served.

【夏の花鳥風月 Nature and events in summer】

深緑●Dark green leaves
春の樹々などの薄い緑色も、夏になると深い（濃い）緑色になり、夏を演出する。
The light green leaves of spring darken as summer progresses, providing a bold background to summer events.

あじさい●Japanese hydrangea
淡青紫色など、さまざまな色がある。6月中旬から開花する初夏を代表する花である。
There are several varieties of Japanese hydrangea, with many colors from light blue to violet. This plant begins to bloom in mid-June and is a representative flower of early summer.

ひまわり●Sunflowers
夏を代表するひまわりだが、アメリカ中西部が原産。主に一重咲きだが、八重もある。
Sunflowers are prevalent in midsummer in Japan, but are actually native to the Midwest of the U.S.A. The flower is mostly single-petaled but there are double-petaled varieties, too.

あさがお●Morning glory
名のごとく夏の朝に咲くあさがおは、奈良時代に薬用植物として渡来した。
As the name indicates, this plant blooms in early morning in summer. Morning glory was imported in the Nara Era as a medicinal plant.

しょうぶ●Iris
端午の節句に用いられる。北海道から九州に分布する。花期は5〜6月で夏の季語である。
The iris is used in *Tango-no-Sekku* (Boys' Festival). This plant is found from Hokkaido to Kyushu. The flowering season is from May to June, and iris is used as a seasonal word reflecting summer in composing *haiku*.

山ゆり●Gold-banded lily
7〜8月に開花する日本国有のゆり。大きな花で強い香りがする。根は食用になる。
This is a lily native to Japan and comes into flower in July and August. The flower is large and has a strong odor. The root is edible.

ハスの花●Lotus flower
花期は5〜6月で、白やピンク（薄紫）の花を咲かせる。ハスの花はレンゲ（蓮花）といわれる。
The flowering season of the lotus is from May to June, and its flower is white or pink (or light purple). *Hasu-no-hana* is the generally used Japanese word for lotus flower but *renge* is another Japanese term referring to this plant.

夏の海●The sea in summer
夏の強い日差しでキラキラと輝く夏の海。海開きはまさに夏の風物詩である。
The sea in summer glitters under the burning sun. The opening of the beaches in summer is a special attraction for swimmers.

大阪の天神祭り Tenjin Festival in Osaka

夏祭り Summer Festivals

日本全国で5月から8月にかけて大小さまざまな夏祭りが催される。その多くは、田植え祭り、祓、魂祭り、神幸祭になるが、祭りの数日前からその地方は祭り一色になる。豪華絢爛な神輿や山鉾を担ぐ人々のエネルギーと見物客とのエネルギーで日本の暑い夏はより熱くなる。

From May to August, summer festivals of all scales are held all over Japan. They are mostly rice planting festivals, purification festivals, festivals of souls or *shinkosai* (A Shinto festival featuring the parade of *mikoshi*). On the days before the festival, the area begins to fill with the festival atmosphere. The energy of the young people carrying magnificent *mikoshi* (portable shrine) on their shoulders and the excitement of spectators seem to bring the summer heat to a peak.

夏祭りの歴史と由来 Origin and history of summer festivals

　現在の夏祭りは、半てんと股引（パッチ）を着た男衆が神輿を担ぎ、金魚すくい、お面屋などの露店が並び、夏の風物詩になっている。夏祭りは半年を無事にすごせたことの祝いや、災いが起きないよう鎮めるためのものが多い。夏祭りですぐ思いだすのが神輿だが、これは古くから伝わる〝神幸祭り〟になる。神輿の中に祀られた神体から発する強い神力によってその土地の邪霊を追い払い、幸せを願うものだ。華麗な山鉾巡行で有名な京都の祇園祭は、平安時代に流行した疫病は、荒ぶる死者によって引き起こされると考えられてはじまった。

　他には花火大会、盆祭り（盆踊り）、ほおずき市、朝顔市なども夏祭りのひとつと考えられている。

Today's summer festivals feature *mikoshi* carried by young men wearing *hanten* (short coat) and *matahiki* (drawers) and street stalls of goldfish scooping, masks, etc., comprising the festival attractions in summer. Most summer festivals are observed to thank the gods for a peaceful and happy life in the past half year or to prevent any disaster and appease the spirits of the deceased. Summer festivals remind us of *mikoshi*, which is the feature of *shinkosai*. *Shinkosai* is held to exorcise evil spirits from the district by the power of the gods generated by worship in *mikoshi* and to pray for happiness. The Gion Festival in Kyoto, well known for the parade of splendid *yamahoko* (floats), was started in the Heian Era when people thought that the epidemics that prevailed in those days were caused by the avenging spirits of the dead.
Fireworks displays, the Bon Festival (featuring *bon-odori* dances), *hozuki* (Japanese lantern plant) markets and morning glory markets are also regarded as summer festivals.

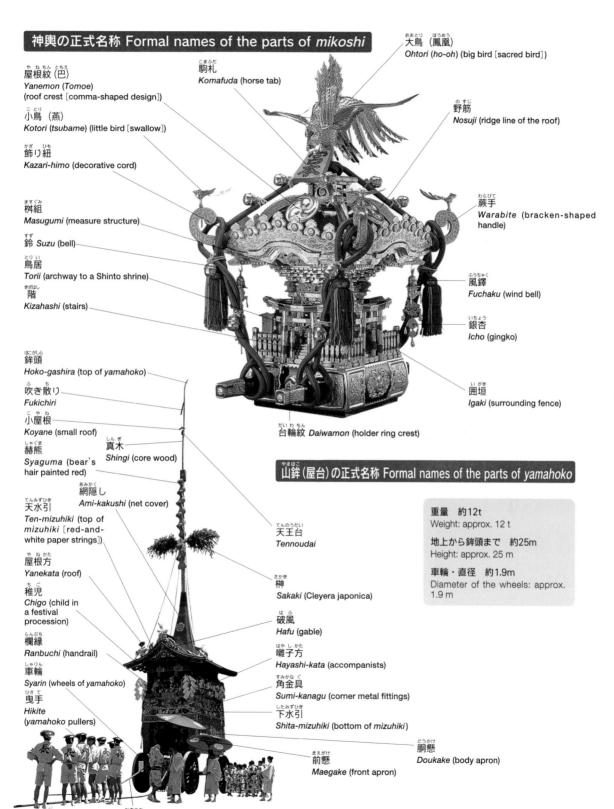

神輿の正式名称 Formal names of the parts of *mikoshi*

屋根紋（巴）
Yanemon (Tomoe)
(roof crest [comma-shaped design])

小鳥（燕）
Kotori (tsubame) (little bird [swallow])

飾り紐
Kazari-himo (decorative cord)

桝組
Masugumi (measure structure)

鈴 Suzu (bell)

鳥居
Torii (archway to a Shinto shrine)

階
Kizahashi (stairs)

駒札
Komafuda (horse tab)

大鳥（鳳凰）
Ohtori (ho-oh) (big bird [sacred bird])

野筋
Nosuji (ridge line of the roof)

蕨手
Warabite (bracken-shaped handle)

風鐸
Fuchaku (wind bell)

銀杏
Icho (gingko)

囲垣
Igaki (surrounding fence)

台輪紋 Daiwamon (holder ring crest)

鉾頭
Hoko-gashira (top of yamahoko)

吹き散り
Fukichiri

小屋根
Koyane (small roof)

赫熊
Syaguma (bear's hair painted red)

真木
Shingi (core wood)

網隠し
Ami-kakushi (net cover)

天水引
Ten-mizuhiki (top of mizuhiki [red-and-white paper strings])

屋根方
Yanekata (roof)

稚児
Chigo (child in a festival procession)

欄縁
Ranbuchi (handrail)

車輪
Syarin (wheels of yamahoko)

曳手
Hikite (yamahoko pullers)

天王台
Tennoudai

榊
Sakaki (Cleyera japonica)

破風
Hafu (gable)

囃子方
Hayashi-kata (accompanists)

角金具
Sumi-kanagu (corner metal fittings)

下水引
Shita-mizuhiki (bottom of mizuhiki)

前懸
Maegake (front apron)

胴懸
Doukake (body apron)

引綱 Hiki-tsuna (pulling ropes)

山鉾（屋台）の正式名称 Formal names of the parts of *yamahoko*

重量　約12t
Weight: approx. 12 t

地上から鉾頭まで　約25m
Height: approx. 25 m

車輪・直径　約1.9m
Diameter of the wheels: approx. 1.9 m

日本三大祭り Top three summer festivals

日本全国に数多くの夏祭りがある中でも特に日本屈指の夏祭りということで日本三大祭りがある。ここではそんな三大祭りを紹介する。

The top three summer festivals are the most popular festivals among the many summer festivals in Japan. These festivals are outlined below.

神田祭り Kanda Festival

東京・外神田にある通称、神田明神こと神田神社。毎年五月中旬におこなわれるのが日本三大祭りのひとつ〝神田祭り〟だ。神田祭りの起源は今から約1300年前だが、江戸時代には〝天下祭り〟といわれるほど豪華な祭りだった。本祭りの神幸祭には90基近い神輿がねり歩き、町中や神田神社の境内を担ぎ手と見物客で埋め尽くす。

Kanda Festival is dedicated to Kanda Shrine, commonly known as Kanda Myojin, in Sotokanda, Tokyo. This festival is held in mid-May every year. It dates back about 1,300 years and was such a splendid event in the Edo Era that it was nicknamed "Tenka-matsuri (whole country's festival)." At *shinkosai*, the main part of this festival, nearly 90 *mikoshi* parade, and *mikoshi* carriers and spectators fill the town and the precincts of Kanda Shrine.

天神祭り Tenjin Festival

毎年七月二十四、二十五日におこなわれる大阪府北区の天満宮の天神祭り。疫病の流行する夏を無事にすごせるよう祈願したのがはじまりで、1000年以上もの歴史ある祭りだ。見処は二十五日におこなわれる斎船に神鉾を乗せ、堂島川へ漕ぎ出す船渡御の光景だろう。

Tenjin Festival is observed on July 24 and 25 each year at Tenman Shrine in Kita-ku, Osaka. It originated as an event for praying for good health during summer when epidemics often broke out. This festival has a history of over 1,000 years. The best scene is probably that of *funatogi* in which the sacred halberd (*kamihoko*) on the purified boats (*iwaibune*) sail the Dojima River on July 25.

祇園祭 Gion Festival

京都市東山区祇園町の八坂神社(祇園社)の祇園祭は、平安時代に流行した疫病や災厄除去を、八坂神社に祀られている素戔嗚尊等に願った御霊会にはじまる。見処は十七日におこなわれる32基の山鉾巡行と神幸祭だ。「コンコンチキチン　コン　チキチン」のお囃子とともに豪華絢爛な山鉾は、まるで時代絵巻のようだ。この祇園祭、国内外の見物客で大変賑わい、有料観覧席も設けられている。

(問合せ：京都市観光協会 ☎ 075-752-0227)

The Gion Festival held at Yasaka Shrine (Gion Shrine) in Gion-machi, Higashiyama-ku, Kyoto, originates in the *goryo-e* (festival for the soul) dedicated to Susanoo-no-Mikoto, a Shinto deity worshipped at Yasaka Shrine, to pray to the deity for elimination of epidemics and disasters prevalent in the Heian Era. The best attractions are the parade of 32 floats and *shinkosai* held on July 17. The parade of the magnificent floats accompanied by the festival refrain, "*kon-kon-chiki-chin, kon chikichin*," resembles the scenes in Heian picture scrolls. During the Gion Festival, Kyoto is crowded with visitors from home and abroad, and you can reserve one of the special paid stands established for viewing the parade. (Contact: Kyoto City Tourist Association, Tel: 075-752-0227)

短い東北の夏をおしむかのように繰り広げられる夏祭り。中でも豪華で幻想的なねぶたとハネト（踊子）が有名な青森市の〝ねぶた祭り〟、190本もの竿灯がユラユラと揺れる幻想的な秋田県の〝竿灯祭り〟、豪華絢爛な笹飾りが有名な宮城県の〝仙台七夕祭り〟が、旧国鉄が定めた東北三大祭りといわれている。

In the Tohoku (north eastern Honshu) region, summer festivals are held as if to mourn the short summer. The many summer events in this region include the Nebuta Festival in Aomori, which is well known for splendid *nebuta* (floats) and *haneto* (dancers), the Kanto Festival in Akita Prefecture where as many as 190 *kanto* (long poles decorated with many paper lanterns) are paraded, the lanterns swinging slowly and dreamily, and the Sendai Tanabata Festival in Sendai, Miyagi Prefecture, famous for gorgeous decorations on long bamboo stalks, are known as the Top Three Tohoku Festivals, which were selected by the former Japanese National Railways.

ねぶた祭り Nebuta Festival

青森県弘前市の〝ねぶた祭り〟を真似て、安永年間（1772〜1781年）に灯籠を持ち歩きながら踊ったのが起源とされている。昭和23年（1948年）に港祭りとねぶた祭りが一緒になり、現在のような祭りになった。武者絵などを張ったねぶたとハネトと呼ばれる踊り子たちが、はねながら「ラッセラッセ」の掛け声とともに踊る姿が見処。

This festival is said to be modeled on the Nebuta Festival in Hirosaki, Aomori Prefecture; in the An-ei period (1772-1781), people danced bringing lanterns in their hands. In 1948, Aomori unified the Harbor Festival and the Nebuta Festival into one, which became the Nebuta Festival as seen today. The best scenes are *nebuta* (the magnificent floats made using pieces of paper with pictures of warriors, etc.) and the dances performed by *haneto* shouting "*Rasse, rasse!*"

竿灯祭り Kanto Festival

宝暦年間（1751〜1764年）に真夏の病魔や邪気を払うための〝ねぶた流し〟として灯籠を持ち歩いたのがはじまりの秋田県の竿灯祭り。現在は五穀豊穣を願って、長さ12m、重さ50kgもの大若射といわれる大きな竿灯をはじめ、中、小約190本もの竿灯を額、肩、平手などに載せながらねり歩く姿は圧巻。

The Kanto Festival in Akita Prefecture has its origin in the *Nebuta Nagashi* (ceremony of floating lantern on the water) observed in the Horeki period (1751-1764) when people paraded with lanterns to purify themselves and protect against illnesses in summer and evil spirits. At present, to pray to the gods for bumper crops, carriers parade along the street holding *kanto*, including some very large ones 12 m long and weighing 50kg. The highlight is a parade of about 190 *kanto* carried on the foreheads, shoulders, hands, etc. of the carriers.

仙台七夕祭り Sendai Tanabata Festival

日本三大七夕祭りにも数えられる宮城県仙台市の七夕祭り。定禅寺通りを中心に中央通りの一番町まで、豪華絢爛な笹飾りが続く。商売繁盛、無病息災などを願って、和紙飾りや、紙衣、千羽鶴、短冊、巾着、吹き流し、投網、屑籠の七つ道具が飾られた笹飾りが、約3000本もたつ姿はまさに圧巻だ。

The Sendai Tanabata Festival in Sendai, Miyagi Prefecture, is one of the top three *Tanabata* festivals in Japan. Jozen-ji Street and Chuo Street up to Ichiban-cho are adorned with splendid bamboo stalk decorations. To pray for good business and health, about 3,000 bamboo stalks are adorned with seven types of paraphernalia, i.e., paper clothes, paper cranes, *tanzaku* (pieces of paper) each bearing a *tanka* (31-syllable Japanese poem), *kinchaku* (drawstring money pouch), streamers, cast nets and wastepaper baskets, are really magnificent spectacles.

夏祭りを楽しむレシピ
Recipe to enjoy Summer festivals

焼きとうもろこし
しょう油の焼けた香りと、とうもろこしの甘さが美味しい

about
10
min

Grilled Corn on the Cob
The savory smell of burned soy sauce makes sweet corn tastier

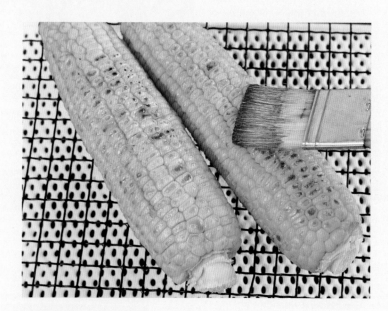

■材料・2人分
とうもろこし ……………2本
しょう油 ………………適量

■ Ingredients (serves 2)
2 ears of corn
Soy sauce

【作り方】

1 とうもろこしの皮をむき、ひげを取る。とうもろこしにラップをし、電子レンジで3〜5分加熱する。

2 1のラップをはずし、とうもろこしを焼き網に乗せ、転がしながら全体を焼く。焼き色がついてきたら、しょう油をハケで2〜3回塗りながら、香ばしく焼く。

【DIRECTIONS】

1 Remove the husk and floss from the corn. Wrap the corn with plastic wrap, and microwave for 3 to 5 min.

2 Remove the wrap, and place the corn on a grill mesh. Grill the corn while turning it so that it is grilled evenly. When the corn begins to brown, put brush soy sauce on the surface a few times, so that the savory aroma comes out.

86　夏を彩る日本の歳時記と和食

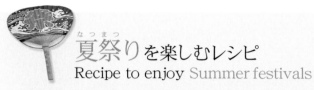

<ruby>夏祭<rt>なつまつ</rt></ruby>りを楽しむレシピ
Recipe to enjoy Summer festivals

焼きいか
お祭りの屋台でおもわず買ってしまう香ばしい焼きいか

about
12
min

Grilled Squid
The savory aroma of grilled squid is so tempting that you cannot simply pass a street stall selling grilled squid at a festival

■材料・2人分
するめいか（胴の部分）…2杯
酒 …………………小さじ2
しょう油 …………大さじ3
サラダ油 …………適量
七味唐辛子 ………適量
マヨネーズ ………適量

■ Ingredients (serves 2)

2 *Surume-ika* Japanese common squid (body part)
2 tsps *sake*
3 Tbsps soy sauce
Vegetable oil
Shichimi-tougarashi seven-spice chili mix
Mayonnaise

【作り方】

1 するめいかの胴の中を水洗いし、軟骨を抜き取る。

2 胴に斜めに切り込みを数本入れる。

3 焼き網を空焼きし、サラダ油を薄く塗り、**2**のいかを並べて両面をさっと焼く。

4 酒、しょう油を合わせたタレをハケで**3**のいかに塗りながら、全体を香ばしく焼く。

5 好みで七味唐辛子をふりかけたマヨネーズでいただく。

【DIRECTIONS】

1 Wash the inside of the squid, and remove the cartilage.

2 Make several shallow cuts on the surface of the squid.

3 Preheat the grill mesh, and thinly apply the vegetable oil. Place the squid on the mesh, and grill both sides quickly.

4 Put the mixture of the *sake* and soy sauce on the surface while grilling the squid slowly, so that the savory aroma comes out.

5 Add mayonnaise sprinkled with *shichimi-tougarashi*, if you like.

キャベツたっぷりお好み焼き

ソースの香りが食欲をそそり、キャベツたっぷりでとてもヘルシー

about
15
min

"As-You-Like-It" Pancake Containing Lots of Cabbage

The aroma of sauce stimulates your appetite. It's very healthy with a lot of cabbage

■材料・2人分（2枚分）

キャベツ	200g
青ねぎ	10本
大和いも	50g

A［薄力粉（ふるっておく） ……100g
　だし汁 ……3/4カップ

B［天カス ……大さじ2
　紅しょうが ……少々

卵	2個
豚ばら肉の薄切り	6枚
サラダ油	大さじ1

〈トッピング〉

ソース	適宜
青のり	適宜

▓ Ingredients (for 2 pancakes)

7 oz cabbage
10 green onions
1 3/4 *yamato-imo* yam

A［ 3 1/2 oz *hakurikiko* low-gluten cake flour (sifted)
　3/5 U.S. cup stock

B［ 2 Tbsps deep-fried *tempura* batter
　Beni-shoga red pickled ginger

2 eggs
6 slices pork belly
1 Tbsp vegetable oil

<Topping>
Okonomi sauce (Thick Japanese-style Worcester sauce)
Green laver

【作り方】

1 キャベツは粗いせん切りに、青ねぎは小口切りにする。

2 大和いもは皮をむいてすりおろし、Aと混ぜて生地を作る。

3 2の生地の2分の1の量を小さいボウルに入れ、2等分にした1のキャベツ、青ねぎ、Bと卵を1個割り入れたらスプーンなどでざくざく刻むように混ぜる。

【DIRECTIONS】

1 Cut the cabbage into coarse strips, and the green onions into rounds.

2 Peel the yam, and grate. Mix with **A** to make batter.

3 Put a half of the batter into a small bowl, add a half of the cut cabbage, the cut green onions, the ingredients of **B**, and 1 egg, and roughly mix the ingredients with a spoon.

4 フライパンにサラダ油を熱して弱めの中火にし、**3**を丸く流し入れたら豚ばら肉の薄切りを3枚ずつのせ、表面がふつふつとしてきたらひっくり返す。豚ばら肉の薄切りが焼けたらもう一度ひっくり返してさらに約1〜2分焼く。生地を押して弾力があれば焼き上がり。同じようにもう1枚焼く。トッピングをかけていただく。

4 Heat the vegetable oil in a frying pan, and turn down the heat to medium-low. Pour the mixture prepared in **3** onto the pan, and place 3 slices of pork belly on top. When the surface of the batter begins to form bubbles, turn over. When the pork is cooked, turn the pancake over again, and heat for 1 to 2 min. Press the pancake, and if it is resilient, it's done. Make another pancake likewise. Serve with the topping.

コラム
Column

キャベツの栄養と効能
Nutrients and Efficacy of Cabbage

　お好み焼きに使用するキャベツには、ビタミンU（キャベジン）が多く含まれている。このビタミンU（キャベジン）は、胃腸の粘膜の新陳代謝を活発化し、初期の胃潰瘍や十二指腸潰瘍を回復させる働きがあることで知られている。

　また、免疫力を高め、風邪を予防するなどの働きがあるビタミンCが多く、キャベツの葉4枚程度で一日の必要なビタミンCをカバーできるといわれている。さらに食物繊維が豊富なため、便秘解消にもなり、ダイエット食品としても注目されている。

　さらにキャベツに含有されているアリルイソチオシアネート、インドールがガンを抑制し、ペルオキシダーゼが発ガン性物質の活性化を抑制することがわかっている。

Cabbage, an indispensable ingredient of the "as-you-like-it" pancake, contains a high value of Vitamin U (cabagin). Vitamin U (cabagin) is known for its effects in activating the metabolism of the gastric mucosa, thus curing early-stage stomach ulcers and duodenal ulcers. Cabbage also contains a lot of Vitamin C, which is effective in preventing colds by enhancing the immune system. It's said that 4 leaves of cabbage contains the daily necessary amount of Vitamin C. Since the vegetable is also rich in dietary fiber, it helps to ease constipation and is attracting attention as a slimming food.

Additionally, it is found that allyl isothiocyanate and indole contained in cabbage prevent cancer, and peroxydase prevents cancer-causing substances from being active.

コラム

Column

お好み焼きの種類
Varieties of *Okonomiyaki*, or "As-You-Like-It" Pancakes

日本全国でお好み焼きは食べられているが、中でも〝関西風お好み焼き″〝広島風お好み焼き″〝東京風 (江戸前) お好み焼き″が有名である。

関西風お好み焼きは、大阪を中心に神戸、京都などが中心だが、現在は全国区といっても過言ではないだろう。関西風お好み焼きの特徴を簡単に紹介すると、生地にキャベツ、青ねぎ、豚ばら肉、天かす、卵を入れてよく混ぜ合わせたものを鉄板で焼くこと。

ちなみに関西風お好み焼きは、当初こんにゃくや豆の具を入れて、しょう油味で食べる「ベタ焼き」「チョボ焼き」というものだったらしい。

広島風お好み焼きは、生地と具材を混ぜ合わせず、生地の上にのせていくのが特徴。つまり、関西風のように最初から生地と具材を混ぜないことが、大きく異なる。生地を裏返したり、のせる回数が多いので、お店では自分で焼くことはなく、焼いてくれる。また、使用するソースはおたふくソースに限られる。

東京風 (江戸前) お好み焼きは、最初に鉄板に薄く生地を作り、その上にキャベツ、肉などの具材をのせ、最後に残った生地をまわしかけて裏返して焼き上げるのが基本だ。

Okonomiyaki pancakes are popular across Japan. Of them, especially famous varieties are "Kansai-style," "Hiroshima-style," and "Tokyo-, or *Edomae*-style."

The Kansai-style pancakes were mainly eaten in Osaka, Kobe, and Kyoto, but it is not an exaggeration to say that they now enjoy nationwide popularity. Simply put, the Kansai-style pancakes feature cabbage, green onions, pork belly, bits of deep-fried *tempura* batter, and eggs mixed well, before being cooked on an iron plate.

By the way, the origin of the Kansai-style pancake is said to be *beta-yaki*, or *chobo-yaki*, which contained such ingredients as the *konnyaku* devil's tongue cake and beans, and served with soy sauce.

Hiroshima-style *okonomiyaki* is unique in that the ingredients are put on the batter, instead of being mixed with it. Unlike Kansai-style, ingredients are not mixed with the batter before being cooked. At Hiroshima-style *okonomiyaki* restaurants, customers do not cook on iron plates on their tables by themselves, unlike other-style *okonomiyaki* restaurants, because there are many things to do, such as turning over the pancakes and placing the ingredients in several portions. Instead, staff cook for customers. *Otafuku*-brand sauce is the only sauce used for Hiroshima-style *okonomiyaki*.

To make Tokyo-style (*Edomae*) *okonomiyaki*, basically, a thin layer of batter is made first, and cabbage, pork, and other ingredients are placed on top. Then, the remaining batter is poured onto the ingredients, and turned over.

花火大会 Fireworks displays

夏の夜空を彩る打上げ花火。世界でも最も美しく、壮大といわれる日本の花火。また、家庭では〝せんこう花火〟などをはじめとするさまざまな〝おもちゃ花火〟がされるほど日本の夏を代表する風物詩の代表といっても過言ではない花火には、どのような歴史があり、由来があるのだろうか……。

Skyrockets decorate the night sky in summer. Japanese fireworks are said to be the most beautiful and spectacular in the world. At home, people enjoy a wide variety of toy fireworks, including *senko-hanabi* (small sparklers). Summer in Japan is celebrated everywhere with fireworks, but what is their origin and history?

花火の歴史と由来 Origin and history of fireworks in Japan

　日本の花火は中国から伝えられたといわれている。紀元前三世紀には中国で爆竹が使用されているし、六世紀には火薬が使われると同時に花火も造られたといわれているが、これは諸説あり定かではない。

　日本人で最初に花火を見たのは、徳川家康だといわれている。1613年に駿府城内で外国人（南蛮人）がおこなった花火を見物したと、『駿府政治録』という日記・政治録に書かれているらしい。

　江戸時代になると花火を専門に扱う火薬屋が登場する。その代表が1659年に初代弥兵衛が〝おもちゃ花火〟を売り出した「鍵屋」である。そしてもうひとつが、鍵屋の手代（番頭の下）だった清吉がのれん分けして1810年に両国広小路に店を構えた「玉屋」である。

　しかし、1843年玉屋が失火、店はもちろんのこと半町ほどの火事になり、財産没収、江戸お構い（追放）となり、一代で家名断絶になってしまった。ちなみに鍵屋は〝宗家花火鍵屋〟として今なお続いている。

　江戸時代は花火専門職の花火を〝町人花火〟と呼び、大名らが配下の火薬職人に命じた花火は〝武家花火〟、水戸藩、尾張藩、紀州藩の徳川家の花火を〝御三家花火〟と呼んだ。また、江戸だけではなく、九州、愛知、長野などでも花火があげられていたらしい。

　明治時代に入ると海外から多くの薬品が輸入され、今までに出せなかったさまざまな色や、明るくなって、日本の花火は大きく変化することになる。大正時代になると花火製作はさらに活発になり、技術も向上していく。芯を入れた〝芯物花火〟、芯が二重に入る〝八重芯〟、芯が三重の〝三重芯〟などが出来上る。

Fireworks in Japan were originally imported from China. In the 3rd century B.C., firecrackers were already used in China. It is thought that gunpowder began to be used and fireworks were made simultaneously in the 6th century in China, but this is uncertain.

Tokugawa Ieyasu, the first *shogun* of the Tokugawa regime, is said to be the first person in Japan who saw fireworks. *Sunpu-Seijiroku*, a diary and record of political events, reports that Ieyasu viewed the fireworks staged by a foreigner (European visitor) at his Sunpu Castle in 1613.

In the Edo Era, merchants specializing in gunpowder appeared. Representative of these merchants was the firm Kagiya, whose founder Yahei introduced toy fireworks. Another was the firm Tamaya, founded by Seikichi, a clerk (reporting to the head clerk) at Kagiya, who was given a branch of his own by Kagiya, at Ryogoku-hirokoji, Edo, in 1810.

写真提供：大仙市
Photo by courtesy of Daisen City

But in 1843, Tamaya caused a fire and not only the store but the neighboring districts were burnt down. Seikichi forfeited his assets and was expelled from Edo, and the name of Tamaya vanished from the fireworks business scene. On the other hand, Kagiya has continued until today as the leader of the fireworks industry.

In the Edo Era, there were three categories of fireworks displays. Tradesmen's firework displays were held by firework specialists, Warriors' firework displays were held by pyrotechnists by order of a *daimyo* and other warriors and *Gosanke* (three families') firework displays were sponsored by the three Tokugawa families, Mito, Owari and Kishu. Fireworks seem to have been held not only in Edo but also in Kyushu, Aichi, Nagano and some other areas.

In the Meiji Era (1869-1912), many chemicals began to be imported from abroad, which led to great changes in fireworks in Japan: many new colors were added, and fireworks became brighter. In the Taisho Era (1912-1926), the manufacture of fireworks grew more active and the manufacturing techniques were improved further. New types of fireworks, such as fireworks with wicks in them, double-wick fireworks and triple-wick fireworks, were introduced.

歌川広重の「名所江戸百景 両国花火」
（東京都江戸東京博物館・複製禁止）

On Hundred Sights in Edo: Fireworks at Ryogoku by Utagawa Hiroshige (by courtesy of the Edo-Tokyo Museum, Tokyo; reproduction prohibited)

日本で最古の花火大会 Oldest fireworks display in Japan

　記録に残っているもので、日本最古の花火大会は、〝隅田川花火大会〟といわれている。亨保17年（1732年）の大飢饉で多くの餓死者が出たことと、疫病が流行したために、八代将軍の徳川吉宗が犠牲になった人々の慰霊と悪病退散を祈って、隅田川（大川）で水神祭をおこない、両国橋周辺の料理屋が幕府の許可をもらい花火を上げたのが、〝両国の川開き〟で、現在の〝隅田川花火大会〟のはじまりである。

The oldest recorded fireworks display in Japan is said to have been the Sumida River Fireworks Display. In the serious famine in 1732, many people starved to death and epidemics prevailed. Tokugawa Yoshimune, the eighth *shogun*, held a festival for the water god along the Sumida River to console the spirits of deceased persons and to pray for the epidemics to end. On that occasion, restaurants around the Ryogoku Bridge displayed fireworks by permission of the government. This was the River Festival at Ryogoku, the origin of the Sumida River Fireworks Display today.

日本全国で数多くの花火大会が催されるが、その中でも日本三大花火といわれているのは、秋田県の〝大曲全国花火競技会〟、新潟県長岡市の〝長岡祭り花火大会〟、茨城県土浦市の〝土浦全国花火競技会〟になる。

The top three fireworks displays, selected from many fireworks displays held throughout Japan, are the Ohmagari National Fireworks Display in Akita Prefecture, the Nagaoka Festival Fireworks Display in Nagaoka, Niigata Prefecture, and the Tsuchiura National Fireworks Display in Tsuchiura, Ibaraki Prefecture.

※写真提供：大仙市 Photos by courtesy of Daisen City

大曲全国花火競技会
Ohmagari National Fireworks Display

毎年八月の第4土曜日の秋田県大仙市の雄物川河畔でおこなわれるのが、全国の花火師が技を競い合う〝大曲全国花火競技会〟だ。この花火大会の名物は、花火師が造った新作はもちろんのこと、なんといってもフィナーレを飾る〝ワイドスターマイン〟だ。これは約7分間にわたって続けざまに打ち上げられるため、まさに壮大で鮮やかな光と色彩に目が奪われてしまうことだろう。

This fireworks display is held at the riversides of the Omono River in Daisen, Akita Prefecture, on the fourth Saturday in August every year, where pyrotechnists from all over the country compete to show off their skills. The features of this event are the newly designed fireworks of pyrotechnists and in particular, the Wide Star Mine displayed at the finale. This show lasts about seven minutes during which fireworks are let off in quick succession, amazing viewers with the dazzling display of bright light and colors.

土浦全国花火競技会
Tsuchiura National Fireworks Display

茨城県土浦市の桜川河畔でおこなわれるのが〝土浦全国花火競技会〟である。通常花火大会や競技会は夏におこなわれることが多いが、この競技会は十月初旬に実施される。大正十四年（1925年）にはじまった競技会は、〝十号玉〟〝スターマイン〟〝創造花火〟の3部門を全国の花火師が競う。

This fireworks display takes place at the riversides of the Sakura River in Tsuchiura, Ibaraki Prefecture. Fireworks displays and competitions are usually held in summer, but this event is held in early October. At the Tsuchiura Fireworks Display started in 1925, pyrotechnists from all over Japan compete in three sections: No.10 fireworks, Star Mine fireworks, and newly designed fireworks.

長岡祭り花火大会
Nagaoka Festival Fireworks Display

新潟県長岡市でおこなわれる〝長岡祭り花火大会〟は、毎年八月二、三日に信濃川河畔で実施される。2日間で2万発もの華麗なる花火が夜空を彩る。放浪の画家・山下清の切り絵でも有名だ。天保十一年(1840年)に長岡藩主・牧野忠雅によって打ち上げられたのがきっかけで、大正時代に実寸三尺の〝正三尺玉〟が打上げに成功したことから、全国に知られるようになった。

This display is held on August 2 and 3 each year at the riversides of the Shinano River in Nagaoka, Niigata Prefecture.

As many as 20,000 fireworks color the night sky in the two days. This fireworks display is also famous for the paper cutting by Kiyoshi Yamashita, the vagabond painter. The origin is the fireworks display in 1840 sponsored by Makino Tadamasa, the lord of the domain of Nagaoka. The success in the display of *sei-sanjaku-dama*, fireworks with a diameter of precisely three *shaku* (one *shaku* = approx 30.3cm), made this event widely known throughout Japan.

打ち上げ花火の種類 Type of fireworks

【割物花火】
Warimono fireworks

菊、牡丹、八重芯菊、三重芯菊(菊花残光)や、魚、ハートなどの型物などを割物という。
Fireworks having the shape of an object, such as a chrysanthemum, peony, double-petaled chrysanthemum (having afterglow), fish, and then heart, are named *warimono* fireworks.

【創造花火】
Newly designed fireworks

全国の花火師たちが技を競う競技大会で見られるのがこの創造花火だ。まさに花火師の数だけの種類がある。
These fireworks can be seen in national fireworks displays where pyrotechnists from all over the country compete to show their skills. They are as various as the number of pyrotechnists.

【スターマイン】
Star mine fireworks

同時に数種もの花火を打ち上げた見事なスターマイン。色合いや形の織り成すハーモニーがきれいだ。
Several different fireworks let off simultaneously are called star mine fireworks. These are beautiful and show the harmony of diverse colors and shapes.

※写真提供：大仙市 Photos by courtesy of Daisen City

七夕祭り *Tanabata* (Star) Festivals

七月七日の七夕の夜に、天の川で隔てられた彦星と織姫が年に一度だけ会うことができるといわれる。そんな七夕の日に短冊に願いごとを書いて笹竹に吊るすと、願いごとがかなうといわれている。ここでは、そんな七夕の由来や日本三大七夕を紹介している。

Legend has it that Vega and Altair, who are separated by the Milky Way, are allowed to meet only once a year on the night of *Tanabata* or July 7. It is said that if you write your wish on a *tanzaku* (a strip of paper) and hang it on a bamboo grass, your wish will be granted. This section describes the origin of *Tanabata* and the top three *Tanabata* festivals in Japan.

七夕祭りの歴史と由来 Origin and history of *Tanabata* (Star) Festivals

　七夕は中国の牽牛星（彦星）と織女星（織姫）の伝説による。織姫は天帝の娘で機織の上手な働き者で、彦星も働き者だったので天帝は二人の結婚を認めたのだが、二人は夫婦生活が楽しく、働かなくなってしまった。天帝は怒り、二人を天の川を隔てて引き離した。年に一度だけ、七月七日に会うことをゆるされたが、雨がふり天の川の水が増えると会うことができない話が七夕伝説である。

　日本にはこの伝説が奈良時代に伝わり、宮中では七夕を〝しちせき〟と呼んでいたが、後に〝たなばた〟と呼ばれるようになった。七夕の〝たな〟は棚〝はた〟は機織りのことで、女性は機織りや裁縫の技能向上を願った布の端切れを笹竹につけて軒先に出して織姫にあやかって祈願したといわれる。

　また、短冊や色紙形に自筆で願いごとを書いて、字の上達を願ったともいわれている。さらに年に一度しか会えない悲しい恋物語であることから、恋愛の成就を願う行事でもある。

Tanabata derives from the Chinese legend of Vega and Altair. Vega was the daughter of the Lord of Heaven and a hard worker good at weaving and Altair was also a hard-working young man. Thus the Lord permitted their marriage, but their married life was so happy that they stopped working diligently. The Lord became angry and separated them by the Milky Way. They were permitted to meet just once a year on July 7. But when heavy rains fell on the day, the river water increased and prevented their date. This is the *Tanabata* legend.

This legend was imported into Japan in the Nara Era. People in the court called *Tanabata shichiseki* at first but began to use *Tanabata* instead later. The Japanese word Tanabata is composed of *tana* (=shelf) and *hata*, which is pronounced euphonically as *bata* and refers to weaving; therefore it is said that women prayed to gods for improved weaving and sewing skills by putting pieces of cloth on a bamboo grass and placing it in front of their house, trying to share Vega's skill in weaving.

It is also said that people prayed for improved skill in writing characters by writing their wish on a *tanzaku* or *irogami* (a piece of fancy paper) in their own hand. Additionally, because the event is based on the sad love story of Vega and Altair who can meet only once a year, *Tanabata* is also an event for praying for the fruition of love.

日本三大七夕 Top three *Tanabata* Festivals in Japan

日本全国の家庭や学校、商店などで楽しまれている七夕だが、豪華絢爛な七夕祭りの中でも三大がある。

The top three *Tanabata* Festivals are the best of the many events held by families, schools, stores, and the like throughout Japan.

仙台七夕祭り
Sendai Tanabata Festival

宮城県仙台市では「タナバタさん」と呼ばれる仙台七夕祭りは、700年以上の伝統を誇っている。伊達藩主の伊達政宗が、女性や子供たちに奨励したのがはじまりで、その後、武家や商家の間で流行し、現在に至っている。豪華な吹き流しを飾った1500本以上の大きな竹飾りが商店街を彩る。

Commonly known as "*Tanabata*-san" in Sendai, Miyagi Prefecture, this festival takes pride in its long history of over 700 years. The origin is an event that Date Masamune, the Lord of the domain of Date, encouraged women and children to hold. Later the festival became popular among warriors and merchants and has continued until the present. More than 1,500 bamboo stalks with splendid streamers on them decorate shopping centers.

平塚七夕祭り
Hiratsuka Tanabata Festival

昭和二十五年（1950年）に、戦後の商業振興のひとつとして催されたのが神奈川県平塚市の七夕祭りだ。駅前の商店街には、大きくて豪華な吹き流しや、くす玉などが飾られた竹飾りが並び、夜にはライトアップされて、とても幻想的である。他には七夕パレード、ミス七夕コンテストなどの催しもある。

This event was first held in 1950 in Hiratsuka, Kanagawa Prefecture, as a means of promoting commerce after the war. The shopping arcades in front of Hiratsuka Station are adorned with bamboo decorations with gorgeous, large streamers, *kusudama* (large decorative paper balls), etc., which are lit up and provide a fantastic sight at night. Other features include *Tanabata* parades and beauty contests for appointing a Miss *Tanabata*.

安城七夕祭り
Anjo Tanabata Festival

愛知県安城市で昭和二十九年（1954年）に、"夏の観光資源"としてスタートしたのがはじまりの安城七夕祭り。各商店が毎年自慢の竹飾りを競い合うため、豪華絢爛な吹き流しや短冊などの飾りが披露され、その年の最優秀が決められる。毎年8月上旬の3日間おこなわれる。

The Anjo Tanabata Festival originated in 1954 in Anjo, Aichi Prefecture, as an event for tourists in summer. The stores compete in their bamboo decorations and magnificent streamers, *tanzaku* and other features are displayed, with the year's best ones being selected. This festival is held for three days in early August every year.

お盆 *Obon*

先祖の精霊を迎え、供養するために盆棚を作り、季節の野菜や果ものなどを供える。家族や親戚が一同に集まり、懐かしい顔が揃う時でもある。皆んなで先祖の精霊を迎えるためにお墓を清掃し、盆踊り、精霊流しをして精霊を慰め、送り出す。けっして忘れてはいけない日本の伝統行事である。

During *obon*, people make *bon-dana* (bon altar) to make offerings of seasonal vegetables and fruit, and to welcome and pray for the spirits of their ancestors. It is one of the times of the year when family and relatives come together. People clean their ancestors tombs to welcome the spirits, and dance *bon-odori* (*bon* dance) and perform *shoryou-nagashi* (releasing of spirits). *Obon* is a very important traditional Japanese celebration.

お盆の歴史と由来 Origin and history of *obon*

　先祖の精霊を迎え、供養する期間（七月または、八月十三日から十六までの4日間）をお盆という。正式的には〝盂蘭盆会〟といわれる。この盂蘭盆会とはインドのサンスクリット語のウラバンナ（逆さ吊りという意味）を音写したものだ。

　ある日、神通力をもつ者が、仏教の開祖であるお釈迦様の弟子の一人の目連尊者の亡き母親が餓鬼道に落ち、逆さ吊りにされて苦しんでいるということを知った目連尊者は、お釈迦様にどうしたら母親を助けられるかと聞いたところ、「夏の修業が終わった七月十五日（旧暦）に僧侶を招き、供ものをささげて供養すれば母を救うことができる」とのこと。お釈迦様の教え通りにしたところ、目連尊者の母親は極楽往生が出来たというのだ。それ以来七月十五日（旧暦）に先祖に感謝し、供養する日（お盆）になったのである。

　日本では推古天皇の十四年（606年）に、お盆の行事がおこなわれたという。その後、お盆の行事は地方によってさまざまな様式になったが、先祖の霊が帰ってくる日として定着している。

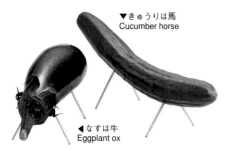

▼きゅうりは馬
Cucumber horse

◀なすは牛
Eggplant ox

きゅうりを馬、なすを牛に見立てるが、これは、馬は足が速いことから「あの世から早く家に帰ってくるように」と願いを込め、牛は歩みが遅いため、「あの世に帰るのが遅くなるように」という願いが込められている

A cucumber is used to depict a horse because horses are swift, reflecting the people's wishes for the spirits to arrive early from the other world. Conversely an eggplant is used to depict an ox because they are slow, reflecting people's wishes for the spirits to take their time returning.

The time of year when people welcome and pray for their ancestors (four days from the 13th to 16th of either July or August) is called *obon*. The official name for this celebration is "*ura-bon-e.*" This word is a phonetic derivation of the sanskrit word *Ullambana* (to hang upside down).

One day, Mahamaudgalyayana, a disciple of Shakyamuni Buddha, the founder of Buddhism, learns from a person with supernatural powers that his deceased mother has fallen to the realm of hungry spirits and is in great agony being hung upside down. Mahamaudgalyayana then asks Shakyamuni Buddha how he can save his mother to which Shakyamuni Buddha replies, "After you have finished your summer practice, on July 15th (old calendar), invite a monk to your home, make offerings, and pray for your mother. By doing so, she will be saved." Mahamaudgalyayana did as Shakyamuni Buddha instructed and his mother was able to enter paradise. Ever since that time, July 15th (old calendar) has been considered the day for giving thanks and for praying for one's ancestors, or *obon*. It is said that *obon* was first practiced in Japan in the 14th year of the reign of Emperor Suiko (606). Since then, while the celebration has taken on a variety forms region to region, it still remains the day when the spirits come home.

お盆になる前に仏壇などを清掃し、墓の掃除をし、故人（ご先祖様）の好物や果もの、野菜などを用意する。十一日か十三日に供花（盆花）を飾る。現在、都会であまり見かけることはなくなったが、盆棚（精霊棚、先祖棚ともいう）を作り、季節の野菜や果もの、ご飯、餅、団子などの他に、きゅうりやなすに割箸や竹で足をつけて牛や馬（ご先祖様の霊の送迎用）を作り供える。

十三日の夕方に迎え火として門口などで燃やす火をたよりにご先祖様の霊が家に来るとされる。盆提灯や盆灯籠もまた迎え火のひとつである。また、広場に集まってされる盆踊りは、帰ってきた精霊を供養する踊りで、古くは正装して輪を作り「南無阿弥陀仏」を唱えながら回っていたのが、現在のような手振りが加わった民謡踊りへと変化したものである。

迎えた霊が、再び帰るための案内として十五日の夕方には〝送り火〟として門口などで火が燃やされる。ちなみに京都の夏の風物詩になっている〝大文字の送り火〟もこのひとつである。

送り火が終わると精霊流し（精霊送りともいう）がおこなわれる。この精霊流しは、当初盆棚の敷もの（精霊薦）に供えものを包み、線香などとともに海に流したり、近くの川に流された。その後、わら船や精霊船などや灯籠などを舟に載せて川に流すようになった。

お盆の期間は、地方によって異なるが、魚などの生ぐさみや肉類を食べず、季節の野菜などを使った煮もの、ちらし寿し（野菜ちらし寿し）、赤飯などの精進料理が食べられる。

Before *obon*, people clean their *butsudan* (ancestral altar), their tombs, and prepare foods, fruit and vegetables that the deceased (ancestors) enjoyed. *Kuge* (flowers of *obon*) are arranged on the 11th or 13th. People make *bon-dana* (*bon* altars, also called *shoryo-dana* [spirit altar] or *senzo-dana* [ancestor altar]), prepare vegetables and fruit that are in season. They also cook rice, rice cakes, and rice dumplings, and also use chopsticks or bamboo sticks to make oxen and horses from cucumbers and eggplant (these are what the ancestors ride on as they make their way to and from this world). These practices are seen less and less in the cities, however.

It is said that our ancestors arrive at our homes guided by *mukaebi* (welcoming fire), the fire that we light at the entrance of our home on the evening of the 13th. *Bon-chochin* (paper *bon* lanterns) and *bon-dourou* (stone *bon* lanterns) are also a form of *mukaebi*. The *bon-odori* dance, in which people get together to perform in large open spaces, is a means of expressing prayers for our ancestors. Traditionally, people used to dress up in formal clothing and dance in circles chanting "*namu amidabutsu*" but it has changed over the years into a folk dance accompanied by unique hand gestures.

On the evening of the 15th, people burn *okuribi* (sending off fire) near their house's entrance to serve as a guide for the spirits to return to where they came from. The famous "*daimonji no okuribi*" of Kyoto is also a form of *okuribi*.

When *okuribi* is finished, people perform *shoryo-nagashi* (also called *shoryo-okuri*). *Shoryo-nagashi* (releasing of spirits) has its origins in people using the underliner (*shourogomo*) used for the *bon-dana* to wrap offerings, placing incense on them, and then releasing them onto the ocean or river. Later, people began using little boats made of hay, *shoryo-bune* (spirit boats) and lanterns placed on boats.

While customs differ from region to region, people generally refrain from eating fish or meat during *obon*, and enjoy *shojin-ryori* (vegetarian cooking) such as cooked vegetables, *chirashi-zushi* with only vegetables, and *sekihan* (red rice).

お盆の期間は煮ものや赤飯などといった精進もの（精進料理）が食べられる

During *obon*, people enjoy *shojin-ryori* (vegetarian cooking) such as cooked vegetables and *sekihan* (red rice).

盆踊りの歴史と由来 Origin and history of *bon-odori*

　平安時代に空也上人によってはじめられた念仏踊り（正装して輪を作り「南無阿弥陀仏」を唱えながら回る）が、盂蘭盆会の行事と結びついたといわれている。

　この盆踊りは、戻って来た精霊を慰め、送り出すための踊りだといわれている。また、戻って来た精霊が供養のおかげで成仏できたことを表わす踊りともいわれている。さらには、戻って来た精霊たちを踊りに巻き込みながら送り出すためとか、悪霊や亡者たちを踊りながら追い出すものという地方もある。

Nenbutsu-odori ([chanting dance] where people dress up in formal clothing and dance in a circle while chanting "*namu amidabutsu*"), which was first started by a learned monk named Kuuya Shonin in the Heian Era, was later adopted by the people as one of the events of *urabone*.

It is said that *bon-odori* is a dance to comfort and send off the spirits of our ancestors and for expressing how the returning spirits were able to become Buddha through our prayers. Another version says that it is a dance where the returning spirits dance amongst the living before leaving. Then in some regions, it is said that people dance to cast bad spirits away.

日本三大盆踊り Three major *bon-odori* in Japan

戻って来た精霊を慰め、送り出すといわれる盆踊り。現在は踊りを楽しむだけのものが増えているが、今なお昔ながらの伝統を守っている盆踊りがある。ここではそんな三つの盆踊りを紹介する。

In many regions of Japan, *bon-odori* are performed to comfort and send off returning spirits. While in many regions it has become an event where people simply enjoy dancing, there are some that still follow age old traditions. We would like to introduce you to three such *bon-odori*.

西馬音内盆踊り
Nishimonai Bon-Odori

秋田県羽後町で700年以上の歴史を持つ盆踊りで、先祖供養や豊年祈願のためにはじめられた。女性は端縫いの衣装を着て優雅に踊る。また黒い覆面（彦三頭巾）をかぶった踊り手が登場するなど幻想的な盆踊りである。毎年八月十六から十八日の2日間、西馬音内本町通りで夕方から翌日の朝方まで夜を徹して繰り広げられる。

This *bon-odori* held at Ugomachi in Akita has a history going back over 7 centuries. It originated as an event to pray for people's ancestors and for a rich harvest. Women dress in costumes called *hanui* and dance gracefully. There is also an element of mystery where dancers with black masks over their heads (*hikosazukin*) join in. Dancers dance throughout the night from dusk until dawn during this event which is held each year from August 16th to 18th on the Honmachi Street in Nishimonai.

郡上踊り
Gujo-Odori

毎年七月上旬から九月初めまでの岐阜県郡上市の各地でおこなわれる郡上踊り。特に八月十三日から十六日の4日間のお盆の日には、笛、太鼓、三味線を囲んで、〝かわさき〟、〝三百〟、〝春駒〟〝猫の手〟などといわれる10種類もの踊りを地元民、帰省客、観光客の数千人から1万人以上で踊る光景は圧巻である。

Gujo-odori are performed each year from early July to early September in various places of Gujo City in Gifu. The events held during the 4 days of *obon*, from August 13th to 16th, are particularly spectacular where thousands and sometimes even more than 10,000 locals, former locals, and tourists come together, encircling performers of traditional flute, drum, and shamisen to dance 10 variations of dances called by names such as "*kawasaki*," "*sanbyaku*," "*harukoma*," and "*nekonoko*."

阿波踊り
Awa-Odori

この阿波踊りが盆踊りのひとつであることはあまり知られていないが、れっきとした盆踊りである。毎年八月十二日から十五日に徳島県の各市町村で開催される。中でも徳島市で開催される徳島阿波踊りは、参加960連以上（踊りのグループ）、踊り子10万人以上もが参加する。また、各市町村で選ばれた選抜隊で競われる選抜阿波踊り大会では、一糸乱れぬ〝女踊り〟や、エネルギッシュな〝ケンカ踊り〟、〝男踊り〟などを見ることができる。ちなみにこの阿波踊りにも日本三大があり、徳島県の阿波踊りはもちろんのこと、埼玉県の〝南越谷阿波踊り〟、東京都の〝高円寺阿波踊り〟になる。

It is not generally known that the *awa-odori* is a form of *bon-odori*. These events are held in various towns and villages in Tokushima between August 12th and 15th each year. In particular, the Tokushima Awa-Odori held in Tokushima City attracts over 960 "rens" (dancing groups) or a total of over 100,000 dancers. In addition, the Select Awa-Odori event, which features selected groups from each municipality, is famous for the precisely choreographed "*onna-odori*" as well as the energetic "*kenka-odori*" and "*otoko-odori*." The "three greatest" *awa-odori* in Japan are, first and foremost, the Tokushima Awa-Odori, followed by the Minami Koshigaya Awa Odori of Saitama and Koenji Awa Odori of Tokyo.

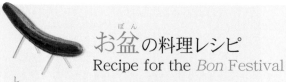

お盆の料理レシピ
ぼん

Recipe for the *Bon* Festival

凍み豆腐の煮もの

だし汁を吸い込んだ凍み豆腐は郷愁を感じさせるやさしい味わい

about
35
min

Freeze-dried *Tofu* Simmered in Seasoning

Seasoning-soaked freeze-dried *tofu* has a gentle taste that makes you nostalgic

■材料・2人分	
絹ごし豆腐	1丁
にんじん	1/2本
干ししいたけ	3枚
ゆでたけのこ	1/2本
いんげん	3本
ごま油	大さじ1/2
A ┌ 干ししいたけの戻し汁	適量
│ だし汁	1カップ
└ 酒	大さじ1
B ┌ 砂糖	大さじ1
│ しょう油	大さじ1
└ みりん	大さじ1

Ingredients (serves 2)

1 cake *Kinugoshi-tofu* fine-grained *tofu*
1/2 carrot
3 dried *shiitake* mushrooms
1/2 boiled bamboo shoot
3 pods of kidney beans
1/2 Tbsp sesame oil

A ┌ Liquid used for softening dried *shiitake* mushrooms
│ 4/5 U.S. cup stock
└ 1 Tbsp *sake*

B ┌ 1 Tbsp sugar
│ 1 Tbsp soy sauce
└ 1 Tbsp *mirin* sweet cooking *sake*

※調理時間に絹ごし豆腐を凍らせる時間は含まれていない
※The cooking time does not include the time for freezing the *kinugoshi-tofu*

【作り方】

1 絹ごし豆腐は半分に切ってから2cmの幅に切り、バットなどにあけて冷凍庫に半日以上入れて凍らせて凍み豆腐を作る。

※冷凍庫を使えば、家庭でも簡単に凍み豆腐ができる。

2 1の凍み豆腐を取りだし、常温において自然解凍させ、軽く絞って水けをきる。

3 干ししいたけは水に漬けて戻し、包丁で軸を切り取り半分に切る。戻し汁はとっておく。

4 にんじんとゆでたけのこは水洗いして水けをきり、にんじんは皮をむき、それぞれ乱切りにする。いんげんは水洗いして筋を取り、塩を加えた湯（分量外）で塩ゆでし、ざるにあけて水けをきり3〜4cmの長さに切る。

5 鍋にごま油をひいて中火にかけ4のにんじん、ゆでたけのこ、3の干ししいたけを入れて炒め、全体に油がなじんだら、2の凍み豆腐、Aを加える。

6 5が煮立ってきたら弱火にし、Bを加えて7〜8分ぐらい煮込む。

7 6に4のいんげんを散らし、器に盛りつける。

【DIRECTIONS】

1 Cut the *tofu* in half, and then into 3/4 inch strips. Put the *tofu* in a cooking tray, and leave it in a freezer for more than 12 hours to make freeze-dried *tofu*.
※Freeze-dried *tofu* can be made easily in a freezer at home.

2 Take the frozen *tofu* out, and leave it to defrost at room temperature. Lightly drain the *tofu*.

3 Soak the dried *shiitake* mushrooms in water to soften. Chop off the mushrooms' stalks, and cut them in half. Put aside the liquid used for softening the mushrooms.

4 Wash the carrot and boiled bamboo shoot, and drain. Peel the carrot. Cut the carrot and bamboo shoot into wedges while rotating them. Wash the pods of kidney beans, and string. Boil the kidney beans in salty water (extra quantity of salt), drain on a basket, and cut into lengths of about 1 1/2 inches.

5 Heat the sesame oil in a pot over a medium flame, and stir-fry the cut carrot, bamboo shoot, and the cut mushrooms. When the surface of the vegetables absorbs the oil, add the freeze-dried *tofu* and **A**.

6 When it comes to the boil, add **B**, and simmer for 7 to 8 min.

7 Put the ingredients of **6** in a serving dish, and sprinkle the kidney beans prepared in **4** on top as a finishing touch.

コラム

Column

凍み豆腐ってどんな豆腐？ **What Is Freeze-dried *Tofu*?**

　凍み豆腐とは、おもに信州や東北地方の農村地帯で保存食として誕生したものだ。
　夕方に朝作った豆腐の水をよくきり、その豆腐を約1cm厚に切り、板の上に並べ外に置く。翌朝その豆腐はよく凍っている。それをすげ草でひとつずつ編み、約10日間外で干して出来上がる。

Freeze-dried *tofu* originated mainly in rural areas of Nagano Prefecture and the Tohoku region (northern Japan) as preserved food.
In the evening, drain the *tofu* that was made in the morning, cut it into about 3/8 inch slices, neatly place them on a board, and leave it outdoors to let the *tofu* freeze. Next morning, tie the hard-frozen *tofu* slices with sedge stalks one by one, and hang them outdoor for about 10 days to dry.

お盆の料理レシピ
ぼん

Recipe for the *Bon* Festival

みょうがのちらし寿し

暑い夏を忘れさせてくれる、みょうがの甘酢漬けを使ったすがすがしいちらし寿し

about
60
min

Chirashi-Zushi with *Mioga*

Chirashi-zushi garnished with sweet-vinegared *mioga* is refreshing enough to relieve you from the summer heat

■材料・2人分

米 …………1.5合	みょうがの甘酢漬け…3本
水 …………270cc	★みょうがの甘酢漬けは、
昆布 ………10cm分	P105を参照にして作る。
	しょうが …………1片
┌ 酢 ……大さじ2	大葉 ……………5枚
A 砂糖 大さじ1と1/2	ちりめんじゃこ …15g
└ 塩 ……小さじ1/3	白ごま ……大さじ2

▥ Ingredients (serves 2)

1 1/8 U.S. cups rice	3 sweet-vinegared
1 1/8 U.S. cups water	*mioga*
4 inch *konbu* kelp	★To make sweet-vinegared
	mioga, see p.105.
┌ 2 Tbsps vinegar	1 knob ginger
A 1 1/2 Tbsps sugar	5 green perilla leaves
└ 1/3 tsp salt	1/2 oz dried baby sar-
	dines
	2 Tbsps white sesame
	seeds

【作り方】

1 寿し飯を作る。
米は炊く30分前にといでざるに上げておき、炊飯器に水とさっと洗った昆布を入れて炊き、約10分蒸らしたら、飯台またはボウルにAを合わせて作った寿し酢を数回に分けて加え、ご飯をしゃもじで切るように混ぜ合わせ、うちわであおいでつやを出す。

2 みょうがの甘酢漬けは縦半分に切ってから薄切りにし、しょうがは針しょうがにして水にさらしてから水けをしっかりときり、大葉は約6〜7mmくらいの角切りにしておく。

3 1の寿し飯にちりめんじゃこ、白ごま、2のみょうがの甘酢漬け、大葉を加えて混ぜてちらし寿しを作る。

【DIRECTIONS】

1 Make vinegared rice.
Wash the rice 30 min before cooking, and drain on a sieve. Place the rice in a rice cooker, add water and the lightly rinsed *konbu* kelp, and cook. After leaving the rice cooker covered for about 10 min to allow the grains to settle, put the rice in a bowl or wooden *sushi* bowl, and add **A** in several parts. Use a flat wooden spoon to mix the rice quickly in a cutting motion, while cooling it with a hand fan to make the rice shiny.

2 Cut the sweet-vinegared *mioga* lengthwise first, and then slice it. Cut the ginger into needle-thin strips, soak it in water, and drain well. Cut the green perilla leaves into about 1/4 inch squares.

3 Add the dried baby sardines, white sesame seeds, sliced sweet-vinegared *mioga*, and the cut green perilla leaves to the vinegared rice and mix them.

みょうがの甘酢漬け
Sweet-vinegared *Mioga*

【作り方】

1 ホーローなどの小鍋にAを合わせて加熱して甘酢を作り、冷ましておく。

2 みょうがは大きければ半分に切り、約60秒〜90秒熱湯に入れてゆで、ざるに上げて水けをきり、熱いうちにガラスなどの耐酸性の容器に入れて1の甘酢を注ぎ入れる。

3 ラップを容器に密着させ、半日くらい漬ける。完全に冷めたら冷蔵庫で保存する。

【DIRECTIONS】

1 Heat **A** in a small enameled pan (or other kind of pan), and leave it to cool.

2 If the *mioga* is large, cut it in half. Boil the *mioga* for 60 to 90 sec, and drain on a basket. Put the *mioga* in a container of glass or other acid-resistant material, and pour the sweetened vinegar prepared in **1**.

3 Seal the bowl with plastic wrap, and leave it for about half a day. When it cools down completely, store it in a refrigerator.

■材料・みょうが6本分		▓ Ingredients (for 6 mioga)	
みょうが ……… 6本		6 *mioga*	
A	酢 ……… 1/3カップ	**A**	1/3 U.S. cup vinegar
	水 ……… 2/3カップ		2/3 U.S. cup water
	砂糖 ……… 約50g		1 3/4 oz sugar
	塩 ……… 小さじ1/2		1/2 tsp salt

コラム
Column

夏の風物詩「ほおずき市」の由来
The origins of *"hozuki-ichi"* [*hozuki* market], a summer tradition

　毎年七月九日から十日の2日間、東京の浅草の浅草寺に〝ほおずき市〟が立つ。実はこれも夏祭りのひとつである。かつては、東京の愛宕神社で最初に市が立ったのだが、浅草寺の功徳日（ご利益が四万六千日分ある）に七月十日が当たるため、より盛大になったといわれる。

　古くからほおずきは「ほおずきを水に鵜呑みにすれば、大人は癪を切り、子供は虫の気を去る」といって薬草として使われていた。その後、赤とうもろこしを吊るしていた農家だけが落雷からまぬがれたとあって、赤とうもろこしが売られたが不作の年があり、代わりに赤い〝ほおずき〟が雷除けのお守りとして売られるようになったのだ。

　また、精霊が迎え火や提燈の灯を頼りに帰るといわれることから、精霊が迷わないように、盆棚に赤いほおずきを提燈に見立てて飾るという説もある。

　現在は、ほおずきはもちろんのこと、盆栽、ミニ盆栽なども売られて、とても盛大な市になっている。

Each year, for two days on July 9th and 10th, the *hozuki* market is held at Asakusa in Tokyo. This is also one of the summer festivals of Japan. The first markets were originally held at Atago Shrine in Tokyo, but because July 10th fell on a *kudokubi* (day of merit) of Sensoji Temple (the day being worth 46,000 days of blessings), the festival here became much more popular.

Hozuki has traditionally been considered to have medicinal value as can be seen in old descriptions that say "When swallowed whole with water, *hozuki* reduces aggravation in adults and eliminates tantrums in children." Later in history, when the story spread that houses that hung red corn were spared lightning strikes, people purchased red corn as a lucky charm. However, because corn crops were subject to shortages during some years, vendors began selling *hozuki*—which are also red—as lucky charms for preventing lighting strikes.

Another theory says that the red *hozuki* were placed on *bon-dana* to mimic lanterns to guide spirits who were guided home by *mukaebi* and lanterns.

The festival has now grown very popular, with vendors selling not only *hozuki*, but *bonsai* and mini *bonsai* as well.

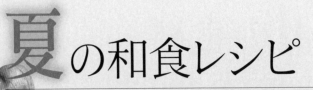

夏の和食レシピ

Recipes of Japanese Food in Summer

夏を彩る旬の食材
Seasonal Ingredients in Summer

初夏の梅雨、そして真夏の強い日差しをいっせいに浴びた野菜たちが、たわわに実をつける季節。真っ赤になったトマト、みずみずしいきゅうり、表皮が艶々と光るなす、甘いとうもろこしなどの野菜類。脂ののった真あじ、白身で美味しいしろぎすをはじめ、こち、あゆ、いさきなど魚介類が店頭をにぎわす。夏の旬の食材で暑い夏を乗り越えたい。

This is the time of year when we are blessed with vegetables that have benefited from the rains during the rainy season early in summer and the intense sunshine of summer. Bright red tomatoes, juicy cucumbers, eggplants with shiny skin, and sweetcorn are just some of the vegetables of summer. The fish stores are also full of fattened horse mackerel, delicious Japanese whiting, flathead, sweetfish, and chicken grunt. People overcome the hot summer days with foods that are in season in summer.

※本書で紹介する食材の旬は基本的なものを紹介している。地方によって異なる場合もある。
※The typically best season for the ingredients in this book is given, and this may differ in some areas.

おくら（秋葵）
Okra

東北アフリカ原産のおくらは、日本には幕末に渡来したといわれる。カルシウム、カロチン、ビタミンCなどを含み、独特なぬめりがある。あえもの、炒めものなどに使われる。

Originally from north eastern Africa, okra was introduced to Japan near the end of the Edo Era. Rich in calcium, carotene, and Vitamin C, okra has a characteristic stickiness. It is often used in *aemono* (marinated dishes) or *itamemono* (stir-fried dishes).

えだまめ（枝豆）
Edamame (green soybean)

えだまめは、実はだいずのさやが緑色のうちに収穫したものだということはあまり知られていない。ゆでたものはもちろん、豆を炒めもの、煮ものにしても美味しい。

It is not commonly known that *edamame* are soybeans harvested while the pods are still green. They are excellent when boiled, as well as stir-fried or simmered in broth.

そらまめ（空豆、蚕豆）
Broad beans

北アフリカ原産だが、日本には天平8年（736年）に中国を経てインドの僧が伝えた。塩ゆでしたものは、ほくほくとしていて甘味があって美味しい。

Originally from eastern Africa, this bean was introduced to Japan by an Indian monk via China in 736. When cooked in salted water, these beans give a potato-like texture with a sweet flavor.

きゅうり (胡瓜)
Cucumbers

ほてった体を冷やしてくれるきゅうり。表面のとげが新鮮なものが新しい証拠。サラダ、あえもの、漬けものをはじめ、中国ではスープや炒めものなどにも使用される。

Cucumbers help cool us down on hot summer days. You can tell how fresh they are from the tiny prickles on their surface. Cucumbers are used in salads, *aemono* or pickles. In China, cucumbers are also used in soups and *itamemono*.

うめ (梅)
Ume (Japanese apricot)

春には青かった梅も、6月中旬以降になると実も大きくなり黄色く色づいたり、赤くなって収穫期になる。梅干しはもちろんのこと、梅酒、ジャムなどにもされる。

Ume that were still green in the spring grow larger and turn yellow or red in June, at which point they are ready to harvest. *Ume* are used to make *umeboshi* (pickled *ume*), *umeshu* (*ume* wine) and jam.

しょうが (生姜)
Ginger

地下の塊茎を食用とするが、よくすりおろして薬味などにするのは、前年に収穫した種しょうが (ひねしょうが) になる。他には根しょうが、葉しょうが、軟化しょうががある。

The ginger we eat is the stem tuber of the ginger plant. The ginger we grate for garnish is the seed ginger (*hine-shoga*) which was harvested the previous year. Other types of ginger include root ginger, leaf ginger, and softened ginger.

みょうが (茗荷)
Mioga

北海道から沖縄まで自生する日本原産の野菜のひとつのみょうが。独特な香りは薬味はもちろんのこと、漬けもの、酢のもの、天ぷらなどに使用される。

Mioga is an indigenous vegetable of Japan that can be found in the wild from Hokkaido to Okinawa. Its unique flavor makes it excellent for garnishing and pickling. It is also often *sunomono* (vinegared dishes) or included in *tempura*.

トマト (小金瓜、蕃茄)
Tomatoes

今や品種が数多くあるトマト。ビタミンA、ビタミンC、ミネラルを多く含む健康野菜。生食 (サラダなど) はもちろんのこと、ソース、ケチャップ、ジュースなどにされる。

There are currently a wide variety of tomatoes, which contain large amounts of Vitamins A, C, and minerals. Tomatoes can be eaten raw (in salads for example) or cooked to make sauces and ketchup or pressed to make juice.

にがうり (苦瓜)
Nigauri (bitter melon)

沖縄名のゴーヤーで知られているにがうり。名のごとく苦いのが特徴。ビタミンCやミネラルを多く含む。炒めものはもちろん、天ぷら、酢のもの、あえものなどに使用する。

Nigauri is otherwise known by their Okinawan name *goya*. Just as the name *nigauri* (*nigai* = bitter *uri* = melon) suggests, they have a characteristic bitterness to them. *Nigauri* contains large amounts of Vitamin C and minerals. It is often used in *itamemono*, *tempra*, *sunomono*, or *aemono*.

とうもろこし（玉蜀黍）
Corn

今やハニーバンタムのように甘味種（スイートコーン）が多く作られている。皮とひげを取りゆでるか、焼いていただくのがポピュラーだが、サラダやスープなどにも使用する。

Sweet varieties of corn such as honey bantam have gained popularity over the years. A popular way of enjoying corn is to first remove their husk and silk, and then either boiling or grilling them on the cob. Corn is also excellent in salads and soups.

たまねぎ（玉葱）
Onion

たまねぎは血液をサラサラにする効果などがあるため、健康野菜としても人気がある。サラダなどの生食はもちろんのこと、揚げもの、煮込み、炒めものなど、料理法は多い。

Onions are popular as a healthy vegetable because they invigorate the blood. They can be enjoyed raw in salads and are also excellent *agemono*, stewed, or *itamemono*.

なす（茄子）
Eggplant

夏の野菜の代表ともいえるなす。小丸なす、卵形なす、丸なす、中長なす、長なす、大長なす群に分類できる。焼きもの、炒めもの、煮もの、天ぷら、漬けものなどにされる。

The eggplant is a vegetable that represents summer. They come in different shapes and sizes such as small and round, egg-shaped, round, medium and long, long, and large and long. They are good to use in *yakimono* (grilled food), *itamemono* and *nimono* (simmered dishes), as well as in *tempura* and pickles.

アスパラガス
Asparagus

グリーンとホワイトがある。ホワイトは軟白させるために土寄せをして日光をシャットアウトして作られる。サラダ、あえもの、おひたし、天ぷらにされる。

Asparagus come in green and white. White asparagus are made by banking up soil around them to shield them from sunlight as they grow and make them whiter and softer. Asparagus are excellent in salads, *aemono*, *ohitashi* (boiled food), and in *tempura*.

じゃがいも（馬鈴薯）
Potatoes

さまざまな品種があるじゃがいもだが、一般的なのは、だんしゃくいも（男爵薯）、メークイーンだろう。煮もの、炒めもの、サラダ、揚げものなどに使用する。

Potatoes come in a wide range of varieties. The most popular ones are probably the *danshaku* and may queens. Potatoes are used in *nimono* or *itamemono*, as well as in salads and *agemono* (deep-fried dishes).

あゆ（鮎、香魚）
Sweetfish

夏の川魚を代表するあゆ。養殖ものと天然ものとがあるが、天然ものはスイカの香りがする。塩焼き、田楽、刺身の他に、稚あゆは天ぷらにすると美味しい。

Sweetfish is a popular type of river fish caught during the summer. They are available either wild or farmed, and the wild ones have a watermelon-like flavor. People enjoy these grilled with salt or *miso*, or as a *sashimi*. Sweetfish fry are often used in *tempura*.

うなぎ(鰻)
Eels

天然ものと養殖ものがあるが、売られているのはほとんど養殖ものになる。ビタミンAが多く、夏ばてに効くとされている。蒲焼き、白焼き、炒めもの、蒸しものにされる。

While eels are either caught wild or farmed, most of the eels sold in stores are most likely farmed. Eels contain large amounts of Vitamin A and are said to be good for relieving summer fatigue. They are *kabayaki* (grilled with sauce) or *shirayaki* (grilled without sauce), *itamemono* or steamed.

あなご(穴子)
Conger eels

一年中捕れるが、特に夏に脂がのって美味しいとされる。蒲焼きはもちろんのこと、天ぷら、炒めもの、煮ものなどにされる。江戸前ものの代名詞となっている。

Conger eels are available throughout the year, but the ones caught in summer are rich in healthy oils and taste delicious. These are excellent for *kabayaki* (grilled with sauce), *tempura*, *itamemono*, and *nimono*. This is one of the more famous of *Edomae* fishes (fish caught in Tokyo Bay).

真あじ(真鰺)
Horse mackerel

一年中出まわる真あじだが、夏に脂がのって特に美味しいといわれる。あじとは味がいいことから名づけられた。塩焼き、刺身、煮つけ、揚げもの、酢のものなどにする。

Horse mackerel are available throughout the year, but the ones caught in summer are especially rich in healthy oils and taste delicious. The fish got its Japanese name "*aji*" because they taste (*aji*) good. They are excellent when grilled with salt, *sashimi*, simmered, *agemono* or *sunomono*.

いさき(伊佐木、伊佐幾、鶏魚)
Chicken grunt

初夏が旬とされるいさきだが、冬の肝や白子が入っているのも美味しい。身がやわらかいので塩焼き、煮つけにされるが新鮮なものは刺身にしたい。また、ムニエルにもよい。

While traditionalist maintain that chicken grunt come into season early in summer, their liver and roe in winter are delicacies in their own right. Chicken grunt have soft flesh so they are often grilled with salt and simmered with soy sauce, and fresh ones make excellent *sashimi*. They are also great as a meuniere.

かつお(鰹)
Skipjack tuna

初夏のかつおは、秋のものに比べてあまり脂がのっておらず、すっきりとした味で人気がある。刺身はもちろんのこと、煮もの、揚げもの、漬け丼などに適している。

Skipjack tuna in early summer are not as fatty as the ones caught in autumn, giving them a smooth flavor. Skipjack tuna makes great *sashimi*, and they are excellent when simmered with soy sauce or *agemono*. They also make a great *zuke-don* (marinated fish with soy sauce on white rice).

その他の旬の食材
Other Seasonal Ingredients

らっきょう(辣韭) ●Shallot
ゆうがお(夕顔) ●White flowered gourd
しろうり(白瓜) ●Oriental pickling melon
にんにく(大蒜) ●Garlic
れたす ●Lettuce
ピーマン ●Green pepper
じゅんさい(蓴菜) ●Water shield
こち(鯒) ●Flathead
しろぎす(白鱚) ●Japanese whiting
はも(鱧) ●Pike eel
すずき(鱸) ●Japanese sea bass perch
かんぱち(間八、勘八) ●Great amberjack
ひらまさ(平政) ●Amberjack
とびうお(飛魚) ●Flyingfish
まだこ(真鮹) ●Common octopus
いか(烏賊) ●Squid
しゃこ(蝦蛄) ●Mantis shrimp
あわび(鮑) ●Abalone

フルーツトマトの白ワインのジュレがけ

about **8** min

ほのかな酸味と甘味のあるフルーツトマトを白ワインのジュレでさっぱりといただける爽やかな一品

Fruit Tomatoes with White Wine Jelly Sauce

A refreshing dish of sweet and slightly sour fruit tomatoes with white wine jelly

■ 材料・3人分

フルーツトマト	……………6個

A [はちみつ ……… 大さじ1/2
　　レモン汁 ……… 小さじ1/2

B [粉ゼラチン ………… 4g
　　水 ………… 大さじ2

C [水 ………… 大さじ5
　　砂糖 ………… 大さじ4
　　白ワイン ……… 1カップ
　　レモン汁 ……… 大さじ1

ミント ………………… 適宜

Ingredients (serves 3)

6 fruit tomatoes (a tomato that is sweet like fruit is called fruit tomato)

A [1/2 Tbsp honey
　　1/2 tsp lemon juice

B [4 g powdered gelatin
　　2 Tbsps water

C [5 Tbsps water
　　4 Tbsps sugar
　　4/5 U.S. cup white wine
　　1 Tbsp lemon juice

Mint leaves

※調理時間にゼリーを固める時間は含まれていない

※The time required for the jelly to set is not included in the time for cooking.

■作り方

1 フルーツトマトはへたをくり抜いて、熱湯に入れてから冷水につけて皮を湯むきにし、ボウルに入れて**A**でマリネし、冷蔵庫で冷やしておく。

2 **B**の水に粉ゼラチンを入れてふやかしておく。

3 ホウロウなどの鍋に**C**の水と砂糖を入れて煮とかし、白ワインを入れてアルコールを飛ばしてから火を止め、電子レンジ（600W）で30秒加熱して溶かした**2**とレモン汁を入れて混ぜ合わせ、タッパーなどに入れて粗熱が取れたら冷蔵庫で冷やし固める。

4 器に**1**のフルーツトマトを入れ、上に**3**をかけ、ミントを飾る。

■DIRECTIONS

1 Remove the calyxes of the tomatoes by cutting out the top part, blanch, and peel in cold water. Put the tomatoes in a bowl, marinate with **A**, and leave in a refrigerator.

2 Put the gelatin in the water of **B** to soak.

3 Put the water and sugar of **C** in an enameled pot (or other kind of pot), and heat to melt the sugar. Add the white wine, and evaporate the alcohol before turning off the heat. Add the gelatin (melted in a microwave [600 W] for 30 sec) and the lemon juice, and mix. Put the mixture in a plastic container with a lid. After letting it cool slightly, leave in a refrigerator to set the jelly.

4 Put the tomatoes prepared in **1** in a serving dish, pour the jelly sauce prepared in **3** over the tomatoes, and garnish with the mint leaves.

おくらのジュレあえ
Marinated Okras with Jelly Sauce

■材料・2人分

おくら	8本
塩	少々
A 粉ゼラチン	2g
水	大さじ1
B だし汁	大さじ4
酒	大さじ1
しょう油	大さじ1/2
塩	小さじ1/4
みりん	大さじ1

■ Ingredients (serves 2)

8 okras
Small quantity of salt

A 2 g powdered gelatin
1 Tbsp water

B 4 Tbsps stock
1 Tbsp *sake*
1/2 Tbsp soy sauce
1/4 tsp salt
1 Tbsp *mirin* sweet cooking *sake*

【作り方】

1 **A**の水に粉ゼラチンを入れてふやかしておく。

2 小鍋に**B**を入れてひと煮立ちさせたら、**1**を入れて煮とかし、タッパーなどに入れ、粗熱が取れたら冷蔵庫で冷やし固める。

3 おくらはがくの部分をぐるりとむいてから、塩でこすって板ずりをし、熱湯でゆでて冷水に取って水けをキッチンペーパーなどでしっかりとふく。

4 **3**のおくらを**2**であえて、器に盛りつける。

[DIRECTIONS]

1 Put the gelatin in the water of **A** to soak.

2 Put **B** in a small pan and bring it to the boil. Add the soaked gelatin to dissolve, and put the ingredients in the pan in a plastic container with a lid. After letting it cool slightly, leave in a refrigerator to set the jelly.

3 Peel the top part of the okras, and roll them on a cutting board with salt. After boiling them, soak them in cold water, and dry well with kitchen paper.

4 Put the okras in a serving dish, and marinate them with the jelly sauce prepared in **2**.

about **5** min

プチトマトのにんにく焼き

プチトマトの美味しさとにんにくの風味がベストマッチでビールやワインに最適

Fried Cherry Tomatoes with Garlic

Delicious cherry tomatoes and the flavor of garlic make the best match, and go well with beer and wine

■材料・2人分

プチトマト	……………1パック
にんにく	……………1/2片
チャイブ	……………4〜5本
オリーブ油	………大さじ1
塩・黒こしょう	………少々

Ingredients (serves 2)

1 pack cherry tomatoes
1/2 clove garlic
4-5 stalks chives
1 Tbsp olive oil
Small quantity of salt and pepper

■作り方

1 プチトマトはへたを取り、にんにくは芽を取って薄切りに、チャイブは刻んでおく。

2 フライパンにオリーブ油と**1**のにんにく、プチトマトを入れて加熱し、プチトマトの皮がはじけてきたら、塩・黒こしょうをし、火を止めて皿に盛り、**1**のチャイブをふりかければ出来上がり。

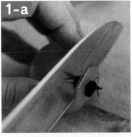
1-a

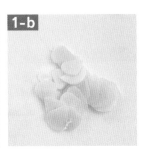
1-b

2

■DIRECTIONS

1 Remove the calyxes of the cherry tomatoes. Remove the sprout of the garlic, and slice. Chop the chives.

2 Put the olive oil, sliced garlic, and cherry tomatoes in a pan, and heat. When the skin of the tomatoes begins to break, season them with salt and pepper, and turn off the heat. Put on a serving dish, and sprinkle the chopped chives as a finishing touch.

コラム
Column
トマトの栄養と効能
The Nutrients and Efficacy of Tomatoes

ドイツなどの欧州では「トマトが赤くなると医者が青くなる」といわれるほど、トマトの栄養と効能は豊富である。

そんなトマトには、赤い色素を作るリコピンをはじめ、ルチン、ビタミンA、ビタミンCが豊富に含まれている。他にはビタミンH、ビタミンPが含まれている。

リコピンは老化の原因といわれる活性酸素を抑制する働きや、抗ガン作用がある。ルチンは血圧を下げる作用があるため、高血圧の人におすすめ。また、血液をサラサラにしてくれる効果もあることで知られている。

ビタミンA、ビタミンCは免疫力を強化し、風邪を予防する。ビタミンH、ビタミンPはお互いの相乗効果でコラーゲンを作ったり、血管を強くしてくれる働きをする。

Tomatoes are rich in nutrients and have high efficacy; it is commonly said that "a tomato a day keeps the doctor away" in Germany and other parts of Europe.

Tomatoes contain high values of lycopene, which is a red pigment, rutin, Vitamin A, and Vitamin C. Vitamins H and P are also found in tomatoes.

Lycopene reduces active oxygen, which responsible for the progress of aging, and prevents cancer. Rutin is effective for reducing blood pressure, and is thus recommended to hypertensive people. Rutin is also known to prevent blood from clotting.

Vitamins A and C enhance immunity, preventing a cold. Vitamins H and P produce collagen and enhance blood vessels by their synergistic effects.

about 5 min

きゅうりとセロリの塩昆布あえ

手軽にできて、食欲のない暑い日に最適なあえもの

Cucumber and Celery Mixed with Salted *Konbu* Kelp

This easy-to-cook mixed dish is best when it's very hot and you have no appetite

■材料・2人分

きゅうり	1本
セロリ	1/3本
みょうが	1本
塩	少々
ごま油	小さじ1/2
塩昆布	10g

▥ Ingredients (serves 2)

1 cucumber
1/3 stalk celery
1 *mioga*
Small quantity of salt
1/2 tsp sesame oil
1/3 oz salted *konbu* kelp

■作り方

1 きゅうりは所々皮をむいて乱切りに、セロリは筋を取ってから斜め薄切り、みょうがは縦半分に切ってから斜め薄切りにして水にさらしてからざるに上げて水けをきる。

※水にさらしたみょうがの水けをよくきること。水けをよくきらないと、仕上がりが水っぽくなり、味が薄くなるので注意したい。

2 ボウルに**1**のきゅうり、セロリ、みょうがを入れ、塩、ごま油、塩昆布であえれば出来上がり。

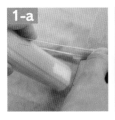

1-a 1-b

■DIRECTIONS

1 Partially peel the cucumber, and cut into wedges while rotating it. String the celery, and slice diagonally. Cut the *mioga* in half lengthwise first, and then slice diagonally. Soak the *mioga* in cold water, and drain on a basket.

※Drain the *mioga* well. Otherwise, the dish will be watery when finished, and its taste will be too weak.

2 Put the cut cucumber, celery, and *mioga* in a bowl, and mix with the salt, sesame oil, and salted *konbu* kelp.

きゅうりとトマトのさっぱりあえ

Cucumber and Tomato with a Refreshing Dressing

■材料・2人分

きゅうり	1/2本
玉ねぎ	1/8個
トマト	1個

A	レモン汁	大さじ1
	はちみつ	小さじ1
	塩	小さじ1/4
	EX.オリーブ油	小さじ1

■ Ingredients (serves 2)

1/2 cucumber
1/8 onion
1 tomato

A
1 Tbsp lemon juice
1 tsp honey
1/4 tsp salt
1 tsp extra virgin olive oil

【作り方】

1 きゅうりは縦半分に切ってから斜め薄切り、玉ねぎは薄切りにして水にさらし、ざるに上げて水けをきる。

2 トマトは皮を湯むきし、約1.5cm角に切って種を取る。

3 Aを合わせてたれを作る。

4 **1**のきゅうり、玉ねぎ、**2**のトマトをボウルに入れて**3**であえる。

【DIRECTIONS】

1 Cut the cucumber in half lengthwise first, and then slice diagonally. Slice the onion, soak in cold water, and drain on a basket.

2 Peel the tomato by blanching, cut into 1/2-inch cubes, and remove the seeds.

3 Mix the ingredients of **A** to make the dressing.

4 Put the cut cucumber, onion, and tomatoes in a bowl, and mix them with the dressing.

なすのソテーとしょうがのソース

about **10** min

油との相性抜群のなすをしょうがソースでいただく

Sautéed Eggplant with Ginger Sauce

Serve eggplants, which perfectly match oil, with ginger sauce

■ 材料・2人分

なす ………………………2本
万能ねぎ ………………………5本
黒こしょう ………………………少々
オリーブ油 …………大さじ3

A
┌ しょうが（すりおろし）
│　　……………………小さじ1
│ 長ねぎ（みじん切り）
│　　……………………小さじ1
│ 酢 …………………大さじ2
│ しょう油……大さじ1と1/2
└ 砂糖 ……………………小さじ1

■ Ingredients (serves 2)

2 eggplants
5 *bannou-negi* onion
Small quantity of black pepper
3 Tbsps olive oil

A
┌ 1 tsp grated ginger
│ 1 tsp chopped *naga-negi* onion
│ 2 Tbsps vinegar
│ 1 1/2 Tbsps soy sauce
└ 1 tsp sugar

1 Aを合わせてドレッシングを作っておく。

2 なすは斜め切りにして水にさらしてアクを抜いてから、水けをしっかりときっておく。万能ねぎは小口切りにする。

3 フライパンにオリーブ油を熱し、2のなすを両面こんがりと焼いて皿に盛り、1のドレッシングをかけ、2の万能ねぎと黒こしょうを散らしていただく。

 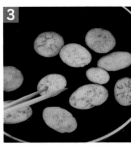

■DIRECTIONS

1 Mix the ingredients of **A** to make the sauce.

2 Cut the eggplants diagonally, and soak in water to remove harshness. Thoroughly drain the eggplants. Cut the *bannou-negi* onion into rounds.

3 Heat the olive oil in a frying pan, and fry the eggplants on both sides till brown. Place the eggplants on a serving dish, pour the sauce over them, and sprinkle the *bannou-negi* onion and the black pepper.

コラム

Column

なすの種類
Kinds of Eggplants

　なすは6～9月頃に多く市場に出まわる夏野菜の代表だが、現在は安定して生産されているため、一年中店頭に並んでいる。

　スーパーなどでよく見かけるなすといえば、中長なす（約10～15cm）が主流で、他には煮ものや漬物によく使用される長なす（約20～25cm）があり、おもに九州で栽培されている大長なす（約28～40cm）などがある。

　他には田楽などによく使用される米なす、漬け物に使用される小丸なす、煮ものや田楽、しぎ焼きなどに使用される丸なすの加茂なす（京野菜のひとつ）が店頭に並ぶ。

　また、大阪で栽培されている皮がやわらかく、多汁質で浅漬けや生食できる水なすも短い期間だが市場に出まわるようになった。

Eggplants are a typical summer vegetable that are abundant on the market from around June to September. But they are available throughout the year today thanks to stable production.

The variety most commonly seen at supermarkets and grocery stores is *chunaga-nasu*, or medium-long eggplant (about 4 to 5 inches long). Also commonly available are *naga-nasu*, or long eggplant (about 8 to 10 inches long), which is often used for simmered dishes or pickles, and *oo-naganasu*, or large long eggplant (about 11 to 16 inches long), which is grown mainly in Kyushu.

Others include *bei-nasu*, or American eggplant, which is used for *dengaku* (roasted eggplant with *miso*), *komaru-nasu*, or small round eggplant, used for pickles, and *kamo-nasu* (traditionally grown in Kyoto), a type of round-shaped eggplant, used for simmered dishes, *dengaku*, and *shigiyaki* (roasted eggplant with sweet miso sauce).

Mizunasu, or water eggplant, has also come to be available on the market recently though for a short period. The variety grown in Osaka features soft skin and watery flesh. It is edible raw, and good for short-time pickling.

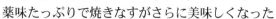

焼きなすの薬味がけ

薬味たっぷりで焼きなすがさらに美味しくなった

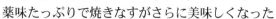

about **15** min

Grilled Eggplant with Condiments

Plenty of condiments make grilled eggplants more delicious

■材料・2人分

なす	3本
万能ねぎ	5本
みょうが	2本

A
香菜	3本
紫玉ねぎ	1/8個
しょうが	1/2片
にんにく	1/2片

B
黒酢	大さじ2
はちみつ	大さじ1
しょう油	大さじ1と1/2
白ごま	小さじ1

Ingredients (serves 2)

3 eggplants
5 *bannou-negi* onion
2 *mioga*

A
3 sprigs coriander
1/8 purple onion
1/2 knob ginger
1/2 clove garlic

B
2 Tbsps black vinegar
1 Tbsp honey
1 1/2 Tbsps soy sauce
1 tsp white sesame seeds

■作り方

1 Aはすべてみじん切りにし、ボウルに合わせたBと合わせてたれを作っておく。

2 万能ねぎは小口切りにし、みょうがは縦半分に切ってから斜め薄切りにし、水にさらしてから水けをきっておく。

3 なすはへたを切ってから皮に切り込みを数本入れ、グリルなどに入れて皮が真っ黒になるまで焼いてから氷水につけて、竹串などを使いながら皮をむき、水けを軽くキッチンペーパーなどでふき取り、食べやすい大きさに切る。

4 1のボウルに3のなす、2の万能ねぎ、みょうがを入れてあえ、器に盛りつける。

■DIRECTIONS

1 Chop all the ingredients of **A**, and mix with **B** in a bowl to make the dressing.

2 Cut the *bannou-negi* onion into rounds. Cut the *mioga* in half lengthwise first, and then slice diagonally. Soak in water, and drain.

3 Cut the calyxes off the eggplants, and make several shallow cuts on the skin. Grill the eggplants under a cooking grill until the surface is burned black. Soak them in chilled water, and peel with a bamboo skewer or other utensil. Paper-dry the eggplants lightly, and cut into bite-size pieces.

4 Mix the cut eggplants, the cut *bannou-negi* onion, and *mioga* with the dressing in the bowl, and arrange them in a serving dish.

焼きなす
Grilled Eggplant

■材料・2人分

なす	4本
しょうが	1片
大葉	2枚
かつお節	少々
だし汁	大さじ3
しょう油	大さじ1と1/2

■ Ingredients (serves 2)

4 eggplants
1 knob ginger
2 green perilla leaves
Small quantity of dried bonito flakes
3 Tbsps stock
1 1/2 Tbsps soy sauce

【作り方】

1 なすはへたに包丁の刃先を当てて、がくの下側を切り落とす。なすの皮に縦1cm幅の浅い切り目を入れる。

2 焼き網を熱し、なすを並べて強火で時々転がしながら全面をよく焼く。皮がパリパリし、中がやわらかくなっていたら火からおろして氷水に放し、皮をむく。

3 しょうがは皮をむいてすりおろす。だし汁としょう油を合わせてだし割りじょう油を作る。

4 なすを食べやすい大きさに切って器に盛り、大葉、かつお節、3のおろししょうがを添え、だし割りじょう油をかけていただく。

[DIRECTIONS]

1 Apply the blade edge of a knife at the boundary between the stem and calyx, and chop off the stem. Make a 3/8-inch long vertical shallow incision on the skin.

2 Heat a cooking grill, and place the eggplants on it side by side. Grill the surfaces completely by occasionally rolling on the grill. When the skin is crispy and the inside soft, remove from the heat, and peel while soaking in chilled water with ice.

3 Peel the ginger, and grate. Mix the stock and soy sauce.

4 Cut the eggplants into bite-sized pieces, and arrange in a bowl. Garnish with the green perilla leaves, dried bonito flakes and grated ginger. Pour on the stock/soy sauce mixture prepared in **3**. above.

じゃがいもと玉ねぎの煮もの

about **30** min

栄養たっぷりの皮つきじゃがいもと牛肉、玉ねぎの相性が最高

Simmered Potato and Onion

Nutrition-rich potatoes with the skin, beef, and onion go perfectly together

■材料・2人分

じゃがいも（小粒）	250g
玉ねぎ	1/2個
いんげん	5本
牛ばら薄切り肉	100g
サラダ油	大さじ1
だし汁	2カップ

A [砂糖 大さじ2
日本酒 大さじ2

B [しょう油 大さじ2
みりん 大さじ1

■ Ingredients (serves 2)

8 3/4 oz potatoes (small)
1/2 onion
5 pods kidney beans
3 1/2 oz thinly sliced beef plate
1 Tbsp vegetable oil
1 2/3 U.S. cups stock

A [2 Tbsps sugar
2 Tbsps *sake*

B [2 Tbsps soy sauce
1 Tbsp *mirin* sweet cooking *sake*

■作り方

1 じゃがいもは皮つきのままよく洗い、玉ねぎはくし形切り、いんげんは筋を取り、塩（分量外）を入れた湯でさっとゆで、約3〜4cmの長さに切っておく。

2 牛ばら薄切り肉は食べやすい大きさに切り、さっとゆでてこぼして余分な油を落としておく。

3 鍋にサラダ油を熱し、**1**の玉ねぎ、じゃがいもを炒め全体に油がまわるようになったら、**2**の牛ばら薄切り肉を加えて炒め合わせる。

4 **3**の鍋にだし汁を入れ、弱めの中火で約15分アクを取りながら煮る。じゃがいもに串を刺してすっと通るように煮えてきたら、**A**を入れてひと煮立ちさせ、**B**を加えて落としぶたをしながら弱火で煮汁が少なくなるまで煮て、彩りに**1**のいんげんを散らしていただく。

■DIRECTIONS

1 Wash the potatoes with the skin well. Cut the onion into wedges. String the kidney beans, briefly boil in salty water (extra quantity salt), and cut into lengths of about 1 1/2 inches.

2 Cut the sliced beef into bite-size pieces. Blanch to remove excess fat.

3 Heat the vegetable oil in a pot, and stir-fry the cut onion and washed potatoes. When the surface of the ingredients absorbs the oil, add the beef, and stir-fry.

4 Pour the stock into the pot, and simmer over a medium-low heat for about 15 min, while skimming off the scum. When the potatoes are soft enough for a skewer to go in smoothly, add **A**, and bring it to the boil. Add **B**, place a drop lid on the ingredients, and continue simmering over a low heat till most of the liquid is gone. Sprinkle the kidney beans prepared in **1** to add a touch of green before serving.

肉豆腐
Simmered Beef and Tofu

■材料・2人分

木綿豆腐	1丁
牛ロース薄切り肉	150 g
玉ねぎ	1/2個
糸こんにゃく	1/2玉
あさつき	5〜6本

A		
	水	1/2カップ
	砂糖	大さじ3
	酒	大さじ3
	みりん	大さじ1
	しょう油	大さじ3
	塩	小さじ1/4

サラダ油	大さじ1
七味唐辛子	適宜

【作り方】

1 木綿豆腐は4cmの角切りにする。

2 玉ねぎは皮をむきくし形切りに、牛ロース薄切り肉は食べやすい大きさに切る。

3 糸こんにゃくは水洗いして5cmの長さに切り、熱湯で1〜2分ゆでてアクを抜き、ざるにあけて水けをきる。

4 あさつきは水洗いして水けをきり、笹うち（斜め薄切り）にする。

5 鍋にサラダ油をひいて中火にかけ、**2**の牛肉を入れて炒め、牛肉の色が変わってきたら**2**の玉ねぎ、**3**の糸こんにゃくを加えて炒める。

6 **5**の全体に油がなじみ軽く火が通ってきたら、**1**の木綿豆腐、**A**を加え、味が染み込むように煮汁をまわしかけながら煮込む。

7 器に**6**を盛りつけ、**4**のあさつきを散らし、好みで七味唐辛子をかけていただく。

■Ingredients (serves 2)

1 cake *momen-tofu*, coarse-grained *tofu*
5 1/4 oz thinlysliced beef loin
1/2 onion
1/2 lump devil's tongue shred
5 or 6 leaves *asatsuki* chive

A
  4/5 U.S. cup water
  3 Tbsps sugar
  3 Tbsps *sake*
  1 Tbsp *mirin* sweet cooking *sake*
  3 Tbsps soy sauce
  1/4 tsp salt

1 Tbsp vegetable oil
Shichimi tougarashi seven-spice chili mix

[DIRECTIONS]

1 Cut the coarse-grained *tofu* into cubes of 1 1/2-inch thickness.

2 Peel the onion and cut using the wedge-cut technique. Cut the beef into bite-sized pieces.

3 Rinse the devil's tongue shred in cold water and cut into 2-inch lengths. Boil for 1 to 2 min to eliminate bitterness. Drain on a sieve.

4 Rinse the *asatsuki* chives in cold water and drain. Slice thinly into diagonal pieces.

5 Heat the vegetable oil in a pot over a medium heat. Fry the beef prepared in **2**. above. When the beef starts to turn white, add the onion and devil's tongue shred and fry.

6 When the entire surfaces of the ingredients absorb the oil and are cooked lightly, add the *tofu* and **A**. Pour the simmering liquid over the ingredients in a circular motion to let them seasoned thoroughly.

7 Arrange the ingredients in a bowl. Sprinkle the *asatsuki* chives on top and *shichimi tougarashi* seven-spice chili mix as an option.

うざく

about
15
min

食欲の落ちる夏でもさっぱりといただける栄養満点の一品

Uzaku

This nutrition-rich dish is refreshing even when you have poor appetite due to the summer heat

■材料・2人分

うなぎの蒲焼き	1/2尾
きゅうり	1/2本
酒	適量
塩	小さじ1/2
A ┌ 酢	50cc
├ 薄口しょう油	大さじ1
└ みりん	大さじ1/2

■ Ingredients (serves 2)

1/2 grilled eel with sauce
1/2 cucumber
Sake
1/2 tsp salt

A ┌ 1/5 U.S. cup vinegar
├ 1 Tbsp light soy sauce
└ 1/2 Tbsp *mirin* sweet cooking *sake*

124　夏の和食レシピ

■作り方

1 うなぎの蒲焼きに酒を少々塗り、オーブントースターで軽く焼き、約1cm幅に切る。

2 きゅうりは水洗いし、水けをきり縦半分に切り、斜め薄切りにする。ボウルに塩水（水100cc〈分量外〉に、塩を合わせる）を作り、きゅうりを約5分ひたし、しんなりしたら水けを絞っておく。

※きゅうりの水けをしっかり絞らないと、仕上がりが水っぽくなるので注意しよう。

3 Aを合わせて三杯酢を作る。1のうなぎ、2のきゅうりに、それぞれ三杯酢を適量加えてあえ、器に盛る。

■DIRECTIONS

1 Apply a small quantity of *sake* to the grilled eel, and lightly heat in a toaster oven. Cut the eel into 3/8-inch-wide pieces.

2 Wash the cucumber, and drain. Cut it in half lengthwise first, and then slice thin diagonally. Make salty water by dissolving the salt in 2/5 U.S. cup water (extra quantity) in a bowl. Soak the cucumber in the bowl for about 5 min. When the cucumber softens, squeeze out the water.

※Note that if the water is not squeezed out well, the finished dish will be watery.

3 Blend the ingredients of **A** to make *sanbaizu* dressing. Mix the eel prepared in **1** and drained cucumber with a proper quantity of the dressing, and arrange in a serving dish.

コラム
Column

うなぎの栄養と効能
Nutrients and Efficacy of Eel

「土用の丑の日のうなぎ」は、夏バテに効くとよくいわれるが本当だろうか……。

うなぎにはビタミンA、ビタミンB群、ビタミンD、ビタミンE、タンパク質、脂質、ヨードが含まれている。特にビタミンAはいわしの100倍、牛肉の200倍もある。

ビタミンAは免疫力を高める働きや美肌効果があり、風邪予防に最適。ビタミンB群は疲労回復に効果があり、老化を防ぐビタミンE、代謝をよくするヨードをはじめ、動脈硬化や心筋梗塞、脳血栓の予防に有効なEPA（エイコサペンタエン酸）、脳細胞を活性化させる痴呆症予防、抗ガン作用、コレステロール値低下作用のあるDHA（ドコサヘキサエン酸）が含まれている。

It's often said that eating eel on the midsummer day of the Ox is effective for curing summer fatigue.

Eel contains Vitamin A, B-complex vitamins, Vitamin D, Vitamin E, protein, lipid, and iodine. The value of Vitamin A is especially high—100 times that of sardine, and 200 times that of beef.

Vitamin A is effective in enhancing immunity, and good for skin care. It is also very effective in preventing colds. The B-complex vitamins are effective for recovery from fatigue. Vitamin E has anti-aging effects, and iodine enhances the metabolism. Eel also contains EPA (eicosapentaenoic acid), which is effective in preventing arterial sclerosis, myocardial infarction, and cerebral thrombosis, and DHA (docosahexaenoic acid), which activates brain cells, thus preventing dementia, combating cancers, and reducing cholesterol levels.

トマトとおくらの夏煮もの

夏野菜を代表するトマトとおくらにだしがしみて、冷え冷えで美味しい

Simmered Tomato and Okra, Summer Style

Tomato and okra, two typical summer vegetables, soaked with stock, are chilled and tasty

■材料・2人分

トマト（中） ……………2個
おくら ……………………2本
だし汁 ………………1カップ

A [酒 …………………大さじ2
　　 塩 ………………小さじ1/2

B [片栗粉 …………大さじ1/2
　　 水 …………………大さじ1

■ Ingredients (serves 2)

2 tomatoes (medium size)
2 okra pods
4/5 U.S. cup stock

A [2 Tbsps *sake*
　　 1/2 tsp salt

B [1/2 Tbsp starch powder
　　 1 Tbsp water

※調理時間に冷やす時間は含まれない
※The time required for cooking does not include the time for cooling the ingredients.

■作り方

1 トマトはへたをくり抜いて、熱湯に入れてから冷水につけて皮を湯むきにする。

2 おくらはがくの部分をぐるりとむき、塩（分量外）でこすって板ずりをしてから熱湯でゆでて冷水にさらしてから水けをきる。

3 鍋にだし汁を入れ、**A**で調味したら**1**のトマトを入れて軽く煮て、**B**で水溶き片栗粉を作って入れとろみをつけ、そのまま粗熱を取って冷蔵庫で冷やす。

4 **3**を器に盛りつけ、**2**のおくらを斜めに切ったものを添える。

 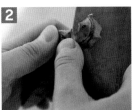

■ DIRECTIONS

1 Remove the calyxes from the tomatoes by cutting out the top part, blanch, and peel in cold water.

2 Peel the top part of the okra pods, and roll them on a cutting board with salt (extra quantity). Boil them, put into cold water, and drain.

3 Put the stock in a pot, and season with **A**. Cook the tomatoes prepared in **1** in the pot briefly, and add the mixture of **B** to thicken the soup. After cooling down slightly, refrigerate it.

4 Arrange the tomatoes with the diagonally cut okra on a serving dish.

コラム
Column

おくらの栄養
Nutrients of Okra

日本でもよく食べられるおくらだが、実は原産地はアフリカで、紀元前2世紀のエジプトですでに栽培されていたといわれている。

おくらの特徴ともいえるネバネバのもとには、ペクチン、ムチンなどが含まれている。他にはビタミンB1、ビタミンC、ビタミンE、カルシウム、βカロチンなどが含まれている。

ペクチンは血糖値の上昇を抑えてくれるし、糖尿病の予防、整腸作用があるため便秘の改善に効果がある。ムチンはたんぱく質の吸収を抑えてくれる働きをする。

またビタミン群は疲労回復や美肌に役立つので、疲れたなと思ったらおくらをすすんで食べたいものだ。

おくら
Okra

Okra, commonly eaten in Japan, originally comes from Africa. It is said that okra was grown in Egypt as early as in the second century BC.

The sticky substance, which is characteristic of okra, contains pectin and mucin. Vitamin B1, Vitamin C, Vitamin E, calcium, and beta-carotene are also contained.

Pectin prevents rising of blood sugar levels and diabetes. It also helps ease constipation, thanks to its effect of calming intestinal disorders. Mucin restricts the absorption of protein.

The vitamins are effective for recovery from fatigue and good for skin care. So, if you feel tired, have okra.

あじのたたき
脂ののったあじを大葉、みょうがなどの薬味でいただく

Chopped Raw Horse Mackerel
Enjoy fat-rich Japanese horse mackerel served with green perilla leaves, *mioga*, and other condiments

■**材料・2人分**

真あじ（刺身用）	1尾
長ねぎ	約2cm
しょうが	小1片
みょうが	1/2個
大葉	3枚
しょう油	適量

▒ Ingredients (serves 2)

1 whole horse mackerel (for *sashimi*)
About 3/4 inch *naga-negi* onion
1 small knob ginger
1/2 *mioga*
3 green perilla leaves
Soy sauce

■作り方

1 しょうがは皮をむき、みじん切りにする。長ねぎはみじん切りにする。みょうがは根の部分を切り取り、縦に薄くスライスする。大葉は水洗いして、2枚は飾り用に、1枚はせん切りにする。

2 真あじはP291を参照して三枚おろしにして、腹骨をすき取る。包丁で皮をひき取り、もしくは手で皮を取り、小骨を指先でさぐりながら骨抜きでていねいに抜き取り、斜めに細切りにする。

3 2のあじの細切りに1のしょうが、長ねぎを加え、軽くあえる。

4 器に1の大葉をしき、3のたたきを盛り、1のみょうが、せん切りの大葉を添える。しょう油でいただく。

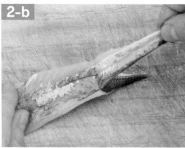

■DIRECTIONS

1 Peel the ginger, and chop fine. Chop fine the *naga-negi* onion. Cut off the root part of the *mioga*, and cut lengthwise into thin slices. Rinse the green perilla leaves, and cut one leaf into thin strips, and set aside two leaves as decoration.

2 Fillet the horse mackerel (see p.291). Thinly shave off the lower part of the inner surface of the fillets to remove the belly bones. Skin the fish by pulling the skin with a kitchen knife or your hands. Use bone tweezers to carefully pull out small bones, while feeling about with your fingers. Cut the fillets diagonally into thin strips.

3 Lightly mix the cut horse mackerel with the ginger and *naga-negi* onion prepared in **1**.

4 Lay one of the green perilla leaves on a serving dish, arrange the mixture of **3**, and garnish with the strips of perilla leaves. Serve with soy sauce.

自家製黒さつま揚げ

自分で作るから格別に美味しいさつま揚げ。風味、歯ごたえがたまらない

about **15** min

Home-made Brown *Satsuma-Age*

Fried fish cakes are especially tasty if made at home. Their flavor and texture are simply irresistible

■ 材料・2人分

真いわし	2尾（正味240g）

A	長ねぎ（みじん切り）	約7〜8cm分
	しょうが汁	小さじ1/2
	みそ	小さじ1/2
	酒	小さじ1
	片栗粉	小さじ1

にんじん	約2cm（約20g）
ごぼう	約3〜4cm（約20g）
いんげん	2本
ししとう	2本
揚げ油（サラダ油）	適量
おろししょうが	適量
しょう油	適量

■ Ingredients (serves 2)

2 whole Japanese sardines (8 1/2 oz)

A
About 3 inches *naga-negi* onion (chopped)
1/2 tsp ginger juice
1/2 tsp *miso*
1 tsp *sake*
1 tsp starch powder

3/4 inch (2/3 oz) carrot
1 1/2 inches (2/3 oz) burdock
2 pods kidney beans
2 *shishitou* bell peppers
Vegetable oil for frying
Grated ginger
Soy sauce

■作り方

1 真いわしはP291の真あじを参照して三枚おろしにし、腹骨をすき取り、包丁でたたいてみじん切りにする。Aを加えたらすりこぎでよくねばりが出るまですり混ぜてすり身を作る。

2 ごぼうは包丁で皮をこそげ、ささがきにし、水にさらしてペーパータオルなどでしっかり水けをとる。にんじんは皮をむき、せん切りにする。いんげんは筋を取り、斜め薄切りにする。ししとうは楊枝などを刺して、数カ所に穴を開ける。

3 1のいわしのすり身に2のごぼう、にんじん、いんげんを加え混ぜて6等分し、小さめの小判型にする。

4 170℃に熱した揚げ油で3をこんがりと揚げる。2のししとうは素揚げする。さつま揚げとししとうを器に盛りつけて、おろししょうがを添える。しょう油をつけていただく。

■DIRECTIONS

1 Fillet the Japanese sardines (see p.291). Thinly shave off the lower part of the inner surface of the fillets to remove the belly bones. Chop the flesh with a kitchen knife. Add **A** and grind well with a wooden pestle until sticky.

2 Scrape off the skin of the burdock, and shave. Soak in water, and paper-dry well. Peel the carrot and cut into julienne strips. String the kidney beans, and slice diagonally. Pierce the *shishitou* bell peppers with a toothpick to make several small holes.

3 Mix the burdock, carrot, and kidney beans prepared in **2** with the ground fish meat. Divide the paste into 6 equal parts, and form into flat ovals.

4 Heat the vegetable oil to 340°F, and deep-fry the formed paste till brown. Deep-fry the *shishitou* bell peppers prepared in **2**. Arrange the fried fish cakes and the bell peppers on a tray, and garnish with grated ginger. Serve with soy sauce.

バリエーション

★どんな魚でもさつま揚げはできるが、市場に出まわっているさつま揚げによく使われる食材は、すけそうだらやさめ、えそなど2種類の食材を混ぜたものが多い。

★一般家庭でさつま揚げを作る場合は、まず新鮮な魚を入手することが第一歩だろう。入手しやすいのは、真あじ、さんま、いしもち（にべ）、そして地方によっては、とびうおがあげられる。

★真あじを使用すると意外にさっぱりとしたものに仕上がる。いしもち（にべ）を100％使用した練りものは高級品として知られている。とびうおは独特な風味があるため、野趣あふれるさつま揚げになる。

▲真あじ
Horse mackerel

▲さんま
Pacific saury

VARIATION

★Any fish can be used for *Satsuma-age*, but those available in stores are mostly made of a mixture of 2 different fish, such as walleye pollack, shark, and lizardfish.

★The first step for making home-made *Satsuma-age* is to obtain fresh fish. Easily obtainable fish include horse mackerel, Pacific saury, white croaker, and *nibe* croaker. In some regions, flying fish is also available.

★Horse mackerel makes *Satsuma-age* lighter than you may expect. Fish paste made from white croaker or *nibe* croaker is known as a luxury foodstuff. Flying fish gives *Satsuma-age* a rustic flavor, due to the fish's distinctive taste.

about
25
min

あじの梅しそフライと骨せんべい

あじで梅干しと大葉を巻いて揚げたおしゃれな一品

Fried Horse Mackerel Rolls and Fried Fish Bones

A stylish dish of pickled *ume* and green perilla leaves rolled with horse mackerel

■材料・2人分

真あじ	2尾
梅干し	2個
大葉	4枚
小麦粉	適量
溶き卵	1個分
パン粉	適量
揚げ油（サラダ油）	適量
塩・こしょう	適量

■ Ingredients (serves 2)

2 whole horse mackerels
2 pickled plums
4 green perilla leaves
Flour
1 beaten egg
Breadcrumbs
Vegetable oil for frying
Salt and pepper

■作り方

1 真あじはP291を参照して三枚おろしにする。身は腹骨をすき取り、小骨を骨抜きで取る。中骨は捨てないで取っておく。

2 大葉は縦半分に切る。梅干しは種を取り、包丁でたたいておく。

3 1の真あじの身に2のたたいた梅をぬり、2の大葉をのせて、くるくると巻き、表面に軽く塩・こしょうをする。

4 3に小麦粉、溶き卵、パン粉の順で衣をつけ、巻き終わりを楊枝で止める。

5 4を170℃に熱した揚げ油でカラッと揚げる。1の中骨は約160℃でパリッと香ばしくなるまで揚げ、塩・こしょうをふる。

6 5のフライの楊枝を取り、骨せんべいとともに器に盛り合わせる。

1-a

1-b

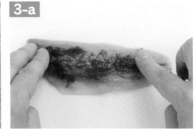
3-a

3-b

4-a

4-b

■DIRECTIONS

1 Fillet the horse mackerel (see p.291). Thinly shave off the lower part of the inner surface of the fillets to remove the belly bones. Use bone tweezers to pull out small bones. Put the backbones aside.

2 Cut the green perilla leaves in half lengthwise. Remove the stone of the pickled plums, and chop the flesh with a kitchen knife.

3 Place the chopped pickled plums on the horse mackerel fillet prepared in **1**, add the green perilla leaves, and roll. Lightly sprinkle salt and pepper on the surface of the roll.

4 Coat the fish rolls with, first, the flour, second, the beaten egg, and then the breadcrumbs, and pierce the end of the roll with a toothpick to prevent it from opening.

5 Deep-fry the fish rolls with coating until crisp in the vegetable oil heated to 340°F. Deep-fry the backbones at 320°F until crisp, and sprinkle with salt and pepper.

6 Remove the toothpicks from the fried rolls, and arrange on a serving dish together with the fried bones.

about
40 min

薬味たっぷり かつおのたたき
かつおに薬味をたっぷりと添えてさっぱりといただく

Bonito *Tataki* with an array of Condiments
Enjoy refreshing raw bonito with its surface slightly grilled, garnished with an array of condiments

■材料・2人分

かつお（刺身用おろし身・皮つき）	1/2節
しょうが	1片
にんにく	1片
万能ねぎ	2本
みょうが	1個
大葉	2枚
ピーマン	1/4個
塩	適量
ぽん酢しょう油	適量

 Ingredients (serves 2)

1/2 block bonito (prepared for *sashimi* with skin)
1 knob ginger
1 clove garlic
2 *bannou-negi* onions
1 *mioga*
2 green perilla leaves
1/4 green sweet pepper
Salt
Ponzu soy sauce (citrus-juice-mixed soy sauce)

■作り方

1 しょうがは皮をむき、すりおろす。にんにくは皮をむき、薄切りにする。万能ねぎは水洗いして、小口切りにする。みょうがは根の部分を切り落とし、薄い輪切りにする。大葉は水洗いをし、せん切りにする。ピーマンはへたと種を切り取り、せん切りにする。

2 かつおは熱したフライパンで表面をさっと焼き、氷水（分量外）を入れたボウルに入れ冷やし、水けをペーパータオルなどでふき取る。

3 2のかつおを、約1cmの厚さに切り、切り口に軽く塩をふり約20〜30分おく。

4 3のかつおを器に盛り、1の薬味をあしらい、ぽん酢しょう油をかける。

■DIRECTIONS

1 Peel the ginger, and grate. Skin the garlic, and slice thinly. Rinse the *bannou-negi* onion, and cut into small rounds. Cut off the root part of the *mioga*, and slice thinly into rounds. Rinse the green perilla leaves, and cut into thin strips. Remove the calyx and seeds of the green sweet pepper, and cut into thin strips.

2 Quickly fry the surface of the bonito in a heated frying pan, chill in iced water (extra amount), and paper-dry.

3 Cut the bonito into 3/8 inch-thick slices, and sprinkle salt on the cross section of the slices. Leave them for 20 to 30 min.

4 Arrange the sliced bonito on a serving dish, garnished with the condiments prepared in **1**, and pour over the *ponzu* soy sauce.

コラム
Column

初かつおと戻りかつおの違い
Difference between the Season's First Bonito and Returning Bonito

よく初かつおと戻りかつおという言葉を聞くが、この違いはどこにあるのだろうか……。

かつおは日本列島の南岸を流れる黒潮に乗ってエサを求めて北上し、北海道から三陸沖に達すると、今度は向きを変えて南下する習性がある。

北上する時のあっさりした身のかつおを初かつおと呼び、エサをいっぱい食べて栄養を蓄えた脂ののった南下するかつおを戻りかつおとか下りかつお、トロかつおと呼ばれる。

江戸時代には「女房を質屋にいれても食いたい初かつお」といわれるほど、庶民にとっては初かつおは高級魚だったらしい。また、江戸っ子の見栄がよくわかる言葉でもある。

You may often hear the words "*hatsu-katsuo*," or the first bonito of the season, and "*modori-katsuo*," or retuning bonito. But what is the difference?

Bonito have the habit of traveling north in search of food, riding on the Japan Current along the southern coast of the Japanese archipelago. When they reach the areas from Sanriku to Hokkaido, they change direction, and start traveling down south.

When bonito are traveling north, their flesh contains less fat. They are called "*hatsu-katsuo*." When they are traveling south, their flesh contains lots of fat as they've taken in lots of food, and stored much nutrition. They are called "*modori-katsuo*," "*kudari-katsuo*," or "*toro-katsuo*."

During the Edo Era, "*hatsu-katsuo*" was an expensive foodstuff for ordinary people, as shown in the saying that "*hatsu-katsuo* is worth eating even if you have to pawn your wife to do so." This phrase also indicates the vanity of *Edokko* (people born in Edo, present-day Tokyo).

きすの天ぷら

口の中できすの甘い身がほろっとほぐれていく

Japanese Whiting *Tempura*

Sweet meat of Japanese whiting melts in your mouth

■材料・2人分

きす（天ぷら用開き身）	………	4〜6枚
小麦粉	………	適量
大葉	………	4枚

A
だし汁	………	100cc
しょう油	………	大さじ2
みりん	………	大さじ2

B
小麦粉	………	60g
卵黄1個＋冷水	………	合わせて120cc

揚げ油（サラダ油）	………	適量
大根おろし	………	適量
レモン（くし形切り）	………	2切れ

■ Ingredients (serves 2)

4-6 Japanese whiting (cut open for *tempura*)
Flour
4 green perilla leaves

A
2/5 U.S. cup stock
2 Tbsp soy sauce
2 Tbsp *mirin* sweet cooking *sake*

B
2 oz flour
1/2 U.S. cup mixture of 1 egg yolk and chilled water

Vegetable oil for frying
Grated *daikon* giant white radish
2 lemon wedges

■作り方

1 きすの水けをペーパータオルなどでよくふき取る。大葉は水洗いし、ペーパータオルなどで水けをふき取る。

2 Bを合わせて天ぷら衣を作る。
※水が冷えていない場合には、衣に氷を1〜2個落とすとよい。

3 Aを合わせて天つゆを作り、温める。

4 鍋に揚げ油を入れて熱し、適温にする。1のきすに薄く小麦粉をはたき、2の天ぷら衣を薄くつけ、揚げ油に入れてカラリと揚げる。大葉は表側に薄く小麦粉をはたき、小麦粉をはたいた面のみに天ぷら衣を薄くつけ、カラッと揚げる。器に盛り、大根おろしとレモンを添え、温めた天つゆを添える。
※レモン汁と塩でいただくのもおすすめ。

■DIRECTIONS

1 Dry the Japanese whiting well with kitchen paper. Rinse the green perilla leaves, and paper-dry.

2 Mix the ingredients of **B** to make the batter.
※ If the water is not chilled, put 1-2 cubes of ice into the batter.

3 Mix the ingredients of **A** to make the *tempura* sauce, and warm.

4 Put the vegetable oil in a pot, and heat to an appropriate temperature. Dust the fish prepared in **1** with flour, coat with the batter thinly, and deep-fry till crisp. Dust the outer surface of the green perilla leaves with flour, thinly apply the batter only to the flour-dusted surface, and deep-fry until crisp. Arrange the *tempura* on a serving dish, and garnish with lemon and the grated giant white radish. Serve with the warmed *tempura* sauce.
※ *Tempura* is also good with lemon juice and salt.

バリエーション

きす釣りをした人はわかるだろうが、外道（狙った魚以外のこと）で、よくメゴチが釣れるが、これをさばいて天ぷらにすると絶品。

★メゴチのさばき方

1 メゴチをザルに入れて、塩をふって手でもみ洗いしてぬめりを出し、水洗いしてぬめりを取る。

2 1のメゴチをまな板に置き、背ビレの後方から前方まで包丁で切り、頭部の後方に包丁を入れ、皮を残すように切り込みを入れる。

3 2を裏返して頭をもって後方に引っ張ると、腹わたと皮が一緒に取れる。

4 3を中骨に沿って包丁を尾の近くまで入れる。片側も同様にし、中骨を切り取る。

2 背ビレを切り、頭部の後方に包丁を入れる
Cut off the dorsal fin, and make a deep cut at the back of the head.

3 2を裏返して頭を持って後方に引っ張る
Turn over the fish, hold the head, and pull it back.

VARIATION

Those who have ever fished for Japanese whiting may know this already, but *megochi*, or Richardson dragonet is often an unex-pected catch when trying to catch whiting. Prepare *megochi* and cook *tempura*. It's very good.

★How to prepare *megochi*

1 Put *megochi* in a basket, and sprinkle with salt. Wash them by rubbing with your hands to allow the slimy substance to come out, and rinse off the slime.

2 Place the fish on a cutting board. Cut off its dorsal fin by sliding a kitchen knife from the back end of the fin toward the head, and make a deep cut at the back of the fish's head, while leaving the ventral skin underneath uncut.

3 Turn over the fish, hold the head, and pull it back. The gut and the skin can be removed together.

4 Cut the body of the fish along the backbone to the point near the tail. Do this on the other side, too, and cut off the backbone.

ほたてと野菜のかき揚げ

サクッサクッとした衣とほたてと玉ねぎ、さつまいもの甘さが美味しい

Scallop and Vegetable Mixed *Tempura*

The crispiness of fried batter, and the sweetness of scallop, onion, and sweet potato make the *tempura* tasty

■ 材料・2人分

ほたて貝柱	2個
さつまいも	1/3本（約100g）
玉ねぎ	1/6個
三つ葉	6本
A ┌ 小麦粉	60g
└ 卵黄1個＋冷水	合わせて120cc
小麦粉	適量
揚げ油（サラダ油）	適量
B ┌ だし汁	100cc
│ しょう油	大さじ2
└ みりん	大さじ2
大根おろし	適量
しょうが（おろし）	適量

■ Ingredients (serves 2)

2 scallop adductors
1/3 sweet potato (about 3 1/2 oz)
1/6 onion
6 trefoil stalks

A ┌ 2 oz flour
  └ 1/2 U.S. cup of mixture of 1 egg yolk and chilled water

Flour
Vegetable oil for frying

B ┌ 2/5 U.S. cup stock
  │ 2 Tbsp soy sauce
  └ 2 Tbsp *mirin* sweet cooking *sake*

Grated *daikon* giant white radish
Grated ginger

■作り方

1 ほたての貝柱は約1.5cmの角切りにし、ペーパータオルなどでしっかりと水けをふいておく。

2 さつまいもは水洗いし、皮つきのまません切りにし、水にさらしてからペーパータオルなどでしっかりと水けをきる。玉ねぎはへたを切り取り、皮をむいて薄切りに、三つ葉は水洗いして約2cmの長さのざく切りにする。

3 Aを合わせて天ぷら衣を作る。ボウルに卵黄と冷水をよく混ぜ合わせておき、ふるった小麦粉を一度に入れ、菜箸でざっくりかき混ぜる。粉やだまが残っている状態でよい。

4 Bを合わせて天つゆを作り、温める。

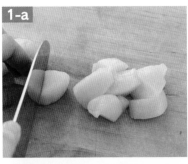

■DIRECTIONS

1 Cut the scallop adductors into 1/2-inch cubes, and paper-dry well.

2 Wash the sweet potato with water, and cut into narrow strips with skin. Soak in water, and paper-dry well. Remove the top part of the onion, skin, and slice thinly. Rinse the trefoil, and cut into 3/4 inch lengths.

3 Mix the ingredients of **A** to make the batter. Mix the egg yolk and chilled water well in a bowl. Add sifted flour, and mix roughly with long chopsticks. It is all right even if some flour or lumps remain unmixed.

4 Mix the ingredients of **B** to make the *tempura* sauce, and warm.

5 小さいボウルに**1**のほたて、**2**の野菜類を1/4ずつ入れ、小麦粉を少々を加えて全体にまぶす。それに**3**の衣をつなぎ程度に大さじ1～2杯加え、さっくりと合わせる。

6 揚げ油を約170℃に熱し、**5**を静かに油に落とし、箸で周りを整えながらカラリと揚げ、器に盛り、**4**の天つゆと大根おろし、しょうがを添える。

1と2の具材をボウルに入れ、小麦粉を少し加えて全体にまぶす。

Put the ingredients of 1 and 2 into a bowl, and dust them with a small quantity of flour.

つなぎ程度に大さじ1～2杯の衣を加える。

Add 1 to 2 Tbsps of batter, to bind the ingredients.

5 Put the scallop cubes in a small bowl, and 1/4 each of all vegetables prepared in **2**, and dust them with a small quantity of flour. Add 1 to 2 Tbsps of the batter prepared in **3**, and roughly mix so that the ingredients come together.

6 Heat the vegetable oil to 340°F. Slowly drop the mixture of **5** into the oil, and fry till crisp, while using chopsticks to shape the *tempura* into a circle. Arrange the *tempura* on a serving dish, and serve with the *tempura* sauce prepared in **4**, grated *daikon* radish, and ginger.

バリエーション

★ほたて貝柱の代わりに、小柱、さくらえび、しらうお、むきえび（小）、いかの細切りなどでもよく合う。新鮮なさくらえび（生か釜あげ）やしらうおが手に入ったら、ぜひかき揚げで楽しんでいただきたい。

★さつまいもの代わりに、新しょうがをせん切りにしたものや、にんじん、ごぼうのせん切りも美味しい。また、春菊のやわらかい葉の部分を入れても香り高いかき揚げになる。紅しょうがを加えると、見ためもきれいで、今までのかき揚げとは違う風味を楽しめるので一度ためしてみてほしい。

※写真の上がいかの細切り、下がむきえび
The photo shows squid rectangles (above) and shelled small shrimps (below).

VARIATION

★ Scallop adductors can be replaced by smaller adductors of other shellfish, *sakura* shrimps, whitebait, shelled small shrimps, or squid rectangles. When fresh *sakura* shrimps (either raw or boiled), or fresh whitebait are available, try mixed *tempura*.

★ Instead of sweet potato, thin strips of young ginger, carrot and burdock are also good for the mixed *tempura*. Tender leaves of *shungiku*, or garland chrysanthemum, can add a stronger flavor to the mixed *tempura*. Try red pickled ginger shreds, as they will give a look and flavor that are different from those of conventional *tempura*.

コラム

Column

かき揚げと天ぷらの語源と由来
The Etymologies and Origins of *Kakiage* (Mixed *Tempura*) and *Tempura*

かき揚げは材料と衣を掻き混ぜて揚げるのが語源とされている。

ちなみにそば屋さんの天ざるを注文すると、多くのお店では、えびに野菜の天ぷらの場合が多いが、天ざるの元祖は、芝えびと小柱を使ったかき揚げなのだそうだ。

天ぷらの歴史は古く、室町時代に長崎を訪れた西洋人が伝えたといわれる、南蛮料理のひとつである。

天ぷらの語源はポルトガル語で〝調理〟を意味する「tempero・テンポラ」や、スペイン語で〝天上の日、魚肉の揚げものを食べる日〟を意味する「templo・テンペロ」などの説がある。

天ぷらは当時の庶民には食べられない高級品だったが、江戸時代に入ると立ち食いの屋台が登場し、庶民に愛されるようになった。

その当時の天ぷらは、いか、芝えび、こはだ、はしら（小柱）、あなごなどの江戸前ものを串に刺したものを揚げ、どんぶり鉢の天つゆにつけて食べていた。

The word "*kakiage*" is said to come from the method of cooking—"*kaki-mazeru* (mix)" the ingredients and batter, and "*ageru* (fry)."
Incidentally, when you order *tenzaru*, or buckwheat noodles accompanied by *tempura* at noodle restaurants, most of them serve shrimp and vegetable *tempura*. But it's said that the original version of *tenzaru* came with the *kakiage* mixed *tempura* of *Shiba* shrimps and small shellfish adductors.

Tempura has a long history. it's said that Westerners who visited Nagasaki in the Muromachi Era first brought *tempura* to Japan. It was one of the Spanish or Portuguese dishes that were introduced in the period.
Regarding the etymology of *tempura*, it's said that the word originally came from "*tempero*," a Portuguese word that means "to cook." Another view is that it came from a Spanish word "*templo*," meaning holy days when people eat fried fish or meat.

In the early days, *tempura* was too expensive for ordinary people, but in the Edo Era, *tempura* stalls appeared and contributed to making the food popular among ordinary people.

In those days, fish ingredients from Tokyo Bay, such as squid, *Shiba* shrimps, Japanese shad, shellfish adductors, and conger eels, were fried on skewers. Diners dipped the skewers in *tempura* sauce in a large bowl.

絵は江戸時代の天ぷら屋台の風景。ちなみに中央がいかの鉄板焼き屋、右が料理がなんでも四文（よんもん）の四文屋である。

The picture shows a tempura stall in the Edo Era. In the center is a stall serving squid fried on an iron plate. On the right is a flat-priced stall offering all items at 4-*mon*.

おくら納豆やっこ

おくらと納豆のネバネバが美味しい

Tofu with Okra and *Natto*

Slick okra and *natto* fermented soybeans are tasty

■材料・2人分

木綿豆腐	1丁
ひきわり納豆	1パック
おくら	2本
うずらの卵黄	2個
刻みのり	少々
しょう油	大さじ1と1/2
だし汁	大さじ3
辛子	小さじ1/4

■ Ingredients (serves 2)

1 block *momen-tofu*, coarse-grained *tofu*
1 pack chopped natto fermented soybeans
2 pods okra
2 yolks of quail eggs
Small quantity of shredded *nori* seaweed
1 1/2 Tbsps soy sauce
3 Tbsps stock
1/4 tsp mustard

■作り方

1 おくらはまな板の上にのせ、塩（分量外）をまぶして板ずりをし、さっとゆでてざるにあけ、冷水に漬けて水けをきり、へたを取り小口切りにする。

2 冷水で冷やした木綿豆腐を好みの大きさに切って水けをきる。

3 2の豆腐を器に盛り、ひきわり納豆をのせてまん中にくぼみを作り、そこにうずらの卵黄を入れる。

4 ボウルにしょう油、だし汁、辛子を入れてよく混ぜてたれを作る。

5 3に1のおくらと刻みのりを散らし、4のたれをかけていただく。

■ DIRECTIONS

1 Place the okras on a cutting board, sprinkle with salt (extra quantity) and roll them. Boil them briefly, soak in cold water, and drain. Remove the calyxes, and cut into rounds.

2 Cut the *tofu* chilled in cold water into bite-size pieces, and drain.

3 Place the cut *tofu* on a serving dish, put the *natto* on top, and make a dent in the center to hold the quail egg yolk.

4 Mix the soy sauce, stock, and mustard in a bowl to make sauce.

5 Sprinkle over the cut okra, and the shredded *nori* seaweed. Serve with the sauce prepared in **4**.

きゅうりザーサイやっこ

ザーサイの塩けが豆腐と相性が最高

Tofu with Cucumber and Zha Cai

The salty taste of Zha cai Chinese pickles best matches with *tofu*

■材料・2人分

絹ごし豆腐	1丁
きゅうり	1/2本
ザーサイ	20 g

A ┌ 白ごま ……… 大さじ1
　├ ごま油 ……… 大さじ1
　└ しょう油 ……… 大さじ1

■ Ingredients (serves 2)

1 block *kinugoshi-tofu* fine-grained *tofu*
1/2 cucumber
2/3 oz zha cai Chinese pickles

A ┌ 1 Tbsp white sesame seeds
　├ 1 Tbsp sesame oil
　└ 1 Tbsp soy sauce

■作り方

1 ザーサイは4〜5時間ぐらい水につけて、塩抜きをする。

2 冷水で冷やした絹ごし豆腐を好みの大きさに切り、軽く水けをきる。

3 きゅうりは水洗いしへたを切り取り、**1**のザーサイとともに粗みじん切りにする。

4 ボウルに**A**を入れてよく混ぜてたれを作り、**3**を加えてあえる。

5 器に**2**の絹ごし豆腐を盛りつけ、**4**をのせていただく。

■ DIRECTIONS

1 Soak the zha cai pickles in water for 4 to 5 hours to remove the salt.

2 Cut the *tofu* chilled in cold water into bite-size pieces, and drain.

3 Rinse the cucumber, and remove the calyxes. Coarsely chop the zha cai together with the cucumber.

4 Blend the ingredients of **A** well in a bowl to make the sauce, add the chopped zha cai and cucumber, and mix.

5 Arrange the cut *tofu* on a serving dish, put the mixture of **4** on top before serving.

ゴーヤ塩焼きそば

about **15** min

ほろ苦いゴーヤと塩味の焼そばがたまらなく美味しい

Salt Fried Noodles with Bitter Melon

The slight bitterness of bitter melon and salt-seasoned fried noodles are irresistibly good

■材料・2人分

蒸し中華麺	2玉
豚ばら薄切り肉	80g
ゴーヤ	1/2本
長ねぎ	1/2本
にんにく	1片
赤唐辛子	1本
サラダ油	大さじ1
酒	大さじ1
中華スープ	大さじ2
塩・黒こしょう	少々

■ Ingredients (serves 2)

2 portions steamed Chinese noodles
2 4/5 oz sliced pork belly
1/2 bitter melon
1/2 *naga-negi* onion
1 clove garlic
1 red chili pepper
1 Tbsp vegetable oil
1 Tbsp *sake*
2 Tbsps Chinese soup
Small quantity of salt and black pepper

■作り方

1 豚ばら薄切り肉は食べやすい大きさに切り、ゴーヤは縦半分に切って種とわたを取り除いてから薄切りにする。長ねぎは斜め薄切り、にんにくはみじん切り、赤唐辛子はへたを切り取り、種を抜いて輪切りにする。

2 蒸し中華麺は耐熱皿にのせてラップをし、電子レンジ（600W）で1分30秒加熱する。

3 フライパンにサラダ油を熱し、**1**のにんにく、赤唐辛子、豚ばら薄切り肉を炒めたら、**1**の長ねぎ、ゴーヤを順に入れてから**2**を入れ、酒、中華スープを加えて塩・黒こしょうで味を調える。

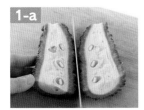
1-a

1-b

■DIRECTIONS

1 Cut the pork belly into bite-size pieces. Cut the bitter melon in half lengthwise, remove the seeds and pulp around them, and slice thinly. Slice the *naga-negi* onion diagonally. Chop the garlic finely. Remove the calyx and the seeds of the red chili pepper, and cut into rounds.

2 Put the steamed Chinese noodles in a heat-resistant dish, and cover it with plastic wrap. Microwave (600w) the noodles for 1min 30 sec.

3 Heat the vegetable oil in a frying pan, and stir-fry the chopped garlic, cut red chili pepper, and pork belly slices, and add the *naga-negi* onion first, and then the sliced bitter melon. Put the noodles in, add the *sake* and Chinese soup, and season with salt and black pepper.

コラム
Column

ゴーヤの栄養と効能
Nutrients and Efficacy of Bitter Melon

　沖縄を代表する野菜のゴーヤ（にがうり）は、ゴーヤチャンプルーなどで食されているが、今や日本全国に普及し、さまざまな料理で食べられるようになった。

　ゴーヤの特長ともいえる苦味のもとであるククルビタシンというフラボノイド類が含まれているが、これが免疫力を強化してくれて、糖尿病やガンの予防に効果がある。

　また、ビタミンCも多く、やはり免疫力を強化してくれるため、風邪の予防に効果がある。ゴーヤのビタミンCは熱に強く、熱を通してもほとんど失われることはない。

　他には食物繊維、ビタミンB1、ビタミンB2、βカロテン、カリウムなどが含まれている。

ゴーヤ（にがうり）
goya (bitter melon)

The bitter melon, locally called *goya*, is one of the typical vegetables grown in Okinawa, where "*goya champuru*," or stir-fried bitter melon, among others, is a popular dish. But today the vegetable is popular across Japan, and cooked in various ways.

The bitterness, the unique taste of bitter melon, contains cucurbitacin, a type of flavonoid. It enhances immunity, and thus prevents diabetes and cancer.

Bitter melon also contains a high content of Vitamin C. Since Vitamin C also has immunity-enhancing effects, it prevents colds. The Vitamin C contained in bitter melon is resistant to heat. So Vitamin C remains even if the vegetable is cooked.

Also contained in bitter melon are dietary fiber, Vitamin B1, Vitamin B2, beta-carotene and potassium.

長いもそうめん

食欲の落ちる暑い夏に最適な一品

about **10** min

Chinese Yam, *Somen* Style

Best for hot summer days when you have little appetite

■材料・2人分

長いも	15cm
水菜	1株
とんぶり	大さじ2
いくら	大さじ2
めんつゆ	1/4カップ

■作り方

1 長いもは皮をむき、スライサーなどでごく細いせん切りにする。

2 水菜は3cmの長さに切り、とんぶりは目の細かいざるなどに入れて水洗いして、水けをきっておく。

3 ボウルに**1**の長いもと**2**のとんぶりを入れてあえて器に盛り、**2**の水菜をちらし、いくらを盛りつけ、めんつゆをかけていただく。

■Ingredients (serves 2)

6 inch Chinese yam
1 bundle *mizuna* potherb mustard
2 Tbsps kochia seeds
2 Tbsps salmon roe
1/5 U.S. cup dipping sauce for noodles

■DIRECTIONS

1 Peel the Chinese yam, and cut into very thin strips with a mandolin slicer or other device.

2 Cut the *mizuna* into 1 1/2 inch lengths. Rinse the kochia seeds in a fine mesh sieve, and drain.

3 Mix the cut yam and the kochia seeds in a bowl, and arrange the mixture in a serving dish. Sprinkle over the cut *mizuna* and salmon roe. Pour the dipping sauce before serving.

秋を彩る
日本の歳時記と和食

Japanese Events and Food in Autumn

秋の歳時記と和食

Events and Food in Autumn

涼しい風が吹き、空に秋雲がたなびき、虫たちの鳴き声が秋の到来を教えてくれる。暑くもなく、寒くもなく過ごしやすい日々が続き、〝食欲の秋〟〝スポーツの秋〟〝読書の秋〟ともいわれる。たわわにみのった稲穂に赤とんぼが止まる。山々の樹々が色づく紅葉。月がきれいに見える澄んだ夜空が続く仲秋。また、収穫を祝う秋祭りがおこなわれるなど、冬の前の秋はなにかと忙しい。そんな秋の食卓を飾るのは、さんま、いわし、さばなどの脂ののった魚介類と栄養たっぷりの根菜などの野菜だ。

The cool breeze, autumn clouds in the sky and the chirping of insects announce the arrival of autumn. Neither hot nor cold, these are comfortable days. No wonder the season is often referred to as "autumn, the season for good appetites," "autumn, the season for playing sports" and "autumn, the season for reading." Red dragonfly perch on ears of rice that are ready to harvest, the trees in the hills turn yellow and red, and the clear mid-autumn sky is perfect for moon viewing. And with harvest festivals, autumn is quite a busy time of year. The foods that adorn our dinner tables during autumn include seafood that is rich in oils such as saury pike, sardines, and mackerel, as well as nutritious roots and leaf vegetables.

【秋の花鳥風月 Nature and Events in Autumn】

紅葉●Autumn colors

山々の樹々の葉が赤や黄色、オレンジに色づく紅葉。秋を代表する花鳥風月である。
The leaves on the trees in the hills begin to turn red, yellow and orange, heralding the end of summer and the beginning of autumn.

ひがん花●Spider lily

彼岸の頃に真っ赤な花を咲かせるひがん花。別名まんじゅしゃげ（曼珠沙華）と呼ぶ。
The spider lily blooms at around the time of *higan* or the equinox. It is also known by the name *manjushage*.

コスモス●Cosmos

漢字で秋桜と書くように秋を代表する花で、赤、白、桃色などの色がある。
The name of this flower, which represents autumn, is written "autumn cherry blossom" in *kanji*. It comes in many colors including red, white, and pink.

稲穂●Ears of rice

夏に青々としていた稲も黄金色になり、穂がたわわに育ち頭をたれる。
Ears of rice, which are green in summer, turn golden in autumn, and bend over with their weight.

すすき●Eulalia

秋の七草のひとつに数えられるすすき。風に揺れるさまは、まさに秋の風物詩。
Eulalia is one of the seven plants of autumn. Eulalia swaying in the breeze is a typical autumn sight.

くり●Chestnuts

いががパクっと開き、くりの実が見える。くりは日本の風物詩のひとつだろう。
The prickly burs open to reveal the shiny brown chestnuts inside. Chestnuts are an important part of the autumn tradition of Japan.

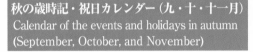

月見●Moon viewing

仲秋（中秋）といわれる九月中旬の月見の日。月見団子などを供えて月を愛でる。
Mid-September, which is referred to as *chushu* or mid-autumn, is the time for moon viewing. People enjoy eating *tsukimi-dango* (moon viewing rice dumplings) whilst they appreciate the moon.

赤とんぼ●Red dragonflies

アキアカネの雄、ミヤマアカネの雄などを秋を感じさせてくれる赤とんぼという。
Male *akiakane* and *miyamaakane* dragonflies are referred to as red dragonflies, and give us real feeling of autumn.

秋の歳時記・祝日カレンダー（九・十・十一月）
Calendar of the events and holidays in autumn (September, October, and November)

敬老の日・九月の第三月曜日●Keirō-no-hi (Respect for the Aged Day)—Third Monday of September

月見・九月中旬〜十月上旬の満月●Tsukimi (Full Moon Viewing)—on the full moon night from the middle of September to the beginning of October

秋分の日・九月二十三日●Autumn Equinox Day—September 23
※年によって二十二日もある。
※Some years have this event on September 22.

お彼岸・九月二十〜二十六日●Ohigan (Equinoctial Week)—from September 20 to 26

体育の日・十月第2月曜日●Taiku-no-hi (Health and Sports Day)—Second Monday of October

紅葉狩り・九月中旬〜十一月●Momiji-gari (Viewing the Autunm Colors)—from October to November

文化の日・十一月三日●Bunka-no-hi (Culture Day)—November 5

七五三・十一月十五日●Shichi-go-san (Seven-Five-Three)—November 15

勤労感謝の日・十一月二十三日●Kinrō-kansha-no-Hi(Labor Thanksgiving Day)—November 23

紅葉狩り Momiji-gari (Viewing the Autumn Colors)

北国の標高の高い山から徐々に低い山、そして里山と紅葉のはじまり、桜とは
逆に南下していく紅葉。風が冷たくなり、秋風が吹きはじめると青々としてい
た山の樹々が赤や黄色などに変化していくようすは、まさに日本の秋を代表する風物
詩である。

Starting in the high altitudes in northern Japan, autumn colors eventually creep down in altitude and latitude, in the opposite direction of the advance of cherry blossoms in spring. As the winds become chillier, the green leaves of the hills gradually turn red and yellow. These sights are truly a part of the autumn traditions of Japan.

紅葉狩りの歴史と由来 Origin and history of *momiji-gari*

　平安時代の貴族たちが紅葉狩りを楽しんでいたといわれる。そのようすは、「今日は嵯峨の紅葉、昨日は大原の紅葉、明日は貴船の紅葉」とうたわれている。また、『万葉集』や『源氏物語』などにも紅葉狩りがうたわれている。

　その後、江戸時代になると四季の移ろいを楽しむこの紅葉狩りは、当初、将軍や武家の間で、その後に商人、そして庶民にも親しまれるようになった。江戸時代の八代将軍・徳川吉宗は、当時桜の名所で知られる江戸の飛鳥山に桜とカエデの苗を植えたといわれる。明治時代になると紅葉を見るために、多くの市民が旅行までして紅葉狩りをしたという。

　そんな紅葉狩りの〝狩り〟は、当初貴族たちが獣や野鳥、小動物を捕まえる（狩猟）意味だったが、それが果ものなどを採る意味にも使われるようになった。今なお残っているいちご狩り、ぶどう狩りなどがそうである。その後、狩猟をしない貴族が草花を観賞することを〝狩り〟に例えたともいわれる。

The poem "Today the autumn colors of Saga, yesterday the autumn colors of Ohara, and tomorrow the autumn colors of Kifune" illustrates how the nobles of the Heian Era enjoyed viewing the autumn colors. The *Manyo-shu* (Collection of a Myriad Leaves) and *Genji Monogatari* (The Tale of Genji) both make references to viewing autumn colors.

Later, in the Edo Era, the custom of viewing the autumn colors as a way of enjoying the transition of the seasons was enjoyed by the *shogun* and the *samurai* class, and then later by the merchant class, and still later by the commoners. The 8th *shogun*, Yoshimune Tokugawa, is said to have planted seedlings of cherry and maple on Asukayama, a popular flower viewing location during the Edo Era. In the Meiji Era, large numbers of people traveled to different parts of the country just to view the changing colors.

The word "*gari*=*kari* pronounced euphonically meaning hunting" in *momiji-gari* (literally, autumn color hunting) derived from the actual hunting of animals and birds small and large in which the nobles engaged. Gradually, people began using the word to refer to fruit picking. This usage can still be seen in expressions such as *ichigo-gari* (strawberry hunting) or *budo-gari* (grape hunting). Later, nobles who did not have a taste for hunting began to use the word for occasions where they gathered together to appreciate plants and flowers.

戸隠の鬼女紅葉伝説 The legend of Momiji (autumn colors), the demon woman of Togakushi

いい伝えは諸説あるが、今から1000年以上も昔、現在の長野県長野市の戸隠の地に、〝紅葉〟という女性が移り住んできたことからこの伝説ははじまる。当初、村人たちと仲よく暮らしていた紅葉は、荒倉山の〝鬼の岩屋〟という洞穴を根城にして、〝おまん〟という怪力の女性らの手下とともに悪事をはたらくようになり、村人を大変困らせていた。

この話が都に届き、平維茂が鬼狩りを命ぜられた。どうにかこうにか鬼の岩屋近くに到着した維茂軍は、紅葉のようすを探るために酒宴を催した。一説には旅の修業僧になりすました紅葉がそれを探りに来て、維茂に毒酒をすすめたが無事だったとか、維茂が毒酒を紅葉にすすめ、酔い伏したところを斬りすてたともいわれる。しかし、有力ないい伝えによると、維茂軍が勝ち進むと、紅葉が鬼の姿になって妖術を使って維茂軍を大いに悩ませたという。しかし、維茂は、八幡大菩薩を念じつつ剣をふるい、紅葉を斬りすてたともいわれる。

これが、長野県長野市戸隠の〝鬼女紅葉伝説〟であり、紅葉狩りの由来ともいわれている。

While there are a number of variations to the story, one begins over 1,000 years ago when a woman named Momiji moved to Togakushi in what is now Nagano City in Nagano Prefecture. At first Momiji got along well with the people of the village, but soon, she set up camp in a cave called "Onino Iwaya (cave of demons)" on Mt. Arakurayama with women who belonged to a gang led by Oman, a woman of monstrous strength, and began terrorizing the villagers.

This news traveled to the capital city of Kyoto. Upon learning of the villagers plight, Tairano Komimochi ordered a demon hunt. Once Komimochi and his army managed to make it to the Onino Iwaya, he decided to hold a banquet to spy on Momiji. One version says that Momiji, disguised as a traveling monk, visited the banquet to offer poisoned *sake* to Komimochi but failed to take his life. Another version says that Komimochi's soldiers offered poisoned *sake* to Momiji, and once she was drunk and asleep, they killed her. But the most prevalent version says that as Komimochi's men marched forward, Momiji transformed into a demon and caused Komimochi's army much aggravation. Ultimately, however, Komimochi fought the demon woman, all the while praying to the Great Hachiman Bodhisattva and successfully defeated his enemy.

This is the "legend of Momiji, the demon woman" of Togakushi and presents another possible origin for the word momiji gari or "autumn color hunting."

紅葉する代表落葉樹 Typical deciduous trees that change their colors

【イロハモミジ・鶏爪楓】
Japanese maple

東北地方南部以西から九州に分布。別名イロハカエデとも呼ばれ、真っ赤に色づく落葉樹の代表でもある。
This tree grows in areas west of southern Tohoku and as far south as Kyushu. It is also known by the name *irohakaede*, and is a classic example of a deciduous tree that turns red.

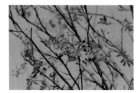

【ナナカマド・七竈】
Mountain ash

秋になると紅葉や真っ赤な実がつく落葉高木。北海道から九州に分布。比較的低山や里山に多く見られる。
This is a tall deciduous tree whose leaves change color, and which bears a bright red fruit. This tree grows in areas ranging from Hokkaido to Kyushu, mostly in relatively low lying mountains and hills.

【イチョウ・銀杏・公孫樹】
Gingko

秋になると黄色く色づき、晩秋になると落ちるイチョウの葉。中国原産の落葉高木で、北海道から沖縄まで分布する。
This tree's leaves turn yellow in autumn and fall in late autumn. Originating in China, this tall deciduous tree grows in areas ranging from Hokkaido to Okinawa.

【ヌルデ・白膠木・塩膚木】
Nurude (Chinese sumac)

別名フシの木とも呼ばれる。日本各地に分布する落葉小高木で、乳白色の樹液で物を塗ることからヌルデといわれる。
This tree is also called the "*fushinoki*." This is a medium deciduous tree found throughout Japan. It is called "*nurude*" as its white sap is used in painting.

紅葉狩りを楽しむレシピ
Recipe to enjoy autumnal foliage

豆腐ときのこの炊き込みご飯
秋を代表する食材のきのこを炊き込みごはんでいただく

about 12 min

Mixed Rice featuring *Tofu* and Mushrooms
Enjoy mushrooms, autumnal delicacies, in mixed rice

■材料・2〜3人分

米	2カップ
木綿豆腐	1/2丁
油揚げ	1/2枚
しめじ	1/3パック
しいたけ	2枚
えのき	1/3袋
さやいんげん	2〜3本
サラダ油	大さじ1
だし汁	1と3/4カップ
酒	大さじ2
砂糖	小さじ1
みりん	大さじ1
薄口しょう油	大さじ2
塩	小さじ1/4

【作り方】

1 米は炊く30分前にとぎ、ざるに上げて水をきっておく。

2 具材の下ごしらえをする。木綿豆腐をキッチンペーパーにはさみ、軽く重しをして水けを切って、粗めに崩しておく。
油揚げはざるにのせ、熱湯を回しかけ、油抜きをし、2cmの長さの短冊に切る。
しめじは石突きを取り小房に分け、しいたけは石づきと軸を切り取り、薄切りにする。えのきは根の方を切ってから、長さを半分に切る。

3 鍋に油を熱し、2のしめじ、しいたけ、えのき、油揚げを炒め、全体に油が回ったら2の豆腐を入れてさらに炒める。
材料に軽く火が通ったら酒、砂糖、みりんを入れて、薄口しょう油、塩を加えてからめる。

4 炊飯器に1の米とだし汁、3の具と汁を入れてかき混ぜたら炊く。

5 炊き上がったら10分ほど蒸らし、具をかき混ぜる。塩（分量外）ゆでし、小口切りにしたさやいんげんを散らしていただく。

■ Ingredients (serves 2 or 3)

1 2/3 U.S. cups rice
1/2 block *momen-tofu*, coarse-grained *tofu*
1/2 cake *abura-age* deep-fried *tofu*
1/3 pack *shimeji* mushrooms
2 *shiitake* mushrooms
1/3 bag *enokidake* mushrooms
2-3 pods kidney beans
1 Tbsp vegetable oil
1 1/2 U.S. cups stock
2 Tbsps *sake*
1 tsp sugar
1 Tbsp *mirin* sweet cooking *sake*
2 Tbsps light soy sauce
1/4 tsp salt

【DIRECTIONS】

1 Wash the rice 30 min before cooking, and drain on a sieve.

2 Prepare ingredients. Wrap the coarse-grained *tofu* with kitchen paper, and place a weight on top to drain. Coarsely break the *tofu*. Put the *abura-age* in a sieve, and pour over boiling water in a circular motion to remove excess oil. Cut the *abura-age* into 3/4-inch long rectangles. Cut off the hard tip of the *shimeji* mushrooms, and separate into small portions. Remove the stem of the *shiitake* mushrooms, and thinly slice. Cut off the lower part of the *enokidake* mushrooms, and cut in half lengthwise.

3 Heat the oil in a pot, stir-fry the *shimeji*, *shiitake*, *enokidake*, and *abura-age*. When the surface of the ingredients has absorbed the oil, add the *tofu*, and stir-fry further.
When the ingredients are lightly cooked, add the *sake*, sugar, and *mirin* sweet cooking *sake*, as well as the light soy sauce, and salt, to allow the ingredients to be covered by the sauce.

4 Put in a rice cooker the drained rice, the stock, and the ingredients with sauce prepared in **3**. Mix and cook.

5 When the cooking is done, keep the cooker covered for about 10 min to allow the grains to settle. Open the lid, and mix the rice. When serving, sprinkle over the kidney beans (boiled in salty water 〈extra quantity〉, and cut into rounds).

里いもの鶏あんかけ

里いものねっとり感と鶏ひき肉のあんかけのとろみが美味しい

about
25
min

Taros with Thick Chicken Dressing

The sticky texture of taros and the thickened dressing with ground chicken make the dish tasty

■材料・4人分	
里いも	400g
┌ だし汁	1と1/2カップ
┌ 砂糖	大さじ4
A 酒	大さじ1
└ 薄口しょう油	大さじ2
黄ゆず	適宜
鶏ひき肉	100g
┌ だし汁	3/4カップ
B 砂糖	大さじ2
└ しょう油	大さじ2
片栗粉	大さじ1/2

■ Ingredients (serves 4)

14 oz taros

A
- 1 1/4 U.S. cups stock
- 4 Tbsps sugar
- 1 Tbsp *sake*
- 2 Tbsps light soy sauce

Yellow *yuzu* Japanese lime rind
3 1/2 oz ground chicken

B
- 3/5 U.S. cup stock
- 2 Tbsps sugar
- 2 Tbsps soy sauce

1/2 Tbsp starch powder

【作り方】

1 里いもは水で洗って、たわしでこすりながら泥をよく落とす。里いもの上下を平らに切り落し、側面の皮を上から下へ丸みをなぞって形よく皮をむき、水をはったボウルに入れていく。

2 1のボウルの水を捨て、塩（分量外）をひとつまみふり入れて手でよくもんでぬめりを取り、水で洗ってざるに上げる。鍋にたっぷりの水と里いもを入れて強火にかけ、煮立ったら火を弱めて2～3分ゆでる。ざるに上げてゆで汁を切り、さっと表面のぬめりを水で洗う。

3 鍋にAのだし汁と2の里いもを入れて火にかけ、煮立ったら中火にし、Aの砂糖を入れて落としぶたをして2～3分煮たら、Aの酒、薄口しょう油を加えてアクをすくいながら煮汁が1/3量になるまで煮ていく。

4 別の鍋にBのだし汁と砂糖、しょう油を入れて中火で煮立て、鶏ひき肉を入れてよく混ぜる。鶏ひき肉に火が通ったら同量の水（分量外）で溶いた片栗粉を回し入れてあんを作る。

5 器に3の里いもを入れ、3の煮汁をはり、上から4の鶏あんをかけ、黄ゆずのせん切りを乗せていただく。

【DIRECTIONS】

1 Wash the taros with water, while using a brush to remove mud. Cut off the top and bottom parts of the taros to make both sides flat, and peel them, while moving a kitchen knife in several downward strokes to nicely shape them. Put them in water in a bowl.

2 Drain the bowl, sprinkle a pinch of salt (extra quantity) on the taros, and rub them to remove the slime. Rinse the taros, and drain in a sieve. Put the taros and a generous quantity of water in a pot, and heat over a high flame. When it comes to the boil, turn down the heat to low, and boil for about 2 to 3 min. Drain the taros in a sieve, and quickly rinse off the slime on the surface of the taros.

3 Put the stock of **A** and the taros in a pot, and heat. When it comes to the boil, turn down the heat to medium and add the sugar of **A**. Place a drop lid on the taros, and simmer for 2 to 3 min. Add the *sake*, light soy sauce of **A**, and simmer, while skimming off the scum, until the quantity of the liquid is reduced to 1/3.

4 Put all the ingredients of **B** in another pot, and bring it to the boil over the medium heat. Add the ground chicken, and stir well. When the chicken is cooked, pour in a circular motion a mixture of starch powder and the same quantity of water (extra quantity) to thicken the dressing.

5 Arrange the taros in a serving dish, add the simmering liquid of **3**, and pour over the thickened dressing of **4**. Sprinkle over julienne strips of *yuzu* before serving.

コラム *Column*

里いもの栄養と効能 Nutrients and Efficacy of Taros

あの里いものぬるぬるはムチンによるもので、このぬるぬるが肝臓を丈夫にし、胃潰瘍や腸炎を予防する効果がある。

他には食物繊維、ビタミンB1、ビタミンB2、カリウムを含んでいる。食物繊維の一種であるガラクタンが脳細胞を活性化させ、ボケや老化を防止する。カリウムは高血圧を改善し、コレステロールを下げる効果がある。

The slime of taros contains mucin, which is effective for maintaining a healthy liver and prevents stomach ulcers and enteritis.

Taros also contain dietary fiber, Vitamin B1, Vitamin B2 and potassium. A type of dietary fiber called galactan makes brain cells active, thus preventing aging and dementia. Potassium lowers high blood pressure, and cholesterol.

七五三 *Shichi-Go-San* or Celebration of 3, 5, and 7-Year-Old Children

三歳は男の子と女の子、五歳は男の子、七歳は女の子の成長や今までの無事を祝う〝七五三〟。この七五三という数字には日本ならではの考え方や歴史が含まれている。現在はイベント化している七五三だが、古き良き時代の七五三をもう一度ふり返ってみたい……。

Boys and girls of 3 years of age, boys of 5, and girls of 7 are celebrated for their healthy growth so far and their continuous healthy growth is prayed for. The numbers represent the unique concept and history of Japan, but the traditional ceremony is almost an "event" in the present day. It is worthwhile looking back into the history to see how the ceremony was performed in the good old days.

七五三の歴史と由来 Origin and history of *Shichi-Go-San*

　十一月十五日に催される七五三は、三歳は男の子と女の子、五歳は男の子、七歳は女の子の成長を祝う行事である。かつては、七五三は子供が無事に育ったことのお礼や、健やかに成長することを願って神社や氏神にお参りに行く〝宮参り〟がおこなわれたが、現存の都会では写真スタジオで借衣装で着かざり、記念写真をとり、お祝いの食事をする七五三が増えているようだ。

　古くから二、三歳になると剃っていた髪をたくわえる〝髪置き〟、五歳では初めて袴を着る〝袴着の祝い〟、七歳では大人の帯を締める〝帯直しの祝い〟があったものが、江戸時代に武家の間で定着したといわれている。

　七五三が十一月十五日におこなわれるのは、江戸三代将軍の徳川家光の四男の徳松（のちの五代将軍・徳川綱吉）の体が弱く、宣明暦（中国暦のひとつで、太陰太陽暦の暦法のこと）で占ったところ、鬼宿日の十一月十五日に五歳の祝い（一説によると徳松の三歳の〝髪置き〟の儀がおこなわれた日ともいわれる）をすると丈夫になるといわれ、祝いをしたのがはじまりといわれている。さほど医学の発達していない江戸時代では、五歳から七歳まで無事に育つということは、祝いにあたいしたのだ。

The *Shichi-Go-San* ceremony performed on November 15 is originally a prayer for the healthy growth of children. Parents used to take their children to the local shrine or the guardian god to give thanks for the children's healthy growth until then and pray for their continuous sound growth (*Miya-mairi*). In the modern age, many families go to a photo studio to have commemorative photos taken, with the children adorned in rented costumes. A celebratory dining-out then follows.

In olden times, children were allowed to let their hair grow rather than having it shaved at the age of 2 or 3 (*Kami-oki*), put on *hakama* (divided skirt for men) for the first time at 5 (*Hakama-gi-no iwai*), and tied the *obi* (belt) worn by grown-ups (*Obi-naoshi-no iwai*) at 7. This custom became established among the *samurai* warrior families in the Edo Era.

The ceremony takes place on November 15 because, according to an account, Tokumatsu (later to become Tokugawa Tsunayosi, the 5th *shogun*), the 4th son of Tokugawa Iemitsu, the 3rd *shogun* of the Edo Shogunate, born weak, was told by an augur that he would be strong if his 5th birthday was celebrated on November 15, or *Kishuku-nichi*, by the *Senmyo-Reki* (one of the Chinese lunar calendars). Another account goes that November 15 was the day when Tokumatsu received the *Kami-oki* ceremony at the age of 3. It was a matter of congratulations that a child grew healthily up to the age of 5 or 7 in the Edo Era when medicine was underdeveloped.

千歳飴と七五三の関係 *Chitose-Ame* and *Shichi-Go-San*

七五三には千歳飴がつきものだが、千歳飴にはどんな由来があり、何を意味しているのだろうか……。千歳飴は鶴、亀、松竹梅といった縁起物が描かれた長い袋に入っている。もちろん飴も長く、紅白の色になっている。これは長くのびる（末永く生きてほしい）ことと、これまで無事に育ったことへの祝いで紅白になっているのだという。

ちなみにこの千歳飴、江戸・浅草の飴売りの七兵衛という人が、売りはじめたという説と、大阪の平野甚左衛門という人が江戸に出て、売りはじめたとされる説がある。

Chitose-ame and *Shichi-Go-San* are closely related to each other. *Chitose-ame*, a Japanese candy, is packed in a long bag printed with various good-luck symbols such as the crane, turtle, and *Sho-Chiku-Bai* (pine, bamboo, and Japanese apricot). The candies are slim and long, and colored red and white. Their length is indicative of longevity and the red and white colors are said to express congratulations for sound health. Some say Shichibei, a candy merchant in Asakusa, Edo (present-day Tokyo), started selling *chitose-ame* while others believe Jinzaemon Hirano, Osaka, was the first seller of *chitose-ame* in Edo.

七五三の祝い膳 Festive Meals of *Shichi-Go-San*

かつての七五三の祝いは、親類縁者を自宅に招いて盛大におこなわれていた。地方によって異なるが七五三の代表的な祝い膳は、特に三歳の祝いを〝真魚の祝い〟といって真鯛の塩焼きや、車えび、伊勢えびなどの魚介類が使われていたらしい。

今でもこのような伝統を守っている地方もあるが、現在はあまり気にすることなく、子供たちの好きなものが作られているようだ。

Shichi-Go-San was once extravagantly celebrated at home inviting as many relatives as possible. Festive meals differed in according to the region. A typical festive meal for children of 3 years of age (called *Mana-no-iwai*) included red sea bream grilled with salt, as well as dishes with tiger prawn, lobster, and other seafood.

Some regions still observe this tradition, but foods liked by children are generally served today.

三歳の祝いは〝真魚の祝い〟といわれ、新鮮な真鯛の塩焼きが祝い膳に並ぶ
Celebration of children of 3 years of age is called "*Mana-no-Iwai*," which comes with fresh red sea bream grilled with salt and served on the table.

七五三を楽しむレシピ
しちごさん
Recipe to enjoy the *Shichi-go-san* children's festival

さつまだんご
さつまいもの甘さと栗の食感は子供たちだって大好き

about
20
min

Sweet Potato Balls
Kids love the sweetness of sweet potatoes and the texture of chestnuts

■材料・6個分

さつまいも	1/2本
栗の甘露煮	2〜3粒
バター	5g
砂糖	大さじ1
卵黄	少々

Ingredients for 6 balls

1/2 sweet potato
2 - 3 chestnuts cooked in syrup
1/6 oz butter
1 Tbsp sugar
Small quantity of egg yolk

【作り方】

1 栗の甘露煮は粗く刻んでおく。

2 さつまいもは皮を所々むいて適当な厚さの輪切りにし、水にさらしてアクを抜き、鍋に水（分量外）とともに入れ、串がすっと通るようになるまで煮たら、ざるに上げて水けをきり、熱いうちにボウルに入れてつぶす。

3 2にバターと砂糖を加えて混ぜたら1の栗の甘露煮を加えて混ぜ、6等分に丸めて、溶いた卵黄を塗る。

4 3をアルミホイルをしいたトースターの天板にのせて焼き、焼き色がつけば出来上がり。

〖DIRECTIONS〗

1 Chop the chestnuts coarsely.

2 Peel the sweet potato randomly, cut into rounds of an appropriate thickness, and soak in water to remove the harshness. Put the potato and water (extra quantity) in a pot, and boil until soft enough for a skewer to pass through smoothly. Drain in a sieve, and mash in a bowl while hot.

3 Mix the butter and sugar with the mashed sweet potato, and the chestnuts prepared in **1**, and make 6 balls of an equal size. Apply the beaten egg yolk.

4 Place the balls on the aluminum-foil-covered baking tray of a toaster oven, and bake till they begin to brown.

七五三を楽しむレシピ
しちごさん

Recipe to enjoy the *Shichi-go-san* children's festival

じゃがボール
こんなおしゃれなお菓子を七五三に作ってあげたい

about
20
min

Potato Ball
Why don't you make such a fashionable snack for the *Shichi-go-san* festival?

■ 材料・6個分

じゃがいも（中）	1個
ハム	1枚
プロセスチーズ	20g
マヨネーズ	大さじ1/2
パセリ（みじん切り）	少々
塩・こしょう	少々
卵黄	少々

■ Ingredients for 6 balls

1 potato (medium size)
1 slice of ham
2/3 oz processed cheese
1/2 Tbsp mayonnaise
Small quantity of finely-chopped parsley
Small quantity of salt and pepper
Small quantity of egg yolk

【作り方】

1 ハムとプロセスチーズは約5mm角に切る。

2 じゃがいもは皮をむき、適当な大きさに切り、塩（分量外）を入れた湯で串がすっと通るまでゆでたら、鍋の水を捨てて空炒りするように水分をとばす。

3 2のじゃがいもが熱いうちにボウルに入れてつぶし、塩・こしょう、マヨネーズを加えてよく混ぜる。粗熱が取れたら1のハムとプロセスチーズ、パセリのみじん切りを加えて混ぜ、6等分に丸め、溶いた卵黄をぬる。

4 3をアルミホイルをしいたトースターの天板にのせて焼き、焼き色がつけば出来上がり。

【DIRECTIONS】

1 Cut the ham and processed cheese into about 1/5-inch squares.

2 Peel the potato, and cut into bite-size pieces. Boil the potato in boiling salty water (extra quantity of salt) until soft enough for a skewer to pass through smoothly. Drain the pot, and heat the potato to allow the water to evaporate.

3 Mash the potato in a bowl while hot, and mix well with the salt, pepper, and mayonnaise. When the potato cools slightly, add the ham and processed cheese prepared in **1** and the parsley, and mix them. Make 6 balls of an equal size, and apply the beaten egg yolk.

4 Place the balls on the aluminum-foil-covered baking tray of a toaster oven, and bake till they begin to brown.

その他の秋の歳時記 Other Seasonal Events in Autumn

本書で〝紅葉狩り〟〝七五三〟の秋を代表する歳時記を紹介したが、秋にはまだまだたくさんの行事がある。ここでは秋になると各地方でおこなわれる〝運動会〟、弁当をもって里山や高原に行く〝行楽〟、先祖の霊を供養する〝彼岸〟、満月を愛でる〝月見〟を紹介する。

The typical autumnal events of *Momiji-gari* (autumn color viewing) and *Shichi-Go-San* are introduced in this book. There are many other events in autumn. Some of them - *undo-kai* (athletic meets) held in various regions, *koraku* (holiday-making with a lunchbox in the forested hillsides), *Higan* (memorial services for the ancestors), and *Tsukimi* (full moon viewing) - are described below.

運動会の歴史と由来 Origin and history of *undo-kai* (athletic meets)

　暑い夏がすぎ、涼しい秋風が吹く九月から十月上旬になると運動会が催されるが、日本で最初におこなわれた運動会は、明治七年（1874年）に、東京・築地にあった海軍兵学校で英語教師をしていたイギリス人のストレンジ氏の指導によっておこなわれた〝競闘遊戯会〟だといわれている。

　その後、明治十一年（1878年）に札幌農学校（現在の北海道大学）で〝遊戯会〟が開催され、数年で北海道内の小中学校に広まったといわれる。その後、森有礼文部大臣（第二代）が体育の集団訓練を目的ですすめたことにより、日本全国の学校で運動会が開催され、現在に至っている。

　明治時代には、学校の運動場も整備されていない地方もあり、寺や神社の境内で学生と市民が一緒にしたともいわれている。ちなみに運動会という言葉は、明治十六年（1883年）の東京大学の運動会が最初といわれている。

明治三十三年（1900年）におこなわれた札幌農学校（現在の北海道大学）の第19回遊戯会のようす
北海道大学附属図書館所蔵（複製禁止）

A scene from the 19th playgame meeting held in 1900 at Sapporo Agricultural College (currently Hokkaido University); courtesy of Hokkaido University Library (reproduction prohibited)

The *undo-kai* season lasts from September through the early October when the heat of late summer is gone and autumn brings in cool breezes. The first *undo-kai* held in Japan is said to be *Kyoto-yugi-kai* (competitive playgame meeting) held in 1874 under the supervision of F. W. Strange, an English teacher of the naval academy in Tsukiji, Tokyo.

Later, a playgame meeting was held at Sapporo Agricultural College (currently Hokkaido University) in 1878. Within several years, *undo-kai* had reportedly spread to the elementary schools and junior high schools all over Hokkaido. Arinori Mori, the second minister of education of the Meiji government, vigorously promoted *undo-kai* for the purpose of group training in gymnastics. The athletic meets spread to schools all over Japan as we see today.

In the Meiji Era, not all schools had a playground. In some regions, students enjoyed exercises and sports meets in the precincts of a temple or a shrine together with the citizens. The term *undo-kai*, which is generally used today, was first used in the athletic meet held at the University of Tokyo in 1883.

行楽の歴史と由来 Origin and history of *koraku* (holiday-making)

　日本では古くから、農耕などの忙しい仕事の前の春と収穫が終了した秋に、野山や海辺、川辺に行って遊んだり、弁当を持って行って食べる習慣があった。

　春の行楽は三月三日の雛の日に由来するが、秋は豊穣や自然の恵みに感謝しながら、紅葉真っ盛りの山の温楽地（湯治場）などに季節の野菜などを持ち込み、体を休めたのである。

　江戸時代の東北地方では、春や秋になると身欠きにしんの煮つけ、凍み豆腐、厚揚げの煮つけ、青菜のおひたし、握った指のあとがついているてんのこ握りなどをお重に詰めたものを〝お野掛け弁当〟といって、野遊びを楽しんだといわれる。

It was a long-established custom for the Japanese to go out and play in the fields, seashore, or riversides by bringing lunchboxes before the busy farm work started in spring and after harvesting in autumn.

Koraku in spring is derived from *Hina-Matsuri* (Girls' Festival) on March 3. In autumn, people used to carry seasonal vegetables and other food to spend a relaxing time in a *tojiba* (therapeutic bath) in a spa nested in the mountains full of rich red and yellow leaves, giving thanks for the autumn harvest and appreciating the blessings of nature.

In the Edo Era, people in the Tohoku district used to enjoy going out for diversions by bringing *Onokake* lunchboxes in spring and autumn. The lunchbox contained herrings that had been cut open, dried, and cooked in soy sauce, frozen *tofu*, thick-fried *tofu* cooked in soy sauce, boiled greens, and *tennoko-nigiri* (rice ball with marks of the hands that shaped the ball), which are put together in tiered food boxes.

彼岸の歴史と由来 Origin and history of *Higan* (memorial services for the ancestors)

　〝彼岸〟は春分と秋分の日の年2回ある。この彼岸は仏教のサンスクリット語で「パーラミター（波羅密多）」の漢訳の〝到（至）彼岸〟からきている。

　彼岸とは、この世と来世の間に横たわる大きな河の向こう岸（彼岸）にいる霊が、苦しみのない安楽な〝極楽浄土〟に成仏してほしいと、先祖や亡き人の霊を祈り供養することである。

　彼岸には新しい花や、お萩をはじめとする故人の好物を供え、線香をあげて読経をする。そして墓参りをし、墓前墓石をきれいにし、新しい花を供え、線香をあげて、手を合わせて拝礼する。この時は、家族の近況報告や感謝の気持ちを念じるだけで、お願いごとをしてはいけないとされている。

彼岸に供えられるお萩
Ohagi offered in *Higan*

The *Higan* ceremony is observed twice a year or at the spring and autumnal equinox. *Higan* is a Japanese translation of the Chinese phrase, "arriving on the other shore," which comes from Sanskrit "paramita."

In the *Higan* ceremony, people wish that the spirits on the other shore (*higan*) of a large river lying between this world and the next safely reach the agony-free, comfortable land of perfect bliss (*Gokuraku-jodo*) where they would attain Buddhahood.

People offer fresh flowers and *ohagi* (rice balls coated with red bean jam) and other favorite foods of the deceased. Priests visit the house, burn incense, and recite a sutra. The party then visits the graves, cleans tombs, offers fresh flowers, burns incense, and joins their hands in prayer. It is customary to report to the ancestors, say, how the family is getting on and express thankfulness; they are told not to make a wish.

陰暦では七月から九月の秋で、仲秋（中秋）になる八月十五日（現在の九月上旬）が、一年で最も月が美しいとされる名月（十五夜）といわれる月見に当たる。

　月見はもともと中国の各地でおこなわれていた里いもの収穫祭だという説がある。それが奈良時代から平安時代に日本に伝わり、宮廷行事となったといわれる。その当時の貴族たちは、〝観月の宴〟と称して詩歌を詠んだり、池に船を浮かべて、水面に映る月を酒を飲みながら楽しみ、詩歌を詠んだといわれる。

　中国では月見に月餅を供えるが、日本では月がよく見える縁側や部屋などに〝すすきの穂〟を飾り、〝月見団子〟〝果もの〟〝田畑の初もの〟などを供えるのが一般的だが、地方によっては里いもや豆、栗などの秋を代表する食材を供える所もあるらしく、〝いも名月〟ともいわれる。

　すすきには月の神が降りてくる力があるといわれているし、月見の日（十五夜）の月光を浴びると不老長寿にあやかれるといわれるいい伝えがある。

The autumn season is from July through September in the lunar calendar. The full moon on the 15th night of August (*Chushu*) in the lunar calendar (the beginning of September in the current calendar) is said to be the most beautiful in the year, and is called *Jugoya* (15th night - harvest moon). People cherish viewing *Jugoya*, which is called *Tsukimi* (full moon viewing).

The origin of *Tsukimi* is said to go back to a harvest festival for taros celebrated in various areas of China. The ceremony was then introduced to Japan in the Nara or Heian Era, where it became a traditional court event. The aristocrats at that time enjoyed the *Kangetsu-no-Utage* (banquet for viewing the Jugoya harvest moon) by composing poems and drinking *sake* on a boat while watching the moon reflected on the water of the pond.

In China, people make offerings of *geppei* (moon cakes) in China. In Japan, generally, *susuki-no-ho* (ears of Japanese pampas grass) is used to decorate verandas or rooms commanding a fine view of the moon. The offerings include *tsukimi-dango* (moon-viewing dumplings), fruit, and the first of the new crops of the rice paddies and fields. In some areas in Japan, the offerings are taros, beans, chestnuts, and other ingredients representative of autumn, hence the harvest moon is called *Imo-Meigetsu* (taro harvest moon) in these areas.

Japanese pampas grass is said to have the power through which the god of the moon comes down. It is also said that longevity is expected when you are bathed in moonlight on the night of *Tsukimi* or the night of the harvest moon.

日本三大名月 Three Best Places to Admire the Harvest Moon in Japan

日本全国で美しい名月（十五夜）が見られるが、中でも三大といわれる名月を紹介する。

You can view the splendor of the harvest moon (*Jugoya*) everywhere in Japan. As a guide, the three most famous places for viewing the harvest moon are introduced below.

石山寺
Ishiyama-dera Temple

滋賀県大津市の石山寺は、崖などの石山で形成された小高い丘に寺院があり、紫式部が「源氏物語」をこの寺院で書いたとされる。そんな石山寺からの名月を〝石山の秋月〟と呼び、近江八景のひとつに数えられている。

Ishiyama-dera Temple, Ohtsu City, Shiga Prefecture, is located on a low hill formed by cliffs and stony mountains. Some say Murasaki Shikibu, a famous woman writer in the Heian Era, wrote *Genji Monogatari* (The Tale of Genji) while staying at this temple. The harvest moon viewed from Ishiyama-dera Temple is specially called *Ishiyama-no-Shugetsu* (autumn moon of Ishiyama), and is one of the *Ohmi-Hakkei* (eight scenic views of the Ohmi region).

姨捨山長楽寺
Obasute-yama Choraku-ji Temple

長野県千曲市の姨捨山にある長楽寺は、四十八枚田の水を張つた段々の田んぼの一枚ごとに月が映つて見えることから、〝田毎の月〟と呼ばれ、名月の名所として知られている。

Choraku-ji Temple, on Obasute Mountain, Chikuma City, Nagano Prefecture, is the place to view the moon reflected on each of the 48 terraced rice paddies when these are filled with water (*Ta-Goto-no Tsuki*, moon on each paddy). The spectacular view attracts multitudes of people to this famous harvest moon-viewing spot.

大沢池
Ohsawa-ike Pond

京都市右京区嵯峨にある大覚寺にある大沢池。嵯峨天皇によって造られた池で、当時はこの池に龍頭船などの屋形船を浮かべ、池に映る月の美しさを楽しんだといわれる。現在も仲秋の名月の時期になると、屋形船を浮かべ満月の夜を楽しんでいる。

Ohsawa-ike Pond is located in the premises of Daikaku-ji Temple in Saga, Ukyo-ku, Kyoto. The pond was constructed by the order of the Emperor Saga. At that time, *yakata-bune* (Japanese-style houseboat for dining and pleasure) such as *ryuto-sen* (dragon-head ship) was set afloat on the pond to view the moon and its reflection on the water. At present, houseboat services are run around the time of the harvest moon to welcome many people who enjoy the night of the full moon.

運動会・行楽を楽しむレシピ
Recipe to enjoy sports days and outings

巻き寿し
子供たちの大好きなえびフライと、大人でも楽しめるたくあん、チーズを巻き寿しにする

about
40
min

Sushi Roll
Roll fried prawns, a children's favorite,
takuan pickles and cheese that adults would also enjoy

■ 材料・4本分

寿し飯…4本分(約600g)	マヨネーズ …大さじ1
焼きのり …………4枚	塩 ……………適量
	こしょう ……適量
〈えびフライ巻き〉	揚げ油(サラダ油)…適量
殻つきえび ………6本	
	〈たくあんチーズ巻き〉
〈衣の材料〉	たくあん ………40g
小麦粉 …………適量	プロセスチーズ …30g
溶き卵 …………適量	きゅうり …縦1/2本
パン粉 …………適量	大葉 ……………6枚
	白ごま …………適量
レタス ………2〜3枚	
ミニアスパラ …6〜8本	
ウスターソース ……	
…………小さじ1/2	

■ Ingredients for 4 rolls

21 oz vinegared rice (for 4 rolls)
4 sheets toasted *nori* seaweed

〈**Fried prawn rolls**〉
6 shell-on prawns

〈**Fry coating**〉
Flour
Beaten egg
Breadcrumbs

2 - 3 leaves of lettuce
6 - 8 mini asparagus

1/2 tsp Worcester sauce
1 Tbsp mayonnaise
Salt
Pepper
Frying oil (vegetable oil)

〈***Takuan* and cheese rolls**〉
1 1/3 oz *takuan* pickled *daikon* giant white radish
1 oz processed cheese
1/2 cucumber
6 green perilla leaves
White sesame seeds

【作り方】

1 えびフライ巻きの準備をする。
殻つきえびは背わたを取り、尾を残して殻をむいて、揚げた時に曲がらないようえびの腹側に切れ目を3〜4カ所入れる。それに軽く塩・こしょうし、小麦粉、溶き卵、パン粉の順に衣づけする。中温の揚げ油でカラリと揚げる。

2 レタスは適当な大きさにちぎる。ミニアスパラはさっと塩ゆでにする。ウスターソースとマヨネーズを合わせる。

3 たくあんチーズ巻きの準備をする。
たくあんはせん切りに、きゅうりは太めの棒切りに、プロセスチーズは5mm角に切る。大葉は水洗いし、ペーパータオルなどで水けをふき取り、固い軸を取る。

4 巻きすに焼きのりをおき、寿し飯(約150g)をのせ、手前を1cm、向こう側を2cmくらい残すように広げる。寿し飯の中央は少しぼませ、そこに具材をおくようにする。

5 えびフライ巻きは、**2**のレタスをしき**1**のえびフライと**2**のミニアスパラをのせ、**2**のウスターソースとマヨネーズを合わせたソース少々をかける。えびの尾は両側にはみ出すように置いて巻くと飾りになってよい。たくあんチーズ巻きは、**3**の大葉をしき、**3**のたくあんときゅうりをのせ、プロセスチーズと白ごまをふる。

6 **5**の具材の部分を手で押さえながら、巻きすごと待ち上げて寿し飯の手前と向こう側を合わせるようにして巻き上げる。巻きす全体をきっちり締めるよう巻いたら、清潔な塗れ布巾で両端を軽く押さえて形を整え、包丁で食べやすい大きさに切る。切るたび包丁を清潔な塗れ布巾で拭うと切りやすい。

【DIRECTIONS】

1 Preparing the fried prawn rolls.
Devein the prawns, and shell them, leaving the tails on. Make 3 to 4 cuts on the belly side so that the prawns will not bend when fried. Lightly sprinkle with salt, pepper, and coat with the flour first, beaten egg second, and finally breadcrumbs. Fry in the oil heated to a medium temperature, until crisp.

2 Tear the lettuce into proper-size pieces. Briefly boil the mini asparagus in salty water. Mix the Worcester sauce and mayonnaise.

3 Preparing the *takuan* and cheese rolls.
Cut the *takuan* into julienne strips and the cucumber into thickish bar rectangles. Cut the cheese into 1/5-inch cubes. Rinse the green perilla leaves, paper-dry, and remove the hard stalks.

4 Place a *nori* seaweed sheet on a *maki-su* bamboo mat. Put the vinegared rice (about 5 1/4 oz) on the *nori* sheet, and spread leaving 3/8 inch at the bottom and 3/4 inch at the top uncovered. Cut a long shallow hollow in the center of the spread rice, where the ingredients will sit.

5 To make the prawn roll, place the torn lettuce, fried prawns, and the boiled mini asparagus, and add a small quantity of the mixed sauce of Worcester sauce and mayonnaise. Place the prawns in such a way that their tails will stick out from both ends, when rolled. The tails are used for decoration. For *takuan* and cheese rolls, place the green perilla leaves, put on the cut *takuan* and cucumber, and sprinkle over the cheese and white sesame seeds.

6 Lift the near edge of the bamboo mat and *nori* sheet together, while holding the ingredients with your hands, and bring over to meet the far edge of the sheet. After firmly pressing the roll, shape it by gently pressing both ends using a moistened clean cloth. Cut crosswise into bite-size pieces. Clean the knife with a moistened clean cloth after each cutting. This will make the cutting smooth.

運動会・行楽<ruby>行楽<rt>こうらく</rt></ruby>を楽しむレシピ
Recipe to enjoy sports days and outings

吹き寄せいなり

具材がいっぱい入ったおしゃれないなり寿しを自然の中で楽しむ

about
50
min

Mixed *Sushi* Pockets

Enjoy these lovely *sushi* pockets containing various ingredients in the open air

■ 材料・16個分

寿し飯		2合分
油揚げ		8枚
A	だし汁	400cc
	砂糖	大さじ5
	みりん	大さじ3
	しょう油	大さじ3
しいたけ		3枚
えのき		1/2束
B	だし汁	100cc
	しょう油	小さじ2
	砂糖	大さじ1/2
	酒	大さじ1/2
	みりん	大さじ1/2

れんこん		約60g
C	酢	大さじ2
	砂糖	大さじ1
	塩	ひとつまみ
	水	大さじ3
さつまいも		約100g
黒ごま		大さじ1
ゆず		1/4個分
三つ葉		16本
塩		適量

■ Ingredients for 16 pockets

Vinegared rice, cooked with 1 1/2 U.S. cups rice
8 slices *abura-age* deep-fried *tofu*

A
- 1 2/3 U.S. cups stock
- 5 Tbsps sugar
- 3 Tbsps *mirin* sweet cooking *sake*
- 3 Tbsps soy sauce

3 *shiitake* mushrooms
1/2 bundle *enokidake* mushrooms

B
- 2/5 U.S. cup stock
- 2 tsps soy sauce
- 1/2 Tbsp sugar
- 1/2 Tbsp *sake*
- 1/2 Tbsp *mirin* sweet cooking *sake*

About 2 oz lotus root

C
- 2 Tbsps vinegar
- 1 Tbsp sugar
- Pinch of salt
- 3 Tbsps water

1/3 sweet potato (About 3 1/2 oz)
1 Tbsps black sesame seeds
1/4 *yuzu* Japanese lime
16 trefoil stalks
Salt

【作り方】

1 油揚げをまな板にのせ全体を箸で転がしてから、湯通しして油抜きする。長さを半分に切り指で袋を開く。鍋に油揚げとAを入れ、中火にかける。煮立ったら落としぶたをして、弱火で20〜30分煮てそのまま冷まし、味を含ませる。

2 しいたけは半分に切り、さらに薄切りにする。えのきは石突きを取り2cmの長さに切り、Bと合わせて煮る。

3 れんこんは皮をむき、小さないちょう切りにし、さっと塩ゆでして熱いうちにCに漬けて甘酢れんこんを作る。

4 さつまいもは皮つきのまま1cm角に切り、さっと水洗いし、塩少々を加えてやわらかくなるまでゆでる。

5 ゆずは皮をそぎ、せん切りにする。中身は絞っておく。三つ葉は長いままさっと塩ゆでにする。

6 寿し飯が少し温かいうちに、それぞれ汁けをきった2、3、4、5のゆずの皮と絞り汁、黒ごまを加えて切るように混ぜ、16等分して軽く握っておく。

7 1の油揚げの汁けを軽く絞り、6の寿し飯を詰め、全体を軽く握る。それを5の三つ葉で結ぶ。

【DIRECTIONS】

1 Roll the *abura-age* deep-fried *tofu* on a cutting board with a chopstick. Blanch it to remove excess oil. Cut in half crosswise, put the *abura-age* and the ingredients of **A** into a pot, and heat over a medium flame. When it comes to the boil, cover with a drop lid, and turn down the heat to cook for 20 to 30 min. Allow it to cool, so that the *abura-age* absorbs the liquid.

2 Cut the *shiitake* mushrooms in half, and thinly slice. Remove the bottom part of the *enokidake* mushrooms, and cut into 3/4-inch lengths. Simmer these mushrooms in the mixture of **B**.

3 Peel the lotus root and cut into small quarter rounds. Boil in salty water, and soak in the mixture of **C** while hot, to make sweet-vinegared lotus root.

4 Cut the sweet potato into 3/8-inch cubes with skin, rinse quickly, and boil in water with a small quantity of salt until they become soft.

5 Shave off the rind of the *yuzu*, cut the rind into julienne strips, and squeeze juice from the flesh. Briefly boil in salty water the trefoil without cutting.

6 While the vinegared rice is still slightly warm, add the drained mushrooms prepared in **2**, the sweet-vinegared lotus root, boiled sweet potato, the cut *yuzu* rind and juice, and the black sesame seeds, and mix with the rice in a cutting motion. Divide the rice into 16 equal parts, and coarsely shape into balls.

7 Lightly squeeze the liquid out of the *abura-age* prepared in **1**, fill with the rice, and shape by lightly pressing the entire surface. Tie the *abura-age* pocket with the boiled trefoil stalks.

運動会・行楽<ruby>行楽<rt>こうらく</rt></ruby>を楽しむレシピ
Recipe to enjoy sports days and outings

フライドチキン

子供たちだって大好きなフライドチキンは運動会、行楽に最適

about
30
min

Fried Chicken

Ideal for sports days and outings,
as fried chicken is everybody's favorite, including kids

■材料・2人分

鶏もも肉	2枚
塩・こしょう	少々
小麦粉	適宜
揚げ油	適宜
レモンの輪切り	適宜
クレソン	適宜

〈衣の材料〉

小麦粉	100g
おろしにんにく	適宜
水	少々
酒	100cc
塩	少々
黒こしょう（粗挽）	適宜

■ Ingredients (serves 2)

2 boneless chicken thighs
Small quantity of salt and pepper
Flour
Frying oil
Sliced lemon
Watercress

〈**Ingredients for coating**〉
3 1/2 oz flour
Grated garlic
Small quantity of water
2/5 U.S. cup *sake*
Small quantity of salt
Black pepper (coarsely ground)

【作り方】

[下ごしらえ]

1 ボウルに小麦粉、おろしにんにく、水、酒を入れ、泡立て器でゆっくりと泡立てないようにかき混ぜる。泡立て器を持ち上げて上から衣がとぎれないように、スルスルッと落ちるまでなめらかになったら衣の完成。塩、黒こしょうを加えてさっと混ぜ合わせる。

2 鶏もも肉は、余分な脂身を取り除き、1枚を8等分に切る。

3 2の鶏もも肉全体に塩・こしょうをふりかけ、下味をつける。
バットに小麦粉を広げ、下味をつけた鶏肉を押しつけるように表面にしっかりとつけ、余分な粉ははたき落とす。

4 揚げ油を中火で熱し、170℃に温めておく。

[衣をつけて揚げる]

1 下ごしらえ**3**の鶏もも肉を、下ごしらえ**1**の衣にくぐらせ衣が均一につくようにし、下ごしらえ**4**の油の中に入れる。一度に入れる量は3〜4個が目安。中火にし、時々揚げ箸で鶏肉を持ち上げてひっくり返しながら火が中まで通るまでじっくり揚げていく。
★中火にしないと周りの衣だけが焦げ、肉の中まで火が通らないので注意したい。

2 **1**がきつね色に揚げ色がつき、鶏肉全体が浮いてきたら火が通った証拠。油をきりながら揚げバットに取り上げて油をきっておく。

3 **2**を器に盛り、クレソン、レモンの輪切りを添えていただく。

【DIRECTIONS】

[Preparations]

1 Put in a bowl the flour, grated garlic, water, and *sake*, and mix with a whisk. Move the whisk carefully so that bubbles are not formed. Lift the whisk to see if the batter is smooth enough to fall unbroken. If so, the batter is ready. Add the salt and black pepper, and lightly mix.

2 Remove excess fat from the boneless chicken thighs, and cut each thigh into 8 equal pieces.

3 Sprinkle the entire surface of the chicken with the salt and pepper for preliminary seasoning.
Spread the flour on a cooking tray, press the chicken to cover the entire surface with the flour, and dust off excess flour.

4 Heat the frying oil over a medium flame to 340°F.

[Coating and frying]

1 Dip the chicken prepared in **3** in the batter prepared in **1** to evenly coat the chicken. Put 3 to 4 pieces in the heated frying oil at a time. Fry the chicken over a medium heat until fully cooked, while occasionally lifting and turning with chopsticks.
★Make sure the flame is medium. Otherwise, the coating will burn before the chicken is fully cooked.

2 When the chicken browns, and begins to float in the oil, it's ready. Remove the chicken from the oil, while draining, and place on a draining tray.

3 Arrange the fried chicken on a serving dish, garnishing with the watercress and sliced lemon.

いも煮

里いも、大根、牛肉にだしがしみ込んで体の芯まで温まる一杯

about
30
min

Stewed Taros

A bowl of stock-soaked taros, *daikon* radish and beef warms you up from inside

■材料・2人分

里いも …………………………… 5〜6個	A 酒 …………………………… 1/2カップ
長ねぎ …………………………… 1本	砂糖 …………………………… 大さじ2
大根 …………………………… 3cm	しょう油 …………………………… 大さじ2
こんにゃく …………………………… 1/2枚	みりん …………………………… 大さじ1
牛切り落とし肉 …………………………… 150g	
だし汁 …………………………… 3カップ	

■ Ingredients (serves 2)

5 -6 taros
1 *naga-negi* onion
1 1/5 inches *daikon* giant white radish
1/2 cake *konnyaku* devil's tongue
5 1/4 oz hashed beef
2 1/2 U.S. cups stock

A ⌈ 2/5 U.S. cup *sake*
  ⌊ 2 Tbsps sugar

2 Tbsps soy sauce
1 Tbsp *mirin* sweet cooking *sake*

【作り方】

1 里いもはよく洗い、皮の上下を切り落としてから皮をむき、大きければ半分に切る。耐熱皿にのせてラップをし、電子レンジ（600W）で3分加熱する。

2 長ねぎは斜切り、大根は皮をむき半月切り、こんにゃくは塩（分量外）でもんで水洗いしたら水からゆでてアクを抜き、小さくちぎっておく。

3 鍋にだし汁と**1**の里いも、**2**の大根、こんにゃくを入れて煮立てたら弱めの中火にし、**A**を入れて里いもがやわらかくなるまで煮る。里いもに串がすっと入るようになったら牛切り落とし肉をばらすように入れてアクを取りながら煮込み、しょう油とみりんを入れて味を調え、**2**の長ねぎを入れてひと煮立ちさせたら出来上がり。

【DIRECTIONS】

1 Wash the taros well, cut off the top and bottom parts, and peel. Cut in half, if large. Place the taros on a heat-resistant tray, cover with plastic wrap, and microwave (600 w) for 3 min.

2 Cut the *naga-negi* onion diagonally. Peel the *daikon* radish, and cut into half moons. Rub the *konnyaku* devil's tongue cake with salt (extra quantity), rinse, put in a pot with water, and bring it to the boil to remove any bitterness. Tear the *konnyaku* devil's tongue cake into small pieces after boiling.

3 Put in a pot the stock and taros prepared in **1**, the cut *daikon* radish and torn *konnyaku*, and cook. When the soup comes to the boil, turn down the heat to medium, add **A**, and cook until the taros become soft. When the taros are soft enough for a bamboo skewer to pierce them smoothly, add the beef while loosening the chunks, and continue cooking while skimming off the scum. Season with the soy sauce and *mirin*, put the cut *naga-negi* onion in, and bring it to the boil briefly.

コラム

Column

"いも煮会"って何？　どんなことをするの？
What is *imo-ni-kai*? What do you do?

　今や日本全国で知られている "いも煮会" だが、江戸時代の元禄の頃、山形県の最上川で働く船頭たちが、荷もつが届くのを何日も待つ間に、前々から里いもを買い求めておき、棒だらなどと一緒に煮て、飲み食いしたのが "いも煮" のはじまりといわれている。

　その後、昭和初期になると、養蚕農家の人たちが、秋の養蚕後に最上川の河原で繭業者から経費を出してもらい、里いもはもちろんのこと、きのこ、牛肉などを入れた豪華ないも煮会を繭業者を招待しておこなったのが、現在のいも煮の原形といえる。

　その後、いも煮会は各地区の青年団の女性たちとの出会いの場になり、一般の人たちにも広く普及していくことになり、今では山形県内だけではなく、日本全国の川原でされるようになった。これも日本独特な秋を楽しむ行楽のひとつではないだろうか……。

　本家本元の山形県山形市では、「日本一の芋煮会フェスティバル」と銘うって、毎年九月の第1日曜日に馬見ヶ崎河川敷で、約6mもの大鍋で、里いも、牛肉、こんにゃく、ねぎなどを入れた約50,000人分のいも煮を作り、市民や観光客に配布している。

Imo-ni-kai (*imo-ni* gathering) is popular all over Japan today. In the Genroku period of the Edo Era, the boatmen plying the Mogami River, Yamagata Prefecture, waiting day after day for the arrival of enough goods to carry, cooked taros, which had been stored as provisions, together with dried cod and other foodstuff. This was said to be the start of *imo-ni* (taro cooking).

Later in the early Showa Era, silk-raising farmers, with expenses paid by cocoon buyers, held a gorgeous *imo-ni* gathering using not only taros but also mushrooms and beef and invited the cocoon buyers. This was the original form of *imo-ni-kai* of the present day.

Imo-ni-kai then became the venue for meeting women for the members of young men's associations in various regions. It became popular among other people as well. At present, *imo-ni-kai* is held not only in Yamagata Prefecture but also everywhere in Japan, where there is a dry riverbed. *Imo-ni-kai* is indeed one type of *koraku* (holiday-making) in autumn unique to Japan.

In Yamagata City, Yamagata Prefecture, where this festive event took place for the first time in Japan, Japan's largest *imo-ni-kai* festival is held on the Mamigasaki Dry Riverbed on the first Sunday of September every year. To cook *imo-ni*, ingredients such as taros, beef, devil's tongue, *naga-negi* onion, etc. are put into a large pan of about 6 meters in diameter. The food is enough to serve about 50,000 citizens and sightseers.

秋の和食レシピ

Recipes of Japanese Food in Autumn

秋を彩る旬の食材
Seasonal Ingredients in Autumn

食欲の秋ともいわれ、四季の中で最もさまざまな食材が店頭に並ぶ秋。秋を代表する野菜といえば、さつまいも、さといも、かぼちゃ、まつたけなどのきのこ類などがあげられる。魚介類としてはなんといってもさんまやいわし、さばなどが脂がのって美味しくなる。秋の食材を彩ってくれる食材を、焼きもの、煮もの、揚げものなどの調理で楽しみたい。

Autumn is the appetite-stimulating season. The greatest variety of ingredients of all seasons of the year is offered in stores. Vegetables representative of the autumn season include sweet potatoes, taros, pumpkins, and *matsutake* (pine mushroom). Seafood is also abundant. Pacific saury, sardine, and mackerel are particularly juicy. These representative autumnal ingredients are cooked by grilling, simmering, or frying.

※本書で紹介する食材の旬は基本的なものを紹介している。地方によって異なる場合もある。
※The typically best season for the ingredients in this book is given, and this may differ in some areas.

さといも（里芋）
Taro

さといもの芋の部分は、実は茎が肥大したものだ。代表的なものには、石川早生、石川小芋、土垂、やつがしら、えびいもなどがある。煮もの、汁もの、蒸しものなどに使われる。

The ball of a taro is actually the stem that has become fat. Typical taros include *Ishikawa-wase* (early taro originally cultivated in Ishikawa Village, Osaka), *Ishikawa-koimo* (new taros formed on top of old ones; from Ishikawa Village), *dodare*, *yatsu-gashira* (eight-headed new taros on an old one), and *ebi-imo* (shrimp taro). Taros are a favorite ingredient in *ni-mono* (simmered dishes), *shirumono* (soups), and *mushimono* (steamed dishes).

ながいも（長薯）
Chinese yam

日本全国で栽培されるやまいものひとつで、スーパーなどでよく見かけるのがこのながいもである。皮をむいて短冊切りにするとサクサクと食感もよく、すっていただいても美味しい。

Chinese yam, a kind of Japanese taro, is cultivated all over Japan. It is a popular food easily available in supermarkets and other stores. Pare the skin and cut into rectangles and enjoy the crunchy texture. It also tastes good when crushed in a mortar.

とうがん（冬瓜）
Wax gourd

冬の瓜と書くが秋が旬になる。皮が厚く、果肉は白色の多汁である。皮を厚めにむき、果肉を煮もの、炒めもの、スープ、吸いものの実などに使用される。

Tougan (wax gourd) in Japanese literally means "gourd of winter" but is most delicious in autumn. The skin is thick and the white flesh is succulent. The skin is pared rather thickly, and the flesh is used in simmered or *itamemono* (stir-fried dishes) and as an ingredient for clear soup.

さつまいも (薩摩芋)
Sweet potato (*Satsuma-imo*)

さつまいもの由来は薩摩 (現在の鹿児島県) 経由で日本各地に伝播したためといわれている。さまざまな品種があるが、ベニアズマ、ベニコマチ、べにあか (紅赤) などが有名。

The Japanese name of *Satsuma-imo* (*Satsuma* potato) comes from the Satsuma region (currently Kagoshima Prefecture), from where the vegetable spread all over Japan. Various breeds are available, famous ones including *beni-azuma* (crimson easterly), *beni-komachi* (crimson beauty), and *beni-aka* (crimson red).

かぼちゃ (南瓜)
Pumpkin

かぼちゃは、日本かぼちゃと西洋かぼちゃに分類することができる。日本かぼちゃは黒皮、菊座が、西洋は芳香青皮甘栗、黒皮栗が代表になる。煮もの、天ぷらなどにされる。

Pumpkins are generally classified into Japanese and Western pumpkins. Typical Japanese pumpkins include *kuro-kawa* and *kiku-za*, while typical Western ones include *hoko-aokawa-amakuri* and *kurokawa-kuri*. Pumpkins are an ingredient used in simmered dishes, *tempura*, and many other dishes.

ほうれん草 (菠薐草)
Spinach

ほうれん草には東洋系品種と西洋系品種に大別することができる。東洋系品種は葉が薄く、根もとが赤いのが特徴。西洋系は葉が厚く、根の色は赤いが淡い。

Spinach is generally classified into Oriental and Western kinds. The Oriental variety has thin leaves and is red at the root. The Western variety has thick leaves and is light red at the root.

しゅんぎく (春菊)
Garland chrysanthemum

別名きくな (菊菜) ともいわれるしゅんぎくは、実は日本原産ではなく、地中海沿岸地方が原産になる。今や日本の鍋料理はもちろんのこと、おひたしなどに欠かせない野菜である。

The origin of the garland chrysanthemum, also known as the crown daisy, is not Japan but the Mediterranean region. The garland chrysanthemum is indispensable for Japanese one-pot dishes. The vegetable is also an essential item for *ohitashi* (boiled vegetables eaten with soy sauce).

まつたけ (松茸)
Matsutake mushroom

国内産はもちろんのこと、中国産、アメリカ産、カナダ産などの輸入ものが数多く出まわっている。香りが高く、焼きもの、蒸しもの (土瓶蒸し)、炊き込みご飯などに使う。

In addition to the domestic ones, many imported products are on the market, including those from China, U.S., and Canada. With rich aroma, *matsutake* is a favorite ingredient for roasted and grilled dishes as well as steamed dishes, such as *dobin-mushi* (steamed clear soup with chicken, etc. in a clay pot). It is also used in *takikomi-gohan* (steamed rice with chicken, fish, and vegetables).

れんこん (蓮根)
Lotus root

れんこんは、はすの地下 (水中) 茎が肥大したもの。日本古来の野菜と思っている人も多いだろうが、1500年以上前に渡来した野菜である。煮もの、揚げものなどにされる。

A lotus root is actually the underground (underwater) stem of a lotus that has become fat. Many people believe lotus roots are a vegetable of Japan from olden times but it came to Japan more than 1,500 years ago. Lotus roots are used in *nimono* and *agemono* (deep fried dishes).

ぎんなん（銀杏）
Gingko nut

ぎんなんは銀杏の種子で10月中旬から下旬に成熟する。食用部分は硬い殻の中の外種皮を除いたもの。新しいものはきれいな濃緑色をしている。焼いたり、蒸しものなどに使う。

Gingko nuts, the seeds of the gingko tree, mature from the middle through the end of October. The edible part is covered by hard shell. The outer skin is peeled off before cooking. New gingko nuts are colored clear dark green. The nuts are cooked by grilling. They are also an ingredient for steamed dishes.

くり（栗）
Japanese chestnut

9月下旬から10月中旬にかけて成熟するくりの実。天然ものもあるが、市場に出まわるのは栽培ものがほとんど。ゆでたり、くりご飯、正月用のきんとん、お菓子などに使われる。

The chestnut matures in late September through mid-October. Natural chestnuts are available, but most on the market are cultured ones. Chestnuts are generally boiled. They are also used in *kuri-gohan* (chestnut rice) and *kuri-kinton* (mashed sweet potatoes with sweetened chestnuts) of New Year dishes as well as in confectionary.

ゆず（柚子）
Japanese lime

酢のもの、鍋料理、土瓶蒸しなど幅広く使用されるゆず。すがすがしい香りが料理を一層引き立ててくれる、日本を代表する調味用柑橘といってよいだろう。

Japanese lime (*yuzu*) is extensively used in various dishes such as vinegared dishes, one-pot dishes, and *dobin-mushi* (steamed clear soup with chicken and other ingredients in a clay pot). The refreshing scent brings out the flavor of the other ingredients. Japanese lime is a representative seasoning citrus fruit of Japan.

かわはぎ（皮剥）
File fish

硬い皮を剥いでから調理することから名がついたかわはぎ。秋から肝が大きくなり美味しくなる。煮つけ、鍋料理の具、肝と一緒にいただく刺身（肝あえ）は絶品。

File fish or *kawa-hagi* (literally "peel off skin") is so named because it is skinned before cooking. With the fully enlarged liver, the fish is especially tasty in autumn. It is generally boiled with soy sauce, and is also a favorite ingredient for one-pot dishes. It makes a superb *sashimi* food when combined with a dressing prepared from its liver (*kimo-ae*).

さんま（秋刀魚）
Pacific saury

秋を代表する味覚のひとつのさんま。秋に三陸沿岸から南下するものが脂がのって美味しいとされる。塩焼きはもちろんのこと、新鮮なものは刺身にもされる。

Pacific saury (*sanma*) is one of the most prominent seasonal foods of autumn in Japanese cuisine. Pacific saury going south off the *Sanriku* coast are at their best in this season when they put on fat. They are normally grilled with salt. Fresh *sanma* is also served as *sashimi*.

さば（鯖）
Mackerel

真さばとごまさばがいるが、真さばは秋になると脂がのって美味しくなる。ごまさばは夏が美味しいとされる。酢のもの、煮もの（味噌煮込み）、揚げものなどにされる。

There are chub mackerel and dotted mackerel. The former is fatty and tasty in autumn, while the latter is best eaten in summer. Mackerel is a favorite ingredient for *sunomono* (vinegared dishes), simmered dishes (miso-stewed dishes), and *agemono*.

たちうお（太刀魚）
Atlantic cutlassfish

立ったまま泳ぐことや、体が刀のように平たく、銀色に輝いているのが名の由来。ほぼ一年中出まわるが、脂がのった秋が一番美味しい。塩焼き、煮つけ、ムニエルなどにする。

Tachiuo (standing fish) or the Atlantic cutlassfish is so named in Japanese because it swims standing up or, to express it another way, the body is flat and silvery as a sword (*tachi* = sword, *uo* = fish). The Atlantic cutlassfish is eaten throughout the year but is tastiest in autumn when it puts on fat. It is salt-grilled, boiled with soy sauce, or served as a meunière.

いわし（鰯）
Sardine

真いわし、うるめいわし、片口いわしが食用にされる。特に真いわしは、秋になると大型になり、脂がのって美味しくなる。新鮮なものは刺身、煮つけ、塩焼きなどにされる。

Ma-iwashi (true sardine), *urume-iwashi* (round herring), and *katakuchi-iwashi* (Japanese anchovy) are edible. *Ma-iwashi*, in particular, gets larger, fattier, and tastier in autumn. Fresh sardines are also served as *sashimi*, boiled with soy sauce, or salt-grilled.

いしもち（石持）
White croaker

いしもちは頭部内にまるで石のような硬い耳石があるのが名の由来。正式名称はしろぐちになる。こちらは釣りあげた時にグーグーとぐちをいっているように鳴くことから。

Ishimochi (stone keeper) meaning white croaker in Japanese is so named because the otolith in the head is as hard as stone. The official name is *shiroguchi* (white grumbler) because the fish murmurs as if grumbling when landed.

さけ（鮭）
Salmon

私たちがよく食べているのは、しろさけ（白鮭）のことで、秋になると秋ざけとか秋あじとも呼ばれ、新巻きにされる。切り身は焼きもの、バター焼き、煮ものなどにされる。

Japanese people usually eat *shirosake* (white salmon). In autumn, salmon is called *aki-zake* (autumn salmon) or *aki-aji* (autumn taste), and processed into *ara-maki* (the guts are removed and the cavity is filled with salt) for preservation. Fillets of the salmon are served grilled (with or without butter) or boiled.

かき（牡蠣）
Giant Pacific oyster

身が太る晩秋から冬に美味しいかきは、300年ほど前から広島湾で養殖されていたという。みそでいただく土手鍋はもちろんのこと、焼き、揚げ、炒めものにもよく合う。

The giant Pacific oyster gets larger in autumn and winter, when it tastes good. Culture reportedly started about 300 years ago in Hiroshima. *Dote-nabe* (a one-pot specialty with *miso*) is most enjoyable, while grilled, deep-fried, and stir-fried oysters are also delicious.

その他の旬の食材
Other Seasonal Ingredients

セロリ●Celery
やまといも（大和薯）●Yam
じねんじょ（自然薯）●Japanese yam
しいたけ（椎茸）●Japanese mushroom
まいたけ（舞茸）●Hen of the woods
なめこ（滑子）●*Nameko* mushroom
そば（蕎麦）●Buckwheat noodles
りんご（林檎）●Apple
なし（梨）●Pear
かき（柿）●Persimmon
くるみ（胡桃）●Persian walnut
かつお（鰹）●Skipjack tuna
わかさぎ（公魚）●Japanese smelt
ししゃも（柳葉魚）●*Shishamo* smelt
いとよりだい（糸撚鯛）●Goldenehread
めじな（目仁奈）●Largescale black fish
あかがい（赤貝）●Bloody clam
はぜ（鯊）●Goby

かぼちゃときのこのサラダ

about 15 min

かぼちゃの甘さとカッテージチーズの爽やかな酸味が美味しい

Pumpkin and Mushroom Salad

The sweetness of pumpkin and the refreshing tartness of cottage cheese make this a tasty dish

■材料・2人分

かぼちゃ	1/8個
しめじ	1/2パック
プチトマト	4個
クレソン	1/2束
カッテージチーズ	30g
A ┌ EX.オリーブ油	大さじ1
├ レモン汁	大さじ1
└ 塩・黒こしょう	少々

■ Ingredients (serves 2)

1/8 pumpkin
1/2 pack *shimeji* mushrooms
4 cherry tomatoes
1/2 bundle watercress
1 oz cottage cheese

A ┌ 1 Tbsp extra-virgin olive oil
├ 1 Tbsp lemon juice
└ Small quantity of salt and black pepper

■作り方

1 かぼちゃは種とわたを除き、ラップをして電子レンジ（600W）で2分強加熱してから1cmの薄切りにする。しめじは石突きを切って小房にわけ、プチトマトは半分に切り、クレソンは茎の硬い部分と葉に切り分ける。

2 耐熱ボウルに**1**のかぼちゃ、しめじ、クレソンの茎を入れてラップをして電子レンジ（600W）で2分加熱し、**A**を入れてあえる。

3 **2**が冷めたら**1**のプチトマト、クレソンの葉、カッテージチーズを加え、皿に盛りつける。

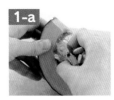 1-a
 1-b

■DIRECTIONS

1 Remove the seeds and pulp of the pumpkin, and cover with plastic wrap. Microwave (600 w) for 2-plus min, and cut into 3/8-inch-thick slices. Cut off the hard tip of the *shimeji* mushrooms, and separate into small portions. Cut the cherry tomatoes in half lengthwise. Cut the watercress to separate the hard stalks from the leaves.

2 Place on a heat-resistant tray the cut pumpkin, *shimeji* mushrooms, and the watercress stalks, cover with plastic wrap, and microwave (600 w) for 2 min. Add the ingredients of **A** and mix.

3 When it cools down, add the cherry tomatoes, watercress leaves prepared in **1**, and cottage cheese, and arrange on a serving dish.

かぼちゃのサラダ
Pumpkin Salad

■材料・2人分 / ■ Ingredients (serves 2)

材料・2人分	Ingredients (serves 2)
かぼちゃ ……………1/6個	1/6 pumpkin
玉ねぎ ……………1/8個	1/8 onion
レーズン …………大さじ1	1 Tbsp raisin
A サワークリーム …大さじ2 レモン汁………大さじ1 シナモンパウダー …少々 塩・黒こしょう ……少々	**A** 2 Tbsps sour cream 1 Tbsp lemon juice Small quantity of cinnamon powder Small quantity of salt and black pepper
エンダイブ ……………少々	Small quantity of endive

【作り方】

1 かぼちゃは種とわたを除き、ラップをして電子レンジ（600W）で2分強加熱し、皮を取り除き、一口大に切ってさらに電子レンジで3分加熱する。

2 ボウルに**1**のかぼちゃを入れて熱いうちに半分くらいフォークなどでつぶす。

3 玉ねぎはみじん切りにし、水でさらしてから水けをよく絞る。

4 **2**のかぼちゃに**A**、**3**の玉ねぎ、レーズンを加えてあえ、エンダイブを添えた器に盛る。

[DIRECTIONS]

1 Remove the seeds and pulp of the pumpkin, and cover with plastic wrap. Microwave (600 w) for 2-plus min, and remove the skin. Cut into bite-size pieces, and microwave again for 3 min.

2 Put the pumpkin in a bowl, and half-mash with a fork while hot.

3 Chop the onion finely, soak in water, and drain.

4 Mix **A**, the drained onion, and the raisins with the pumpkin prepared in **2**. Arrange on a serving dish, garnishing with the endive.

about **20** min

かぼちゃとしめじの甘酢炒め

かぼちゃとしめじが甘酢風味の飽きのこない美味しさに

Sweet-Vinegar-Sautéed Pumpkin and *Shimeji* Mushrooms

Thanks to the sweetened-vinegar, pumpkin and *shimeji* mushrooms, this dish refreshes with no cloying aftertaste

■ 材料・2人分

かぼちゃ	1/8個
しめじ	1/2パック
玉ねぎ	1/4個
赤唐辛子	1本
サラダ油	大さじ2
薄力粉	大さじ1

A
黒酢	大さじ1
酒	大さじ1
はちみつ	大さじ1
しょう油	大さじ1/2

塩・黒こしょう	少々

▨ Ingredients (serves 2)

1/8 pumpkin
1/2 pack *shimeji* mush-rooms
1/4 onion
1 red chili pepper
2 Tbsps vegetable oil
1 Tbsp *hakurikiko* low-gluten cake flour

A
1 Tbsp black vinegar
1 Tbsp *sake*
1 Tbsp honey
1/2 Tbsp soy sauce

Small quantity of salt and black pepper

■作り方

1 かぼちゃは種とわたを取り、ラップをして電子レンジで（600W）1分強加熱してから1cmの厚さの一口大に切る。耐熱皿にのせてさらに2分強、電子レンジで加熱してから、薄力粉を薄くはたきつける。

2 しめじは石突きを切って小房に分け、玉ねぎはくし形切りに、赤唐辛子はへたを切り取り、種を抜いて小口切りにする。

3 フライパンにサラダ油を熱し、**2**の赤唐辛子、玉ねぎ、しめじ、**1**のかぼちゃの順に炒め、塩・黒こしょうをし、合わせた**A**のたれを加えて炒め合わせる。

■DIRECTIONS

1 Remove the seeds and pulp of the pumpkin, and cover with plastic wrap. Microwave (600 w) for 1-plus min, and cut into 3/8-inch-thick bite-size pieces. Put the pumpkin on a heat resistant tray, and microwave again for 2-plus min. Dust the pumpkin with the *hakurikiko* flour.

2 Cut off the hard tip of the *shimeji* mushrooms, and separate into small portions. Cut the onion into wedges. Remove the calyx and seeds of the red chili pepper, and cut into small rounds.

3 Heat the vegetable oil in a frying pan, stir-fry in the order of the red chili pepper, onion, *shimeji* mushrooms, and pumpkin. Sprinkle with the salt and black pepper, add the mixture of **A**, and stir-fry further.

かぼちゃとほうれん草のバター焼き

Butter-Sautéed Pumpkin and Spinach

■材料・2人分

かぼちゃ	1/8個
ほうれん草	3株
玉ねぎ	1/4個
ベーコン	2枚
バター	10g
塩・黒こしょう	少々

■Ingredients (serves 2)

1/8 pumpkin
3 whole spinach
1/4 onion
2 slices bacon
1/3 oz butter
Small quantity of salt and black pepper

【作り方】

1 かぼちゃは種とわたを除き、ラップをして電子レンジ（600W）で2分強加熱して5～6mmの厚さに切る。玉ねぎは薄切りに、ベーコンは1.5cmの幅に切る。

2 ほうれん草は塩（分量外）を入れた熱湯でゆでてから、水にさらしてアクを抜き、水けをよく絞って約3～4cmの長さに切る。

3 フライパンにバターを溶かし、**1**のベーコン、玉ねぎ、かぼちゃ、**2**のほうれん草を炒め合せ、塩・黒こしょうをする。

[DIRECTIONS]

1 Remove the seeds and pulp of the pumpkin, and cover with plastic wrap. Microwave (600 w) for 2-plus min, and cut into 1/5-inch-thick pieces. Slice the onion thinly. Cut the bacon into 1/2-inch-wide pieces.

2 Boil the spinach in salty water (extra quantity of salt), and soak in water to remove harshness. Squeeze off water, and cut into about 1 1/2-inch lengths.

3 Melt the butter in a frying pan, sauté the cut bacon, onion, pumpkin and the spinach, and season with salt and black pepper.

里いもの白煮

里いも美味しさと美しさを最大限引き出した白煮

Simmered Taros, *Shira-ni* Style

This pale-colored simmered dish brings out the taste and beauty of the taros to the maximum

■材料・2人分

里いも …………………約250g
だし汁 …………………1カップ

A
┌ 砂糖 …………………大さじ1
│ 塩 ……………………小さじ1/4
│ 薄口しょう油 …大さじ1/2
└ みりん …………………大さじ1

絹さや …………………4〜5枚

Ingredients (serves 2)

8 3/4 oz taros
4/5 U.S. cup stock

A
┌ 1 Tbsp sugar
│ 1/4 tsp salt
│ 1/2 Tbsp light soy sauce
│ 1 Tbsp *mirin* sweet cook-
└ ing *sake*

4 - 5 snow peas

■作り方

1 里いもはよく洗い、上下を切り落としてから縦に6面になるように皮をむき（六方むき）、塩（分量外）でもんで水洗いしてから、鍋に水と入れてゆで、煮立ったら約3〜4分弱火で煮立て、ざるに上げて水洗いしてぬめりを取る。

2 絹さやは筋を取り、塩（分量外）を入れた熱湯でゆでておく。

3 鍋に**1**の里いもとだし汁を入れ、煮立ってきたら火を弱め、落としぶたをして約10分煮込み、**A**を順に入れて味つけをし、さらに味がしみ込むように約7〜8分煮込む。

4 器に**3**の里いもと、**2**の絹さやを盛りつけていただく。

■DIRECTIONS

1 Wash the taros well, cut off the top and bottom parts, and peel vertically in 6 strokes (*roppou-muki*). Rub the taros with salt (extra quantity), and rinse. Put the taros and cold water in a pot, and heat. When it comes to the boil, turn down the heat to low, and continue cooking for 3 to 4 min. Drain in a sieve, and rinse to remove the slime.

2 String the snow peas, and put in boiling salty water (extra quantity of salt) to boil.

3 Put the taros and the stock in a pot. When it comes to the boil, turn down the heat, cover the taros with a drop lid, and simmer for about 10 min. Put the seasonings of **A** in the listed order, and continue simmering for 7 to 8 min to allow the taros to absorb the seasonings.

里いもの煮っころがし
Taro Tumbles

■材料・4人分

里いも	400g
だし汁	1カップ
酒	大さじ1と1/2
みりん	大さじ1と1/2
砂糖	大さじ3
しょう油	大さじ1と1/2
黄ゆず	適宜

■ Ingredients (serves 4)

14 oz taros
4/5 U.S. cup stock
1 1/2 Tbsps *sake*
1 1/2 Tbsps *mirin* sweet cooking *sake*
3 Tbsps sugar
1 1/2 Tbsps soy sauce
Yellow-colored *yuzu* rind

【作り方】

1 里いもは水で洗い皮をむく。

2 鍋にだし汁、酒、みりん、砂糖、しょう油と**1**の里いもを入れて煮る。

3 **2**の里いもがやわらかくなったら鍋をゆすって転がしながら煮詰める。

4 里いもを器に盛り、黄ゆずの皮をおろし金でおろして上に散らす。

【DIRECTIONS】

1 Wash the taros in cold water, and peel.

2 Place the stock, *sake*, *mirin*, sugar, soy sauce and taros in a pot, and simmer.

3 When the taros in the pot become tender, shake the pot while still simmering so that the taros tumble around.

4 Arrange the taros in a bowl, and sprinkle over the grated yellow-colored *yuzu* rind.

4 Arrange the taros in a serving dish, and garnish with the snow peas.

里いものみそ煮

煮汁がからみあった里いも、長ねぎと鶏ひき肉がよく合うおかず

about **25** min

Simmered Taros in *Miso*

Taros, *naga-negi* onion, and ground chicken go well in *miso*

■材料・2人分

里いも	4〜5個（200g）
長ねぎ	1本
しょうが	1片
鶏ひき肉	80g
ししとう	6本
サラダ油	大さじ1
だし汁	1/2カップ

A
酒	大さじ1
砂糖	大さじ1
みそ	大さじ1
みりん	大さじ1
しょう油	小さじ1

B
片栗粉	大さじ1/2
水	大さじ1

Ingredients (serves 2)

4 - 5 taros (7 oz)
1 *naga-negi* onion
1 knob ginger
2 4/5 oz ground chicken
6 *shishitou* bell peppers
1 Tbsp vegetable oil
2/5 U.S. cup stock

A
1 Tbsp *sake*
1 Tbsp sugar
1 Tbsp *miso*
1 Tbsp *mirin* sweet cooking *sake*
1 tsp soy sauce

B
1/2 Tbsp starch powder
1 Tbsp water

■作り方

1 里いもはよく洗い、上下を切り落として、縦に6等分になるように切ってから皮をむき鍋に水と入れてゆで、煮立ったら約4〜5分弱火で煮立てざるに上げておく。

2 長ねぎは3cmの長さに切り、しょうがはみじん切りにしておく。

3 鍋にサラダ油を熱し、**2**のしょうがと鶏ひき肉を炒め、ぽろぽろになってきたら**2**の長ねぎと**1**の里い

もを加えて炒め合わせ、ししとうを加える。

4 全体に油がまわったらだし汁と混ぜ合わせた**A**を入れて煮込み、煮汁が少なくなってきたら**B**で水溶き片栗粉を作り、回しかければ出来上がり。

■DIRECTIONS

1 Wash the taros well, and cut off the top and bottom parts. Cut lengthwise into 6 equal pieces, and peel. Put the taros in cold water, and boil. When it comes to the boil, turn down the heat to low, boil for 4 to 5 more min, and drain in a sieve.

2 Cut the *naga-negi* onion into 1 1/5-inch lengths. Finely chop the ginger.

3 Heat the vegetable oil in a pan, and stir-fry the chopped ginger and the ground chicken. When the chicken becomes loose and crumbly, add the cut *naga-negi* onion and the taros, stir-fry further, and add the *shishitou* bell peppers.

4 When the surface of the ingredients absorbs the oil, add the mixture of the stock and **A**, and simmer. When the amount of the liquid is reduced, pour the mixture of **B** in a circular motion.

コラム
Column

里いもの種類
Kinds of Taros

私たちがスーパーなどでよく見かけ、里いもといっているのは、きぬかつぎなどに使用する小型の石川小芋、その小芋より大きい石川早生、関東地方で多く栽培されている土垂のことだろう。

また、近年関東地方のスーパーなどでもよく見かけるようになった、京都野菜のひとつに数えられるえびいもや、たけのこいも（京いも）がある。えびいもはえびのように曲がっているのが名の由来で、えびいもと棒たらとを煮た〝いも棒〟という料理などによく使われる。

たけのこいも（京いも）
Takenoko-imo (Kyo-imo)

The kinds of taros commonly available at supermarkets are "*Ishikawa koimo*," small taros often used for *kinukatsugi*, or boiled taros; "*Ishikawa-wase*," larger than "*Ishikawa koimo*"; and "*dotare*," which is commonly grown in the Kanto region.
Recently, "*ebi-imo*," a Kyoto-brand vegetable, and "*takenoko-imo (Kyo-imo)*" have become available in supermarkets recently in Kanto.
"*Ebi-imo*" is so called because it bends like "*ebi*" or shrimp. "*Ebi-imo*" is often cooked with dried cod, or "*bou tara*." This dish is called "*imo-bou*."

きぬかつぎ

about **15** min

皮に包まれた白い身のねっとりした食感が美味しい

Kinukatsugi Boiled Taros
White flesh of taros with the skin is sticky and good

■材料・2人分

里いも（小粒）	6個
ゆず皮	少々
黒ごま	少々
塩	少々

▓ Ingredients (serves 2)

6 taros (small)
Small quantity of *yuzu* Japanese lime rind
Small quantity of black sesame seeds
Small quantity of salt

■作り方

1 里いもは皮をよく洗い、皮の3分の1あたりに包丁で**切込み**を一周ぐるりと入れる。

2 蒸気の上がった蒸し器で、**1**の里いもをやわらかくなるまで**強火**で蒸す。

3 ゆず皮をせん切りにする。

4 **2**の里いもがやわらかくなったら、キッチンペーパーなどにくるんで上の3分の1皮をむき、せん切りにした**3**のゆず皮と黒ごまを散らして、塩をつけていただく。

■DIRECTIONS

1 Wash the taros well, and make a shallow cut at about 1/3-inch from the top.

2 Heat the steamer. When steam starts to escape, add the taros, and steam over a high heat until soft.

3 Cut the *yuzu* rind into julienne strips.

4 Wrap the softened taros in kitchen paper, and peel the top 1/3 part. Sprinkle on the cut *yuzu* rind and the black sesame seeds, and serve with salt.

コラム
Column

きぬかつぎの由来
The Origin of *Kinukatsugi*

きぬかつぎとはけっして里いもの種類の名前ではなく、小粒の里いも(石川小芋など)の皮の3分の1を切り取って、蒸した料理のことである。

きぬかつぎとは、平安時代の身分の高い女性が外出する時に1枚の布や単小袖をかぶったことを衣被(きぬかず、かずき)と呼んでいた。

この衣被をかぶった様子に、里いものきぬかつぎ(上部の皮をむいて白くなっている)が似ていることから名づけられたのが、きぬかつぎの由来である。

小粒の里いも
Small taros

Kinukatsugi is not the name of a taro species, but a steamed dish of small taros (*Ishikawa-koimo* and other kinds), with its top 1/3 part peeled.

The term *kinukatsugi* came from "*kinukazu*," or "*kazuki*," which was a practice among noblewomen in the Heian Era of covering their heads with a piece of cloth or a type of *kimono* called *hitoe-kosode* when they went out.

The *kinukatsugi* taros with their heads peeled white were likened to noblewomen wearing cloth on their head. This is the origin of the term *kinukatsugi*.

ごぼうとれんこんのそぼろ煮

滋味深いごぼうとれんこんの風味と歯ごたえがたまらなく美味しい

Simmered Burdock and Lotus Root with Ground Beef

The daintiness of burdock and the flavor and crispy texture of lotus root make this dish irresistibly good

■材料・2人分

ごぼう	…………	1/2本
れんこん	…………	1/2節
牛ひき肉	…………	約80g
ごま油	…………	小さじ2
だし汁	…………	1/2カップ
A [酒	…………	大さじ1
砂糖	…………	大さじ1
B [しょう油	…………	大さじ1
みりん	…………	大さじ1

▥ Ingredients (serves 2)

1/2 burdock
1/2 lotus root
About 2 4/5 oz ground beef
2 tsps sesame oil
2/5 U.S. cup stock

A [1 Tbsp *sake*
1 Tbsp sugar

B [1 Tbsp soy sauce
1 Tbsp *mirin* sweet cooking *sake*

■作り方

1 ごぼうは包丁で皮をこそいで斜め切りにして水にさらし、れんこんは乱切りにして水にさらし、ざるに上げて水けをきる。

2 鍋にごま油を熱し、**1**のごぼうとれんこんを入れて炒め、油がまわったら牛ひき肉を入れて炒め合せる。

3 **2**のひき肉の色が変わったらだし汁を入れ、ひと煮立したら**A**を加えて落としぶたをして煮込み、**B**を加えてさらに弱火で煮ふくめる。

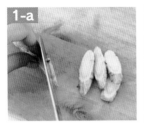
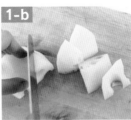

■DIRECTIONS

1 Scrape off the skin of the burdock with a kitchen knife and slice diagonally. Soak in water, and drain in a sieve. Cut the lotus root into wedges while rolling it, soak in water, and drain in a sieve.

2 Heat the sesame oil in a pot, and stir-fry the drained burdock and lotus. When the surface of the ingredients has absorbed oil, add the ground beef, and stir-fry.

3 When the color of the ground beef has changed, add the stock, bring it to the boil, and add **A**. Cover the ingredients with a drop lid, simmer, add **B**, and continue simmering over a low heat until the ingredients absorb the seasoned stock.

コラム
Column

ごぼうとれんこんの栄養と効能
Nutrients and Efficacy of Burdock and Lotus Roots

ごぼうには他の野菜に比べて栄養はあまり豊富ではないが、食物繊維、炭水化物のイヌリンを多く含んでいる。食物繊維は便秘を解消してくれたり、改善してくれるため、コレステロールやガンの原因になる有害物質を排泄してくれる働きもある。イヌリンは血糖値の上昇を抑えるため糖尿病に効果があるし、腎臓の機能を高める働きがある。

れんこんは食物繊維、ビタミンC、カリウム、ムチンなどを含んでいる。食物繊維はごぼうと同じ働きをする。ビタミンCは免疫力を高めてくれるため、疲労回復などの効果や風邪予防、美肌効果がある。カリウムは塩分を体外に排出するのを助けてくれるため、高血圧の人はすすんでとりたいものだ。

れんこん
Lotus Roots

ごぼう
Burdock

Though not as nutritious as many other vegetables, burdock contain a high amount of dietary fiber and inulin, a kind of carbo-hydrate. Dietary fiber helps relieve or ease constipation, thus excretes cholesterol and harmful cancer-causing substances. Inulin prevents the blood sugar level from rising, and is thus effective against diabetes. It also helps to enhance kidney functions.

Lotus roots contain dietary fiber, Vitamin C, potassium, and mucin. Dietary fiber is effective as mentioned above. Vitamin C enhances immunity, and is thus effective for relieving fatigue, preventing colds, and making the skin beautiful. Potassium helps to eliminate saline matter, therefore, is recommended for those with high blood pressure.

きのこのバター炒め

about **10** min

秋の味覚を代表するきのこをバターでさっと炒めより美味しくいただく

Butter Sautéed Mushrooms

Enjoy mushrooms, autumnal delicacies, simply sautéed in butter

■ 材料・2人分

しめじ	……………1/2パック
しいたけ	……………2個
エリンギ	……………1本
長ねぎ	……………1/2本
にんにく	……………1片
オリーブ油	………大さじ1
バター	……………15g
塩・黒こしょう	………少々
白ワイン	………大さじ2
砂糖	……………小さじ1/2
レモン汁	……………小さじ1
イタリアンパセリ	……少々

▓ Ingredients (serves 2)

1/2 pack *shimeji*
mushrooms
2 *shiitake* mushrooms
1 king oyster mushroom
1/2 *naga-negi* onion
1 clove garlic
1 Tbsp olive oil
1/2 oz butter
Small quantity of salt and
black pepper
2 Tbsps white wine
1/2 tsp sugar
1 tsp lemon juice
Small quantity of flat-leaf
parsley

■作り方

1 しめじ、しいたけ、エリンギは根元を切り、しめじは小房に分け、しいたけは十字に切り、エリンギは半分の長さに切って薄切りに、長ねぎは斜め薄切りに、にんにくは薄切りにする。

2 フライパンにオリーブ油、バターと1のにんにくを入れて加熱し、香りがしてきたら1の長ねぎを入れて炒め、全体に油がまわったら、1のしめじ、しいたけ、エリンギを入れて炒め合わせ、塩・黒こしょうをし、白ワインと砂糖を入れてアルコールをとばすように煮立たせたら、レモン汁をふり入れて火を止め、皿に盛りつけ、イタリアンパセリを添える。

■ DIRECTIONS

1 Remove the bottom part of the *shimeji*, *shiitake* and king oyster mushrooms. Separate the *shimeji* into small portions. Cut the *shiitake* into 4 pieces. Cut the king oyster in half crosswise, and slice thinly. Cut the *naga-negi* onion diagonally. Thinly slice the garlic.

2 Heat the olive oil and butter in a frying pan, and put in the garlic. When the aroma of the garlic begins to rise, add the cut *naga-negi* onion. When the surface of the onion has absorbed the oil, stir-fry the cut *shimeji*, *shiitake* and king oyster, and sprinkle with the salt and black pepper. Add the white wine and sugar, and bring to the boil to allow the alcohol to evaporate. Pour over the lemon juice, and turn off the heat. Arrange in a serving dish, and garnish with the parsley.

きのこのバターホイル蒸し

Mushrooms with Butter Steamed in Foil Wrap

■材料・2人分

しいたけ	3枚
エリンギ	2本
えのき	1/2束
しめじ	1/2パック
バター	大さじ2
塩・こしょう	適量
白ワイン	小さじ2
万能ねぎ	適量
レモン	適量
しょう油	適量

■ Ingredients (serves 1)

3 *shiitake* mushrooms
2 king oyster mushrooms
1/2 bundle *enokidake* mushrooms
1/2 pack *shimeji* mushrooms
2 Tbsps butter
Salt and pepper
2 tsps white wine
Bannou-negi onion
Lemon
Soy sauce

【作り方】

1 しいたけとエリンギは、包丁で軸に十字に切れ目を入れ、指で4つくらいに裂く。えのきとしめじは石突きを取り小房にわける。万能ねぎは小口切りに、レモンはくし切りにする。

2 アルミホイルに1のきのこ類をのせる。軽く塩こしょうし、バターをのせ、白ワインをふって、アルミを閉じ、グリルかオーブントースターで焼く。

3 中に熱が入ったらアルミを開け、1の万能ねぎを散らし、レモンのくし切りを添える。お好みでしょう油をたらしていただく。

[DIRECTIONS]

1 Put a shallow crosscut on the *shiitake* and king oyster mushrooms with a kitchen knife, and tear with fingers into about 4 pieces. Cut off the bottom part of the *enokidake* and *shimeji* mushrooms, and separate into small portions. Cut the *bannou-negi* onion into small rounds. Cut the lemon into wedges.

2 Put all the mushrooms prepared in **1** on an aluminum foil sheet, sprinkle with salt and pepper, add the butter, and sprinkle over the wine. Close the foil wrapper, and grill in a griller or toaster oven.

3 When the ingredients are cooked, open the foil wrapper, sprinkle with the cut *bannou-negi* onion, and garnish with the lemon wedge. Add soy sauce if you like.

さんまの塩焼き
秋を代表する脂ののったさんまを定番の塩焼きでいただく

Salt Grilled Saury
Enjoy salt-grilled *sanma* saury, a standard way of cooking oil-rich sauries, a typical autumnal delicacy

■ 材料・1人分

さんま	1尾
塩	適量
大根おろし	適量
すだち	1/2個

▓ Ingredients (serves 1)

Sanma saury
Salt
Grated *daikon* giant white radish
1/2 *sudachi* citrus

■作り方

1 さんまは水洗いする。

2 1のさんまの水けをペーパータオルなどでふき取り、飾り包丁を入れ、各ヒレに化粧塩をする。
※尾はアルミホイルで包むと、焦げずにきれいに仕上がる。

3 グリルをよく熱し、盛りつける側（手前から見て頭が左）から焼く。6〜7割火が通ったら、裏返して中火で焼く。

4 3のさんまを器に盛り、大根おろし、すだちを添える。

焼き網やグリルにさんまが入らない場合は、さんまの各ヒレに化粧塩をしてから中央から切り、焼く方法もある。

If the fish is too long for the grill, cut in half after applying salt (kesho-jio) to the fins.

■DIRECTIONS

1 Rinse the saury.

2 Paper-dry the fish, make shallow decorative cuts on its body, and apply salt to the fins to prevent them from scorching (kesho-jio).
※ If wrapped with aluminum foil, the tail will cook nicely.

3 Heat a grill well, and grill first the side of the fish that faces up when served. (The head is on the diner's left side.) When the saury is about 60 to 70 percent done, turn it over, and grill the other side on medium heat.

4 Arrange the fish on a serving dish, and garnish with the grated *daikon* radish and *sudachi* citrus.

あじの塩焼き
Salt Grilled Horse Mackerel

■材料・1人分

真あじ	1尾
塩	適量
はじかみ	1本

■Ingredients (serves 1)

1 horse mackerel
Salt
Sweet-vinegared ginger stick

【作り方】

1 P290の真あじの塩焼き用を参照して、下処理をする。

2 1の真あじの各ヒレに化粧塩をする。
※尾はアルミホイルで包むと、焦げずにきれいに仕上がる。

3 グリルをよく熱し、盛りつける側（手前から見て頭が左）から焼く。6〜7割火が通ったら、裏返して中火で焼く。

4 3の真あじを器に盛り、はじかみを添える。

【DIRECTIONS】

1 Prepare the fish. (See p.290 for the preparation of salt-grilled horse mackerel.)

2 Apply salt to the fins to prevent them from scorching (kesho-jio).
※ If wrapped with aluminum foil, the tail will cook nicely.

3 Heat a grill well, and grill first the side of the fish that faces up when served. (The head is on the diner's left.) When the fish is about 60 to 70 percent done, turn it over, and grill the other side on medium heat.

4 Arrange the horse mackerel on a serving dish, and garnish with the sweet vinegared ginger stick.

さんまの有馬煮
ありまに

about **25** min

脂ののったさんまにピリッとした実山椒の相性が最高

Simmered Saury, *Arima-ni* Style

Fat-rich saury goes perfectly with the pleasant tingling sensations of *sansho* Japanese pepper grains

<table>
<tr><td>

■材料・2人分

さんま ・・・・・・・・・・・・・・・・・・・・・・・・・・・・・・2尾
しょうが ・・・・・・・・・・・・・・・・・・・・・・・・・・・1片

	水	50cc
	酒	50cc
A	酢	大さじ1
	砂糖	大さじ1
	しょう油	大さじ1

実山椒の佃煮 (市販品) ・・・・・・・・・・・・小さじ2
木の芽 ・・・・・・・・・・・・・・・・・・・・・・・・・・・・・・適宜

</td><td>

Ingredients (serves 2)

2 sauries
1 knob ginger

	1/5 U.S. cup water
	1/5 U.S. cup *sake*
A	1 Tbsp vinegar
	1 Tbsp sugar
	1 Tbsp soy sauce

Misansho no tsukudani, soy-sauce simmered *sansho* Japanese pepper grains (available in stores)
Kinome young leaves of *sansho*

</td></tr>
</table>

1 さんまはうろこを取り、頭と尾を切り取り、約4～5cmの筒切りにする。内蔵を取り出し、水洗いしてペーパータオルなどでよく水けをふき取る。

2 しょうがは皮をむき、せん切りにする。

3 鍋に**2**のしょうがと**A**を入れて煮立たせ、**1**のさんまを加えて再度煮立たせアクを取る。

4 **3**に実山椒の佃煮を加え、落としぶたをして中弱火で約15分煮込む。器に盛り、木の芽を添える。

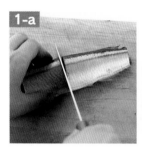
1-a

1-b

■DIRECTIONS

1 Scale the sauries. Cut off the head and tail, and cut the body into 1 1/2 to 2-inch long round pieces. Remove the guts, rinse, and paper-dry well.

2 Peel the ginger, and cut into julienne strips.

3 Put the cut ginger and the ingredients of **A** into a pot, and bring the liquid to the boil. Put in the saury prepared in **1**, bring it to the boil again, and skim off the foam.

4 Add the *sansho* grains, cover the fish with a drop lid, and simmer on a medium-low heat for about 15 min. Arrange in a serving dish, and garnish with the young *sansho* leaves.

コラム
Column

有馬煮って何？
What is "*Arima-ni*," or *Arima*-ni Style Simmered Dish?

有馬煮とは実山椒を使って食材を煮る料理法のこと。甘辛く佃煮風に炊いたものが多い。

昔、兵庫県の有馬地方(神戸市にありながら、六甲山の北側に位置しているため、山深く、自然が豊富な地で知られている) が山椒の産地だったことが、有馬煮の由来である。実山椒と一緒に材料を煮ることによって、日持ちがする保存食となったのだろう。

さんま、いわしなどの魚類はもちろんのこと、肉類の有馬煮、実山椒だけの有馬煮をつかった有馬煮ご飯などがある。

実山椒　*Misansho*

"*Arima-ni*," is a way of cooking ingredients with *sansho* grains, often simmered with sugar and soy sauce like *tsukudani* preserved food.

The name "Arima" comes from the Arima area in Hyogo Prefecture, which used to be a production center of *sansho*. (Although the area is part of the major city of Kobe, it is located on the northern side of Mt. Rokko and has a mountainous, rich natural environment) People probably made preserved food by simmering ingredients with *sansho* grains.

Ingredients for *Arima-ni* include fish such as sauries and sardines, as well as various meats. *Arima-ni* rice uses only *sansho* grains.

about **25** min

いわしの梅煮
いわしのくさみを梅干しがおさえてくれて滋味溢れる味に

Simmered Sardines with Pickled Plums
Pickled plums reduce sardine's distinctive odor, and make this dish savory

■ 材料・2人分

真いわし	……………………………	4尾
梅干し	……………………………	2個

A
水	……………………………	50cc
酒	……………………………	50cc
砂糖	……………………………	大さじ1
みりん	……………………………	大さじ1/2
しょう油	……………………………	大さじ1と1/2

しょうが（薄切り）	……………	4枚
大葉	……………………………	4枚

Ingredients (serves 2)

4 sardines
2 *umeboshi* pickled plums

A
1/5 U.S. cup water
1/5 U.S. cup *sake*
1 Tbsp sugar
1/2 Tbsp *mirin* sweet cooking *sake*
1 1/2 Tbsps soy sauce

4 slices of ginger
4 green perilla leaves

■作り方

1 真いわしはうろこを包丁でこそげ取り、頭と尾を切り取り、腹わたを取って、血合いなどを水で洗い、水けをペーパータオルでふく。

2 水洗いした大葉は、せん切りにする。

3 梅干しは楊枝で数カ所に穴をあけておく。鍋に梅干しとA、しょうがの薄切りを入れ、煮立ったら1を入れ、落としぶたをして弱めの中火で約15分煮る。

4 器に3の真いわし、梅干しを盛りつけ、2の大葉のせん切りを添える。

1-a
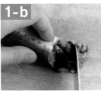
1-b

■DIRECTIONS

1 Scrape off the scales of the sardines with a kitchen knife. Cut off the head and tail, gut, and rinse the dark-colored part. Paper-dry the fish.

2 Rinse the green perilla leaves, and cut into julienne strips.

3 Prick several holes on the surface of the plums with a tooth pick. Put into a pot the plums, add the ingredients of **A**, and ginger slices. When it comes to the boil, add the fish, cover with a drop lid, and simmer over a low-medium heat for about 15 min.

4 Arrange the fish and plums on a serving dish, and garnish with the strips of green perilla leaves.

さんまの梅煮
Simmered Sauries with Pickled Plums

■材料・2人分

さんま		2尾
梅干し		2個
A	水	50cc
	酒	50cc
	砂糖	大さじ1
	みりん	大さじ1/2
	しょう油	大さじ1と1/2
しょうが		適量
針しょうが		適量

■ Ingredients (serves 2)

2 sauries
2 *umeboshi* pickled plums

A
- 1/5 U.S. cup water
- 1/5 U.S. cup *sake*
- 1 Tbsp sugar
- 1/2 Tbsp *mirin* sweet cooking *sake*
- 1 1/2 Tbsps soy sauce

Ginger
Ginger needles

【作り方】

1 さんまはうろこを包丁などで取り、水洗いしたら4～5cm長さの筒切りにし、内蔵を取り出し、洗ってよく水けを取る。

2 鍋に梅干し（楊枝でつついておく）とA、薄切りのしょうがを入れ、煮立ったら1を入れ、落としぶたをして弱めの中火で約15分煮る。

3 2のさんまを盛りつけて、針しょうがを添える。

【DIRECTIONS】

1 Scale the sauries with a kitchen knife, and rinse. Cut off the head and tail, and cut the body into 1 1/2 to 2-inch long round pieces. Remove the guts, rinse, and paper-dry well.

2 Put into a pot the pickled plums (pricked with a toothpick), add the ingredients of **A**, and the sliced ginger. When it comes to the boil, put in the fish, cover with a drop lid, and simmer over a low-medium heat for 15 to 20 min.

3 Arrange the fish in a serving dish, garnishing with the ginger needles.

さばのおろし煮

about **30** min

大根おろしで揚げたさばが、さっぱりと食べられる

Simmered Mackerel with Grated *Daikon*

Grated giant white radish lightens the taste of the fried mackerel

■材料・2人分

さば	……………………………	半身

A	しょう油	………………………	小さじ2
	酒	…………………………	小さじ1
	みりん	………………………	小さじ1
	しょうが汁	……………………	小さじ1/2

片栗粉	……………………………	適量
揚げ油（サラダ油）	……………	適量

B	だし汁	………………………	100cc
	酒	…………………………	大さじ1/2
	しょう油	……………………	小さじ1

三つ葉	……………………………	4本
大根おろし	………………………	1/4カップ

■ Ingredients (serves 2)

1 fillet mackerel

A	2 tsps soy sauce
	1 tsp *sake*
	1 tsp *mirin* sweet cooking *sake*
	1/2 tsp ginger juice

Starch powder
Frying oil (vegetable oil)

B	2/5 U.S. cup stock
	1/2 Tbsp *sake*
	1 tsp soy sauce

4 trefoil stalks
1/5 U.S. cup grated *daikon* giant white radish

■作り方

1 さばはそぎ切りにし、**A**を合わせた中に入れ、もみ込んで約20〜30分漬ける。汁けをペーパータオルなどでふき取り、片栗粉をまぶして、170℃に熱した揚げ油でカラリと揚げる。

2 三つ葉は水洗いし、約1.5cmのざく切りにする。

3 鍋に**B**を入れて熱し、煮立ったら大根おろし、**1**を加えて温める。

4 **3**を器に盛り、**2**の三つ葉を散らす。

1-a

1-b

■DIRECTIONS

1 Shave the mackerel, add the mixture of **A**, rub, and marinate for 20 to 30 min. Paper-dry, dust with starch powder, and fry in 340˚F oil until crisp.

2 Rinse the trefoil, and cut into 1/2-inch lengths.

3 Put the ingredients listed in **B** into a pot, and heat. When it comes to the boil, put in the grated radish and the fried mackerel, and warm.

4 Arrange the fish in a serving dish, and sprinkle over the cut trefoil.

さばのみそ煮
Simmered Mackerel in *Miso*

■材料・2人分

さば	半身
長ねぎ	1/2本

A
水	200cc
酒	150cc
砂糖	大さじ2
みりん	大さじ2

しょうが（薄切り）	4枚
みそ	大さじ3

■ Ingredients (serves 2)

1 fillet mackerel
1/2 *naga-negi* onion

A
- 4/5 U.S. cup water
- 3/5 U.S. cup *sake*
- 2 Tbsps sugar
- 2 Tbsps *mirin* sweet cooking *sake*

4 thin slices ginger
3 Tbsps *miso*

【作り方】

1 さばの半身は、1枚を2つに切り、それぞれ飾り包丁を入れる。それを平ざるにのせ、熱湯を回しかけ霜降りにする。
※魚の生ぐさみが取れ、旨味を閉じこめることができるので、必ず霜降りにすること。

2 長ねぎは根もとを切り、約4cmのぶつ切りにしてグリル（またはトースター、フライパン）で焼いて、焼きめをつける。

3 鍋に**A**としょうがの薄切りを加えて火にかけ、煮立ったら**1**を入れ落としぶたをして中火で約10分煮る。
※必ず煮汁が沸騰してから魚を入れましょう。煮汁が沸騰していないと、魚の生ぐさみが出てしまうので注意したい。

4 **3**にみそを溶き入れ、**2**の長ねぎを加えて弱火でとろみがつくまで煮る。

5 **4**のさばと長ねぎを器に盛り、鍋に残ったみそをかける。

[DIRECTIONS]

1 Cut the mackerel fillet in half, and make decorative cuts on the skin surface of each piece. Place the fish on a flat basket, and pour hot water over the fish in a circular motion to blanch.
※Make sure to blanch the fish, as the process removes the fishy odor, whilst retaining the delicious *umami* taste.

2 Cut off the bottom part of the *naga-negi* onion, and cut into 1 1/2-inch lengths. Heat in a grill (or a toaster oven, or a frying pan) until partially brown.

3 Put into a pot the ingredients of **A** and the sliced ginger, and heat. When it comes to the boil, put in the fish, cover with a drop lid, and simmer over a medium heat for about 10 min.
※Do not add the fish until after the liquid comes to the boil. Otherwise, a fishy odor will remain.

4 Put in the *miso* while mixing with the liquid, add the cut *naga-negi* onion, and simmer over a low heat until the liquid thickens.

5 Arrange the fish and *naga-negi* onion on a serving dish, and pour the remaining liquid into the pot.

いわしのチーズ磯辺揚げ

のりの香りがいわしを包み、美味しいおつまみにしてくれる

Isobe-Age Fried Sardine with Cheese and *Nori*

The flavor of *nori* toasted seaweed envelops the sardine, making a tasty snack

■材料・2人分

真いわし	4尾
スライスチーズ	4〜5枚
のり	1枚
A ┌ 小麦粉	60g
└ 卵黄1個＋冷水	合わせて120cc
小麦粉	適量
塩・こしょう	適量
揚げ油（サラダ油）	適量
抹茶塩（抹茶：塩＝2：1で合わせる）	適量

Ingredients (serves 2)

4 sardines
4-5 piece of sliced cheese
1 sheet *nori* toasted seaweed

A ┌ 2 oz flour
└ 1/2 U.S. cup mixture of an egg yolk and chilled water

Flour
Salt and pepper
Frying oil (vegetable oil)
Tea-salt mixture (mix powdered green tea and salt at a ratio of 2:1)

■作り方

1 真いわしは三枚おろし（P291の真あじのさばき方参照）にし、軽く塩・こしょうする。

2 1のいわしの大きさに合わせ1/2〜1/3に切ったスライスチーズをのせ、くるくると巻く。さらに1枚を8等分に細長く切ったのりで巻く。

3 Aを合わせて天ぷら衣を作る。2に薄く小麦粉をまぶし、衣をつけて、170℃の揚げ油でカラリと揚げる。

4 3を器に盛り、抹茶塩を添える。

2-a

2-b

■ DIRECTIONS

1 Fillet the sardines. (See p.291, it's the same method for filleting a horse mackerel.) Lightly sprinkle with salt and pepper.

2 Cut the sliced cheese into 2 or 3 to fit the size of the sardine fillets. Place the cheese on the sardine, and roll up. Wind *nori* seaweed, which has been cut into 8 equal-size strips, around the roll.

3 Mix the ingredients of **A** to make the batter. Dust the rolls with the flour, apply the batter, and deep-fry at 340°F until crisp.

4 Arrange the fried rolls on a serving dish, and serve with the tea-salt mixture.

コラム
Column

磯辺ってどんな意味？
What Does *Isobe* Mean?

のりを食材に巻いて揚げるか、焼いた料理を磯辺という。この磯辺はのりの磯の香りからきているのだろう。

紹介しているレシピはいわしを使用しているが、さんま、真あじ、さばなどでもよく合う。また、大和いもをすったものをのりで包み、油でからりと揚げると、のりはパリッ、中身はトロッとしてなんとも美味しい。

よく屋台で売っている角餅をやわらかく焼いて、しょう油で味つけしたものをのりで包んだ磯辺焼きも、しょう油の焼ける香りとのりの風味がたまらなく美味しく、忘れられない日本の味である。

さば
Mackerel

真あじ
Horse mackerel

Ingredients wound with *nori* toasted seaweed and fried, or grilled are called "*isobe*," meaning seashore. The name probably comes from the flavor of *nori*, which is reminiscent of the smell of the sea.

This recipe involves sardines, but sauries, horse mackerels, or mackerels are also good. Ground yam wrapped with *nori* and fried crisp is also very good, with the crispness of *nori*, and the viscosity of the yam inside.

Isobe-yaki, rectangular rice cakes grilled soft, flavored with soy sauce, and wrapped with *nori*, is a popular food bought from street stalls. With the mouth-watering flavor of grilled soy sauce and *nori*, *Isobe-yaki* has an unforgettable Japanese taste.

かわはぎの肝あえ

濃厚な味の肝に新鮮なかわはぎの身がからんで美味しい

Marinated *Kawahagi* with Liver Sauce

The fresh flesh of *kawahagi*, or thread-sail filefish, marinated with the rich-flavor liver sauce is delicious

■材料・2人分

かわはぎ（刺身用、三枚におろしたもの）
·····························1尾
かわはぎの肝 ···················適量
万能ねぎ ·······················1本
すだち ·························適宜
ぽん酢しょう油 ··················適量

■ Ingredients (serves 2)

1 *kawahagi*, thread-sail filefish (filleted for *sashimi*)
Liver of *kawahagi*
1 *bannou-negi* onion
Sudachi citrus
Ponzu soy sauce (citrus-juice-mixed soy sauce)

■作り方

1 かわはぎのおろし身の薄皮を包丁で、そぎ取る。万能ねぎは水洗いし、小口切りにする。すだちは薄い輪切りにする。

※かわはぎを薄造りや肝あえにする場合は、薄皮を取らないと食感が悪くなるので注意したい。

2 1のかわはぎの身を細造りにする。かわはぎの肝はさっと水洗いし、穴あき玉じゃくしにのせ、そのまま熱湯にくぐらせて霜降りにする。

3 2のかわはぎの肝の水けをキッチンペーパーなどでふき取り、包丁でたたきボウルに入れ、2の細造りの身と軽くあえる。

4 3を器に盛り、1の万能ねぎの小口切りをふり、1のすだちの輪切りを添える。ぽん酢しょう油をかけていただく。

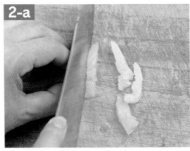
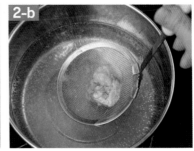

■DIRECTIONS

1 Shave off the filmy skin of the *kawahagi* fillets with a kitchen knife. Rinse the *bannou-negi* onion, and cut into small rounds. Thinly slice the *sudachi* citrus.

※ When making thin-sliced *sashimi* or the liver-marinated dish of *kawahagi*, remove the filmy skin. Otherwise, the texture would be ruined.

2 Cut the fish into narrow strips. Rinse the liver, put on a punched ladle to blanch briefly in hot water and then dip in cold water.

3 Paper-dry the liver, chop with a kitchen knife, and lightly marinate with the fish in a bowl.

4 Arrange the mixture on a serving dish, sprinkle with cut *bannou-negi* onion, and garnish with the sliced *sudachi*. Pour the *ponzu* soy sauce over the top before eating.

たらこ茶漬け

半生に焼いたたらこと煎茶がベストマッチ

Tea-and-Rice with Cod Roe

Medium-done cod roe and green leaf tea are the best match

塩たらこ	1/2腹
三つ葉	適量
煎茶	適量
ご飯	茶碗2杯

■作り方

1 塩たらこは、熱したグリルで表面をさっとあぶり、一口大に切る。

2 三つ葉は水洗いし、ざく切りにする。

3 茶碗にご飯を盛り、**1**の塩たらこと**2**の三つ葉をのせ、熱々の煎茶をたっぷりかけていただく。

■ Ingredients (serves 2)

1/2 salted cod roe
Trefoil stalks
Green leaf tea
2 rice bowls cooked rice

▌DIRECTIONS

1 Briefly grill the surface of the salted cod roe in a heated grill, and cut into bite-size pieces.

2 Rinse the trefoil, and cut coarsely.

3 Put the rice in a rice bowl, place the cut cod roe and trefoil, and pour plenty of hot green tea over the top.

のり茶漬け

焼きのりとわさびがたまらなく美味しい

about **4** min

Tea-and-Rice with *Nori* Seaweed

A combination of toasted *nori* and wasabi are simply delicious

■材料・2人分

焼きのり	1/2枚
わさび	適量
あられ（せんべいをくだく）	適量
だし汁	適量
塩	適量
ご飯	茶碗2杯

■作り方

1 焼きのりを細かく刻む。

2 だし汁に塩を加え温める。

3 茶碗にご飯を盛り、**1**の焼きのりとわさび、あられをのせ、**2**の熱々のだし汁をたっぷりかけていただく。

■ Ingredients (serves 2)

1/2 sheet toasted *nori* seaweed
Wasabi
Arare (broken rice cracker)
Stock
Salt
2 rice bowls cooked rice

■ DIRECTIONS

1 Cut the *nori* seaweed into fine pieces.

2 Add the salt to the stock, and heat.

3 Put the rice in a bowl, put the *nori*, *wasabi*, and *arare* on top, and pour plenty of hot stock over the top.

about **60** min

変わりとろろご飯

栄養たっぷりの大和いもをとろろご飯でいただく。飲んだ後のしめに最適

Rice with Seasoned Yam

Enjoy the nutrition-rich yam and rice. Perfect dish after drinking alcoholic beverages

■材料・3人分

米	1.5合
押し麦	50g
水	360cc
大和いも	200g
A だし汁	3/4カップ
薄口しょう油	大さじ1
みりん	大さじ1
大葉	4枚
おくら	2本
芝漬け	20g

■ Ingredients (serves 3)

1 1/8 U.S. cups rice
1 3/4 oz pressed barley
1 1/2 U.S. cups water
7 oz yam

A ┌ 3/5 U.S. cup stock
　│ 1 Tbsp light soy sauce
　└ 1 Tbsp *mirin* sweet cooking *sake*

4 green perilla leaves
2 pods okra
2/3 oz *shibazuke* pickles

■作り方

1 米と押し麦を合わせてとぎ、炊飯器に入れて水を加え、約30分吸水させてから炊く。
※炊き方はP260・261参照

2 鍋にAを入れて、ひと煮立ちさせて冷ましておく。

3 大和いもの皮をむき、酢水（分量外）につけてからすり鉢ですりおろし、**2**を少しずつ加え、なめらかになるようにすりのばす。

※酢水に皮をむいた大和いもをつけることによって、変色を防ぐ。

4 大葉は角切り、おくらは塩（分量外）をふって、板ずりをして水洗いしてから小口切り、芝漬けはみじん切りにし、**3**のとろろ汁に混ぜる。

5 小丼に**1**のご飯を盛り、**4**をかけていただく。

■DIRECTIONS

1 Wash the rice and pressed barley together, put in a rice cooker, and add the water. After leaving it for about 30 min to allow the grains to absorb water, cook.
(※ See p.260 and 261 for "How to Prepare Boiled Rice.")

2 Put the ingredients of **A** into a pot, bring it to the boil, and let it cool.

3 Peel the yam, soak in vinegared water (extra quantity), and grate in a grinding bowl. Add **A** prepared in **2** a little at a time to mix with the yam using a pestle until smooth.
※ Soaking yam in vinegared water prevents it from turning brown.

4 Cut the green perilla leaves into small squares. Sprinkle salt (extra quantity) on the okra, roll on a cutting board, rinse, and cut into small rounds. Chop the *shibazuke* pickles finely. Mix the cut perilla leaves, okura, and *shibazuke* pickles with the grated yam.

5 Put the rice in a small bowl, and pour the mixture of **4**.

about
25
min

薩摩汁
さつまじる

鹿児島を代表するさつまいもをはじめとする野菜がたっぷりで、ヘルシーな食べるみそ汁

Miso Soup, *Satsuma-Jiru* Style

Healthy *miso* soup full of vegetables including *Satsuma imo*, sweet potato,
main produce from Kagoshima

■材料・2人分

鶏もも肉	1/2枚
さつまいも	1/4本
ごぼう	1/4本
大根	3cm分
にんじん	3cm分
こんにゃく	1/3枚
だし汁	2と1/2カップ
A 酒	大さじ1
しょう油	大さじ1
みそ	大さじ2と1/2
万能ねぎ	2本

▨ Ingredients (serves 2)

1/2 boneless chicken thigh
1/4 sweet potato
1/4 burdock
1 1/4 inch *daikon* giant white radish
1 1/4 inch carrot
1/3 cake *konnyaku* devil's tongue
2 1/8 U.S. cups stock

A 1 Tbsp *sake*
1 Tbsp soy sauce
2 1/2 Tbsp *miso*

2 *bannou-negi* onions

1 鶏もも肉は余分な脂身を取り除いてそぎ切り、さつまいもは輪切りにして水にさらし、ごぼうは皮を包丁でこそいでからささがきにして水にさらし、それぞれアクを抜いたら水きりしておく。

2 大根は皮をむいていちょう切り、にんじんは皮をむいて半月切りにする。こんにゃくは塩（分量外）でもんで水洗いしたら水からゆでてアクを抜き、スプーンなどで小さくちぎり、万能ねぎは斜め切りにしておく。

3 鍋にだし汁、**1**の鶏もも肉、**2**の大根、にんじん、こんにゃく、**1**のごぼうを入れて煮立たせたら、**1**のさつまいもを加えて弱めの中火にし、アクを取りながら約10分煮込む。

4 **3**の具がやわらかくなってきたら**A**を入れて軽く煮込み、器に盛り、**2**の万能ねぎを散らす。

コラム
Column

薩摩汁の由来
The Origin of *Satsuma-Jiru*

薩摩とは鹿児島県のかつての呼び名で、薩摩汁とは薩摩でよく食べられていた汁のことである。

薩摩では古くから闘鶏が盛んで、その闘鶏で死んだ鶏をつぶして、汁を作っていたのが薩摩汁の由来といわれている。

地元では薩摩鶏、油揚げ、桜島だいこん、ごぼう、にんじん、里いも、ねぎ、しょうがなどの野菜を地みそで煮込んで作られる。

Satsuma is a former name of Kagoshima Prefecture. *Satsuma-jiru* was a popular soup in the region.

In Satsuma, cockfighting has traditionally been popular. Cocks that were killed in the cockfighting were made into a soup dish and eaten by the local people. This is believed to be the origin of *Satsuma-jiru*.

In Kagoshima today, they cook *Satsuma-jiru* by simmering Satsuma chicken, *abura-age* deep-fried *tofu*, and various vegetables (including Sakurajima *daikon* radish, burdock, carrot, taro, green onion, and ginger) with locally-made *miso*.

■DIRECTIONS

1 Remove the excess fat of the chicken. Cut the sweet potato into rounds, and soak in water to remove harshness. Scrape off the skin of the burdock with a kitchen knife, shave, and soak in water to remove harshness. Drain the sweet potato and burdock.

2 Peel the *daikon* radish, and cut into quarter-rounds. Peel the carrot, and cut into half-rounds. Rub the devil's tongue cake with salt (extra quantity), rinse, put in cold water, and bring it to the boil to remove harshness. Use a small spoon to cut the cake into bite-size pieces. Cut the *bannou-negi* onion diagonally.

3 Put into a pot the stock, the cut chicken, *daikon* radish, carrot, devil's tongue, and the burdock, and bring the stock to the boil. Add the cut sweet potato, turn down the heat to low-medium, and cook for about 10 min while skimming off the froth.

4 When the ingredients of **3** become soft, add the ingredients of **A**, and continue heating for a moment. Arrange in a serving bowl, and sprinkle the *bannou-negi* onion over the top.

コラム

Column

〝酒の市〟って何？　〝えべっさん〟って何？
What is *Tori-no-Ichi*? What is *Ebessan*?

　〝酒の市〟とは、金銀財宝を飾った熊手が、運を「かっ込む」、を「はき込む」といわれ、開運招福や商売繁盛を願ったもので、江戸時代から浅草の酉の寺（鷲在山長國寺）、各地の鷲神社、大鳥神社で続く行事である。

　十一月の酉の日（十二支）を祭日として、最初に巡ってくる酉の日を〝一の酉〟といってとくに重んじられた。

　熊手は鷲が獲ものをしっかりと捕らえることを〝運を鷲づかみ〟になぞらえて、熊手守りになったといわれる。

　〝えべっさん〟とは大阪の商売繁盛の神様で、正式には〝十日えびす〟といわれる浪速区の今宮戎神社の毎年一月九日から十一におこなわれる祭礼である。

　この今宮戎神社に奉斎しているのは、天照大神、事代主命、外三神になる。その中でも事代主命は、大国主命の子供で、釣り竿に鯛を抱えた豊漁、商売繁盛、田の神様の七福神の一人の戎様である。3日間で約100万人もの参詣者があり、「商売繁盛笹持ってこい」の掛け声で福笹を買い求める。

Tori-no-Ichi Fair is an open-air market held at Juzai-san Chokoku-ji Temple, commonly known as *Tori-no-Tera* (temple of the rooster), in Asakusa, Tokyo. It is also held at many shrines of *washi* (eagle), or *Ohtori* Shrines, throughout Japan. The fair, dating back to the Edo Era, is a popular occasion for townspeople to pray for good fortune and prosperity. Highly decorated bamboo rakes are particularly popular as a charm to bring fortune and business prosperity. It is believed that the treasure-laden rake collects fortunes.
The fair is held on each day of *Tori* (rooster) in November by the lunar calendar, which is determined by the 12 signs of the Chinese zodiac. *Ichi-no-Tori* or the first day of *Tori* is considered to be the most important of all days of *Tori*.
An eagle catches and keeps its prey with its talons fast. Rakes are likened to this action of the eagle and hence the *kumade-mamori* (rake charm) is offered to people to "grasp" fortune fast.
Ebessan (colloquial expression for *Ebisu-sama*), formally called *Toka-Ebisu* (god *Ebisu* on the 10th day), is a festival to thank and pray to the god of business prosperity for the people of Osaka. The festival is held on January 9 through 11 every year at Imamiya Ebisu Shrine in Naniwa-ku, Osaka. Imamiya Ebisu Shrine is dedicated to Amaterasu-Ohmikami (goddess of the sun), Kotoshiro-Nushi-no-Mikoto (god of oracles), and three other gods. Kotoshiro-Nushi-no-Mikoto, son of Ohkuni-Nushi-no-Mikoto, is the god of fishery, business prosperity, and rice paddies. The god is popularly represented as *Ebisu-sama*, one of the Seven Deities of Good Fortune, holding a fishing rod and a red sea bream. Visitors to the festival reach about one million in three days, many purchasing *fuku-zasa* (lucky bamboo grass), shouting with one voice, "Prosperous business, bring the bamboo grass!"

写真提供：今宮戎神社
Photo courtesy of Imamiya Ebisu Shrine

▲大阪の浪速区の今宮戎神社で毎年一月九日から十日の3日間開催される商売繁盛の〝えべっさん〟
The *Ebessan* festival wishing for business prosperity is held at Imamiya Ebisu Shrine, Naniwa-ku, Osaka, lasting 3 days from 9th through 11th of January every year.

写真提供：鷲在山長國寺
Photo courtesy of Juzai-san Chokoku-ji Temple

◀江戸時代から続く商売繁盛の〝酉の市〟は浅草の鷲在山長國寺などで開催される
The *Tori-no-Ichi* fair, dating back to the Edo Era, is the event of wishing for business prosperity. It is held at Juzai-san Chokoku-ji Temple, Asakusa, Tokyo, and many other temples and shrines in Japan.

冬を彩る
日本の歳時記と和食

Japanese Events and Food in Winter

冬の歳時記と和食

Events and Food in Winter

色づいた葉が落ちはじめ、冷たい風が吹き、すすきが揺れ、水が冷たくなるといよいよ冬の季節の到来である。雪の多い地方では厳しい季節だが、それでも冬をすごす知恵と楽しむ豊かな心がある。雪だるま、雪合戦、かまくら、そして温かいこたつで、冬ならではの食材をふんだんに使った鍋料理を皆んなで囲む。これも冬ならではの楽しみだ。そして滋味あふれる根菜は、私たちの体を温めてくれる。自然と調和しながら生活することが、日本人本来の生き方であるということを思い浮かべさせてくれるのが、冬という季節である。

Winter is when the colored leaves fall, a cold wind blows, *susuki* (Japanese pampas grass) sways in the wind, and water is cold to your hands. Winter is a tough season particularly in the snowy regions, yet the Japanese have the wisdom to survive and the rich spirit to enjoy the harsh season - playing snowmen, building *kamakura* (snow hut), and many other diversions. People gather together around the warm *kotatsu* (foot warmer) to enjoy one-pot dishes prepared with bountiful ingredients unique to winter. The occasion is the pleasure of winter. Tasty root vegetables warm us up from inside the body. Living in harmony with nature is the basic way of living of the Japanese - winter is the season that reminds us of this fact.

【冬の花鳥風月 Nature and Events in Winter】

雪景色●Snow Scenes
一夜にしてあたり一面を銀世界にする雪。水墨画を思わせる景色はまさに美しい。
Have the experience of waking up in the morning to find the whole place covered with snow! It is the world of *sumi-e* or ink drawing - all is simple yet full of beauty.

福寿草●*Fukuju-so* (Amur adonis)
黄色の花を咲かせるふくじゅ草。花期は1〜5月になり、新年の季語に使われる。
The season of *Fukuju-so*, with its beautiful yellow flowers, is January through May. *Fukuju-so* is a season word (*kigo*) reflecting winter in composing *haiku* (a Japanese poem of seventeen syllables).

すいせん●Daffodil
花期は1〜5月になり、群生地はみごとだ。花の少ない冬を代表する花である。
The season for daffodils is January through May. A spectacular view presents itself in colonies. The daffodil is a flower typical of winter when few flowers are seen.

寒ぼたん●*Kan-botan* (winter peony)
5月頃の開花だが、冬に咲かせるぼたんを寒ぼたんという。雪と見事にマッチする。
Tree peonies generally come into flower in May. This variety blooms in winter, producing a splendid view against the snow.

さざんか●*Sasanqua* (camellia)
冬に赤、ピンクなどのさまざまな色の花を咲かせて楽しませてくれる。冬の季語である。
Sasanqua blooms in red, pink, and many other colors in winter. It is a season word (*kigo*) for winter in composing *haiku*.

つわぶき●*Tsuwa-buki* (Farfugium japonicum)
茎を食用とされるつわぶき。10〜12月に咲く黄色い小さな花は冬の季語である。
The stem is edible. The small yellow flowers of *tsuwa-buki* coming out in October through December are a season word (*kigo*) for winter in composing *haiku*.

かまくら●*Kamakura* (snow hut)
雪国である東北や上信越地方などの風物詩といってもよいかまくら。中は意外と温かい。
Kamakura is a typical winter diversion in snowy regions such as the Tohoku and Joshin-etsu areas. It is warm inside contrary to expectation.

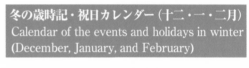

タンチョウ●*Tancho*
北海道東部の湿原に生息している。冬におこなう求愛ダンスを思い出す。
Tancho or Japanese red-crested white cranes live in the marshes in the eastern part of Hokkaido. The famous courtship dance is performed in winter.

大晦日・新年・正月
おお みそ か　しん ねん　しょう がつ

New Year's Eve, New Year, and New Year's Days

大晦日、新年、正月の歴史と由来はもちろんのこと、どのような行事があって、どのようにすごせばよいのか、そしてどのような遊びをしていたのかをここでは紹介している。少しずつながら忘れられている日本の素晴しい伝統の習慣やしきたりをもう一度考えてみたい。

The origin and history of New Year's Eve (*Oo-misoka*), New Year (*Shin-nen*), and New Year's Days (*Shogatsu*) are introduced below. The events people enjoyed and what they did from day to day are also described. Let us look back at the interesting traditions and customs of Japan, which are disappearing today little by little...

大晦日の歴史と由来 Origin and history of *Oo-misoka* (New Year's Eve)

毎月の最終日は〝晦日〟または〝つごもり〟といわれていた。ちなみに二十九日で終わる月は〝九日晦日〟と呼ばれていた。十二月三十一日を大晦日というのは、一年の最後の日なので〝大晦日〟〝大つごもり〟といわれるようになったのが、大晦日の由来である。

The last day of the month is called *Misoka* (day of the hidden moon) or *Tsugomori* (hidden moon). As you may be aware, these terms were created in the age when we were using the lunar calendar. The last day of a month with 29 days is called *Ku-nichi Misoka* (9th-day *Misoka*). December 31 is called *Oo-misoka* (great *Misoka*) because it is the last day of the year. It is sometimes called *Oo-tsugomori* (great *tsugomori*).

大晦日のすごし方 How to spend the day of *Oo-misoka*

昔は時計もなく、太陽の位置で時間を決めていたこともあり、日が沈むと一日が終わると考えられていた。そのため次の日になる前（日が沈む前）に、正月の準備（おせちやしめ飾りなど）をし、大晦日になったら心身を清めて神社にこもり、一晩中起きていて歳神様を迎えていたといわれる。

現在は大晦日の数日前までに家の大掃除を終わらせ、神棚の四手を新しくして榊を立て、お神酒や供えものをする。門口に〝門松〟を置き、玄関に〝しめ飾り〟（しめ飾りには不老長寿を意味する松、竹の子を生ずるため子孫繁栄を表わす竹、実りを象徴する橙、枯れにくい裏白、喜ぶで昆布、家系の伝統で橙などが使われる）を飾り、鏡餅を供える。そしておせち料理を作り、お重に詰めて正月を待つ。

大晦日の夕食は〝年越しそば〟をいただく。この年越しそばの由来は、江戸時代中期に月末にそばを食べる〝三十日そば〟という習慣があり、その習慣が大晦日に年越しそばを食べるようになったといわれる。

年越しそばには「細く長く達者に暮らせるように」とか、そばが切れやすいことから「一年間の苦労を切り

捨て、翌年に持ち越さないように」といった意味がある。ただし地方によっては年越しそばではなく、寿しやいわしを食べる地方もある。

In the old days when there were no clocks and the time was determined by the position of the sun, people thought that the day ended when the sun set. People used to prepare for the New Year (such as preparation of ingredients for *Osechi* —traditional New Year dishes — and hand-making of *shime-kazari* — a Shinto straw festoon decorated with cut paper, etc.) before the next day began, or before the sun set. On the day of *Oo-misoka*, people purified themselves in mind and body, were confined to the shrine, and sat up all night to meet and greet the god of the New Year.

At present, people finish thorough cleaning of the house several days before the day of *Oo-misoka*, replace shide (specially cut paper strips) with new ones on the household Shinto altar, and put the *sakaki* plant and offer *sake* and rice cakes before the altar. They further put up *kado-matsu* (decorative pine trees used in pairs) at the gate, post *shime-kazari* (straw festoons) on the entrance of each house, and offer *kagami-mochi* (rice cakes). Housewives prepare *Osechi* dishes for the New Year and pack them in tiered food boxes to save cooking on the busy New Year's Days. (*Shime-kazari* is made up of pine, a symbol of longevity, bamboo, wishing for a large family associated with rapidly increasing bamboo shoots, straw, representing good harvests, not easily withering *urajiro* ferns, *konbu* (kelp), whose pronunciation in Japanese resembles that of *yorokobu* (rejoice), and bitter oranges, depending on family tradition.)

歳神様にお供えする鏡餅。この鏡餅の形は人の塊、つまり人間の心臓をかたどったものといわれている
A rice cake offered to the year god. It is believed to have been modeled after the soul, or the heart, of a human.

They eat *toshi-koshi-soba* (buckwheat noodles for moving into the New Year) on New Year's Eve. This custom comes from the practice of eating *misoka-soba* (eating buckwheat noodles at the end of a month) in the middle of the Edo Era. This practice has been observed up to now and the Japanese eat *toshi-koshi-soba* on New Year's Eve.

People eat *toshi-koshi-soba* wishing for "living long, strong, and slim like *soba*" or "toil of the past year is severed as the thin *soba* is, and is not carried forward to the New Year." However, *sushi* or sardines are eaten in place of *soba* depending on the region.

新年・正月の歴史と由来 Origin and history of New Year and New Year's Days

　現在、新年といえば一月一日の元旦のことをいうが、江戸時代までは中国の陰陽暦が使われていたため、立春や立春近くの新月の日が初だとされていた。その後、西暦が採用されてから一月一日が新年とされているのだ。

　正月とは年頭の祝いをする三カ日から、松の内（元日から七日、もしくは十五日まで）のことで、歳神様（お正月様）を迎え豊作を祈った日のことである。

Today, New Year means New Year's Day or January 1. Up to the Edo Era when the Chinese lunar calendar was used, the day of the new moon on or near the calendric beginning of spring was New Year's day. Later, the Gregorian calendar was adopted and January 1 has been the New Year since then.

New Year's Days extends from January 1 through the day when the pine decoration is removed (7 or 15 days depending on the region; this period is called *Matsu-no-Uchi* or within pines). The first three days including January 1 are dedicated to celebrating the start of the New Year. During *Matsu-no-Uchi*, people invite and worship the year god (*Oshogatsu-sama*), wishing for a rich harvest for the year.

新年・正月の行事 Events for the New Year and New Year's Days

除夜の鐘が終わると年があけたことになり、神社に〝初詣〟に参拝に行く習わしがある。

初詣はもともと心身を清め大晦日の夕方から、氏神様のおやしろにこもったり、神社の前で夜を明かして歳神様を迎えていた行事である。現在は限られた人のみがおこない、あまりそのようなことはされなくなり、年明けとともに参拝することが多くなった。

また、〝恵方詣〟（干支によって定められたその年の歳徳神がいる方角の神社に参拝する）も初詣だと考えられている。参拝が終わると、破魔矢やお守りを神社にお返しし、新しいものを買い求める。そしておみくじを引き、一年の吉凶を占う。

When the last sound of *Joya-no-Kane* (bell ringing out the old year) is heard, the New Year has arrived. People start for *Hatsu-mohde* (the first visit of the year to a shrine or a temple) at this time.

Hatsu-mohde was originally an event of confining oneself to a shrine of a local deity from the evening of *Oo-misoka* (New Year's Eve) to purify the mind and body. Other people sat up all night in front of a shrine to meet and greet the year god. At present, however, only a limited number of people observe this custom. Most people visit the shrine early morning in the New Year.

Eho-mohde (visiting the shrine located in the direction of the year god determined by the Chinese sexagenary cycle) is also considered *Hatsu-mohde*. After praying before the altar, people return last year's *hamaya* (lucky charm arrow) and *omamori* (talisman) and buy new ones. Then they consult an oracle (*omikuji*) that tells their fortune for the year.

【おみくじ *Omikuji* (written oracle)】
おみくじには大吉、中吉、小吉、末吉、吉、凶、大凶などと書かれている。引いた後のおみくじは、境内の木の枝や2本の木の柱の間に結ぶ。これは神様と〝縁を結ぶ〟という意味がある。凶のおみくじは利き手の反対の手で結べば転じて吉になるといわれる。

Each *omikuji* you draw is written with an oracle such as great blessing (*dai-kichi*), middle blessing (*chu-kichi*), small blessing (*sho-kichi*), near-blessing (*sue-kichi*), blessing (*kichi*), curse (*kyo*), and great curse (*dai-kyo*). After reading it, you tie the oracle paper to the branch of a tree in the premises or between two wooden posts. By doing this, you form a connection with the god. Be sure to tie the curse (*kyo*) oracle paper with your counter-dominant hand. This will turn curse into blessing, they say.

【正しい参拝の仕方 Praying Procedure】

1 鳥居の手前で軽く一礼してから境内に入る。
Lightly bow once before the *torii* (gateway at the entrance to a shrine) and enter the precincts.

2 手水舎の水で両手を清め（洗い）、口をすすぐ。
※左の手のひらに水を受け、その水を口にふくんですすぐこと。
Wash to clean both of your hands and rinse your mouth with the water of *temizu-ya* (water fountain).
※Take the water in your left hand to rinse your mouth.

3 もう一度左手を水で清める。
Clean your left hand once more with the water.

4 神社へ進み、さい銭箱の前で軽く一拝しさい銭を入れ、大鈴を鳴らし、〝二拝二拍手一拝〟（二礼二拍手一礼）をし、小さく一拝する。
※二拝とは深いおじぎを2回、二拍手とは柏手を2回、一拝はもう一度深くおじぎを1回すること。
※二拍手の時に心の中で願いごとをする。
Proceed to the shrine. Lightly bow before the offertory box, make a money offering, ring the big bell, follow the traditional Shinto ritual of two bows, two hand claps, and a final bow. Lastly, perform a light bow.
※ Two bows means two deep bows. Two hand claps means clapping your hands in worship twice. The final bow is a deep bow.
※ Make a wish as you clap your hands.

お年玉の歴史と由来 Origin and history of *otoshi-dama* (money given to children as a gift at New Year)

正月になると子供たちは、親、おじいちゃん、おばあちゃん、親戚などから〝お年玉〟がもらえるが、かつては歳神様の供えものであった〝鏡餅〟は、歳神様の魂がこめられたものと考えられており、これを〝おとしだま〟と呼んでいた。今でもお年玉として子供たちに餅を配る地方があるらしい。

現在はお年玉専用の小さなのし袋にお金を入れて渡すのが通常になっている。

Children receive *otoshi-dama* at New Year from their parents, grandfathers, grandmothers, and relatives. Originally, *otoshi-dama* meant the rice cake that was offered to the year god and hence possessed the soul of the year god within it. Even today, rice cakes are delivered to children as *otoshi-dama* in some regions.

Generally, today, money is put into a small printed envelope, which is exclusively designed for this purpose, and given to children.

お屠蘇とぞう煮の歴史と由来 Origin and history of *otoso* (spiced *sake*) and *zou-ni* (rice cake soup)

おせち料理をいただく前に〝お屠蘇〟をいただくが、これにはどんな意味があるのだろうか……。お屠蘇とは、中国の唐時代の屠蘇庵に住んでいた医者が、風邪予防のために作った薬酒のことで、お屠蘇は「鬼気を屠絶し、人魂を蘇生させる」とされ、一年の邪気を払い、長寿を願って飲まれるようになった。

ぞう煮は歳神に供えた食べものを、新年1番に汲んだ神聖な水と火で一家の主人が雑多に煮たもの。だからぞう煮を漢字で〝雑煮〟と書く。そんなぞう煮は、一年の無病息災を願って歳神様といただく。

ぞう煮は具に各地方の特産品を使用するために、数多くの種類があって、どれもが美味しい。

People drink *otoso* (spiced *sake*) before eating *Osechi* (New Year's meals) in the New Year. What is the meaning of *otoso*? *Otoso* was originally a cold medicine dispensed by a doctor living in a hermitage named *Toso* during the Tang Dynasty, China. The medicine was believed to "stop ghastly things and revive the spirit of a dead person." People took *otoso* to get rid of evil things and wish for longevity at the start of the year.

Zou-ni is made up of various foods that were offered to the year god. They are cooked in mixture (hence called *zou-ni* or "cook unsorted" in Japanese) by the head of the family and using the "sacred" water drawn for the first time in the year. People eat *zou-ni* in the company of the year god, wishing for sound health for the year.

There are many kinds of *zou-ni* dishes because they are cooked in various ways according to regional custom and using ingredients of local specialty. You will never be disappointed by eating any kind of *zou-ni* in Japan.

書き初めの歴史と由来 Origin and history of *kaki-zome* (the first calligraphy of the year)

書き初めは一月二日に好きな言葉や目標を紙に書くことだが、もともとは宮中で年初にくんだ若水で墨をすり、恵方（干支によって定められたその年の歳徳神がいる方角のこと）に向かって書をたしなめたのがはじまりとされている。

書いたものは神棚などに奉納し、その書を小正月（旧暦一月十五日）にどんど焼き（その年に飾った門松やしめ飾り、破魔矢などを持ち寄って焼く。その火で焼いた餅を食べ、一年間の健康を祈願する。正月にお迎えした歳神様を送る意味もある）の火に入れて、灰が高く上がるほど字がうまくなるといわれている。

Kaki-zome is the first writing in the year of one's favorite words or phrases or motto for the year on January 2. It was originally a court custom, where they ground an ink-cake with fresh water collected at the start of the New Year and wrote letters facing the direction of *Eho* (the direction of the year god as determined by the Chinese sexagenary cycle).

The work is dedicated to the god on the household altar. It is then burned in *Dondo-yaki** on the day of *Ko-shogatu* (small New Year - January 15 by the lunar calendar). It is believed that the higher the ashes of your work go up in the sky, the better your writing will become.

***Dondo-yaki**: Burning of the decorative pine trees (*kado-matsu*), sacred straw festoons (*shime-kazari*), lucky charm arrows (*hamaya*), etc., which are collected from all houses in the neighborhood. Using this fire, rice cakes are baked, wishing for health for the year. *Dondo-yaki* is also meant to see off the year god who was the guest during the New Year's Days.

七草がゆの歴史と由来 Origin and history of *nanakusa-gayu* (porridge mixed with seven spring herbs)

一月七日に食べられる七草がゆ。平安時代には一月六日を年取りといって、七日を折り目として、新しい年がはじまるとされていた。そのため七日に「外敵が来ないように」と無病息災の願いを込めて七草 (セリ、ナズナ、ゴギョウ、ハコベラ、ホトケノザ、スズナ、スズシロ) を入れたかゆを食べたのが初まり。

現在では、おせち料理の食べすぎやお酒の飲みすぎで疲れた胃や体に優しいため、食べられることの方が多いようだ。

Nanakusa-gayu is a food eaten on January 7. In the Heian Era, January 6 was the day of *Toshi-tori* (passing of a year) and January 7 the first day of the New Year. They ate seven spring herbs★ on January 7, wishing for sound health and also that "foreign enemies never come upon us."

Today, people eat *Nanakusa-gayu* mainly because they have taken too much *Osechi* and *sake* during the New Year's Days and the stomach and the body are weak. *Nanakusa-gayu* is just fit for such people.

★Japanese parsley (*seri*), shepherd's purse (*nazuna*), cudweed (*gogyo*), chickweed (*hakobera*), henbit (*hotoke-no-za*), turnip (*suzuna*), and daikon (*suzushiro*)

鏡開きの歴史と由来 Origin and history of *kagami-biraki* (opening of the New Year rice cake)

正月に鏡餅を供え、一月十一日にその鏡餅を木づちなどで開き、一年の健康と発展を祝ってお汁粉やぞう煮などにして食べることを〝鏡開き〟という。鏡餅には歳神様が宿るとされ、縁起ものとされているため、けっして刃物で切ったりされないため、切るとか割るとはいわず、開くといわれる。

Kagami-mochi (New Year rice cake) is offered to deities in the New Year. It is "opened" with a wooden hammer on January 11 and the pieces are cooked in *oshiruko* (sweet *azuki*-bean soup with rice cake) or *zou-ni* (rice cake soup), wishing for health and prosperity for the year (*Kagami-biraki* event). The year god dwells in the rice cake, they say, and therefore it is a lucky food. They never use a knife for fear of cutting something divine and lucky. The word "open" is used rather than "cut" or "sever" for *kagami-mochi*.

正月の伝統的な遊び Traditional Games Played on the New Year's Days

古くは正月の遊びといえば、女の子は〝羽根つき〟、男の子は〝凧揚げ〟〝こま回し〟だった。そして家族や友だちとで〝福笑い〟〝かるた〟〝すごろく〟をしたものだ。

羽根つきは羽子板で羽根を打ち合う遊びだが、昔は羽子板を〝こきいた〟、羽根つきを〝胡鬼子勝負〟といって、新年の悪霊払いと一年の吉凶を占うものだった。また、羽根は病気を移す蚊を食べるトンボに見立てられている。ちなみに失敗すると顔に墨を塗るが、これは厄いをもたらす鬼が墨や黒色を嫌いなため、無病息災を願ってのもの。

凧揚げは平安時代に中国から伝わったもので、鎌倉時代に旧暦五月五日の〝端午の節句〟に子供の無病息災を願って揚げられたものが、年の初めに両親が男の子の出生を祝い、無事に成長することを願っておこなわれたものである。

〝かるた〟はポルトガル人が室町時代に伝えた〝うんすんかるた〟が起源だといわれている。それが日本の〝貝覆〟や〝花合わせ〟と結びついて〝花がるた〟という遊びになった。平安時代になると花がるたが、〝歌合わせ〟と結びつき〝歌がるた〟になる。この歌がるたが百人一首のはじまりといわれている。ちなみにかるたはポルトガル語のcarta (手紙、紙板状のもの、トランプ) の意味がある。

福笑いは江戸時代から続くもので、お多福やひょっとこなどの顔の輪かくが描かれた台紙に、目隠しをして眉、鼻、口などの紙片を置いていくが、出来上がったおかしな顔に、おもわず笑いがこぼれる楽しい遊びだ。

すごろくは、さいころを振り、出た目の数だけ石を進め、敵陣へ先に石を全部入れた方が勝ちとするゲームだが、もともとはインドで考えられたもので、日本には奈良時代に中国から伝わったといわれている。

Typical games played on the New Year's Days in the old days were *hane-tsuki* (battledore) for girls and *tako-age* (kite-flying) and *koma-mawashi* (top spinning) for boys. Family games enjoyed with friends invited included *fuku-warai* (make-a-face game), *karuta* (cards), and *sugoroku* (a Japanese snakes and ladders game).

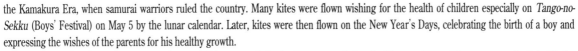

Hane-tsuki is a game of battledore and shuttlecock. The battledore was formerly called *koki-ita* and *hane-tsuki*, a game of *koki-no-ko* (dispelling demons from the New Year and telling the fortune of the year). The shuttlecock was considered to be a dragonfly that catches mosquitoes, a medium that transmits diseases. When you lose, you are smeared on the face with India ink. As the demons are fearful of India ink and black colors, you are protected against evils, and your health is also maintained.

The *tako-age* game was imported from China in the Heian Era. Kite-flying became particularly popular in the Kamakura Era, when samurai warriors ruled the country. Many kites were flown wishing for the health of children especially on *Tango-no-Sekku* (Boys' Festival) on May 5 by the lunar calendar. Later, kites were then flown on the New Year's Days, celebrating the birth of a boy and expressing the wishes of the parents for his healthy growth.

The first *karuta* played in Japan is *un-sun-karuta*, which was taught by the Portuguese during the Muromachi Era. The game was mingled with the Japanese-original *kai-ooi* and *hana-awase* games to become the *hana-garuta* game. In the Heian Era, *hana-garuta* was mingled with the *uta-awase* game to become *uta-garuta* game. This is a primitive form of *hyaku-nin-isshu* (collection of one hundred poems by one hundred poets). *Karuta* has the same meaning as "carta," the Portuguese word for letter, paper board, and playing card.

The *fuku-warai* game, started in the Edo Era, is a favorite New Year pastime until today. The face of an *otafuku* (female) or *hyottoko* (male) is drawn on a large board of paper, on which you place pieces of paper drawn with eye brow, nose, mouth, etc., with a blindfold tied over your eyes. The completed face is funny enough, and you will laugh in spite of yourself together with your other playmates.

Sugoroku is a game where you throw the dice, advance your stone by the number of spots on the dice, and try to place all of your stones in the opponent's territory faster than the opponent to win the game. The game, originally invented in India, came to Japan in the Nara Era via China.

三大凧合戦 Three Major Kite-flying Competitions

男の子の出生を祝ったり、無病息災を願った凧揚げ。今なおお古き良き伝統を受け継ぐ凧合戦の三大。

Kite-flying is an event to celebrate the birth of a boy or wish for his health. The three major kite-flying competitions, inheriting the traditions of the good old days, are introduced below.

白根大凧合戦（新潟県）
Shirone Oh-dako Gassen (Shirone big kite competition), Niigata Prefecture

五十崎大凧合戦（愛媛県）
Ikazaki Oh-dako Gassen (Ikazaki big kite competition), Ehime Prefecture

浜松祭り凧合戦（静岡県）
Hamamatsu Matsuri-dako Gassen (Hamamatsu festive kite competition), Shizuoka Prefecture

年越しそば

細く長く健康で暮らせるよう願い、年を越す前に食べきる

about
30
min

New Year's Eve Noodles

Finish the buckwheat noodles before midnight of New Year's Eve, while praying for a long and healthy life, like the noodles

■材料・2人分

そば（乾麺）	200g	しょう油	60cc
むきえび	60g	みりん	30cc
玉ねぎ	1/6個	砂糖	大さじ1

〈衣の材料〉

小麦粉	60g	水菜	1株
卵黄1個分＋冷水を合わせたもの	120cc	長ねぎ	適量
		揚げ油（サラダ油）	適量

〈麺つゆ〉

だし汁	800cc	七味唐辛子	適宜

■Ingredients (serves 2)

7 oz dried buckwheat noodles
6 small shelled shrimps
1/8 onion

<Ingredients for batter>
2 oz flour
1/2 U.S. cup mixture of an egg yolk and chilled water

<Ingredients for noodle soup>
3 1/3 U.S. cups stock

1/4 U.S. cup soy sauce
1/8 U.S. cup *mirin* sweet cooking *sake*
1 Tbsp sugar

1 plant *mizuna* potherb mustard
Naga-negi onion
Frying oil (vegetable oil)
Shichimi-tougarashi, or seven-spice chili mix

【作り方】

1 麺つゆを準備する。
鍋にみりんを入れ一度沸かして、みりんのアルコール分をとばし、しょう油、だし汁、砂糖を加えて温める。

2 水菜はさっと塩（分量外）ゆでし、水けを絞って3〜4cmの長さに切る。長ねぎは小口切りにする。

3 むきえびは背わたを取り、玉ねぎは薄切りにする。

4 そば（乾麺）はゆでて流水でもみ洗いする。

5 衣・かき揚げを作る。
ボウルに卵黄と冷水を合わせたものに、ふるった小麦粉を一度に入れ、菜箸でざっくりかき混ぜ衣を作る。粉やだまが残った状態でよい。小さなボウルに3のむきえびと玉ねぎを半量入れ、小麦粉（分量外）少々を加えて全体にまぶす。衣を大さじ1〜2杯加えさっくり混ぜる。170℃に熱した揚げ油でカラリと揚げる。残りのたねも同様に揚げる。

6 鍋に湯を沸かし、4のそばを温め、器に盛る。1の麺つゆをはり、5のかき揚げをのせ、2の水菜と長ねぎを添える。お好みで七味唐辛子をかけていただく。

【DIRECTIONS】

1 Prepare the noodle soup.
Boil the *mirin* sweet cooking *sake* in a pot to allow the alcohol to evaporate, add the soy sauce, stock, and sugar, and heat.

2 Briefly boil the *mizuna* potherb mustard in salty water (extra quantity), squeeze off the water, and cut into 1 1/4 to 1 1/2-inch lengths. Cut the *naga-negi* onion into small rounds.

3 Devine the shrimps. Cut the onion in half lengthwise, and then thinly slice crosswise.

4 Boil the dried noodles, and wash in running cold water while rubbing.

5 Make the batter and mixed *tempura*.
Put into a bowl the mixture of an egg yolk and chilled water, add sifted flour at once, and coarsely mix using long cooking chopsticks. Leave some flour or lumps unmixed. Put into a small bowl about a half amount of the shrimps and sliced onion, dust a small quantity of flour (extra), add 1 to 2 Tbsps of batter, and roughly mix. Deep-fry in the oil at 340°F until crisp. Deep-fry the rest of the shrimps and onion likewise.

6 Boil water in a pot, heat the noodles in it, and then transfer them to a serving bowl. Pour over the soup prepared in **1**, place the mixed *tempura*, and garnish with the cut *mizuna* and *naga-negi* onion. Sprinkle with the *shichimi-tougarashi* spice before eating, if you like.

正月料理 *Shogatsu-ryori* (New Year's food)

重箱に詰められたふだん食べられない豪華な料理のおせち。「今年の食事が豊かになりますように」との願いをはじめ、詰められている料理や使用する食材には、さまざまな意味合いや縁起がかつがれている。

Gorgeous *Osechi* (New Year's meal) packed in tiered food boxes is delicious and never eaten at any other time. The food and the ingredients used in *Osechi* have their own meaning and good-luck talismans, including a wish that "all meals be rich this year!"

正月料理の歴史と由来 Origin and history of *shogatsu-ryori* (New Year's food)

正月料理として一番なじみ深いのは、〝おせち〟になるが、このおせちは〝お節供〟の略称で、桃の節句などと同じ節句のひとつである。昔は節句に供える食べものをすべて〝おせち料理〟と呼んでいた。

平安時代の貴族たちが、年のはじめや桃の節句、端午の節句などの五節供に、神前にお供えものをして邪鬼を祓い、そのお下がりをいただき神様の恩恵にあやかったといわれている。この時出されていた料理が〝お節供料理〟と呼ばれていたが、これが現在のおせち料理のもとである。

この時期の神は大きな音や火が苦手といわれており、正月には極力台所に入って音や火を使わないように、正月の事前に保存のきく料理を作り、重箱に詰めておいていたといわれている。また、いつも料理を作っている女性が、正月にはゆっくりできるようにとの考え方もある。

Osechi is the most popular New Year's food now. Originally spelled *Osechiku*, "*Osechi*" meant seasonal festivals such as *Momo-no-sekku* (Girls' Festival). All foods offered in the seasonal festivals were called *Osechi-ryori* in olden times.

In the Heian Era, the aristocrats offered foods on the altar in the Five Seasonal Festivals (New Year, *Mono-no-Sekku*, *Tango-no-Sekku*, and two others) to ward off evil spirits. They ate the foods after the festival to take advantage of the benefits of the god. The dishes served at this time were *Osechiku-ryori*, which is the origin of the present-day *Osechi-ryori*.

Gods at this time were afraid of loud sounds and fire. People prepared preserved foods and put them in tiered food boxes before the New Year arrived so that they did not have to use the kitchen, where fire and sounds are inevitably made, during the New Year's Days. Another possible reason is that women, who were busy making dishes every day, could rest comfortably during the New Year's Days without preparing food for the family.

おせち料理の内容と意味 Ingredients and meaning of *Osechi-ryori*

正月に食べられるおせち料理は、「今年の食事が豊かになりますように」と願いを込めて、ふだん食べられない豪華な食材や縁起ものの食材が使われる。

基本的なおせち料理は、お屠蘇、祝い肴三種（三つ肴）、ぞう煮、煮しめになり、祝い肴三種と煮しめは重箱に詰められた。なぜ重箱に詰めるかといえば、めでたさを〝重ねる〟からきている。

祝い肴三種は関東では田作り（ごまめ）、数の子、黒豆になり、関西では、たたきごぼう、数の子、黒豆が基本だ。

Osechi-ryori served during the New Year's Days is cooked from gorgeous and lucky ingredients that are not eaten in everyday life, with the wish that meals be rich this year.

Basic *Osechi-ryori* consists of *otoso* (spiced sake), *iwai-sakana sanshu* or *mitsu-zakana* (three side dishes), *zou-ni* (rice cake soup), and *nishime* (vegetables and dry foods simmered with soy sauce). *Iwai-sakana sanshu* and *nishime* are packed in tiered food boxes (associated with "superposing happiness").

The three *iwai-sakana* are *tazukuri* or *gomame* (dried anchovy), *kazu-no-ko* (herring roe), and *kuro-mame* (sweetened black beans) in the Kanto area. They are basically *tataki-gobo* ("beaten" burdock), *kazu-no-ko*, and *kuro-mame* in the Kansai area.

【各料理の意味 Meaning of Dishes】

田作り（ごまめ）▶
Tazukuri (Gomame)(Dried young anchovies)

田作り（ごまめ） —— かつては田畑の肥料にされていた片口いわしを使うため、豊作を願う
Tazukuri(Gomame)
(Dried young anchovies) Wish for good harvest: Japanese anchovies were once used as fertilizer for rice paddies and fields.

数の子 —— 卵の数が多いことから、子孫繁栄を願う
Kazu-no-ko
(Herring roe) Wish for being blessed with children: *Kazu-no-ko* literally means "many roes."

黒豆 —— まめに働き（勉強）、まめ（健康）に暮らせることを願う
Kuro-mame
(Sweetened black beans) Wish for working and studying hard and living in good health: In addition to beans, mame means "diligent" in Japanese.

伊達巻 ▶
Date-maki
(Rolled omelet)

伊達巻 —— 伊達者（しゃれ者）たちが着ていたドテラに似ていたことから伊達巻と呼ばれる。巻きものに形が似ていることから、知識が増えるといわれる。
Date-maki
(Rolled omelet) This food is so called because of its resemblance to the *dotera kimono* (worn by a *date-mono* or dandy). It is believed that knowledge increases when you eat *date-maki*, which looks like a rolled book.

昆布巻 —— 「よろこぶ」の語呂合わせで、一年が喜んで生活できるようにと願う
Kobu-maki
(Kelp rolls) Wish for living pleasantly throughout the year: From the harmonious sound between *kobu* (kelp) and *yorokobu* (rejoice)

お多福豆 —— 福が多いことを願って
Otafuku-mame
(Big broad beans) Wish for great happiness: *Tafuku* literally means "much good luck."

紅白なます —— お祝ごとに使う水引をイメージして
Kohaku-namasu
(A dish of raw fish and vegetables seasoned in vinegar and decorated in red-and-white stripes) This food resembles the lucky red-and-white strings used for celebratory envelopes.

昆布巻 ▶
Kobu-maki (Kelp rolls)

ぶりの焼きもの —— ぶりが出世魚であることから、出世を願う
Buri-no-yakimono
(Grilled Japanese amberjack) Wish for a successful career: Japanese amberjack is called by different names as it grows large, which is indicative of a person rising to a high position in their career.

鯛の焼きもの —— 「めでたい」の語呂合わせ
Tai-no-yakimono
(Grilled sea bream) Harmonious sound between *tai* (sea bream) and *mede-tai* (happy)

えびの焼きもの —— ひげが長く、腰が曲がっていることから老人を連想させ、長寿を祈願する
Ebi-no-yakimono
(Grilled shrimp) Wish for longevity: The long barbels and the bent figure remind us of an old man enjoying longevity.

他には〝口取り〟として、紅白かまぼこ、伊達巻、栗きんとん、昆布巻、お多福豆を、〝酢のもの〟として、紅白なます、菊花かぶの酢のもの、ちょろぎ、れんこんの酢のもの(酢蓮・すばす)、〝焼きもの〟として、ぶり、鯛、えびなどになる。

煮しめに使う材料は、くわい、れんこん、里いも、ごぼう、八ツ頭、昆布などが基本だが、地方によって異なる。

Other New Year's foods include *kuchi-tori* or hors d'oeuvres such as *kohaku-kamaboko* (red-and-white boiled fish paste), *date-maki* (rolled omelet), *kuri-kinton* (mashed sweet potatoes with sweetened chestnuts), *kobu-maki* (kelp rolls) and *otafuku-mame* (big broad beans); *sunomono* or vinegared dishes such as *kohaku-namasu* (raw fish and vegetables seasoned in vinegar and decorated in red-and-white stripes), vinegared *kikuka-kabu* (chrysanthemum-shaped turnip), *chorogi* (Chinese artichoke), and vinegared *renkon* (lotus root); and *yakimono* or grilled dishes such as Japanese amberjack, sea bream, and shrimp.

The ingredients used in the simmered dishes basically include *kuwai* (arrowhead), *renkon* (lotus root), *sato-imo* (Taro), *gobo* (burdock), *yatsu-gashira* (new taros on an old one) and *konbu* (kelp). These may vary depending on the region.

【各食材の意味 Meaning of the Ingredients】

くわい ——————— 大きな芽が出ることから、芽が出る (出世する)
Kuwai (Arrowhead)　*Kuwai* shoots big buds, which are considered a sign of success and a successful career.

れんこん ——————— 孔が空いていることから、遠く (先見) が見える
Renkon (Lotus root)　Lotus roots have many holes, representing far sight and the wisdom and power to see into the future.

◀くわい
Kuwai (Arrowhead)

里いも ——————— 子いもがたくさんつくことから、子宝を願う (子孫繁栄)
Sato-imo (Taro)　*Sato-imo*, bearing many new taros, symbolizes a large family with many children. People wish for long-lasting family and prosperity by eating taros.

お重の詰め方(壱の重) How to pack foods in *ichi-no-juu* (first box) of the tiered box

彩りよく、より美味しそうに料理をお重に詰めていくための、コツや基本を壱の重で紹介する。

The basics and useful tips for packing foods in the tiered box, beautiful to see and appealing to the appetite, are introduced below for the case of *ichi-no-juu* (first box).

1 黒豆を小さな器 (ゆず釜、竹筒など) に入れ、お重の中央に置く。次に紅白のかまぼこを、紅が右上にくるように、互い違いに詰める。

Put *kuro-mame* into a small vessel such as *yuzu-gama* (hollowed-out citron) or *take-zutsu* (hollow bamboo container), and place it at the center. Pack the red-and-white *kamaboko* alternately, with the red portion located on the upper-right side of the box.

2 錦玉子、伊達巻を少しずつずらして詰める。

Pack *nishiki-tamago* (yellow and white colored egg cake) and *date-maki* by staggering them a bit.

3 料理と料理の間に仕切りとして、笹の葉や葉らんを置く。

Place bamboo grass leaves or aspidistra leaves between foods to separate them.

4 昆布巻は結び目を上にして重ねて盛り、高さを揃える。

Stack *kobu-maki* one above the other, with the knot facing up. Align the height of the stacks.

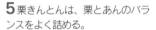

5 栗きんとんは、栗とあんのバランスをよく詰める。

Pack *kuri-kinton*, checking the balance between chestnuts and mashed sweet potatoes.

6 田作り (ごまめ) の頭を左にして重ねて盛り、高さを揃える。
※お頭のある魚、えびなどは頭を左にして詰める。

Stack *tazukuri* (gomame) one above the other, with the head on the left side. Align the height of the stacks.
※Fish cooked whole and shrimps are placed with the head on the left side.

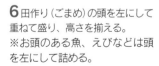

しょうがつ
正月料理
New Year's foods

たづくり
田作り（ごまめ）
ごこくほうじょう
五穀豊穣を願って素朴ながら味わいのあるごまめをいただく

about
10
min

Tazukuri (*Gomame*, or Small Dried Sardines)
Savor the simple but flavorful taste of the *gomame*, while praying for a bumper crop for the new year

■ **材料・4人分**

ごまめ	50g
砂糖	大さじ2
しょう油	大さじ1
水	小さじ2
酒	大さじ1/2
サラダ油	適量

■ Ingredients (serves 4)

1 3/4 oz *gomame*, or small dried sardines
2 Tbsps sugar
1 Tbsp soy sauce
2 tsps water
1/2 Tbsp *sake*
Vegetable oil

【作り方】

1 ごまめは平皿に重ならないように並べ、電子レンジに1分かける。取り出してかき混ぜて再び電子レンジで30秒ずつ4〜5回かける。（冷めた時にごまめがカリカリになっていればOK）。

2 鍋に砂糖、しょう油、水を入れ中火にかけ、煮立って泡が大きくなったら**1**のごまめを入れ、手早くかき混ぜてからめ、火を止めて酒をふって混ぜる。

3 薄くサラダ油を塗ったバットに**2**を手早くあけ、広げて冷ます。

【DIRECTIONS】

1 Scatter the *gomame* on a flat plate so that the fish do not overwrap each other, and microwave for 1 min. Stir, and microwave 4 to 5 times, for 30 sec each. (If the *gomame* is crispy, when cool, it's done.)

2 Put the sugar, soy sauce, and water in a pan, and heat over a medium flame. When it comes to the boil and large bubbles begin to form, put the *gomame* in, and quickly stir to allow the fish to be coated with the sauce. Turn off the heat, sprinkle with the *sake*, and stir.

3 Quickly spread the *gomame* on a cooking tray thinly smeared with vegetable oil, and allow the fish to cool.

正月料理
しょうがつ
New Year's foods

いかの黄金焼き
おうごんやき
黄金に変身したいかが正月の目出たさを演出してくれる

about
15
min

Golden Grilled Cuttlefish
The golden cuttlefish adds happiness to New Year's celebrations

■材料・4人分
もんごういか ·············1杯
卵黄 ·····················1個
塩 ·······················少々
酒 ·······················少々
青のり ···················適量

▨ Ingredients (serves 4)

1 common cuttlefish
1 egg yolk
Small quantity of salt
Small quantity of *sake*
Green laver

【作り方】

1 もんごういかは、足とわた、エンペラを取り除く。胴の皮をむき、開いて表面に鹿の子に切り込みを入れ、縦に2〜3つくらいに切る。身が反らないよう縦横2本ずつ串を打ち、軽く塩をふる。

2 卵黄に塩・酒を加え混ぜる。

3 1のいかはグリルかオーブントースターで、九分どおり焼く。

4 3のいかに2の卵黄を塗って、卵黄が乾くまで焦がさないように焼く。それを2度ほど繰り返し照りよく焼き上げる。

5 4が冷めたら一口大に切り、青のりをふる。
※好みで松葉に黒豆を刺し、金粉を散らしたものを添える。

【DIRECTIONS】

1 Remove the tentacles, guts, and fin of the cuttlefish. Skin the cuttlefish's body, cut open, and put shallow cuts into its surface in the *kanoko* pattern (parallel vertical and horizontal lines or diagonal lines crossing each other). Cut lengthwise into 2 to 3 pieces. Stick 2 skewers each lengthwise and crosswise to prevent the flesh from bending while cooking. Sprinkle with salt.

2 Mix the egg yolk, *sake*, and salt.

3 Grill the cuttlefish in a grill or a toaster oven till 90 percent done.

4 Apply the mixture prepared in **2** on the cuttlefish, and grill until the yolk dries. But do not burn the yolk. Repeat this twice until the egg yolk shines.

5 When the cuttlefish cools down, cut it into bite-size pieces, and sprinkle with green laver.
※ You can garnish the dish with cooked black soybeans skewered on pine needles, and sprinkled with gold leaf flakes.

<ruby>正月<rt>しょうがつ</rt></ruby>料理
New Year's foods

えびの<ruby>旨煮<rt>うまに</rt></ruby>
えびのおかげで正月料理がよりゴージャスになる

about
20
min

Simmered Prawns
Adorn New Year dishes with prawns!

■材料・4人分

有頭えび	……………	8尾
A	だし汁 ……………	250cc
	薄口しょう油 ……	大さじ2
	みりん ……………	大さじ2
	酒 …………………	大さじ2
	砂糖 ……………	大さじ1

■ Ingredients (serves 4)

8 prawns with heads

A
- 1 U.S. cup stock
- 2 Tbsps light soy sauce
- 2 Tbsps *mirin* sweet cooking *sake*
- 2 Tbsps *sake*
- 1 Tbsp sugar

【作り方】

1 有頭えびは背わたを取る。頭の先端とひげ、尾の先を包丁で切り落としておく。

2 鍋にAを入れ火にかけ煮立ったら、1のえびを加えて強火で3分くらい煮る。

3 2のえびに火が通ったら煮汁に漬けた鍋のまま、冷水にあてて冷ます。
※冷めるまで煮汁に漬け、味をふくませること。

【DIRECTIONS】

1 Devein the prawns. Cut off the tips of the heads, filaments, and tails.

2 Put the ingredients of **A** in a pot, and heat. When it comes to the boil, add the prawns, and cook over a high heat for about 3 min.

3 When the prawns are cooked, put the pot in cold water to cool the prawns and the liquid.
※ Leave the prawns in the liquid until cool to allow the seasonings to seep into the prawns.

なます

甘酸っぱく、さっぱり味で美味しい大根、にんじん、赤ピーマンのなます

about
10
min

Namasu Japanese Salad

Sweet and sour salad of *daikon* radish, carrot, and red bell pepper is refreshing and tasty

■材料・2人分

大根	4cm分
にんじん	3cm分
赤ピーマン	1/4個
塩	小さじ1/4
A ┌ 酢	大さじ2
│ だし汁	大さじ4
│ 砂糖	大さじ2
└ 塩	小さじ1/4
ゆず皮（せん切り）	少々

※調理時間に漬ける時間は含まれない

Ingredients (serves 2)

1 1/2-inch *daikon* giant white radish
1 1/4-inch carrot
1/4 red bell pepper
1/4 tsp salt

A ┌ 2 Tbsps vinegar
　 │ 4 Tbsps stock
　 │ 2 Tbsps sugar
　 └ 1/4 tsp salt

Small quantity of *yuzu*, or Japanese lime, rind (thin strips)

※The cooking time does not include the time for marinating

【作り方】

1 大根は皮をむいて約1cmの幅の短冊切り、にんじんは皮をむいて薄切りにして花形に抜き、赤ピーマンは種を取って輪切りにしておく。

★抜いたにんじんのあまりは、味噌汁や、スープなどに利用するとよい。

2 ボウルに1の大根、にんじん、赤ピーマンを入れて塩をふりいれて軽く合わせ、しばらくおいておき、しんなりして水が出てきたら、一度軽く水洗いし、水けを絞る。

3 耐熱容器にAを入れて電子レンジ（600W）で約30〜40秒加熱し、よく混ぜ合わせたら、2の大根、にんじん、赤ピーマンとあえ、ゆず皮のせん切りを加え、1時間以上おいて味をしみこませてからいただく。

【DIRECTIONS】

1 Peel the *daikon* radish, and cut into about 3/8-inch wide rectangles. Peel the carrot, slice thinly, and cut out into flower shape pieces. Remove the seeds of the red bell pepper, and cut into rounds.

★ Use the remaining parts of the carrot for *miso* soup or other kinds of soup.

2 Put the *daikon* radish, carrot, and red bell pepper prepared in **1** in a bowl, sprinkle with salt, and lightly mix. Leave the vegetables until they soften and liquid comes out. Rinse them, and squeeze out excess moisture.

3 Put the ingredients of **A** in a heat-resistant bowl, and microwave (600 w) for 30 to 40 sec. Stir the liquid well, put in the *daikon* radish, carrot, and red bell pepper, and mix. Add the *yuzu* strips, and let stand for more than 1 hour to allow the ingredients to absorb the seasonings before serving.

<ruby>紅白<rt>こうはく</rt></ruby>なます
Red And White Salad

■材料・2〜3人分

大根	200g
にんじん	20g
ゆず皮	少々
塩	少々
〈甘酢の材料〉	
酢	1/4カップ
だし汁	1/3カップ
砂糖	大さじ3
塩	小さじ1/4

■ INGREDIENTS (serves 2 or 3)

7 oz *daikon* giant white radish
2/3 oz carrot
Small quantity of *yuzu* rind
Small quantity of salt
〈For preparing dressing〉
1/5 U.S. cup vinegar
1/7 U.S. cup stock
3 Tbsps sugar
1/4 tsp salt

【作り方】

1 大根とにんじんは皮をむいて4cmの長さのせん切りにする。

2 1をボウルに入れて、塩少々をふり入れてもむ。

★塩もみする時、最初は野菜がかたいので軽くもみ、水が出てきたら、少し力を入れてもむ。

3 甘酢の材料を小鍋に入れて、砂糖が溶けるまで温め、冷ましておく。

4 2の塩もみにしたにんじんと大根の水けをきり、甘酢にゆずの皮のせん切りを入れ、軽くあえてから漬ける。

★1時間くらいおいて味をしみ込ませてからいただく。

【DIRECTIONS】

1 Peel the *daikon* white radish and carrot, and cut into 1 1/2-inch long julienne strips.

2 Place the chopped giant white radish and carrot in a bowl, sprinkle on a pinch quantity of salt and rub together.

★Rub the vegetables lightly at the beginning while they are hard. When liquid appears, press them harder.

3 Place the dressing ingredients in a small pot, and heat until the sugar melts. Let stand until cool.

4 Drain the pressed radish and carrot. Add the *yuzu* rind, cut into julienne strips, to the dressing. Mix the vegetables with the dressing lightly.

★Let rest about 1 hour until the vegetables absorb the seasonings sufficiently.

しょうがつ
正月料理
New Year's foods

鮭のこぶ巻

一年を喜びながら生活できるように願っていただくこぶ巻

about
20
min

Konbu-Rolled Salmon

Enjoy *konbu* kelp rolls, while praying for a happy life in the coming year

■材料・2〜3人分

生鮭	2切れ
塩	少々
早煮昆布	2枚
かんぴょう	20g

A
水	3カップ
酢	大さじ1
酒	大さじ1

B
砂糖	大さじ5
しょう油	大さじ2と1/2

C
みりん	大さじ2
しょう油	小さじ1

Ingredients (serves 2 or 3)

2 fillets unsalted salmon
Small quantity of salt
2 sheets "*hayani*" *konbu*
kelp (soft part of kelp good
for cooking)
2/3 oz dried gourd strips

A
- 2 1/2 cups water
- 1 Tbsp vinegar
- 1 Tbsp *sake*

B
- 5 Tbsps sugar
- 2 1/2 Tbsps soy sauce

C
- 2 Tbsps *mirin* sweet
  cooking *sake*
- 1 tsp soy sauce

【作り方】

1 かんぴょうは塩でよくもみ、少し時間をおく。一度水洗いし、たっぷりの湯で5分くらいゆでて透明感が出て、やわらかくなったらざるに取る。

2 生鮭は塩を少々ふり、一口大に切る。昆布は一度水に漬けてから戻し、ざるに上げて汁けをきって、鮭よりひと回り大きめに切る。鮭を芯にして、昆布を巻きつけ、1のかんぴょうで2重に巻いて結ぶ。

3 鍋に2が重ならないように並べ、Aを入れて沸騰させたら中火にし、Bを入れて、落としぶたをしながら時々アクを取りながら煮る。

4 3の昆布がやわらかく煮えたら、Cを加えて煮ふくめる。照りが出てきたら出来上がり。

【DIRECTIONS】

1 Rub the dried gourd strips with salt, and let it stand for a while. Wash the gourd strips, and boil in deep water for a while until they become soft and slightly transparent. Drain in a sieve.

2 Sprinkle the raw salmon with small quantity of salt, and cut into bite-size pieces. Soak the kelp in water to soften, drain in a sieve, and cut into a size that is large enough to wind the fish. Wind the kelp around the salmon, and tie the doubly wound gourd strip.

3 Arrange the rolls in a pan, (do not pile up), and add the mixture of **A**. When it comes to the boil, turn down the heat to medium, add the mixture of **B**, cover with an *otoshi buta* (drop lid), and simmer while occasionally skimming off the scum.

4 When the *konbu* kelp softens, add the mixture of **C**, and boil down the liquid till the ingredients become glossy.

関東風ぞう煮

あっさりだしで、あっさりいただくのが関東風

about **20** min

Kanto-Style Rice Cake Soup

Kanto-style *zou-ni*, or rice cake soup, is cooked in simple stock

■材料・2人分

角餅	4個
鶏もも肉	80g
にんじん	約3cm
小松菜	2株
かまぼこ	4切れ
三つ葉	適量
ゆず	適量
だし汁	600cc
A ┌ 塩	小さじ1/2
├ しょう油	小さじ2
└ 酒	大さじ1
酒	適量

■ Ingredients (serves 2)

4 rectangular rice cakes
2 4/5 oz boneless chicken thigh
About 1 1/4-inch carrot
2 whole *komatsuna* mustard
4 slices *kamaboko* fish paste
Trefoil stalks
Yuzu Japanese lime
2 1/2 U.S. cups stock

A ┌ 1 tsp salt
├ 2 tsps soy sauce
└ 1 Tbsp *sake*

Sake

【作り方】

1 鶏もも肉は一口大に切り、酒少々をふる。にんじんは短冊切りにする。小松菜はさっと塩(分量外)ゆでし、3〜4cmの長さに切る。かまぼこは薄切りにする。三つ葉は1〜2cmの長さに切る。ゆずは皮をそぐ。

2 角餅をオーブントースターなどでこんがりと焼く。

3 鍋にだし汁を入れ、**1**の鶏肉とにんじんを入れ沸いたらアクを取り、鶏肉に火が通ったら**A**を加える。

4 **3**の鍋に**2**の餅を入れ軽く温め、椀に餅とだし汁を注ぎ入れる。**1**の小松菜、かまぼこ、三つ葉、ゆず皮をあしらう。

【DIRECTIONS】

1 Cut the chicken into bite-size pieces, and sprinkle with a small quantity of *sake*. Cut the carrot into rectangles. Briefly boil the *komatsuna* mustard in salty water (extra quantity of salt), and cut into 1 1/4 to 1 1/2-inch lengths. Slice the *kamaboko* fish paste. Cut the trefoil into 3/8 to 3/4-inch lengths. Shave off small pieces of the *yuzu* peel.

2 Grill the rice cakes in a toaster oven until brown.

3 Heat the stock, cut chicken, and carrot in a pot. When the stock comes to the boil, skim off the scum. When the chicken is cooked, add the mixture of **A**.

4 Put the grilled rice cakes in the pot, and heat. Put into a serving bowl the rice cakes and other ingredients with soup, and garnish with the boiled *komatsuna*, cut *kamaboko*, trefoil, and *yuzu* peel.

コラム

Column

ぞう煮の違い
Variety of *Zou-ni*

　ぞう煮の違いはまず餅の形だ。北海道、東北、関東、東海 (静岡県)、新潟のほとんどは、角餅が主流で、東海、越前、近畿、中国、四国、九州では丸餅を使用する。さらに一部だがあん餅を使用する地方もある。角餅は江戸の文化を受けた土地で、丸餅は京文化の影響を受けた土地と考えられる。

　次に味つけだが、有名なのは京都の白味噌だ。他には四国、中国、近畿などで白味噌が、日本海側では赤味噌が使われている。しょう油や塩で味つけするすまし仕立ては、味噌仕立て以外の地方になる。

　このように地方によってさまざまなぞう煮があるが、今や流通や保存の発達できっちりと区別できなくなっているのが現状だ。

When we talk about varieties of *zou-ni*, we first think of different shapes of rice cakes. Most households in Hokkaido, Tohoku, and Kanto areas as well as Shizuoka and Niigata Prefectures use rectangular rice cakes, while those in Tokai, Echizen, Kinki, Chugoku, Shikoku, and Kyushu areas use round-shaped rice cakes. In some other areas, though not many, people use rice cakes with bean-jam inside. It is believed that rectangular rice cakes are popular in areas under the influence of Edo culture, while round rice cakes are used in areas influenced by Kyoto culture.

Seasonings also differ. Kyoto people famously use "white" *miso*. "White" *miso* is also used in Shikoku, Chugoku and Kinki areas. In areas on the Japan Sea side, "red" *miso* is used generally. Clear soup seasoned with soy sauce or salt is popular in other areas.

Different areas have had different types of *zou-ni*, but today it is increasingly difficult to draw clear lines between areas in terms of *zou-ni* varieties, due to the development of national food distribution systems and storing technology.

節分 せつぶん *Setsubun* (seasonal division)

お父さんが鬼の面を被り、子供たちやお母さんが豆を「鬼は外、福は内」といってぶつける節分。ほほえましい冬を代表する風物詩だが、節分は邪霊災厄を除き、新しい年を迎えるための古くから伝わる大切な行事なのだ。

The father puts on a demon mask and the children and the mother throw beans to the demon while shouting, "In with good fortune! Out with the demon!" This heart-warming event, typical of winter, takes place on the day of *Setsubun*. It has been an important time-honored rite to welcome the New Year by banishing evils and keeping the house from calamity.

節分の歴史と由来 Origin and history of *Setsubun* (seasonal division)

節分とは季節の分かれめのことで、立春、立夏、立秋、立冬の前日をさす。かつては冬から春になる時期を一年の境としていたため、新しい年を迎えるにあたって不浄なことや悪疫をもたらす邪悪なものを追い払う必要があった。

中国では古くから難を除く〝追儺〟がおこなわれており、それが日本に伝わり立春の前日（二月三日・四日）の節分に不浄や悪疫をもたらす鬼を祓う豆をまき、柊挿しがおこなわれるようになった。日本では文武天皇の慶雲三年（706年）に、宮中で初めておこなわれたといわれている。

豆まきに使用する豆は、炒った食べられる豆（地方によっては殻つきの落花生もある）で、歳の数だけ食べると一年を丈夫に暮らすことができるといわれている。豆をまく時の口上は「鬼は外、福は内」が基本だが、地方によって異なる。ちなみに本尊が厄神鬼王や鬼が御祭神であったり、鬼が地名につくなどの場合は、鬼は外とはいわず「鬼は内、福は内」「福は内、悪魔外」「鬼は内、福は内、悪魔外」などといわれる。豆の投げ方は口上をいいながら、下からほおるのが基本になる。

柊挿しは鬼が嫌いだといわれる悪臭を放つ鰯の頭などを焼いて、柊の枝に挿して戸口に置いて除霊をする。にんにくを追加する地方もあるらしい。また、節分の日にいわしを焼いて食べる地方もあるらしい。

Setsubun, or seasonal division, falls on the day before the calendric beginning of each season of spring, summer, autumn and winter. Today, this term specially refers to the day before the beginning of spring. Formerly, transition from winter to spring was considered to be the boundary between years. It was necessary to dispel unclean things and all evils that bring about various plagues before the start of a new year.

In China, *tsuina* has been observed since olden days to dispel harm. The event was imported to Japan, where it was established as a function of the imperial court. They threw beans to banish demons who caused various evil things and plagues. The event also included the rite of *hiiragi-sashi* (insertion of holly branch) to drive devils away by hanging burned sardine heads, skewered to a holly branch. The function was performed on the days (February 3 and 4) immediately before the first day of spring by the traditional Japanese calendar. It is said that this court function was first performed in 706 during the reign of Emperor Monmu.

The beans used in *Mame-maki* (bean throwing) are parched and edible. *Rakkasei*, or peanuts, with shell, are used in place of beans depending on the region. It is believed that one can maintain good health throughout the year by eating the same number of thrown beans as one's age. They shout, in principle, "In with good fortune! Out with the demon (i.e., evils and bad luck)!" as they throw beans. This again varies with the region. They do not say, "Out with the demon" but call out, for example, "In with the demon, in with good fortune," "In with good fortune, out with the devil," or "In with the demon, in with good fortune, out with the devil," in the regions where the Chinese character *oni* (demon) is used in the name of the place. This also applies when the main subject of worship (*honzon*) of a temple is *Yakujin Kio* or the deity of a shrine is a demon. You throw beans from below upwards while shouting as above.

Hiiragi-sashi (insertion of holly branch) is a rite to drive devils away by hanging burned sardine heads giving off a bad smell (the demons are said to dislike the smell), skewered to a holly branch and hung at the door of a house. Garlic is added in some regions. They eat grilled sardines on the day of *Setsubun* in some regions.

恵方巻きの由来 Origin of *Eho-maki* (*Eho sushi* rolls)

　恵方巻きとは〝七福神〟にちなんで七種類の具材を巻いた太巻きのことで、江戸時代末期に大阪の船場で商売繁盛を祈願するために、節分の日に恵方（陰陽道でその年の干支によって定められた、最もよいとされる方角のこと）に向かって食べたのがはじまりである。

　恵方巻きは、目を閉じて願いごとを思いながら、恵方に向かって無言で一本丸ごと食べるのがしきたりになっている。一本丸ごと食べるのは、〝縁を切らない〟ためである。また、途中で食べるのを止めたり、声を出してしまうと願いごとがかなわなかったり、運が逃げるといわれている。

　関西地方の風習だった恵方巻きも、全国のスーパーやコンビニエンスストアで販売されるようになってからは、現在では全国的に知られるようになった。

Eho-maki is a *sushi* roll containing 7 ingredients associated with the Seven Deities of Good Fortune (*Shichi-fukujin*). It was invented at Senba, Osaka, toward the end of the Edo Era to wish for business prosperity. They ate the *sushi* roll on the day of *Setsubun*, facing the direction of *Eho* that was most lucky for the year as determined by the Way of Yin and Yang.

It is customary to eat *Eho-maki* while making a wish in the mind with the eyes closed and without uttering a single word. You will eat the whole roll at a stroke in order not to "lose" ties. Some say that your wish is not heard or the luck runs away from you if you utter a word or stop eating halfway.

Eho-maki is originally the custom of the people in the Kansai region. It is now popular all over Japan, and *Eho-maki* is on sale at supermarkets and convenience stores throughout Japan.

江戸時代末期の大阪・船場が発祥の恵方巻き
Eho-maki originated in Senba, Osaka toward the end of the Edo Era

せつぶん
節分料理
Food for *setsubun*, the last day of winter in the lunar calendar

えほうまき
恵方巻き（太巻き）

一年の無病息災、商売繁盛、幸福を願って太巻きを口いっぱいにほうばる

about 35 min

Ehou-Maki (Thick *Sushi* Roll)

Take a hearty mouthful of a thick *sushi* roll, while praying for your health, good business, and happiness for the year

■ 材料・2本分

寿し飯		2本分（約500g）
干ししいたけ		3枚
A	だし汁（干ししいたけの戻し汁と合わせ）	100cc
	しょう油	小さじ2
	砂糖	大さじ1
	酒	大さじ1/2
	みりん	大さじ1/2
焼き穴子		1尾
卵		2個
B	砂糖	小さじ1
	塩	少々
	酒	小さじ1
きゅうり		縦1/2本
にんじん		縦1/6本
三つ葉		1/2束
でんぶ		大さじ2
焼きのり		2枚
塩		適量
サラダ油		適量

※工程時間に干ししいたけを戻す時間は含まれていません

【作り方】

1 寿し飯を準備する。（P22、23参照）

2 干ししいたけを水で戻しやわらかくなったら、**A**で煮て味をふくませる。冷めたら太めのせん切りにする。

3 焼き穴子は1cm幅に細く切る。

4 卵は溶いて**B**で調味する。フライパンにサラダ油を熱し、卵液を薄く流し、**3**の穴子をのせて縁からくるくると巻く。2本準備する。

5 三つ葉はさっと塩ゆでにする。きゅうりは太めの棒切りにする。にんじんはせん切りにしてさっと塩ゆでにする。

■ Ingredients (for 2 rolls)

1 1/3 oz vinegared rice (for 2 rolls)
3 dried *shiitake* mushrooms

A
2/5 U.S. cup stock (mixed with *shiitake*-soaked water)
2 tsps soy sauce
1 Tbsp sugar
1/2 Tbsp *sake*
1/2 Tbsp *mirin* sweet cooking *sake*

1 grilled conger eel
2 egg

B
1 tsp sugar
Small quantity of salt
1 tsp *sake*

1/2 cucumber
1/6 carrot
1/2 bundle trefoil stalks
2 Tbsps *denbu* shredded and seasoned fish flesh
2 sheets toasted *nori* seaweed
Salt
Vegetable oil

※The cooking time does not include the time for softening the dried *shiitake* mushroom.

【DIRECTIONS】

1 Prepare vinegared rice. (see p.22 and 23)

2 Soften the dried *shiitake* mushrooms by soaking them in water. Simmer the *shiitake* in the mixture of **A** to allow it to absorb the seasonings. When cool, cut the *shiitake* into thick strips.

3 Cut the conger eel lengthwise into 3/8-inch wide strips.

4 Beat the egg, and season with the ingredients listed in **B**. Heat the vegetable oil in a frying pan, thinly spread the beaten egg, place the cut conger eel on top, and roll up the thin omelet by raising the edge first. Make another egg roll likewise.

5 Briefly boil the trefoil in salty water. Cut the cucumber into thickish bar rectangles. Cut the carrot into julienne strips, and briefly boil in salty water.

6 巻きすに焼きのりをおき、1の寿し飯（約250g）をのせ、向こう側を1cmくらい残すように広げる。具材をおくために、寿し飯の中央を少しくぼませる。

7 2、3、4の具材とでんぶを6の中央にのせ、具材とでんぶを手で押さえながら、巻き上げる。巻きす全体をしっかり締めるよう巻いたら、清潔な塗れ布巾で両端を軽く押さえて形を整える。

8 7を包丁で食べやすい大きさに切る。切るたび、包丁を清潔な濡れ布巾で拭うと切りやすい。

6 Place the *nori* sheet on a *maki-su* bamboo mat. Put the vinegared rice (about 8 3/4 oz) on the *nori* sheet, and spread, leaving 3/8-inch at the top uncovered. Cut a long shallow hollow in the center of the spread rice, where the ingredients will sit.

7 Put the ingredients prepared in **2**, **3**, and **4**, and the *denbu* in the center of the rice. Roll up the bamboo mat, while holding the ingredients with your hand. Firmly press the bamboo mat around the roll. Gently push both sides to shape, using a clean moistened cloth.

8 Cut the roll into bite-size portions. Wipe the knife with a clean moistened cloth after each cutting. This will make the cutting smooth.

コラム

Column

恵方巻きの正しい食べ方
Authentic Way of Eating *Ehou-Maki*

大阪では2月3日の節分に商売繁盛、無病息災、幸福を願って太巻寿司（恵方巻）を恵方に向かって丸ごとかぶりつく習慣がある。

恵方とは、陰陽道（自然界の陰陽と、木・火・土・金・水の五行の変化を観察して災厄などを判断し、人間界の吉凶を占う）でその年の干支によって定められた、最もよいとされる方角のことで、その方向に歳徳神（方位神のひとつで、その年の福徳を司る吉神）がいるといわれている。

太巻寿司を切らずにそのまま一本丸かじりするのは、「縁を切らない」という意味がある。そして7種類の具材を使うのは、七福神にちなんで「福を巻き込む」という願いが込められているのだ。

In Osaka, there is a custom of taking a hearty mouthful of a whole *ehou-maki sushi* roll, while praying for good business, health, and happiness, on February 3rd, the *setsubun*, or the last day of winter according to the traditional lunar calendar.

Ehou is the luckiest direction decided based on the year's zodiac sign according to *Onmyodou*, or the way of yin and yang - a way of telling fortune in the human world through the observation of yin-yang in nature, as well as changes in five elements (wood, fire, earth, metal, and water). It is believed that in this direction there is a god called *toshikoku-jin*—one of the deities of directions who controls good luck in the year.

The custom of biting the *ehou-maki* without cutting comes from the idea of not cutting connections. *Ehou-maki*, which contains seven different ingredients symbolizing the Seven Deities of Good Fortune, reflects people's hopes of being blessed by good fortune.

冬の和食レシピ

Recipes of Japanese Food in Winter

冬を彩る旬の食材
Seasonal Ingredients in Winter

夏野菜の多くは暑い夏に体を冷やしてくれるものが多く、冬には私たちの体を温めてくれる根菜が多く出まわる。それらの野菜を使った煮もの、鍋料理は最高。ぶり、はたはた、ひらめなどの多くの魚は脂がのり美味しくなる。それらを使った鍋料理はもちろんのこと、焼きもの、煮つけなどに使用される。また、毛がに、ずわいがに、甘えびなども美味しくなる季節である。

Many summer vegetables cool our body, while many root vegetables warm up our body in winter. *Nimono* (simmered dishes) and *nabe-ryori* (one-pot dishes) using these winter vegetables are superb. Many fish including *buri* (yellow tail), *hata-hata* (sandfish), and *hirame* (bastard halibut) are also delicious because they have plenty of fat in winter. These fish are frequently used in not only one-pot dishes but also *yakimono* (grilled foods) and *nitsuke* (boiled foods). Horsehair crab, snow crab, and northern shrimp are also tasty in winter.

※本書で紹介する食材の旬は基本的なものを紹介している。地方によって異なる場合もある。
※The typically best season for the ingredients in this book is given, and this may differ in some areas.

かぶ (蕪)
Kabu (turnip)

地方によってさまざまな品種があるかぶだが、白かぶと赤かぶに大別することができる。白かぶは漬けもの、煮ものなどにされるが、赤かぶは主に漬けものにされる。

With many species in different regions, *kabu* (turnip) is generally classified into white and red turnips. White turnip is used for pickles and *nimono* (simmered dishes), while red turnip is mainly used for pickles.

だいこん (大根)
Daikon (giant white radish)

多くの品種があるが、市場によく出まわっているのは青首だいこんが多い。一年中出まわるが冬に甘味が増し、みずみずしくなる。主に煮もの、漬けものなどにする。

Although there are also many varieties of *daikon*, the most common on the market is *aokubi* (literally "blue neck") *daikon*. *Daikon* is available throughout the year but gets sweeter and fresher in winter. It is mainly used for *nimono* and pickles.

ねぎ (葱)
Negi (*naga-negi* onion)

鍋料理に欠かせないねぎは、白根が多い千住ねぎ群と青い葉の部分が多い九条ねぎ群、茎が太い加賀太ねぎ群に分類される。焼きもの、汁もの、薬味などに使用される。

Negi is indispensable for one-pot dishes. It is largely classified into *senju-negi* with a large white section, *kujo-negi* with a large blue section (leaves), and *kaga-futo-negi* with a large, thick stem. *Negi* is used in grilled foods and soups and as a condiment.

はくさい（白菜）
Hakusai (Chinese cabbage)

冬の鍋料理や漬けものに欠かせないはくさい。冬になると甘味が増して美味しい。球が詰まっているものがよい。炒めもの、蒸しものなどにも使用される。

Hakusai is an indispensable vegetable for preparing one-pot dishes and pickles in winter. It is more delicious in winter because it is sweeter. The tighter the ball, the better. *Hakusai* is frequently used in *itamemono* (stir-fried dishes) and *mushimono* (steamed dishes).

にんじん（人参）
Nin-jin (carrot)

にんじんはヨーロッパ型とアジア型とがある。市場によく出まわっているのはヨーロッパ型で、金時（京にんじん）はアジア型になる。煮もの、炒めもの、揚げものなどに使う。

Nin-jin is classified into European and Asian varieties. The European variety is very popular in the market. *Kintoki* (*Kyo-ninjin*) is an Asian variety. *Nin-jin* can be eaten in a variety of ways, such as by simmering, stir-frying, or deep-frying.

ごぼう（牛蒡）
Gobo (burdock)

野菜として使用するのは日本だけのごぼう。食物繊維が豊富で、便秘解消やコレステロール値を低下させる健康野菜だ。煮もの、炒めもの、天ぷらなどに使用される。

Gobo is eaten as a vegetable only in Japan. Rich in dietary fiber, the healthy vegetable helps relieve constipation and lower cholesterol. *Gobo* is cooked by simmering and stir-frying. It also makes a good ingredient for *tempura*.

ぶり（鰤）
Buri (yellowtail)

成長とともに呼び名が変わる出世魚の代表。70cm以上をぶりと呼び、40cmクラスをいなだという。寒ぶりは脂がのって美味しいとされ、刺身、焼き、鍋料理などにされる。

Buri is a typical *shusse-uo* (success fish), which is called by different names as it grows larger. *Buri* is 70 cm or larger, while *inada* is the 40-cm class. *Kan-buri* (winter *buri*) is particularly delicious because of its fattiness. It is frequently used in *sashimi* and one-pot dishes, or grilled.

ひらめ（鮃）
Hirame (bastard halibut)

寒びらめといわれるように、冬になると脂がのって美味しくなる。刺身、煮つけ、揚げものなどにされる。腹側が白いのが天然もので、黒斑があるのは養殖ものになる。

Often called "winter *hirame*," this fish is most delicious in winter because it fattens to survive the cold. *Hirame* is a favorite ingredient for *sashimi*. It is also boiled and deep-fried. Natural *hirame* has a white belly, while farmed *hirame* has black spots.

ふぐ（河豚）
Fugu (puffer)

市場（スーパーなど）では毒を処理したしょうさいふぐ、とらふぐなどの身が売られているので、安心して食べることができる。鍋料理、焼き、揚げものに適している。

Usually, *fugu* has poison in its ovaries, but the meat of *shosai-fugu*, *tora-fugu*, etc. in stores and supermarkets is prepared by licensed chefs. *Fugu* is used in one-pot dishes, or eaten grilled or fried.

あんこう（鮟鱇）
Ankou (anglerfish)

見ためはグロテスクだが、あんこうの7つ道具といわれるように捨てるところがないほどさまざまな部位を調理する。肝（あん肝）が大きくなる冬が最も美味しいとされる。

Though it looks grotesque, almost all parts of *ankou* can be cooked, leaving little to discard ("*ankou*'s seven tools" ; the whole fish is separated into 7 groups for cooking, respectively). The fish is a special delicacy in winter when the liver (*ankimo*) grows largest in the year.

あまだい（甘鯛）
Amadai (tilefish)

よく市場に出まわるのは、赤あまだいになる。他には白あまだい（高級）と、黄あまだいがいるが数は少ない。焼きもの、煮もの、蒸しもの、干ものなどにされる。

Aka-amadai (red *amadai*) is most extensively marketed. Also marketed are *shiro-amadai* (white, which is considered high class) and *ki-amadai* (yellow), but only in small quantities. Tilefish are best eaten by grilling, boiling, or steaming, or made into dried fish.

きんめだい（金目鯛）
Kinme-dai (golden-eye bream; alfonsino)

目が金色に輝くのが名の由来。成魚は水深200〜800mに生育している。冬になると脂がのり美味しくなり、煮つけ、塩焼き、刺身、鍋料理などに適している。

The Japanese name derives from the fish's golden eyes. The adult fish inhabit deep ocean waters of about 200 to 800 m. They put on fat and are tasty in winter. *Kinme-dai* is cooked by simmering and salt-grilling, and used for *sashimi* and one-pot dishes.

あこうだい（赤魚鯛、阿候鯛）
Akoh-dai (matsubara's red rockfish)

あこう、めぬけなどと呼ばれるあこうだい。水深400〜700mの岩礁域に生息している。冬に脂がのって、焼き、煮つけ、蒸しもの、鍋料理、汁ものの具などにされる。

Also known as akoh or *menuke*, *akoh-dai* inhabit reefs of 400 to 700 m deep in the sea. They fatten in winter, and are delicious ingredients for grilled, boiled, steamed, and one-pot dishes as well as for soups.

きちじ（喜知次）
Kichiji (bighand thornyhead)

正式名称のきちじより別名のきんき、きんきんの名のほうが通っている高級魚。白身だが脂がのっていて塩焼き、開き干しにしたものの焼きも絶品だ。

Kichiji, a high-class fish, is better known by the aliases of *kinki* and *kinkin*. The fatty white flesh is best cooked by salt-grilling. Dried *kichiji*, with the internal organs removed, is particularly delicious when grilled.

くろまぐろ（黒鮪）
Kuro-maguro (bluefin tuna)

別名ほんまぐろ（本鮪）ともいわれる。日本近海での漁獲量が激減しているため、海のダイヤモンドといわれる。10〜1月が日本近海のくろまぐろの旬になる。

Kuro-maguro is also known as *hon-maguro*. Harvest of this fish is drastically decreasing in the sea off Japan, so that the fish is called "diamonds" of the sea. October through January is the best season for *kuro-maguro* captured in Japanese waters.

ほうぼう（魴鮄）
Houbou (bluefin searobin)

特に冬になると美味しくなり、高級
魚の仲間入りをする。新鮮なものは
刺身、寿し、鍋もの、煮もの、ブイ
ヤベースなどと大活躍する。

Houbou is particularly delicious in
winter, and considered a high-class
fish. Fresh *houbou* is a favorite
ingredient for *sashimi*, *sushi*, one-pot
dishes, and *nimono* as well as
bouillabaisse.

はたはた（鰰、鱩）
Hata-hata (Japanese sandfish)

日本海から北大平洋に分布し、かつ
ては秋田県で多く漁獲されたので、
県魚にもなっている。焼きもの、煮
つけ、鍋料理、汁ものの具など、多
くの料理に使用される。

Hata-hata is found in the areas
extending from the Sea of Japan to
the North Pacific Ocean. It is captured
in quantity in Akita Prefecture and
hence is the prefectural fish of Akita
Prefecture. It is typically cooked by
grilling and boiling and is used in
one-pot dishes and soups.

あまえび（甘海老）
Ama-ebi (northern shrimp)

日本海側ではよく獲れるあまえび。
別名ほっこくあかえびともいわれる
ように、体色が赤く、身が甘いのが
名の由来。新鮮なものは刺身、寿し
種にされる。

Ama-ebi is abundant in the Sea of
Japan. Also known as *hokkoku aka-ebi*
(northern red shrimp), *ama-ebi* has a
red body and sweet flesh. Fresh *ama-
ebi* makes a good ingredient for
sashimi and *sushi*.

けがに（毛蟹）
Ke-gani (horsehair crab)

北海道、東北地方を代表するけがに。
現在は国内産のものより、輸入もの
が多くなっている。殻全体が毛で覆
われているのが名の由来。主にゆで
てから食べられる。

Ke-gani is a representative shellfish of
Hokkaido and Tohoku district, but
imports outnumber the domestic
catch today. *Ke-gani* (hair crab) is so
named because the entire shell is
covered with hair. It is generally
cooked by boiling.

ずわいがに（楚蟹）
Zuwai-gani (snow crab)

産地によって呼び名が変わるずわい
がに。北陸地方ではえちぜんがに
（越前蟹）、山陰地方ではまつばがに
（松葉蟹）と呼ばれる。刺身、焼き、
蒸し、鍋ものにすると最高。

Zuwai-gani has different names in
different regions; *echizen-gani* in the
Hokuriku district and *matsuba-gani* in
the San-in district, for example. Its
delicious taste is best appreciated by
grilling, steaming, and one-pot dishes,
or when served as *sashimi*.

その他の旬の食材
Other Seasonal Ingredients

ブロッコリー●Broccoli
カリフラワー●Cauliflower
みずな（水菜）●Potherb mustard
ほっけ（魸）●Okhostk atka mackerel
ぶだい（部鯛、不鯛）●Parrotfish
むつ（鯥）●Japanese bluefish
みるがい（水松貝、海松貝）●Gaper
とりがい（鳥貝）●Japanese cockle
わたりがに（渡蟹）●Swimming crab
たらばがに（鱈場蟹）●Alaskan king crab
なまこ（海鼠）●Japanese common
sea cucumber
けんさきいか（剣先烏賊）●Swordtip squid
みずだこ（水蛸）●North pacific
giant octopus
うぐい（石斑魚）●Japanese dace

かぶと冬野菜の煮びたし

滋味深いかぶと冬野菜を手軽にできる煮びたしでいただく

about **15** min

Simmered Turnip and Winter Vegetables, *Nibitashi*-Style

Enjoy savory turnips and other winter vegetables in an easy-to-cook dish of *nibitashi*

■ 材料・2人分

かぶ	2個
小松菜	1株
にんじん	約4cm
だし汁	1カップ

A
酒	大さじ1
砂糖	大さじ1
薄口しょう油	大さじ1
みりん	大さじ1

■ Ingredients (serves 2)

2 turnips with leaves
1 whole *komatsuna* mustard
1 1/2-inch carrot
4/5 U.S. cup stock

A
1 Tbsp *sake*
1 Tbsp sugar
1 Tbsp light soy sauce
1 Tbsp *mirin* sweet cooking *sake*

■作り方

1 かぶは葉を約1cm残して切り落とし、皮をむいて8等分のくし形に切り、小松菜はよく洗ってから4cmの長さに切り、にんじんは皮をむいて4cmの長さの短冊に切る。

★かぶの葉は漬けものや炒めものに使用しよう。

2 鍋にだし汁と**1**のかぶを入れて煮立てたら弱火にし、かぶがやわらかく煮えたら、**1**の小松菜、にんじんを加えてさっと煮る。

3 **2**にAを加えて弱火で味を煮ふくませる。

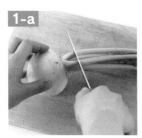

■DIRECTIONS

1 Cut the stalks of the turnips at about 3/8-inch from the round roots. Peel the roots, and cut into 8 equal-sized wedges. Wash the *komatsuna* mustard well, and cut into 1 1/2-inch lengths. Peel the carrot, and cut into 1 1/2-long rectangles.

★ Turnip leaves can be used for pickles or stir-fried dishes.

2 Boil the turnip in the stock, and simmer over a low heat until the turnip softens. Add the cut *komatsuna* and carrot, and cook briefly.

3 Add the mixture of **A** into the pot, and simmer over a low heat to allow the ingredients to absorb the seasonings.

コラム
Column

かぶの栄養と効能
Nutrients and Efficacy of Turnips

かぶは食物繊維が豊富なので、便秘解消、予防に適している。さらにはでんぷんの消化を助けるジアスターゼ、たんぱく質の消化を助けるアミラーゼなどが豊富に含まれているので、胃もたれ、食べすぎ、食欲不振に効果がある。

また、冬の根菜は体を温めてくれるといわれているので、冷え症気味の人はすすんで食べたいものだ。

捨てがちな葉の部分にはビタミンC、カロテン、カルシウム、カリウム、鉄分などが多く含まれているので、みそ汁の具、漬けもの、炒めものなどに使用したい。

Turnips have a high dietary fiber content, which is effective for easing and preventing constipation. In addition, the vegetable also is rich in diastase, which helps digest starch, and amylase, which helps digest protein, and is thus effective in easing an upset stomach, overeating, and poor appetite.

Root crops in winter are recommended to people who have poor circulation, as they are said to warm the body.

Many people throw away the leaves, but they are rich in Vitamin C, carotene, calcium, potassium, and iron. So, try to use turnip leaves for *miso* soup, pickles or stir-fried dishes.

大根の甘辛ステーキ

あまから

たれをふくんだ香ばしい大根をステーキ風にいただく

about **20** min

Salty-Sweet *Daikon* Steak

Enjoy *daikon* radish sautéed like steak, with a richly flavored sauce

■材料・2人分

大根	8cm
オリーブ油	大さじ1
赤唐辛子	1本

A
酒	大さじ1
しょう油	大さじ1
みりん	大さじ2
塩・黒こしょう	少々

糸唐辛子	適宜
あさつき	適宜

■ Ingredients (serves 2)

3-inch *daikon* giant white radish
1 Tbsp olive oil
1 red chili pepper

A
1 Tbsp *sake*
1 Tbsp soy sauce
2 Tbsps *mirin* sweet cooking *sake*
Small quantity of salt and black pepper

Red chili pepper julienne
Asatsuki chives

■作り方

1 大根は皮をむいて2cmの厚さに切り、鍋に米の
とぎ汁（分量外）をひたひたに入れて下ゆでし、や
わらかくなってきたら火を止めて冷めるまでおい
ておく。

2 フライパンにオリーブ油、赤唐辛子、水で洗っ
てから水けをきった**1**の大根を入れて両面焼く。

3 大根に焼き色がついたら**A**を入れて味をふくませ
るように煮からめたら、器に盛り、糸唐辛子をの
せ、あさつきを添える。

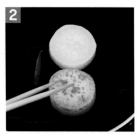

■DIRECTIONS

1 Peel the *daikon* radish, and cut into 3/4-inch
thick rounds. Parboil in water in which rice has
been washed (extra quantity of water) deep enough
to cover the *daikon* radish. When the *daikon* radish
begins to soften, remove from the heat, and let it
stand to cool.

2 Put into a frying pan olive oil, red chili pepper,
and the *daikon* radish, which has been rinsed and
drained. Fry both sides of the *daikon* radish.

3 When the *daikon* browns, add the mixture of **A**,
and continue heating to let the *daikon* absorb the
seasonings. Arrange on a serving dish, place the red
pepper julienne on top, and garnish with the
asatsuki chives.

コラム

Column

大根の使い分け方
How to Use *Daikon* Properly According to Dishes

　大根は部位によって適した料理があるとい
うことを知っているだろうか……。
　大根は上の方が甘く、下にいくほど辛味が
強くなるため、上の部分は大根おろしやサラ
ダなどの生食に適している。中央部分は比較
的やわらかく、みずみずしいのでふろふき大
根や、おでんなどの煮ものに適している。辛
味が強い下の部分は、そばの薬味などに適し
ている。

甘いのでサラダなどに
適している
Good for salad for its
sweetness

中央部は煮ものに適している
Central part is suitable for
simmered dishes

辛味が強いので薬味によい
Good for condiment for its
pungent taste

Do you know that different parts of a *daikon*
radish suit different kinds of dishes?
The upper part of the *daikon* is sweet, and it is
progressively pungent downward. So, the
upper part is good to eat raw, such as in
grated *daikon* or salad. The central part is
relatively soft and juicy, therefore, it is suitable
for simmered dishes like *oden*, or *furofuki
daikon*. The pungent lower part is good for
condiment for *soba* buckwheat noodles.

ぶりの鍋照り焼き

about **20** min

甘辛いたれとぶりの脂ののったやわらかい身がベストマッチ

Buri, Japanese Amberjack, *Teriyaki*

Salty-sweet sauce and fat-rich *buri* are a perfect match

■材料・2人分

ぶり（切り身）	………………	2切れ
塩	………………	適量

A
酒	………………	25cc
しょう油	………………	25cc
みりん	………………	25cc
砂糖	………………	大さじ1

白髪ねぎ	………………	適量
サラダ油	………………	適量

■ Ingredients (serves 2)

2 fillets *buri*, Japanese amberjack (yellow-tail)
Salt

A
1/10 U.S. cup *sake*
1/10 U.S. cup soy sauce
1/10 U.S. cup *mirin* sweet cooking *sake*
1 Tbsp sugar

Shiraga-negi, julienne strips of *naga-negi* onion (use the white part of *naga-negi*)
Vegetable oil

■作り方

1 ぶりは軽く塩をふり、約10分おき、ペーパータオルなどで水けをふき取る。

2 フライパンにサラダ油を入れて熱し、**1**のぶりを両面焼き、余分な油をペーパータオルでふき取る。

3 **2**に**A**を加えて、ぶりに火が通ったら取り出す。

4 **3**のフライパンに残ったたれをそのままとろみが出るまで煮詰める。

5 **3**のぶりを器に盛りつけ、**4**のたれをかけ、白髪ねぎを添える。

1-a　1-b

■DIRECTIONS

1 Lightly sprinkle the *buri* with salt. Let it stand for about 10 min, and paper-dry.

2 Heat the vegetable oil in a frying pan, fry both sides of the fish, and wipe off excess oil with kitchen paper.

3 Add the mixture of **A**, and heat until the fish is cooked. Remove the *buri*.

4 Boil down the remaining sauce in the pan until thick.

5 Arrange the *buri* on a serving dish, pour over the sauce, and garnish with the *shiraga-negi*.

いわしの蒲焼き

Grilled Sardine *Kabayaki*-Style

■材料・2人分

いわし	4尾
長ねぎ	1/2本
ししとう	6本
片栗粉	適宜
サラダ油	大さじ1
酒	大さじ2
砂糖	大さじ1
しょう油	大さじ2
みりん	大さじ1

■ Ingredients (serves 2)

4 sardine
1/2 *naga-negi* onion
6 *shishitou* bell peppers
Starch powder
1 Tbsp vegetable oil
2 Tbsps *sake*
1 Tbsp sugar
2 Tbsps soy sauce
1 Tbsp *mirin* sweet cooking *sake*

【作り方】

1 いわしはP290を参照して手開きにする。

2 **1**の手開きしたいわしに、片栗粉を薄くはたきつける。

3 フライパンにサラダ油を入れ熱し、**2**のいわしを身の方から焼き、こんがりと両面焼いたら取り出す。

4 **3**のフライパンの余分な油はペーパータオルでふき取り、酒、砂糖、しょう油、みりんを入れて煮立て、**3**のいわしを戻し入れてタレを煮からめる。

5 別のフライパンにサラダ油を少量（分量外）熱し、4cmの長さに切った長ねぎとししとうを焼く。

6 皿に**4**のいわしを盛り、**5**の長ねぎ、ししとうを添える。

[DIRECTIONS]

1 Hand-split the sardine. (See p.290 for how to hand-split sardine.)

2 Dust powder starch on the split sardine.

3 Heat the vegetable oil in a frying pan, and fry the inner side of the fish first, and then the outer side, until both sides become brown. Remove the fish.

4 Wipe off extra oil in the pan with kitchen paper, put in the mixture of the *sake*, sugar, soy sauce, and *mirin*, and bring it to the boil. Add the sardines so they are covered with the sauce.

5 Heat a small quantity of vegetable oil (extra) in another frying pan, and sauté the *naga-negi* onion (cut into 1 1/2-inch-long pieces) and *shishitou* green bell pepper.

6 Arrange the sardine on a serving dish, and garnish with the *naga-negi* and *shishitou*.

たらと豆腐のちり蒸し

ホロッとほどける甘いたらの身が美味しい

about 28 min

Steamed Cod and Tofu, *Chirimushi*-Style

Sweet cod meat melts in your mouth. It's so delicious

■ 材料・2人分

たら（切り身）	2切れ
塩	適量
豆腐	1/2丁
ほうれん草	1/4束
昆布（約6〜7cm）	2枚
酒	小さじ2
大根	約5〜6cm
鷹の爪	1本
ぽん酢しょう油	適量

■ Ingredients (serves 2)

2 fillets cod
Salt
1/2 block *tofu*
1/4 bundle spinach
2 sheets *konbu* kelp (2 1/2-inch long)
2 tsps *sake*
2 - 2 1/2-inch *daikon* giant white radish
1 red chili pepper
Ponzu soy sauce (citrus-juice-mixed soy sauce)

■作り方

1 たらは軽く塩をふり約20分おき、ペーパータオルなどで水けを取り、一口大に切る。

2 ほうれん草は水洗いして、さっとゆがいて水けを絞り約4〜5cmに切る。豆腐は2つに切る。

3 大根は皮をむき、箸などで穴を開け、へたを切った鷹の爪を入れてすり、もみじおろしを作る。（詳しくはP67参照）

4 2つの器に昆布をしき、**2**の豆腐と**1**のたらをのせ、酒をふる。

5 蒸し器はP278を参照して温め、**4**の器を蒸し器に入れて強火で約5分蒸し、器を取り出して**2**のほうれん草をあしらい、さらに1〜2分蒸す。

6 **5**が蒸し上がったら、**3**のもみじおろしを適量添え、ぽん酢しょう油でいただく。

■DIRECTIONS

1 Lightly sprinkle the cod with salt, and let it stand for about 20 min. Paper-dry, and cut into bite-size pieces.

2 Wash the spinach, briefly boil and squeeze off the water. Cut into 1 1/2- to 2-inch lengths. Cut the *tofu* in half.

3 Make *momiji-oroshi*. Peel the *daikon* radish, make a hole with a chopstick, stuff with the red chili pepper, and grate. (For details, see p.67.)

4 Place the *konbu* kelp in two bowls, put the cut *tofu*, and cod on top, and sprinkle with *sake*.

5 Heat a steamer (see p.278), place the bowls in it, and cook for about 5 min over high heat. Remove the bowls, and add the boiled spinach. Steam again for 1 to 2 min.

6 When they are ready, take a small quantity of the *momiji-oroshi*, and serve with the *ponzu* soy sauce.

はまぐりの茶碗蒸し
Cup-Steamed Egg Custard with Clams

■材料・2人分

はまぐり（小）	4個
ブイヨン	200cc
卵	2個
牛乳	適量
トマト水煮	1/4缶分（約100g）
玉ねぎ（みじん切り）	大さじ1
オリーブ油	小さじ1
塩・こしょう	適量
イタリアンパセリ	適量

■ Ingredients (serves 2)

4 small clams
4/5 U.S. cup bouillon
2 eggs
Milk
1/4 can boiled tomatoes (about 3 1/2 oz)
1 Tbsp chopped onion
1 tsp olive oil
Salt and pepper
Flat-leaf parsley

【作り方】

1 はまぐりは塩水（分量外）につけて砂出しをする。

2 **1**のはまぐりをブイヨンで煮て身を取り出す。ブイヨンは冷まし、牛乳を加えて250ccにする。

3 小鍋にオリーブ油を入れて熱し、玉ねぎを炒めて、トマト水煮を手でつぶしながら加える。約半量までペースト状に煮詰めたら、塩・こしょうで味を調え、冷ましておく。

4 卵を割り溶いて**2**のブイヨン液と合わせ、塩・こしょうで味を調え、こしておく。

5 器に**3**のトマトソースを各小さじ2杯程度入れ、**4**の卵液を静かに流す。

6 蒸し器はP278を参照して温める。

7 **5**を**6**の蒸し器に入れ、強火で約2分、弱火にて約5分蒸したら、**2**のはまぐりの身をのせ、さらに弱火で約3分蒸す。飾りに残りの**3**のトマトソース、イタリアンパセリを添える。

[DIRECTIONS]

1 Soak the clams in salty water (extra quantity salt) to allow them to expel sand.

2 Boil the clams in the bouillon, and remove the flesh. Cool the bouillon, and add milk to make the liquid of 250cc (1 U.S. cup. + 1 Tbsp).

3 Heat the olive oil in a small pot, sauté the onion, and add the boiled tomatoes while crushing them by hand. Boil down to reduce the amount of the sauce to half to thicken it, season with salt and pepper, and let stand to cool.

4 Beat the eggs, and mix with the bouillon prepared in **2**. Season with salt and pepper, and strain.

5 Put into each bowl about 2 tsps of the tomato sauce prepared in **3**, and then carefully pour the egg mixture into the bowls, respec-tively.

6 Heat a steamer (see p.278).

7 Put the bowls in the steamer, steam for about 2 min over high heat, and 5 min over low heat. Put the clam flesh prepared in **2** on top, and steam for about 3 more min over low heat. Garnish with the remaining tomato sauce, and flat—leaf parsley as a finishing touch.

about **15** min

たらのホイル焼き
ホロッとくずれるたらの身とバターの相性が最高

Aluminum Foil-Grilled Cod
Crumbly cod meat goes perfectly with butter

■材料・2人分

たら（切り身）	2切れ
玉ねぎ	1/8個
れんこん	約2cm
えのき	1/2束
赤ピーマン	1/10個
バター	大さじ1
酒	大さじ2

A
白すりごま	大さじ1
しょう油	大さじ2
砂糖	小さじ1/2
万能ねぎ（小口切り）	2本分

スナップえんどう	2個
塩・こしょう	適量

■ Ingredients (serves 2)

2 fillets cod
1/8 onion
About 3/4-inch lotus root
1/2 bundle *enokidake* mushrooms
1/10 red bell pepper
1 Tbsp butter
2 Tbsps *sake*

A
1 Tbsp ground white sesame seeds
2 Tbsps soy sauce
1/2 tsp sugar
2 *bannou-negi* onions (cut into small rounds)

2 pods snap peas
Salt and pepper

■作り方

1 玉ねぎはへたを切り取り、皮をむいて約7〜8mmの厚さの輪切りに、れんこんは皮をむいて約1cmの厚さの輪切りに、えのきは根もとを切り取り、小房に分ける。赤ピーマンは短冊切りにする。スナップえんどうを塩（分量外）ゆでにする。**A**を合わせてたれを作る。

2 アルミホイルにたらをのせ、軽く塩・こしょうする。

3 2の上に1の玉ねぎ、れんこん、えのき、赤ピーマンの順にのせ、バターをおいて酒をふってアルミホイルを閉じる。グリルかオーブントースターで約10分焼く。

4 3を器に盛り、彩りに1のスナップえんどうをあしらい、1のたれを添える。

■DIRECTIONS

1 Cut off the root of the onion, peel, and cut into about 1/3-inch thick round slices. Peel the lotus root, and cut into 3/8-inch thick rounds. Chop off the base of the *enokidake* mushrooms, and separate into small portions. Cut the red bell pepper into rectangles. Boil the snap peas in salty water (extra quantity salt). Mix the ingredients of **A** to make the sauce.

2 Place the cod on aluminum foil sheets, and lightly sprinkle with salt and pepper.

3 Put on the ingredients in the order of onion, lotus root, *enokidake*, and red pepper. Add butter, and sprinkle with *sake*. Close the foil wrap, and grill in a griller or toaster oven for about 10 min.

4 Place on a serving dish, open the foil, and garnish with the snap peas, and serve with the sauce.

かきのホイル蒸し
Aluminum Foil-Steamed Oyster

■材料・2人分

かき	6粒
長ねぎ	1本
あさつき	5〜6本
みそ	大さじ2
砂糖	大さじ1
牛乳	大さじ1

■Ingredients (serves 2)

6 oysters
1 *naga-negi* onion
5 or 6 leaves *asatsuki* chive
2 Tbsps *miso*
1 Tbsp sugar
1 Tbsp milk

【作り方】

1 かきをざるに入れ、塩（分量外）を全体に軽くまぶし入れ、冷水でふり洗いをし、水けをふき取る。
★ぬめりと汚れを取る。

2 長ねぎは斜め切り、あさつきは小口切りにする。

3 みそに砂糖をよく混ぜ牛乳を入れてよく練り合わせる。

4 アルミホイルに2の長ねぎと1のかきをのせ、3のみそをかけて四方をたたみオーブントースターで10〜15分くらい焼き、あさつきをかけていただく。

[DIRECTIONS]

1 Place the oysters on a sieve and sprinkle salt (except quantity) lightly and wholly on the oysters. Wash the oysters while shaking together with the sieve in cold water and wipe dry.
★This procedure helps to eliminate sliminess and dirt.

2 Cut the *naga-negi* onion diagonally and *asatsuki* chives by using the edge cut technique.

3 Combine the sugar and the *miso* well. Add the milk and mix up thoroughly.

4 Place the *naga-negi* onion and oysters. Pour on the *miso* sauce prepared in **3**, above and close the foil by folding all sides. Bake in an oven toaster for 10 to 15 min. Sprinkle on the *asatsuki* chives before serving.

かきの土手鍋
(どてなべ)

濃厚なみそ味にぷりぷりのかきがからんで美味しい

about **15** min

Oyster hot pot with *Miso*

Strong flavor of *miso* mingled with tender and chewy oysters make a delicious hot pot meal

■材料・2〜3人分

かき（むき身）…………………………	10〜12粒
木綿豆腐…………………………………	1/2丁
しいたけ…………………………………	2枚
大根 ……………………………………	約3cm
ごぼう…………………………………	1/4本
長ねぎ…………………………………	1/2本
せり……………………………………	1/2束
A ┌ 八丁みそ………………………	100g
│ 信州みそ………………………	100g
│ 砂糖……………………………	大さじ1
│ みりん………………………	大さじ3
└ 酒……………………………	大さじ2
だし汁…………………………………	適量

■ Ingredients (serves 2 or 3)

10-12 shucked oysters
1/2 block *momen-tofu* coarse-grained *tofu*
2 *shiitake* mushrooms
About 1 1/5-inch *daikon* giant white radish
1/4 burdock
1/2 *naga-negi* onion
1/2 bundle *seri* Japanese parsley

A ┌ 3 1/2 oz *hatchou-miso*
  │ 3 1/2 oz *Shinshu-miso*
  │ 1 Tbsp sugar
  │ 3 Tbsps *mirin* sweet cooking *sake*
  └ 2 Tbsps *sake*

Stock

■作り方

1 かきは大根おろし（分量外）か塩（分量外）で洗い、水で流してペーパータオルなどで水けをしっかりとふき取る。木綿豆腐は大きめの角切りに切っておく。

2 ごぼうは水洗いし包丁で皮をこそげ取り、ささがきにし水にさらす。大根は皮をむき、いちょう切りにする。長ねぎは斜め切りにする。しいたけは石突きを切り取り、半分に切る。せりは水洗いして約5～6cmの長さのざく切りにする。

3 Aを練り合わせる。

4 土鍋のふちに**3**を適量塗る。**1**のかき、木綿豆腐、**2**のごぼう、大根、長ねぎ、しいたけ、せりを鍋に入れてだし汁をはり、弱火にして、煮えたところからみそとからめながらいただく。
※最後にうどんを入れてもよい。

■DIRECTIONS

1 Clean oysters in grated *daikon* giant white radish (extra) or with salt (extra), rinse in water, and paper-dry well. Cut the tofu into relatively large pieces.

2 Wash the burdock, scrape off the skin with a kitchen knife, shave, and soak in water. Peel the *daikon* radish, and cut into quarter rounds. Cut the *naga-negi* onion diagonally. Cut off the hard tip of the *shiitake* mushroom stems, and cut in half. Wash the *seri* Japanese parsley, and cut into about 2-inch lengths.

3 Mix the ingredients of **A** well.

4 Apply the mixture around the inner edge of an earthenware pot. Put into the pot the oyster, *tofu*, burdock, *daikon* radish, *naga-negi* onion, *shiitake* mushrooms, and *seri* parsley, and pour over the stock. Cook over low heat at the table. Each diner can choose cooked ingredients, while putting *miso* on them.
※ Add *udon* noodles at the end, if you like.

コラム
Column

加熱用かきと生食用かきの違い
Difference between Oysters for Eating Raw and Those for Cooking

スーパーなどで加熱用かきと生食用かきが売られているが、見た目は一緒に見えるが違いはどこにあるのだろうか……。

かきは海水に含まれている菌を吸収しているため、その菌によって食中毒を起こすことがある。この菌を取り除くために、紫外線殺菌装置で殺菌した海水にかきを2～3日おくと菌のいないかきになる。これが生食用で売られているかきである。

つまり殺菌していないのが、加熱用かきになる。ただし菌は加熱すると死んでしまうし、殺菌したものは2～3日エサを食べていないため、身は少しやせ細る。だから鍋やフライなどの加熱する料理には、加熱用のかきの方が美味しく出来上がるのだ。

かき
Oysters

At supermarkets, we see oysters labeled as "edible raw" and "for cooking only." Both look the same. So, what is the difference?
Oysters could cause food poisoning, because they absorb germs in seawater. To remove the germs, they are put in seawater sterilized with ultraviolet beams for a few days. These germ-free oysters are sold as "edible raw" products.
In other words, unsterilized oysters are sold for cooking. But do not worry. Germs are killed if heated. So, for one-pot meals or fried dishes, use oysters "for cooking." They are more delicious than sterilized oysters, which become a bit thin, as they do not take food for a few days.

about **8** min

ぶりしゃぶ

脂ののったぶりをもみじおろしと、ぽん酢としょう油であっさりいただく

Buri Shabu-Shabu

Enjoy fat-rich *buri*, or Japanese amberjack, with spicy-hot grated *daikon* and refreshing citrus-juice-mixed soy sauce

■材料・2人分

ぶり（刺身用さく）…	約10cm
長ねぎ………………	1本
水菜…………………	1/2束
絹ごし豆腐…………	1/2丁
昆布（約10cm）……	1枚
酒……………………	適量
ぽん酢しょう油……	適量
大根…………………	約5〜6cm
鷹の爪………………	1本
ゆず皮（せん切り）…	適量

■ Ingredients (serves 2)

About 4-inch long *sashimi* block *buri* (Japanese amber-jack)
1 *naga-negi* onion
1/2 bundle *mizuna* pot-herb mustard
1/2 block *kinugoshi-tofu* fine-grained *tofu*
About 4-inch *konbu* kelp
Sake
Ponzu soy sauce (citrus-juice-mixed soy sauce)
About 2 1/2-inch *daikon* giant white radish
1 red chili pepper
Yuzu Japanese lime peel (julienne)

■作り方

1 ぶりは約5mmの厚さの平造りにし、皿に盛りつける。

2 長ねぎは縦半分に切り、斜めの薄切りにして、水にさらす。水洗いした水菜は約5〜6cmの長さのざく切りに、絹ごし豆腐は大きめの角切りにし、皿に盛り合わせる。

3 大根は皮をむき、箸などで穴を開け、穴にへたを切り取った鷹の爪を入れてすり、もみじおろし（詳しくはP67参照）を作る。

■DIRECTIONS

1 Slice the *buri* into 1/5-inch-thick pieces, and arrange on a serving plate.

2 Cut the *naga-negi* onion in half lengthwise first, then slice thin diagonally, and soak in water. Wash the *mizuna* potherb mustard, and roughly cut into about 2-inch lengths. Cut the *tofu* into large pieces. Arrange these ingredients on the serving plate.

3 Make *momiji-oroshi*. Peel the *daikon* radish, and make a hole with a chopstick. Insert the red chili pepper (calyx removed) into the hole, and grate. (For details, see p.67.)

4 Put into an earthenware pot a generous amount of water (extra), *konbu* kelp, and small quantity of *sake*, and heat.

5 At the table, dip the *buri* slices in the boiling water, and eat medium-done. Also put in the *naga-negi*, *mizuna* and *tofu*, and eat with the *ponzu* soy sauce with the *yuzu* peel julienne added and the *momiji-oroshi*.
※ Try to wrap the *naga-negi* or *mizuna* with a *buri* slice. It's good.

4 土鍋にたっぷりの水（分量外）と昆布、酒少々を入れて火にかける。

5 1のぶりは4の鍋にくぐらせて半生でいただく。2の長ねぎ、水菜、豆腐を温めて、3のもみじおろし、ゆず皮を入れたぽん酢しょう油でいただく。
※長ねぎや水菜は、ぶりで巻いていただくのがおすすめ。

バリエーション

★しゃぶとは魚の身や脂ののった肉類を、土鍋などに水、酒、昆布を入れて火にかけたものに入れ、身を箸で持ち3〜4回泳がせるようにすることをいう。これによってむだな脂分が落ちるし、身に熱が入るので生で食べる時とは違う食感と甘味が出てくる。

★ぶりしゃぶの代わりには、真だい、きんめだい、まはた、くえ（あら）、ひらめなどの他に、真だこや水だこの薄造りや、ほたて、あわびの薄造りをしゃぶしゃぶしても美味しい。

VARIATION

★ "*Shabu*" means to move thin slices of fish or fat-rich meat held with chopsticks 3 to 4 times sideways, as if to let them swim in boiling water flavored with *sake* and *konbu* kelp boiling in a earthenware pot. This way, the ingredients are slightly cooked, and their excess fat is removed, which changes their texture and makes them sweeter compared to those eaten raw.

★*Buri* can be replaced by slices of red sea bream, alfonsino, sevenband grouper, kelp grouper, or flounder. Common octopus, giant Pacific octopus, scallop and abalone are also good for *shabu shabu*.

コラム

Column

〝出世魚〟ってどんな魚？
What is a *Shusse-uo* Fish?

魚の中には幼魚から成魚までの成長段階で呼び名が変わる魚がいる。それを出世 (世の中に出てりっぱな身分や地位につくこと) になぞらえて〝出世魚〟といわれる。縁起がよいとされお祝いの席などにも使用される。

代表的な出世魚には、ブリ、スズキ、ボラになる。他の魚でも成長段階で呼び名が変わる魚は数多くいるが、古くから白木の台 (祝儀に用いる台) にのせられない魚は出世魚とは呼ばれない。

Some fish are called by different names as they grow larger. They are called *shusse-uo* (successful fish) because of their resemblance to people who succeed in life by acquiring a position or status step by step. *Shusse-uo* is frequently served in ceremonies because it is considered lucky.
Typical *shusse-uo* include Japanese amberjack (*buri*), Japanese seaperch (*suzuki*), and flathead mullet (*bora*). There are many other *shusse-uo* who change their names as they grow, but from olden times, those that are not put on a celebration table made of plain wood (*shiraki*) are not entitled to be called *shusse-uo*.

【代表的な出世魚 Typical *Shusse-uo*】

 ★ブリ・スズキ目アジ科 Japanese amberjack (*buri*), *Carangidae Perciformes*

●関東／ワカシ (15～20cm) →イナダ (40cmクラス) →ワラサ (60～70cm) →ブリ (70cm以上)
※関西でいうハマチは、関東では養殖ものをさす。
Kanto: *wakashi* (15 - 20 cm) → *inada* (40 cm class) → *warasa* (60 - 70 cm) → *buri* (above 70 cm)
※ *Hamachi*, as it is called in Kansai, is the same as cultured *buri* in Kanto.
●関西／ツバス→ハマチ→メジロ→ブリ
Kansai: *tsubasu* → *hamachi* → *mejiro* → *buri*

 ★スズキ・スズキ目スズキ科 Japanese seaperch (*suzuki*), *Percichthyidae Perciformes*

●関東／コッパ→セイゴ (1年魚の25cmぐらい) →フッコ (2～3年魚で50cmぐらい) →スズキ (60cm以上)
Kanto: *koppa* → *seigo* (about 25 cm, 1 year of age) → *fukko* (about 50 cm, 2 to 3 years of age) → *suzuki* (above 60 cm)
●関西／セイゴ→ハネ→スズキ
Kansai: *seigo* → *hane* → *suzuki*

 ★ボラ・ボラ目ボラ科 Flathead mullet (*bora*), *Mugilidae Mugiliformes*

●関東／オボコ (3～18cm) →イナッコ→スバシリ→イナ→ボラ (30cm以上) →トド (5年以上の老成魚)
Kanto: *oboko* (3 - 18 cm) → *inakko* → *subashiri* → *ina* → *bora* (above 30 cm) → *todo* (fully grown fish over 5 years of age)
●関西／ハク (3cm以下) →オボコ (3～18cm) →スバシリ (3～18cm) →イナ (19～30cm) →ボラ (30cm以上) →トド (5年以上の老成魚)
Kansai: *haku* (3 cm or less) → *oboko* (3 - 18 cm) → *subashiri* (3 - 18 cm) → *ina* (19 - 30 cm) → *bora* (above 30 cm) → *todo* (fully grown fish over 5 years of age)

和食の基本

Basics of Japanese Food

美味しいご飯の炊き方

和食のおかずにはご飯が最適。美味しいご飯が炊けるようになりたい

How to Prepare Boiled Rice

Rice is the best accompaniment to Japanese dishes. Let's learn how to make delicious rice

米を購入する時のポイント

米にはコシヒカリ、秋田こまち、ササニシキなどの銘柄が多いが、購入する時のポイントは鮮度が大切なので、袋に記載されている精製年月日に必ず目を通したい。

Important Point When Purchasing Rice

Although there are many rice brands available in Japan, such as Koshihikari, Akita-komachi and Sasanishiki, the most important point is not the brand name but freshness. Always check the polishing date indicated on the bag.

白米の炊き方　*How to Cook Rice*

量の目安
Measuring Suggestions

※右記の目安は多少多くなっている。また、個人差があるので注意したい。
※基本的にはその都度、炊いた方が美味しい。

※The suggestions above may produce slightly more servings than indicated. Also, please note that these are only suggestions, and may vary depending on the appetite of an individual.
※Rice tastes better if cooked each time you have a meal.

2カップ（2合） 12 2/3 oz	▶	1人（3食分） 3 servings
4カップ（4合） 25 2/5 oz	▶	2人（3食分） 6 servings
8カップ（8合） 50 4/5 oz	▶	4人（3食分） 12 servings

【米をとぐ（洗う）】

1 ボウルに水をため、その中に米を入れて素早くかき混ぜてさっと洗い、にごった水を素早く捨てる。
※素早くしないと、米が水に溶けたぬかを吸ってしまうので注意したい。

2 手のひらのつけ根部分を押し返すように20〜30回する。にごった水を捨てる。水がにごらなくなるまで（約3〜4回）繰り返す。

【Washing Rice】

1 Fill a bowl with cold water and add rice. Stir it quickly, and pour off the opaque liquid immediately.
※Quick washing is essential. Otherwise, rice will absorb bran dissolved in water.

2 Fill the bowl with fresh water from the tap. Press the rice repeatedly 20 to 30 times with the heel of the palm to make the grains rub against each other. Pour off the opaque water.

3 2の米をざるなどに上げて、真ん中をくぼませるようにしておく。夏は約30分、冬は約40〜60分が目安。

【ご飯を炊く】

米をとぐ3の水けをよくきり、炊飯器に入れ、分量の水を入れスイッチを入れる。現在の炊飯器は蒸らしも自動的にしてくれる。
※蒸らし機能がないものは炊き上がってもすぐにふたを開けず、そのまま約10分ほど蒸らすとよい。

【炊き上がり】

炊けたらふたを開け、水で濡らしたしゃもじを中釜とご飯の間に入れて底から全体をふんわりと混ぜる。蒸気が飛ぶことにより、ご飯がべったりとせず、ふんわりとしたご飯に仕上がる。

Repeat this procedure about 3 or 4 times until the water becomes almost clear.

3 Drain the rice washed in **2**. above on a sieve. Make a shallow cavity at the center of the rice heap, and let it rest for about half an hour in summer and about 40 to 60 min in winter.

【Cooking Rice】

After draining the rice thoroughly, transfer it to a rice cooker. Add water to cover the rice, and turn on the rice cooker. Rice needs to settle after the heat is turned off, but modern rice cookers handle the whole cooking process up to settling automatically.
※If your rice cooker has no settling function, allow the grains to settle with the cooker covered for about 10 min after it is switched off.

【Finishing】

Open the lid of the rice cooker. Insert a wet *shamoji* or flat wooden spoon between the rice and the inside walls of the cooker, and gently overturn and mix the rice. This finishing process will allow the steam trapped inside the rice to escape, and make the rice crisp and plump.

ご飯を炊く
Cooking Rice

炊き上がり
Finishing

美味しいだしの取り方

和食の基本になる美味しいだしの取り方を覚えよう。いつもの料理が格段にアップするはず……

How to Prepare Basic Stock

Let's learn how to prepare tasty stock, which is the basis of Japanese cooking. It makes usual meals much more delicious

だし汁の材料

Ingredients of Basic Stock

かつお節

かつおを乾燥させて作ったかつお節。表面が赤っぽく黒ずんでいてつやがあり、よく乾燥したものがよい。使うたびに削り器で削って使用したい。

Katsuo-bushi or Dried Bonito Fillet

Katsuo-bushi is a fillet of bonito dried to a wood-like hardness. The surface is a dark reddish color and glossy. Choose one that is completely dried. It must be shaved into flakes before use with a *kezuri-ki* or bonito shaver. Shaving should preferably be done each time the basic stock is prepared, making only the necessary amount of flakes instead of shaving it all at once.

削り節

かつおを薄く削ってパックしたもの。かつお節より香りが落ちるが手軽なので家庭でよく使用される。花がつお、だし節、さば節などがある。

Kezuri-bushi or Packaged Dried Bonito Flakes

Convenient packages with pre-shaved bonito flakes. Although the aroma is somewhat inferior to that of *katsuso-bushi*, they are often used in modern Japanese households due to the convenience they offer. Many variations are also available including *hana-katsuo* with larger flakes, *dashi-bushi* with finer flakes and *saba-bushi* or dried mackerel flakes.

煮干し

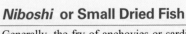

一般的には片口いわしや真いわしの稚魚を煮て干したもので、ジャコ、いりことも呼ばれる。腹が切れていたり、油焼けしたものは避けたい。小ぶりのものがよく、大きいものはクセのある味や臭みが強くなる。

Niboshi or Small Dried Fish

Generally, the fry of anchovies or sardines boiled and dried. They are also called *jako* or *iriko*. Avoid those with a rip in the belly or oxidized oil stains. Smaller ones are better as bigger *niboshi* may taste and smell too strongly.

昆布
Konbu Kelp

昆布はよく乾燥していて、表面に白い粉がふいた肉厚のものがよい。利尻（りしり）昆布、羅臼（らうす）昆布、日高昆布などがある。

Choose completely dried thick *konbu* with white powdery substances on its surface. *Konbu* harvested in the waters off the Rishiri, Rausu and Hidaka regions of Hokkaido are particularly famous.

干ししいたけ
Dried *Shiitake* Mushroom

しいたけを乾燥させたもの。生よりも香りが強くなり、煮ものなどのだし汁によい。

Because the aroma of dried *shiitake* mush-rooms is stronger than raw ones, they are often used for simmered dish stock.

★ だし汁の保存法 ★ How to Store Stock

基本的には作りおきせず、使い切った方がよいが、密封容器に入れ冷蔵庫で2～3日は保存出来る。

In principle, the basic stock should be used up each time it is prepared. However, it can be stored for a few days if it is put in a covered container and kept cool in a fridge.

昆布の水だし汁　*Konbu Kelp Stock*

■材料・4カップ分

昆布 ························· 約20cmの長さのもの1枚
水 ······························· 4カップ

■ Ingredients (Makes 3 1/3 U.S. Cups)

Konbu kelp about 8 inches in length
3 1/3 U.S. cups cold water

【作り方】

1 昆布の汚れを布巾で落とす。

2 ボウルに水を入れ、1の昆布を2～4時間（夏は約2時間、冬は約4時間）入れておく。

3 昆布のだしが出たら、昆布を引き上げる。

【DIRECTIONS】

1 Wipe *konbu* kelp with a cloth to clean.

2 Fill a bowl with cold water and add the kelp cleaned in **1**. above. Let stand for about 2 hours in summer and about 4 hours in winter.

3 Remove the kelp when the stock is ready.

※煮もの、鍋もの、炊き込みご飯などによい。
※使用した昆布、干ししいたけは捨てないで、煮ものや佃煮にするとよい。
※This stock is particularly suitable for simmered dishes, one-pot dishes and *takikomi-gohan*(rice cooked with some other ingredients).
※The used kelp can be reused as an ingredient for a simmered dish or *tsukudani*(salt-sweet preserves).

煮干しのだし汁

■材料・4カップ分

煮干し	約15〜20尾
水	4カップ

【作り方】

1 煮干し1尾ずつ頭と腹わたを取る。

2 ボウルに水を入れ、1の煮干しを入れたら約30分漬けておく。

3 2をそのまま鍋に移し、中火で煮立たせたらすぐに弱火にし、アクを取る。

4 3を5〜10分程弱火で煮たら、ペーパータオルか布巾を目の細かいざるに広げてこす。

■ Ingredients (Makes 3 1/3 U.S. Cups)

15 to 20 pieces of *niboshi* small dried fish
3 1/3 U.S. cups cold water

【DIRECTIONS】

1 Pluck off heads and pinch away entrails of the small dried fish.

2 Fill a bowl with cold water and add the small dried fish. Let stand for about 30 min.

3 Transfer the liquid prepared in **2.** above to a pot, and place it over medium heat. When the liquid comes to the boil, turn down the heat to low immediately. Skim the surface to remove foam.

4 After simmering the liquid over low heat for 5 to 10 min, strain it through a paper towel or a cloth placed over a sieve of fine mesh.

★みそ汁に使用する。
★This stock is suitable for *miso* soups.

昆布とかつお節のだし汁 Konbu Kelp and Katsuobushi Dried Bonito Stock

■材料・4カップ分

昆布	約10cmの長さのもの1～2枚
かつお節 (削り節)	20～30g
水	4と1/2カップ

■ Ingredients (Makes 3 1/3 U.S. Cups)

1 or 2 pieces of 4-inch *konbu* kelp
2/3 to 1 oz *katsuo-bushi* (*kezuri-bushi*)
dried bonito flakes
3 3/4 U.S cups cold water

【作り方】

1 昆布の汚れを布巾で落とす。ボウルに水を入れて約20分漬けておく。

2 1の昆布と水を鍋に入れ中火にかけ、鍋底から細かい泡がたってきたら、すぐに昆布を取り出す。

3 2の汁が沸騰してきたら、かつお節 (削り節) を一気に入れ、火を少し弱め、表面に浮いてくる泡やアクを丁寧に取りながら約2～3分煮る。

4 3の火を止め、かつお節が鍋底に沈んだら、目の細かいざるやペーパータオルなどでボウルに静かに注いでこす。

【DIRECTIONS】

1 Wipe *konbu* kelp with a cloth to clean. Fill a bowl with cold water and add the kelp. Let stand for about 20 min.

2 Transfer the kelp and water prepared in **1.** above to a pot, and place it over medium heat. When small bubbles appear from the pot bottom, remove the kelp immediately.

3 When the liquid begins to boil, add all the dried bonito flakes all at once. Turn down the heat a little, and simmer the liquid for a few minutes while removing the foam thoroughly.

4 Turn off the heat. Wait until all the dried bonito flakes sink to the pot bottom. Strain the liquid through a sieve of fine mesh or paper towel slowly to obtain the clear soup in a bowl.

★煮もの、汁ものによく使用する。
★最後のかつお節の汁は絞らないこと。
★昆布を鍋に入れたまま煮立たせると味が落ちるので注意。
★This stock is suitable for simmered dishes and soups.
★Do not squeeze liquid from the remaining dried bonito flakes.
★Do not boil the liquid while the kelp is inside the pot.

美味しいみそ汁の作り方

家庭の数だけ種類があるみそ汁。母親の味ともいえるみそ汁を美味しく作ろう

How to Prepare Miso Soup

It is said that there are just as many kinds of *miso* soup as there are households. Let's make delicious *miso* soup, a taste of mom's cooking

みその種類

みそは全国に数百種もあると言われる。このみそを分類すると麹（こうじ）の原料による分類（米みそ、麦みそ、豆みそ）、味による分類（甘みそ、甘口みそ、辛みそ）、色による分類（赤みそ、淡色みそ、白みそ）が出来る。みその種類を知ることが美味しいみそ汁を作る秘訣である。

Classification of *Miso*

Miso or soybean paste is said to have hundreds of varieties. *Miso* can be classified in several ways—Rice and soybean-based, barley and soybean-based, and soybean alone-based when basing the classification on the type of ingredients used; very sweet, sweet and salty when based on the taste; and red, light-colored and white when based on the color. It is important to know the types of *miso* that are available to prepare delicious *miso* soup.

信州みそ（米みそ）
Shinsyū-*miso*
(Rice and
Soybean based)

豆みそ（赤みそ）
Soybean based
miso(Red)

白みそ
White *miso*

麦みそ
Barley and
Soybean based
miso

仙台みそ（赤みそ）
Sendai *miso*
(Red)

みそ汁の作り方の基本 *Basic Recipe of Miso Soup*

【作り方】

1 鍋にだし汁（P263～265参照）か水を鍋に入れ、火にかける。

2 火が通りにくいもの（根菜類の大根、かぶ、じゃがいもなど）から入れる。あさりなどの貝類や豆腐は最初から入れる。

3 鍋を強火にかけ、沸騰したら中火にする。

4 具に火が通ったら弱火にし、おたま、万能こし器などに適量のみそを入れ、少しずつ溶かしながら入れる。
※みそを溶かし入れてからは、みその香りが飛ぶので煮立たせないこと。
※みそを一度に鍋に入れてしまうと、味の調整がうまくいかないので少しずつ入れながら好みの味にしていくとよい。
※みそは2種類ほどの合わせたみそを使用すると味わいが増加する。

5 再度中火にし、煮立ってきた煮えばなに長ねぎ、三つ葉、万能ねぎなどを散らし、すぐに火を止める。

【DIRECTIONS】

1 Fill a pot with the dashi stock (See P.260 to 263) or cold water, and place it over heat.

2 Add ingredients. Put anything solid that will take time to cook thoroughly (giant white radish, turnip, potato and other edible roots) first. When using clams such as short-necked clams or *tofu* as an ingredient, put them from the outset.

3 Turn up the heat to high. When the liquid comes to the boil, turn down the heat to medium.

4 Make sure that the ingredients are thoroughly cooked, and turn down the heat to low. Soften an appropriate amount of *miso* in a ladle or strainer, and gradually dissolve it into the liquid.
※Never boil the liquid once you have dissolved *miso* into it because boiling will spoil the flavor.
※Add *miso* gradually while adjusting the taste. You cannot make adjustments if you put the *miso* in all at once.
※If two different types of *miso* are combined and mixed, the flavor of the soup will be further enhanced.

5 Turn up the heat to medium again, and sprinkle chopped *naga-negi* onion, trefoil or *bannou-negi* onion all over the soup. Turn off the heat immediately before it begins to boil.

焼きものの基本とコツ

焼き魚、卵焼きなど、和食には焼きもの料理が数多くあるので基本とコツをマスターしたい

Basics of Grilling and Pan-frying

Japanese meals include a number of grilled or pan-fried dishes, such as grilled fish and omelets. Let's learn the basics and knacks of grilling and pan-frying.

焼き魚

【姿焼き】

焼き魚に使用するものは新鮮なものを選択したい。調理が単純なので材料のよし悪しで美味しさが決定するといっても過言ではない。飾り包丁を入れたら、水けをよくふき取り、ふり塩、化粧塩をしてから焼く。原則は強火の遠火だが、一般家庭ではガスレンジがほとんどになる。それでも片面（盛りつけて表になる方から焼く）を強火で焼き、裏側は最初強火で、仕上げを中火でじっくり焼くと中までしっかり火が通る。

★焼き網★ Cooking Grill

焼き網を使用する場合は、網をよく焼き、サラダ油を少量網に塗ると魚が網にくっつかない。

When using a cooking grill, preheat it thoroughly and apply a small amount of salad oil all over the surface to prevent fish from scorching and sticking to the grill.

Grilled Fish

【*Sugata-yaki* or Grilled Whole Fish】

Choose grilled fish that is as fresh as possible. It is no exaggeration to say that the quality of fish determines the success of the finished dish when considering this simple cooking method. Score the body surface slightly with a knife to ensure the thorough penetration of heat, wipe the whole fish to remove moisture, sprinkle salt and put salt over the fins to prevent scorching. The ideal way to grill fish is to place it over "intense yet distant heat" using charcoal. In modern households, however, gas stoves are commonly used for fish grilling. These gas stoves still suffice if one side of the fish that will be face up when served is grilled over high heat, then the other side over high heat first before reducing it to medium to allow heat to penetrate to the center.

★ガスレンジ★ Gas Stoves

魚をガスレンジで焼く場合は、魚焼き器に水を入れておくと、後かたづけに便利。

When using the broiler compartment of a gas stove to grill fish, put some water in the broiler pan prior to grilling. This will facilitate subsequent cleaning.

【切り身】

切り身の場合は皮のついている表から焼き、美しい焼き目をつける。器に盛りつけた時に表がくるため。裏側は最初強火で、仕上げは中火でじっくり焼くと中まで火が通る。

【Grilled Fillet】

Grill the skin side first, and ensure that the beautifully scorched grid marks are left on the fish. This skin side will face up when served. Grill the other side over high heat first before turning down to medium to ensure the thorough penetration of heat to the center.

レンガで火を調節

ガスレンジの両端にレンガをおき、その上に焼き網をおいて使用すると強火の遠火が可能になる。魚から落ちた脂に火がつき、煙りを出すが吹いて火を消し、煙りを出さないようにしたい。魚の皮に煙り臭さがつき、美味しさを半減させてしまうからだ。

Adjusting Heat with Bricks

If you place one brick on either side of the gas burner and bridge the burner with a cooking grill, it will create the same effect as those with "intense yet distant heat." When the fat drops from the fish onto the grill and catches fire, blow it out immediately so that no smoke is generated. Otherwise, the fish skin will come to smell like smoke, greatly spoiling the taste.

魚をのせる前に網をよく焼いておくと、網に皮や身がついて魚が形崩れするのを防ぐ。
Preheat the cooking grill prior to placing fish on it. In this way, the fish can retain its shape without sticking to the grill.

焦げつかせないコツ

魚を焼く前に焼き網を熱しておくか、網にサラダ油か酢をはけで少量塗ってから焼くと焦げつき防止になる。

Tips for preventing fish from burning

Before placing fish, heat a grill, or apply a small amount of vegetable oil or vinegar to the grill with a brush. This prevents fish from burning on to the grill.

フライパン

【卵焼き】

卵焼き用のフライパンはよく油がなじんだものを使用し、他の調理には使用しないようにしたい。卵が他の材料の臭いを吸収してしまうからだ。

Frying Pan

【Omelet】

Apply a good coating of oil to omelet pans before use. Omelet pans should be used exclusively for making omelets to prevent the smell of other food from affecting eggs.

煮ものの基本とコツ

和食の中でも基本とコツが重要な煮ものは、昔から煮ものが作れれば一人前といわれる

Basics of Simmering

Basic techniques are especially important for simmered dishes. It's long been said that you are a matured cook, if you can make good simmered dishes

鍋

【分量（人数分）に合った鍋を選択したい】

鍋が材料の分量に比べてあまりに大きいと、鍋の中で材料が踊る状態になり、煮崩れの原因になるし、鍋が小さすぎると材料に煮汁がきっちりと回らず芯が残ってしまう原因になるので注意したい。鍋底に材料がきちんとおさまり、材料と材料の間に適当なすき間が出来るぐらいがよいとされる。

Pot

[Select a pot with a size appropriate for the number of servings]

If the pot is too large for the quantity of ingredients, it causes the ingredients to roll and tumble while being boiled, resulting in the loss of their shape. If the pot is too small, on the other hand, the simmering liquid cannot soak into the ingredients deep enough, and their core parts are likely to remain hard and unflavored. Ideally speaking, all ingredients should neatly sit at the bottom of the pot with some space left between each of the ingredients.

材料を入れる順番

【かたく、熱が入りづらい材料から煮る】

材料が何種類かある煮ものは、かたく、熱がなかなか入りづらい材料から順番に煮ることが美味しい煮ものを作るコツ。

Order of Placing Ingredients

[Put hard-to-cook ingredients in first]

When using several kinds of ingredient, put those that are solid and hard-to-cook in first.

落としぶた

【材料に均等に熱が入り、味がしみ込む役割をする】

落としぶた（鍋の大きさの紙やアルミホイル）をすることにより、材料に熱が均等に伝わり、味をしみ込む役割をしてくれる。

Drop-lid

[A convenient tool to distribute heat evenly and help ingredients to soak up flavor]

By covering with a drop-lid(pot-sized paper or aluminum foil),the ingredients can be heated equally and seasoned thorought.

アク取り

【材料から出たアクをこまめに取る】

材料から出たアクはこまめに取りたい。これを
おこたると、出来上がりの色や味が落ちる。

アクは鍋の中心に集めて取るとすく
いやすい。
This foam removing is much easier
if you gather all the foam into the
center of the pot and scoop it out.

Removing Foam

【Remove foam that comes out of the ingredients thoroughly】

Remove foam that comes out of the ingredients
thoroughly. Otherwise, the color and taste when
cooked will be spoilt.

水を入れたボウルを用意し、玉じゃ
くしについたアクを落としてから次
のアクを取る。
Place a water-filled bowl beside you,
and clean the soup ladle used for
removing the foam with the water in
the bowl each time you scoop the foam
out. Remove other foam after cleaning
the ladle.

調味料の順番

【調味料の順番は『さ・し・す・せ・そ』が基本】

昔から伝わる和食の味つけの基本になるさ（砂
糖）、し（塩）、す（酢）、せ（しょう油）、そ（み
そ）の五つの調味料。砂糖は他の調味料に比べ
て浸透が遅いので最初に加え、塩は材料の水
分を出して引き締めてくれる働きや、味を引き
締める役割をする。
酢、しょう油、みそは長く煮ると香りが飛んで
しまうので、数回に分けて加えたり、最後の
仕上げに加えるとよい。

Order of Adding Seasonings

【The most common seasonings used for simmering consist of the 5S's】

The basic and traditional seasonings that are
often used when cooking simmered dishes
consist of the 5S's—*Sato* (sugar), *Shio* (salt), *Su*
(vinegar), *Shoyu* (soy sauce) and *Miso* (soybean
paste) —and these should be added in this order.
Sugar should be stirred into the stock first
because it is hard to penetrate into solid
ingredients while salt extracts their surplus
moisture to tighten the food texture and make the
taste more intense. Vinegar, soy sauce and *miso*
should be added several times or when finishing
off cooking.

煮魚のコツ

煮魚は煮汁が沸騰してから、魚を鍋に入れる
こと。魚の表面がかたまり、旨味が煮汁に出
ることなく美味しい煮魚が出来る。沸騰して
いない状態から魚を入れると、生ぐささが煮
汁に出てしまうので注意したい。煮崩れや鍋
底に魚を焦げつかせない方法として、鍋底に
竹皮を敷いて、その上に魚をのせて煮つける
とよい。

Tips for Simmering Fish

Put fish into a pan only after the simmering liquid
begins to boil. This will harden the fish surface to
prevent the best taste of fish from exuding out into
the liquid. If fish is put in a pot before the liquid
boils, the smell of fish will permeate the
simmering liquid and make it too fishy.To prevent
fish from losing its shape or scorching and sticking
to the bottom of the pot, placing a bamboo sheath
over the bottom of the pot first and then placing the
fish on it is recommended before simmering.

揚げものの基本とコツ

サクッとした揚げものを作りたいもの。そのために揚げものの基本とコツをきっちり覚えよう

Basics of Deep-frying

Let's master the basics of deep-frying to make crispy fried foods

油の適温と見分け方

揚げものをカラッと揚げるためには、材料に適した油の温度を知る必要がある。

野菜の適温	肉類の適温	
約160〜170℃	約160〜170℃	約170〜180℃
───	厚くて大きいもの	ひと口大の小ぶりのもの

Adequate Oil emperatures and Their Determination Method

To make crispy deep-fried dishes, it is important to know which temperature is most adequate for what ingredients.

Vegetables	Meat	
320 to 340°F	About 320 to 340°F	About 340 to 360°F
───	Thick and large	Small bite-size

油の温度の見方

油の温度はてんぷら専用の温度計で見るのが一番よいが、あまり家庭には用意されていない。そんな時は使用する衣を油に落としてみる方法がよいだろう。

How to Determine Oil Temperature

The best way to determine the oil temperature is to use a special thermometer, but this kind of tool is not usually available at home. The alternative way is to put a few drops of batter into the oil and see how they react.

衣を落としてみる
If the few drops of batter

160℃くらい

油に落とした衣は、底に沈むがすぐに浮き上がってくる。

Sink to the bottom of the pan, and float up to the surface quickly–About 320°F

170℃くらい

油に落とした衣は、油の中ほどまで沈みすぐに浮き上がってくる。

Sink halfway to the bottom, and float up quickly–About 340°F

揚げものの順番

天ぷらの盛り合わせのように野菜、魚介類など
ひとつの鍋で数種類の材料を揚げる場合は、
揚げる順番がある。

❶かぼちゃ・さつまいも・にんじん
油に臭いがつかない野菜類を先に揚げる（かた
く、火の通りにくいものから揚げる）。

❷いか・えび・しろぎす
魚介類（えび、いか、しろぎすなど）を揚げる。

揚げものをカラッと揚げるコツ

【作り方】

1 衣の水分をきっちりふき取り、材料に衣をつ
けたら、すぐに揚げる。

2 鍋にたっぷりはった油の中で、材料を泳がせ
るように揚げる。

3 油かすは油を汚し、揚げものがきれいに揚が
らない原因になるので、こまめに取りたい。

4 一度にたくさんの材料を入れると、材料が重
なり揚げむらが出来たり、温度が急激に下がる
ので注意する。温度が下がったら、少し火を強
め、再度適温にしたら火を弱めて、温度を一定
に保つようにする。

5 揚げた揚げものを鍋上で軽く2～3度ふり、網つき
のバットに重ねないようにのせて油をきる。

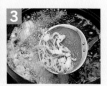

Order in which Ingredients Are Put into Oil

If you need to deep-fry multiple kinds of
vegetable and fish ingredients in the same pan,
care is necessary for the order in which they are
put into oil.

❶ Pumpkin, sweet potato and carrot
Put vegetables with little smell and that are hard
to cook in first.

❷ Squid, shrimp and sillago
Then put in squid, shrimp, sillago and other
seafood.

Tips for Making Deep-fried Dishes Crisp

【DIRECTIONS】

1 Pat dry all ingredients. When coated, they
must be fried immediately.

2 Use plenty of oil, and fry ingredients in such
a way that they are tossed around in the oil.

3 Thoroughly remove the fried batter bits left
after each ingredient is fried before frying
another ingredient. These remnants will cause
the oil to lose clarity, and thereby spoil the
finished look of the dishes.

4 If you put too many ingredients into the pan
all at once, they will overlap with each other
preventing heat from distributing evenly, and
lower the oil temperature rapidly. Should the
temperature be lowered, turn up the heat until
it becomes sufficiently hot again. Maintain a
constant temperature in this way.

5 When retrieving, shake the fried ingredients
lightly a few times above the pot, and drain
them on a draining pan with a rack without
stacking them.

あえもの、酢のものの基本とコツ

美味しいあえもの、酢のものを作る最大のコツは、材料の水けをよく絞ること……

Basics of Preparing Vinegared and Dressed Dishes

The key to making tasty vinegared or dressed dishes is to squeeze out excess water from ingredients

あえもののコツ

【材料の水けをよく絞る】

使用する材料の水けが残っていると、仕上がりが水っぽいものになり、味もぼやけてしまうので、必ず材料の水けをよく絞ってからあえること。また、材料をゆでてから使用する場合は、特に水けをよく絞ってから使用したい。

【あえ衣、たれを作っておく】

材料にあえ衣、たれの材料を別々に加えるのではなく、材料の下処理が終了したら、あえ衣、たれの材料をボウルに入れ、あえ衣、たれを作る。

【材料をよく冷やし、食べる直前に調味料と合わせる】

時間をおくと野菜から水が出て、水っぽくなったり、ぬるいと美味しさが半減するので、材料をよく冷やし、食べる直前に調味料と合わせると美味しくいただける。

酢のもののコツ

【材料の水けをよく絞る】

あえもの同様、使用する材料の水けをよく絞らないと水っぽい酢のものになってしまう。材料を下処理したら、必ずペーパータオルなどでふき取ってから使用したい。

Tips for good dressed dishes

【Squeeze out excess water from ingredients】

If ingredients contain excess water, the dressing would be diluted, spoiling the taste of the finished dishes. So, do not forget to squeeze off excess water before dressing. If ingredients are boiled, water should be squeezed out more carefully.

【Prepare dressing or sauce】

After preparing ingredients, mix seasonings in a bowl to make dressing or sauce, instead of adding the seasonings separately onto the ingredients.

【Chill ingredients well, and season them immediately before serving】

If dressed dishes are let stand for a long time, water would come out from vegetables, diluting the dressing. Also, warm ingredients would spoil the taste of dressed dishes. So, for delicious dressed dishes, chill the ingredients well, and dress them with the mixed seasonings shortly before serving.

Tips for good vinegared dishes

【Squeeze out excess water from ingredients】

Like dressed dishes, vinegared dishes would be diluted, unless excess water is squeezed out. After preparing ingredients, thoroughly remove water, using kitchen paper.

【材料をよく冷やし、食べる直前に調味料と合わせる】
時間をおくと野菜から水が出て、水っぽくなったり、ぬるいと美味しさが半減するので、材料をよく冷やし、食べる直前に調味料と合わせると美味しくいただける。

【Chill ingredients well, and season them immediately before serving】
If vinegared dishes are let stand for a long time, water would come out from vegetables, diluting the dressing. Also, warm ingredients would spoil the taste of vinegared dishes. So, for delicious vinegared dishes, chill the ingredients well, and season them shortly before serving.

合わせ酢の基本・二杯酢の作り方

How to Prepare Basic Vinegar Dressing-Nihaizu or Two-Flavor Vinegar

【作り方】

1 ボウルに大さじ2杯の米酢を入れる。

2 1のボウルに薄口しょう油大さじ2杯を加える。

3 昆布とかつお節で取っただし汁（P265参照）を約30ccを2のボウルに加える。

4 3をさっとかき混ぜて出来上がり。

【DIRECTIONS】

1 Put 2 Tbsps rice vinegar in a bowl.

2 Add 2 Tbsps light soy sauce to the bowl.

3 Add about 1 oz *konbu* kelp and dried bonito stock (See P.265) to the bowl.

4 Stir the mix briefly.

大さじ2杯の米酢
2 Tbsps rice vinegar.

薄口しょう油大さじ2
2 Tbsps light soy sauce.

30ccのだし汁を加える
About 1 oz stock to the bowl.

※三杯酢は、二杯酢にみりんを加えて甘味を出したもの。
※土佐酢は二杯酢や三杯酢にかつお節を加えて煮立たせ、冷ましたもの。

※*Sanbaizu* or three-flavor vinegar is a dressing consisting of *nihaizu* and *mirin* sweet cooking *sake* to emphasize sweetness.
※*Tosa-zu* or Tosa vinegar is made by bringing *nihaizu* or *sanbaizu* with dried bonito flakes to the boil and letting it cool to room temperature.

麺料理の基本とコツ

のどごしの良い美味しい麺料理を楽しむために、麺料理の基本とコツを守ろう

Basics of Cooking Noodles

Stick to the basics of noodle cooking to enjoy good noodles that go down smoothly

乾 麺

そば、うどんをはじめ、そうめん、ひやむぎ
などの乾麺にはさまざまな種類があり、これ
らはいずれも長期間の保存が出来る特徴があ
る。家庭に常備しておけば、いざという時に
も重宝する。麺料理にはもちろんのこと、鍋
料理や吸いものなどにも使用出来る。

Dried Noodles

In addition to *soba* and *udon*, many other
noodles including *somen* or thin wheat noodles
and *hiyamugi* or wheat noodles with a thickness
somewhere between *somen* and *udon*, are also
available in dried form. Dried noodles can be
stored for a long time, and serve as an important
reserve that can be consumed at any time. They
can be used as an ingredient for one-pot dishes
and clear soups as well.

乾麺のゆで方　*How to Boil Dried Noodles*

【作り方】

1 大きめの鍋にたっぷりの湯を沸かす。沸騰し
たら中火にして麺を放射状に広がるように入れ
る。

2 麺を入れて少したったら、麺どうしがつかな
いように箸で軽く混ぜながらゆでる。吹き上が
ってきたら差し水をするか、火加減を調節する。

3 箸で麺を1本取り、水にさらしてから指で切る
か食べてみてゆで加減をみる。

4 ゆで上がったら流水でよくもみ洗いして、麺
のぬめりを取る。

【DIRECTIONS】

1 Fill a large pot with plenty of water, and
bring it to the boil. When it reaches boiling
point, turn down the heat to medium, and add
noodles in such a way that they will spread out
like the spokes of a wheel.

2 A little while later, stir the noodles lightly
with chopsticks to keep them from sticking to
each other. When the boiling water reaches up
to the edge of the pot, either put in some cold
water or reduce the heat.

3 To check whether the noodles are sufficiently
cooked, remove a strand with chopsticks, and
rinse it under cold water. Then, either break it
with the fingers or bite into it to determine its
firmness.

4 When the noodles are cooked to an adequate
firmness, rinse them under cold running water,

※冷たい麺料理の場合はこのまま水けをきって使用する。
※温かい麺料理の場合にはさっと湯通しして温めてから使用する。
※For cold noodle dishes, drain the noodles before serving.
※For hot in-broth noodle dishes, plunge them into a pot of boiling water briefly before use.

rubbing them vigorously to remove surface starch.

生 麺

生麺は乾麺に比べ、味も風味もよく美味しいが、保存がきかないため、なるべく早く食べるようにしたい。基本的には乾麺のゆで方と同じだが、生麺の場合乾燥を防ぐために打ち粉がふってあるので、ゆでる時には打ち粉をよくはらい、手でほぐしながら湯に入れるとよい。

Fresh Noodles

Uncooked fresh noodles are better than their dried counterpart in terms of taste and flavor, but because they are not suitable for long storage, they have to be consumed as soon as possible. The boiling method is basically the same as that for dried noodles. For fresh noodles, however, it is necessary to shake off the powder that has been sprinkled over them to prevent dehydration well before boiling, and loosen the strands when adding them to the pot.

ゆで麺・冷凍麺

うどん、そばなどはすでにゆでてあるものや、ゆでた麺を冷凍してあるものがある。これらはゆでる必要がなく、さっと湯に通すだけで食べられるので、時間がない時や、焼きうどんなどを作る際に便利である。

Cooked / Frozen Noodles

Some noodles including *soba* and *udon* are sold in a cooked or frozen form. They have already been boiled, so there is no need to boil them again. All you need to do is just plunge them into a pot of boiling water just until heated. They are very convenient when there is not enough time to cook or when cooking fried *udon* noodles.

麺をゆでる時のコツ

麺をゆでる時は、大きめの鍋にたっぷりの湯でゆでるのがポイント。また、湯の中で麺が踊るように動いている状態の火加減にするとよい。

Tips for Boiling Noodles

The most important point is to use plenty of water and a sufficiently large pot when cooking noodles. Also, adjust heat so that the boiling water will roll and circulate around the noodles.

蒸しものの基本とコツ

難しいと思われがちな蒸しもの。でも基本とコツさえ覚えれば美味しい蒸しものができる

Basics of Steaming

Many tend to think steamed dishes require special techniques. But actually, making tasty steamed dishes is not difficult if you master the basics and know the knack

蒸し器の使い方と 蒸しかげんの見方

How to Use Steamers and Determine Whether Steaming Is Completed

1 蒸し器に水を入れてふたをし、火にかけ沸騰させる。

2 1が蒸気を出したら、材料を入れた上段の鍋を1の下段の上にしっかりとかぶせる。

3 2の鍋にふたをするが、ふたの水滴が材料に落ちて、水っぽくなったり、表面に穴があいたりして仕上がりが悪くなるので、蒸し器のふたの下に布巾をはさむ。

4 蒸しかげんは竹串を刺してみて、澄んだ汁が出てきたら出来上がり。にごった汁が出てくるのは、中がまだ生煮えの状態なので、もう少し蒸す。

1 Put some water in a steamer water pot, and cover. Bring it to the boil.

2 When steam begins to be expelled from the water pot, remove the lid and place another pot on top of this with *chawan-mushi* cups laid inside.

3 Cover the pot with *chawan-mushi* cups placed inside. When covering the pot, insert a cloth between the lid and pot. This cloth will prevent moisture from dripping from the lid onto the food. Moisture causes food to become watery or creates dents on their surface.

4 *Chawan-mushi* is ready when an inserted bamboo skewer comes out clean. If the skewer is not clean, it means that the inside is still half-cooked, so continue to steam the custard a little longer.

すがたたないようにするには

蒸気がよく出ている蒸し器を弱めの中火で蒸すと、すがたたない。強火で長時間蒸すとすがたってしまう。

すがたってしまった茶碗蒸しの表面。見た目も美しくない上、舌ざわりが悪く、味も落ちる。

Spongy *chawan-mushi* surface. Unsuccessful *chawan-mushi* does not look attractive, and has a coarse texture. It does not taste good either.

How to Prevent *Chawan-mushi* from Becoming Spongy

To prevent the custard from becoming spongy, steam the custard over a lower medium heat while ensuring that a lot of steam is being expelled from the steamer. It becomes spongy if it is steamed over high heat for a long time.

器ごと蒸すには

器ごと蒸すと、取り出す時に熱くて大変、そんな時は蒸し器の上段（器を入れる鍋）に布巾を敷いて、その布巾の上に器を置いて蒸せば、取り出すのに便利。もしくは鍋つかみ用の手袋をつけて取り出してもよい。

How to Take Hot Cups out of the Steamer

Lay a cloth over the bottom of the pot, and place the *chawan-mushi* cups on it prior to steaming. This cloth will keep the cups from coming into direct contact with the hot bottom of the pot. Or you can also use a pair of pot gloves.

蒸し器について

蒸し器には竹製で出来た中華セイロと金属製（ステンレス、アルミ）があるが、家庭では金属製の方が扱いやすい。

Steamer

Roughly speaking, there are two kinds of steamer available in Japan–Chinese-style wood and bamboo steamers and metal (stainless steel or aluminum) steamers. Metal steamers are easier to use for home cooking.

金属製蒸し器
Metal Steamer

使いやすいが、ふたの裏側に湿気がたまり、料理にしずくが落ちるので使用する時は必ず布巾をはさんで使用すること。

A good point about this type of steamer is its ease of use. It, however, tends to form moisture on the inner side of the lid, which will drip onto food unless you insert a cloth between the lid and pot.

鍋料理の基本とコツ

ひとつの鍋をみんなで囲んで、ワイワイ楽しくやるのも日本ならではの食文化のひとつ

Basics of one-pot dishes

It is part of Japanese food culture to sit around a one-pot dishes cooked on the table, while enjoying conversation

食材のくさみを取る

魚の切り身を使用する場合は、切り身に熱湯を回しかけて生ぐさみを取ってから使用したい。
鶏もも肉の場合は、熱湯に入れアクやくさみを取ってから使用するとよい。

熱湯を回しかけ、くさみを取る
Pour hot water in a circular motion and remove the smell.

Remove strong smells of ingredients

Before using a fish fillet, pour hot water in a circular motion, to remove its fishy odor. For boneless chicken thigh, put the meat in boiling water, to remove the scum and smell.

鍋に入れる順番

魚介類、肉類などだしの出るものや、火の通りにくい具材 (ダイコン、白菜のしんの部分など) から先に入れる。貝類、葉菜類などは最後の方に入れること。

Add ingredients in this order

First put into the pot fish or meat, which flavor the soup, and hard vegetables that take time to be cooked such as *daikon* giant white radish or stalks of Chinese cabbage. Put shellfish and leafy vegetables into the pot later.

アクを取る

食材 (特に肉類) を入れるとアクが出るが、このアクをこまめに取って、澄んだだし (スープ) を楽しみたい。

アクはこまめに取ると、澄んだだし (スープ) になる
Constant removal of scum keeps the soup clear.

Skimming off the scum

Scum forms when ingredients, especially meat, are cooked. Skim off the scum frequently to keep the soup clear.

和食の基礎知識

Basic Knowledge of Japanese Cuisine

調理道具

調理道具の特徴を知って使うことによって、料理がさらに美味しくできるはず……

Typical Utensils

Learn about different features of various utensils to use them properly.
This would further improve your cooking

包 丁
Universal Knife

万能包丁
Universal Knife

いろいろな料理に使える。刃の長さが18〜20cmくらいのものが使いやすい。

Can be used for various dishes. One with a 7 to 8-inch long blade is easy to use.

菜切り包丁
Vegetable Knife

大根の輪切り、桂むき、かぼちゃなどのかたい野菜を切るのに適している。刃の長さが17cmくらいのものが使いやすい。

Suitable for slicing *daikon* giant white radish into rounds or paper-thin slices, as well as for cutting pumpkins and other hard vegetables. One with a 6 3/4-inch blade is easy to use.

出刃包丁
Kitchen Carver

肉厚なので、魚をおろしたり、骨つき肉をたたき切る時に便利な包丁。大出刃と小出刃がある。

Because of its thickness, kitchen carvers are often used for filleting fish or cutting chicken with bones. Two sizes, small and large, are available.

柳包丁
Fish Slicer

別名刺し身包丁ともいわれる。魚の刺し身、薄造りなどに使用される。

Fish slicers are often referred to as *"sashimi-bocho"* in Japanese. As the name indicates, they are suitable for preparing *sashimi*.

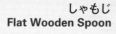

しゃもじ
Flat Wooden Spoon

玉じゃくし
Soup Ladle

みそ汁などの汁ものをすくう時に使用する。

Used for scooping *miso* soup or other types of liquids.

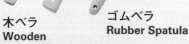

木ベラ
Wooden

ゴムベラ
Rubber Spatula

ご飯を盛る時や、調理中に材料を混ぜたり、裏ごしなどに使用する。

Used for putting boiled rice into bowls, mixing ingredients while cooking and straining.

穴あき玉じゃくし
Ladle with Holes

汁ものの具だけを取る時に便利。また、溶き卵を入れる時などによい。

Convenient for scooping only ingredients from soup. These ladles can also be used when putting an egg into soup while whipping it.

まな板
Cutting Board

食材を切る時に必要なまな板は、木製とプラスチック製がある。木製は食材の臭いが移りやすく、プラスチック製は水に濡れると食材がすべりやすい。

Two types, wooden and plastic, are available. Wooden cutting boards are often left with the smell of ingredients after use while the plastic version becomes slippery when wet.

アルミ鍋
Aluminum Pot

軽く熱が伝わりやすいので煮魚や炒り煮、みそ汁など和食全般に使用できる。

Because of their quick heat transfer qualities, these pots can be used for a wide range of Japanese dishes such as simmered fish, *irini* or dishes simmered until the liquid is gone, and *miso* soup.

ターナー・フライ返し
Turner

煮魚や焼き魚など煮崩れしやすいものを裏返したり、盛りつけたりする時に便利。

Convenient and useful for reversing delicate simmered or grilled fish that loses its shape easily in a pan or on a grill, or for arranging food on plates.

ホーロー鍋
Enamel Pot

酸に強く、さびにくいので煮もの、汁ものによく使用される。

Because these pots are resistant to acid, and difficult to rust, they are often used for simmered dishes and soup.

ボウル
Bowl

食材を洗う、浸す、混ぜる、泡立てる、あえるなど、あらゆる料理の下ごしらえに欠かせない。

A utensil indispensable for cooking, which can be used for rinsing, immersing, mixing, whipping and dressing ingredients.

菜箸・揚げ箸
Kichen Chopsticks

和食には用途に分けて箸を使い分ける。最低2組みは揃えたい。

Several pairs of chopsticks are usually used for different purposes. At least two pairs should always be at hand.

ステンレス鍋
Stainless Steel Pot

耐久性があり煮込み料理や汁ものに最適。

Very durable pots suitable for simmered dishes and soup.

土 鍋
Earthenware Pot

陶器製の鍋で熱の当たりが柔らかく冷めにくい特徴がある。

These pots allow heat to transfer slowly and gently, and retain heat well.

ざる
Draining Basket, Sieve

ボウルと合わせて使うことが多く、食材を洗ったり、水けをきったりするのに用いる。

Often used in combination with a bowl for rinsing and draining ingredients.

蒸し器
Steamer

茶わん蒸しなどの蒸しものに欠かせない。アルミ製のものはふたに水滴が着いて水滴が落ちるので、布巾をはさんで使用する。

A utensil indispensable for cooking steamed dishes such as *chawan-mushi* savory custard. For aluminum steamers, insert a cloth between the lid and pot when steaming to prevent the moisture on the inner side of the lid from dripping onto food.

フライパン
（フッ素樹脂加工）
Fluororesin-processed Frying Pan

焦げつきにくく余計な油を使わないので人気の素材。必要以上に加熱すると樹脂がはがれてしまう。

Frying pans that are currently gaining popularity because they keep ingredients from scorching and require only a little oil. The resin will come off if heated excessively.

落としぶた
Drop-lid

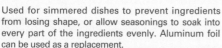

煮ものを作る時に、煮崩れを防いだり、味が全体にしみ込むようにするために使う。アルミホイルでもよい。

Used for simmered dishes to prevent ingredients from losing shape, or allow seasonings to soak into every part of the ingredients evenly. Aluminum foil can be used as a replacement.

巻きす
Bamboo Rolling Mat

巻き寿しを作る時に使う他、ゆでた青菜を絞る時などに使う。

In addition to making *sushi* rolls, these mats can also be used for draining boiled greens.

万能こし器
Strainer

みそ汁を作る際、みそを溶く時に使用する。

Used for straining *miso* when cooking miso soup.

すり鉢・すりこぎ
Grinding Bowl and Pestle

あえものなどのタレを作る時やすったりする時などに使用する。すりこぎは、すり鉢の直径の2倍くらいの長さが使いやすい。

Used for grinding ingredients or when preparing dressing for dressed foods. Pestles should ideally be about twice as long as the diameter of the grinding bowl.

飯台
Wooden *Sushi* Bowl

ちらし寿しなどの寿し飯を作る時に使う。木製なので余分な水分を吸ってくれる。

Used for preparing vinegared rice for garnished *sushi* and other types of *sushi*. Wood absorbs excess moisture.

おろし金
Grater

大根、わさび、しょうがなどをすり下ろす時に使用する。材質は銅製、陶磁器製、プラスチック製などがある。

Used for grating *daikon* giant white radish, *wasabi* horseradish, ginger, etc. They are usually made of copper, ceramic or plastic.

骨抜き
Fish Bone Removing Tweezers

小骨の多い魚（あじ、さばなど）の中骨を取るのに使う。

Used for removing the fine bones of horse mackerel, mackerel, etc.

うろこ取り
Fish Bone Removing Tweezers

魚のうろこは包丁でも取れるが、うろこのかたい魚に使用するとよい。

Scaling can also be done with a knife, but these removers come in handy when scaling hard fish.

<ruby>度量衡表{どりょうこうひょう}</ruby>

MEASUREMENTS

容量　*LIQUID MEASURE*

- 小さじ1＝1 tsp＝5㎖(cc)　● 大さじ1＝1 Tbsp＝15㎖ (cc)
- 1カップ＝1 Japanese cup ＝200㎖(cc)

※1 U.S. cup ＝240 (236) ㎖(cc)

※表の数値はおよその値で換算している。

※The figures in the table indicate roughly converted values.

spoons	㎖	u.s. cup	Japanese cup	ounces
3 Tbsp+1tsp	47㎖ (50㎖)	1/5 cup	1/4 cup	1 1/2 oz
4 Tbsp	59㎖	1/4 cup		2 oz
5 Tbsp+1tsp	79㎖	1/3 cup		
7 Tbsp-1tsp	94㎖(100㎖)	2/5 cup	1/2 cup	3 1/3 oz
8 Tbsp	118㎖(120㎖)	1/2 cup		4 oz
10 Tbsp	142㎖(150㎖)	3/5 cup		5 oz
13 Tbsp+1tsp	200㎖	4/5 cup	1 cup	6 2/3 oz
16 Tbsp	236㎖(240㎖)	1 cup		8 oz
	296㎖(300㎖)	1 1/4 cup	1 1/2 cup	10 oz
	394㎖(400㎖)	1 2/3 cup	2 cup	14 oz
	473㎖	2 cup		
	500㎖	2 1/8 cup	2 1/2 cup	
	560㎖	2 2/5 cup		19 oz
	600㎖	2 1/2 cup	3 cup	
	710㎖	3 cup		
	800㎖	3 1/3 cup	4 cup	
	946㎖	4 cup		

長さ　*LINEAR MEASURE*

- 1cm＝0.39 inches　● 1inche＝2.5 (2.54) cm

CENTIMETERS	INCHES
1.5mm	1/16 in
3mm	1/8 in
5mm	3/16 in
1cm	3/8 in
1.5cm	1/2 in
2cm	3/4 in
2.5cm	1 in

CENTIMETERS	INCHES
4cm	1 1/2 in
5cm	2 in
6.5cm	2 1/2 in
8cm	3 in
9cm	3 1/2 in
10cm	4 in

重量　*WEIGHTS*

- 1 ounces ＝30(28.35)grams
- 1 grams ＝0.035 ounces

GRAMS	OUNCES	POUNDS
5 g	1/6 oz	
10 g	1/3 oz	
15 g	1/2 oz	
20 g	2/3 oz	
30 g	1 oz	
50 g	1 3/4 oz	
60 g	2 oz	
70 g	2 1/2 oz	
80 g	2 4/5 oz	
85 g	3 oz	
100 g	3 1/2 oz	
115 g	4 oz	1/4 lb
140 g	5 oz	
150 g	5 1/4 oz	
170 g	6 oz	
200 g	7 oz	
225 g	8 oz	1/2 lb
300 g	10 1/2 oz	
340 g	12 oz	3/4lb
360 g	12 2/3 oz	
400 g	14 oz	
450 g	16 oz	1lb
500 g	18 oz	
600 g	21 oz	
700 g	24 1/2 oz	
800 g	28 oz	1 3/4 lb

揚げ油の温度　*DEEP-FRYING OIL TEMPERATURES*

160℃／320℉ 165℃／330℉＝low
170℃／340℉ 175℃／350℉＝medium
175℃／350℉ 180℃／360℉＝high

基本的な食材の切り方
Basic Cutting Techniques

輪切り
Rounds

にんじんや大根、なすなどの材料を円形に切ること。材料の皮を薄くむき、用途によって厚さを揃え、均等に切っていく。

A technique used for slicing *daikon* giant white radishes, carrots and other cylindrical ingredients into rounds. Peel the ingredient thinly, and slice it crosswise for rounds of uniform thickness. The thickness depends on how the ingredient is to be used in dishes.

薄切り
Thin Slices

玉ねぎや大根を幅1mm程度の薄さに材料の端から切っていく。スライサーを使えばより均等に仕上がる。

A technique used for slicing onions, *daikon* giant white radishes and other vegetables from one end into rounds of about 1/25-inch thickness. Slicers are handy for realizing a more uniform finish.

斜め切り
Diagonal Cut

長ねぎ、なす、きゅうりなどを厚さを均等に斜めに切っていく。

A technique used for cutting *naga-negi* onions, eggplants, cucumbers and other cylindrical vegetables diagonally. Make sure that the thickness is uniform.

小口切り
Edge Cut

細長い野菜、ごぼう、長ねぎ、きゅうりなどを輪切りの要領で切ること。厚さを揃え、均等に切っていく。

A technique used for slicing burdock, *naga-negi* onions, cucumbers and other long slender cylindrical vegetables into rounds. When slicing, make sure that the thickness is uniform.

せん切り
Julienne Strips

キャベツ、レタス、青じそなどを繊維にそって、薄切りと同様に幅1mm程度に均等に切っていく。

A technique used for cutting cabbages, lettuces, green perilla, etc. very thinly(about 1/25 -inch thick). Vegetables should be cut in the same direction as their grain.

そぎ切り
Shaving Cut

主にしいたけや白菜に使われる切り方。包丁を寝かせるように入れ、そぐように切っていく。

A technique used for *shiitake* mushrooms and Chinese cabbages. Shave vegetables thinly using the knife in such a way that it is almost laid on its side.

半月切り
Half-moons

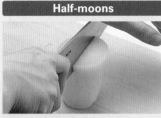

にんじんや大根、きゅうりなどの円筒状の材料を縦半分に切り、輪切りの要領で半月の形に切っていく。

A technique used for cutting carrots, *daikon* giant white radishes, cucumbers and other cylindrical vegetables into half-moons. Cut vegetables in half lengthwise, and then slice them crosswise.

いちょう切り
Quarter-rounds

にんじんや大根などの円筒状の材料を縦4等分に切り、厚さを均等にして、いちょうの葉のように切っていく。

A technique used for cutting carrots, *daikon* giant white radishes and other cylindrical vegetables into quarter-rounds. Cut vegetables in quarters lengthwise, and then slice them crosswise. Make sure that the thickness is uniform.

くし切り
Wedge Cut

トマト、オレンジ、レモンなど球形の材料を縦に6〜8等分に切り、くしのような形にする。

A technique used for cutting tomatoes, oranges, lemons and other spherical foods into wedges. Cut foods lengthwise in sixths or eighths.

短冊切り
Rectangles

拍子切りの要領で材料を長さ4〜5cmに切り、それを繊維にそって薄切りに切っていき、それをそのまま横にたおして幅8mm程度に切っていく。

Cut vegetables into 1 3/5 to 2-inch lengths. Cut them thinly in the same direction as their grain. Lay them on their side, and cut them into rectangles of about 1/3-inch thickness.

細切り
Thin Cut

材料を長さ4〜5cmに切ってから、繊維にそって縦に2mm程度に切っていき、そのまま横にたおして2mm程度に切っていく。

Cut vegetables into 1 1/2 to 2-inch lengths. Cut them lengthwise in the same direction as their grain into rectangles of about 1/12-inch thickness. Lay them on their side, and cut them into thin pieces of about 1/12-inch thickness.

拍子切り
Bar Rectangles

材料を長さ3〜4cmに揃えて切る。繊維にそって厚さ5〜6mmに切っていく。次に切ったものを横にたおし、幅5〜6mm程度に切り、拍子のような形に揃えながら切っていく。

Cut vegetables into 11/5 to 11/2-inch lengths. Cut them in the same direction as their grain into rectangles of 1/8 to 1/4-inch thickness. Lay them on their side, and cut them into bars of 1/8 to 1/4-inch thickness.

さいの目切り
Cube Cut

拍子切りにした材料を端から幅1cm程度に切り、さいころ状にする。

Cut bar rectangles from one end into cubes of about 1/25-inch thickness.

乱切り
Quarter-rounds

包丁を斜めに入れて、野菜を回し、角度を変えながら大きさをほほ一定にして切っていく。

Make diagonal cuts while rotating vegetables a quarter turn between cuts.

針しょうが
Ginger Needles

皮をむいたしょうがを薄切りにし、それを4～5枚重ね繊維にそって針のように細く切っていく。

Slice peeled ginger thinly. Then, cut a stack of 4 to 5 slices in the same direction as their grain into thin needle-like shapes.

あられ切り
Dice Cut

さいの目切りより小さな切り方。材料を長さ4～5cmに揃えて5mm程度の厚さに切り、拍子切りの要領で切っていく。それを端から5mmに大きさを揃えて切っていく。

A technique used for cutting vegetables into cubes with a size smaller than those of the cube cut technique. Cut vegetables into 1 1/2 to 2-inch lengths. Then, cut them lengthwise into rectangles of about 1/8-inch thickness as in the bar rectangles technique. Cut them from one end into 1/8-inch cubes.

ささがき
***Sasagaki* Shavings**

ごぼうの皮をたわしや包丁の背でこそげ落としてから端から5cmくらいのところまで十字に切り込みを入れ、鉛筆を削る要領で端からごぼうを少しずつ回しながらそぎ落としていく。

Scrape off the burdock skin with a *tawashi* kitchen brush or using the back of a knife. Make a lengthwise cross-shape incision about 2 inches deep at one end, and cut it from that end as if you were sharpening a pencil while rotating little by little with the other hand.

みじん切り（玉ねぎ）
Fine Chopping (Onions)

縦半分に切り、そのまま横にたおし幅5mm程度に薄切りに切っていく。次に横から包丁を入れる。端から細かく切っていく。

Cut onions in half lengthwise. Then, with the cut face down, slice them into pieces of about 1/8-inch thickness. Make sideway cuts. Cut them finely from one end.

切り違いきゅうり
Cucumber Peaks

4〜5cmほどの筒切りにしたきゅうりの真ん中に切り目を入れ、切り目に届くように45度斜めに切り込みを入れる。裏返して同じように切り目を入れる。

Cut cucumber into 1 1/2 to 2-inch lengths. Run the knife through the center of a length, and make a diagonal cut(45°) halfway through the cucumber up to the center cut. Make an identical diagonal cut from the other side.

面取り
Bevel-edged Cylinders

主に大根やいも類で使うことが多い切り方。材料の角の部分を包丁の角度を一定にし、左手で大根を回転させながら包丁を送り込み、面を取っていく。

A technique often used for *daikon* giant white radishes and potatoes. Edges of ingredients are beveled for a neat appearance. Apply the knife to the edge of an ingredient at a certain angle, and rotate the ingredient with the left hand.

隠し包丁
Penetration-facilitating Cut

面取りしたものを煮る時に味がしみ込みやすく、火の通りを早くするため、裏面に全体の厚みの1/3くらいまでの十字の切り込みを入れる。

Make a cross-shape incision from one end of a bevel-edged cylindrical ingredient up to about 1/3 of the length. This will facilitate the penetration of seasonings and heat when simmering them.

白髪ねぎ
naga-negi green Onion "Gray Hair" Cut

長ねぎを4〜5cm程度の長さに切り、縦に1本の切り込みを入れてから青い部分を取り除き材料を重ねて、せん切りの要領で細く切っていく。

Cut *naga-negi* onions into 1 1/2 to 2-inch lengths. Make an incision in their center to remove the soft green core. Cut them thinly as in the julienne strips technique.

末広切り
Fan Cut

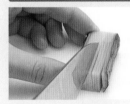

4〜5cmの長さに切り、一片の端を1/4ほど残して縦に細く切り目を入れ、切り目を寝かせるように左右に広げる。

Cut vegetables into 1 1/2 to 2-inch lengths. Make lengthwise cuts at narrow, even intervals through all but 3/8 to 5/8-inch (about 1/4 of the entire length) at one end. Gently spread open the "fan."

しいたけの飾り切り
Shiitake Decorative Cut

生しいたけに3本の切り込みを入れ、切り込みに向かって包丁を左右から斜めに削るように切り込みを入れていく。

Make three incisions on top of each *shiitake* mushroom, and bevel these cuts by inserting the knife diagonally into them.

いわしの手開き　*How to hand-split a sardine*

1 うろこを包丁の背でこそげ取ったいわしの胸びれの後方に、包丁を入れて頭を切り取る。

2 いわしの腹わたを包丁でかきだして取る。

3 中骨に沿って包丁で切り込みを入れる。

4 3の切り込みを入れた箇所に親指を入れ、中骨に沿って尾の近くまで開いていく。

5 身と中骨を手ではがし、尾の近くで手で折り取るか、包丁で切り取る。

1 Scrape off the scales with the back of a kitchen knife. Cut into the back of the fish's pectoral fins, and cut off the head.

2 Scrape out the guts with a knife.

3 Make a cut along the backbone.

4 Thrust your thumb into the cut, and slide along the backbone toward the tail to split the body.

5 Separate the backbone from the flesh, and snap off with your hand or cut off with a kitchen knife near the tail.

真あじの下処理・塩焼き用　*How to prepare a horse mackerel for salt-grilled fish*

1 キッチンバサミで、真あじのエラを切り取る。

2 うろこを包丁でこそげ取ったら、腹側に包丁で切り込みを入れる。

3 2の切り込みから、包丁で腹わたを抜き出し、腹の中を水洗いする。

4 ぜいご（ぜんご）を切り取る。

5 器に盛った時に頭が左にくる側に飾り包丁を入れる。

6 各ひれに化粧塩をする。

1 Cut off the gills with a pair of kitchen scissors.

2 Scrape off the scales with a kitchen knife, and cut into the belly.

3 Use the knife to draw out the guts from the cut, and rinse inside the belly.

4 Cut off the line of hard scales on both sides near the tail.

5 Make decorative cuts on the side that faces up when served with its head on the diner's left.

6 Thickly apply salt to the fins and tail. (*kesho-jio*)

真あじのさばき方・三枚おろし・刺身用　How to fillet a horse mackerel for sashimi

1 真あじの胸びれの後方に包丁を入れる。裏返して反対側も同じように切り、頭を切り離す。

2 包丁を水平にし、腹から尾のつけ根まで切り込みを入れる。

3 包丁で腹わたをかき出す。

4 水をためたボウルの中で血合いを洗い流す。

5 腹側から中骨に沿って2〜3回にわけて徐々に切り込みを入れる。

6 背びれに沿って2〜3回にわけて徐々に切り込みを入れていく。

7 身を横に置き、包丁を入れ、尾と身を一気に切り取る。

8 反対側も**5**から**7**をして身と中骨を切り離す。

9 三枚おろしの出来上がり。

10 腹骨を包丁を寝かせてすき取る。

11 指で皮をつまみ、左手で身を押さえててていねいにはがしていく。

12 毛抜きで血合い骨などをすべて抜き取る。
※指で身をなぞると骨を探しやすい。

1 Cut into the back of the fish's pectoral fins. Turn over the fish, do the same on the other side, and cut off the head.

2 Hold the knife level with the fish, and make a cut from the belly to the bottom of the tail.

3 Use the knife to draw out the guts from the cut.

4 Clean inside the belly in a bowl of cold water.

5 Cut into the fish from the belly, and slide along the backbone in a few strokes.

6 Cut into the fish from the back, and slide along the dorsal fin in a few strokes.

7 Lay the fish, and insert the blade to cut off the flesh from the backbone in one stroke.

8 Turn over the fish, and follow the same process **5** to **7** to separate the flesh from the backbone.

9 Filleting is done.

10 Tilt the blade to shave off the belly bones.

11 Hold the end of the skin with your fingers, and carefully peel, while holding the flesh with your left hand.

12 Use a pair of tweezers to pull out all small bones including those in the dark-colored meat.
※It's easier to find small bones, if you run your finger over the surface of the flesh.

 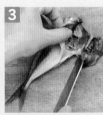 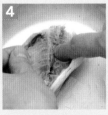  

 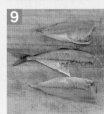  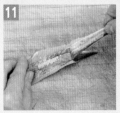 

料理さくいん［50音別］

INDEX [by alphabetical order]

料理さくいん［調理別］

INDEX [by type of cooking]

● 料理制作：藤田 裕子、ハギワラ トシコ、水橋 美紀
● 編集協力：(株)ナヴィ インターナショナル
● 編集・プロデュース：菊池 友彦
● 編集アシスタント：榎 亜以
● 編集担当：田丸 智子(ナツメ出版企画)
● レイアウト：北村 香織、羽田 眞由美〈(株)ナヴィ インターナショナル〉
● 写 真：中島 劭一郎、森岡 篤
● 翻 訳：(株)フルマーク(信濃 葉子、今 博太郎、伴野 昭重、石畠 弘)
● 写真協力：(株)久月 (http://www.kyugetsu.com/index.html)
(株)紀文食品 (http://www.kibun.co.jp/)
(株)ミツカングループ本社 (http://www.mizkan.co.jp/)
(株)宮本卯之助商店 (http://www.miyamoto-unosuke.co.jp/)
TNM Image Archives (http://TnmArchives.jp/)
(財)東京都歴史文化財団イメージアーカイブ (http://www.rekibun.or.jp/)
北海道大学附属図書館 (http://www.lib.hokudai.ac.jp/)
イー葉草・ドット・コム (http://www.e-yakusou.com/)
羽後町企画商工課 (http://www.ugomachi.com/e_ugo/index.html)
郡上市商工観光部観光課 (http://www.gujokankou.com/)
徳島市経済部観光課 (http://www.city.tokushima.tokushima.jp/)
平塚市 (http://www.city.hiratsuka.kanagawa.jp/)
仙台市観光交流課 (http://www.city.sendai.jp/keizai/kankou/)
安城市観光協会 (http://www.city.anjo.aichi.jp/kanko)
新潟市南区産業振興課 (http://www.city.niigata.jp/info/minami/)
浜松市観光コンベンション課 (http://www.city.hamamatsu.shizuoka.jp/)
内子町 (http://www.town.uchiko.ehime.jp/)
弘前市商工観光部観光物産課 (http://www.city.hirosaki.aomori.jp/)
上越市産業観光部 観光局観光企画課
(http://www.city.joetsu.niigata.jp/)
上野観光連盟 (http://www.ueno.or.jp/)

大仙市 (http://www.city.daisen.akita.jp/)
長岡市商工部観光課 (http://www.city.nagaoka.niigata.jp/)
土浦市産業部商工観光課 (http://www.city.tsuchiura.lg.jp/)
千曲市観光協会 (http://www.chikuma-kanko.jp/)
宗教法人 石山寺 (http://www.ishiyamadera.or.jp/)
大覚寺 (http://www.daikakuji.or.jp/)
三春町産業課観光グループ (http://www.town.miharu.fukushima.jp/)
北杜市産業観光部観光課 (http://www.city.hokuto.yamanashi.jp/hokuto/)
本巣市商工観光課 (http://www.city.motosu.lg.jp/)
(社)青森観光コンベンション協会 (http://www.atca.info/)
秋田市企画調整部広報課 (http://www.city.akita.akita.jp/)
神田神社 (http://www.kandamyoujin.or.jp/)
(社)京都市観光協会 (http://www.kyokanko.or.jp/)
大阪天満宮 (http://www.tenjinsan.com/)
木更津市商工観光課 (http://www.city.kisarazu.lg.jp/)
(社)山形市観光協会 (http://www.kankou.yamagata.yamagata.jp/)
鷲在山 長國寺 (http://otorisama.jp/)
今宮戎神社 (http://www.imamiya-ebisu.net/)
ぼうずコンニャクの『市場魚介類図鑑』

ナツメ社Webサイト
http://www.natsume.co.jp
書籍の最新情報(正誤情報を含む)は
ナツメ社Webサイトをご覧ください。

カラー版 英語でつくる和食 食の歳時記

2009年1月6日発行

編著者　　ナヴィ インターナショナル

発行者　　田村正隆

© NAVI INTERNATIONAL, 2009

発行所　　株式会社ナツメ社
　　　　　東京都千代田区神田神保町1-52 加州ビル2F (〒101-0051)
　　　　　電話　03(3291)1257 (代表)　　　FAX　03(3291)5761
　　　　　振替　00130-1-58661

制　作　　ナツメ出版企画株式会社
　　　　　東京都千代田区神田神保町1-52 加州ビル3F (〒101-0051)
　　　　　電話　03(3295)3921 (代表)

印刷所　　東京書籍印刷株式会社

ISBN978-4-8163-4636-1

Printed in Japan

〈定価はカバーに表示してあります〉
〈落丁・乱丁本はお取り替えします〉